99-$16.⁹⁵

P9-DDL-197

LINCOLN FINDS A GENERAL

PRESIDENT ABRAHAM LINCOLN

KENNETH P. WILLIAMS

LINCOLN
FINDS A GENERAL

✳

A Military Study of the Civil War

WITH MAPS BY CLARK RAY

VOLUME ONE

Indiana University Press
Bloomington

© 1949 by Kenneth P. Williams
All rights reserved

No part of this book may be reproduced or utilized in any form
or by any means, electronic or mechanical, including photocopying
and recording, or by any information storage and retrieval system,
without permission in writing from the publisher. The Association
of American University Presses' Resolution on Permission constitutes
the only exception to this prohibition.

Manufactured in the United States of America

Library of Congress Cataloging in Publication Data
Williams, Kenneth P. (Kenneth Powers), 1887–1958.
Lincoln finds a general.
1. United States—History—Civil War, 1861–1865—
Campaigns.   2. Lincoln, Abraham, 1809- 1865—Military
leadership.   3. Generals—United States—History—
19th century.   I. Title.
E470.W765   1985   973.7′3   85-42531
ISBN 0-253-33437-3 (v. 1)
ISBN 0-253-20359-7 (pbk. : v. 1)

Permission to quote copyrighted material is acknowledged to publishers and authors as follows: Appleton-Century-Crofts, Inc.—*General McClellan,* by Peter S. Michie, New York and London, D. Appleton and Company (1915), *General George Brinton McClellan* by W. S. Myers, copyright, 1934, D. Appleton-Century, Inc., *Washington in Lincoln's Time* by Noah Brooks, The Century Company, New York (1895), and *Campaigning with Grant* by Horace Porter, The Century Company, New York (1907); The Bobbs-Merrill Company, Inc.—*Fighting Joe Hooker* by Walter H. Hebert, copyright, 1944, by Walter H. Hebert; Coward-McCann, Inc.— *Conflict; The American Civil War* by George Fort Milton, copyright, 1941, by George Fort Milton; Dodd, Mead & Company, Inc.—*Lincoln and the Civil War* by Tyler Dennett, copyright, 1939, by Dodd, Mead & Company, Inc., *American War of Independence* by F. E. Whitton, copyright, 1931, by F. E. Whitton, *The Generalship of Ulysses S. Grant* by Colonel J. F. C. Fuller, copyright, 1929, by Dodd, Mead & Company, Inc., *Lincoln the President* by James Garfield Randall, copyright, 1945, by Dodd, Mead & Company, Inc.; Doubleday & Company, Inc.—*Recollections and Letters of General Robert E. Lee* by Captain Robert E. Lee; *Encyclopaedia Britannica,* 11th ed.—"Rifles" by Captain C. F. Atkinson; Harper & Brothers—*Reveille in Washington* by Margaret Leech (1941); D. C. Heath and Company—*The Civil War and Reconstruction* by J. G. Randall (1937); Houghton Mifflin Company—*Diary of Gideon Welles* by Gideon Welles (1911), *1914* by Field Marshal Viscount French of Ypres (1919), and *Autobiography* by Charles Francis Adams, Jr. (1916); Little, Brown & Company—*Why Was Lincoln Murdered?* by Otto Eisenschiml (1937); Little, Brown & Company and Atlantic Monthly Press—*Lincoln's War Cabinet* by B. J. Hendrick (1946); Longmans, Green & Company, Inc.— *Stonewall Jackson and the American Civil War* by Colonel G. F. Henderson, and *The Crisis of the Confederacy* by Cecil W. Battine (1905); J. Horace McFarland Company—*The Battle of Gettysburg* by W. E. Storrick (1931); The Macmillan Company—*History of the Civil War* by J. F. Rhodes (1917), *The Biography of the Late Marshal Foch* by Major General Sir George Aston (1929), and *Mr. Secretary* by Ben Ames Williams, Jr. (1940); W. W. Norton & Company, Inc.—*Memoirs of a Volunteer* by John Beatty, copyright, 1946, by W. W. Norton & Company; Oxford University Press—*The Military Genius of Abraham Lincoln* by Colin R. Ballard (1926); G. P. Putnam's Sons—*The Story of the Balti-*

more and Ohio Railroad by Edward Hungerford (1928), and *Ulysses S. Grant and the Period of National Preservation and Reconstruction* by W. C. Church (1926); Charles Scribner's Sons—*The Life and Letters of General George Gordon Meade* by George G. Meade (1913), *Lee's Lieutenants* by Douglas S. Freeman (1942), *R. E. Lee* by Douglas S. Freeman (1934), *Letters from Lee's Army* by Susan Leigh Blackford (1947), and *War Years with Jeb Stuart* by Lt. Colonel W. W. Blackford (1945); University of Alabama Press—*The Civil War Diary of General Josiah Gorgas* by Frank E. Vandiver (1947); The University of North Carolina Press—*George B. McClellan, The Man Who Saved the Union* by H. J. Eckenrode and Bryan Conrad, copyright, 1941, by The University of North Carolina Press, and *I Rode with Stonewall* by Henry Kyd Douglas, copyright, 1940, by The University of North Carolina Press; University of Pennsylvania Press—*South After Gettysburg* by Cornelia Hancock (1937); The University of Wisconsin Press—*Lincoln and the Radicals* by T. Harry Williams; Yale University Press—*A Volunteer's Adventures* by John W. De Forest (1946), and *The Campaign of Chancellorsville* by John Bigelow, Jr. (1910).

To E. A. W. and E. L. W.

PREFACE

LINCOLN's chief military problem was to find a general equal to the hard task the North faced in the Civil War. Though its resources were far in excess of those of the South, they were largely offset by the different roles of the two contestants. The North in the end had to do nothing less than conquer a large area defended by brave armies commanded by some of the best generals this nation has produced. Great superiority in man power and munitions was needed; but it was not sufficient. It was a case of Napoleon's maxim of the necessity of *the man*. The man whom Lincoln found came up the hard way, beginning as commander of a regiment, and ending as General in Chief. He enjoyed no favoritism of superiors, but actually encountered jealousy and distrust; even after he had achieved a notable success, exaggerations and distortions spread harmful rumors behind him.

Ulysses S. Grant remains unique after two world wars; he is still in many ways the most profitable and the most inspiring of all generals to study. He was a soldier's soldier, a general's general. He was always thoughtful of his subordinates, and fitted his instructions to their experience and talents; he never forgot that his superiors had hard problems; he worked tirelessly with what was given him and made no excuses or complaints. He was the embodiment of the offensive spirit that leaves the enemy no rest. He solved problems his own way, not in accordance with maxims, or the doctrines set forth by some school. Thus he was an original contributor to military art and science. He carried no staff manual to study for clues, no check list to scan for anything possibly forgotten. If his orders were logical and covered situations well, it was because he thought that way, not because he could follow a form. As he did not have a highly trained staff of the modern type, one sees in him a remarkable master of detail, as well as

ix

a general who had to make his great decisions without the aid of sub-ordinates selected and trained to help commanders. He began with a small but bold combined operation; he finished with a pursuit that had a perfect ending. Of all the generals in the war—on either side—he alone demonstrated his capacity to command small forces as well as large ones in battle under a great variety of circumstances, and finally to plan and direct the operations of several armies.

Three years of war passed before the historic day in March, 1864, when the experienced and modest Grant met Lincoln, also experienced and equally modest. Behind the General were notable successes; behind the President were months of disappointment with generals who had been unequal to the hard task of conducting offensive operations against the Confederate army commanded by Lee, and who had even missed good chances of shortening the war by destroying Lee's army on his two ventures across the Potomac. It is to the story of those months—months while Grant was maturing in the West—that the present volumes are mainly devoted. How had Lincoln dealt with his other generals? Had he treated them fairly and given them adequate opportunities to display their capacities as commanders? Did he act hastily in changing them, or—judged from modern standards—patiently and leniently? These assuredly are crucial questions in the study of Lincoln. Only by surveying the campaigns of the generals can one form an idea of how Lincoln felt about them on that day when he handed to Grant his commission of Lieutenant General. Later volumes will study the man who drew from his pocket a paper on which he had written his concise words of acceptance.

The Official Records of the war are the chief source. The 128 volumes of the set, thick and heavy, with somber black bindings, look a little forbidding on the shelves of a library. And the main title *The War of the Rebellion* adds to their grimness. But few books even in a great collection contain material that reveals more clearly the character of men. Messages and orders contained in the records, rather than statements made in reports written subsequent to events, have been especially employed. In them we have the most reliable of documents. The work aims to be critical as well as narrative, and other writers are quoted or referred to when their points of view or their words have seemed to be especially striking, or their judgments particularly weighty. In the extensive literature of the war, views in sharp contrast to those here espoused have been set forth; in some instances they are fashionable. I believe that in every really significant case such discordant ideas are noted, and are discussed in the text, the notes, or the appendix.

For the most part the sketches I furnished to Mr. Ray were based upon, and frequently traced from, maps in the two volumes of the atlas that form part of the Official Records, or upon maps in *Battles and Leaders of the Civil War*. Minor discrepancies result from this. The aim has been to keep the maps free from too much confusing detail. The end maps should meet the needs of general orientation. In laying down the railroads on the front map, an effort was made to resolve inconsistencies shown in different maps in the official atlas; and it is hoped that no major error remains in the important strategic lines. In placing the superior numbers that refer to notes, I have had the general reader in mind, rather than the rules followed in technical publications. Judgment in particular cases, rather than a rule, has also determined whether a single page of the Official Records should be cited, or all the pages devoted to a letter or dispatch, where it exceeds the limit of one page.

K. P. W.

Department of Mathematics
Indiana University
March 26, 1949

ACKNOWLEDGMENTS

I‍T IS a pleasure to acknowledge encouragement and assistance that have been received during the writing of the work. Herman B Wells, President of Indiana University; Dean J. W. Ashton of the college of arts and sciences; Dean Stith Thompson of the graduate school; Professor Tracy Thomas, chairman of the mathematics department, were all generous in their approval of a project that took my time away from normal lines of study. President Emeritus William L. Bryan contributed to the background of interest that was essential, and has strengthened some of the convictions that I hold. Throughout the years conversations with him that began on academic questions had the habit of terminating with the Civil War and Grant. Professors R. C. Buley of the department of history, and Oliver Field of the department of government, were instrumental in the expansion of the work beyond the limits originally intended. Dr. Robert A. Miller, director of libraries, and members of his staff have more than met requests that were made of them. Colleagues who have read some of the chapters and made suggestions, or who have answered questions helpfully, are: Professors A. L. Kohlmeier, Cecil K. Byrd, Edward H. Buerig, John M. Hill, Harold E. Wolfe, J. W. T. Youngs, Mr. Charles Harrell, Mr. Ronald Ives, and Mr. Earl Hoff.

Thanks are due to Miss Virginia Watts of the Indiana State Library, to Miss Esther Nugent, Miss Jane E. Rodman, Mrs. Betty Jones, and to Miss Mary Maillard for checking some of the material. Mrs. John W. Bricker of Columbus, Ohio, Mr. Victor Schleicher of Belleville, New Jersey, Mrs. Madge Pickard Palmer of East Paterson, New Jersey, and Dr. A. C. Arnett of Lafayette, Indiana, were helpful readers of some of the chapters. Mrs. C. H. Blackman, Mr. T. L. Nuckols, and Mr. J. S. McBride, chief engineers of the Louisville & Nashville, the

xiii

Chesapeake and Ohio, and the Chicago & Eastern Illinois railroads, respectively, kindly furnished information about parts of their lines during the Civil War. Mrs. Emma Jane Ittner did much of the work on the index and gathered material for some notes and checked quotations and references.

To some persons a special debt is owed. My wife read the entire manuscript, and many pages were improved by her. Colonel Herbert S. Esden was a reader and adviser with whom I have discussed most of the operations and commanders. Captain E. K. Elkins gave generously of his time for several weeks. Through Colonel T. F. Wessels I made the acquaintance of Mr. R. S. Thomas of the Historical Division of the War Department Special Staff, and Major General E. F. Harding, former chief of the division. Mr. Thomas read the manuscript and I had the benefit of some discussion with him. General Harding's experience as an editor, writer, and field commander made him such a reader as an author is not often fortunate enough to find.

CONTENTS

ILLUSTRATIONS

xvii

LINCOLN FINDS A GENERAL

VOLUME ONE

CHAPTER I

A PREVIEW OF A GENERAL

*Until they feel the enemy.**

In the early hours of May 4, 1864—at the beginning of the fourth year of the great American Civil War—the Union Army of the Potomac opened a campaign that was in many ways without precedent in the annals of warfare. For almost a year it would be in constant and close contact with its adversary, the Confederate Army of Northern Virginia. There would be day after day of battle, fiercer and more determined than any armies had ever waged before, interspersed with bitter skirmishes. There would be movements the execution of which would test the courage and skill of the ablest commanders and the most seasoned troops; there would be losses in killed, wounded, and missing that would try the souls of the people who sustained the armies. Finally the end would come miles away in the quiet parlor of an unpretentious house in Appomattox, Virginia—a village until then without fame—when the two Generals in Chief of the North and the South, after a handclasp and a reminiscent conversation, put their signatures to documents that have found a permanent place among the cherished possessions of their people.

The campaign began with the crossing of the Rapidan River, which had separated the rival armies during the winter. Three times in the

---

* The quotations that stand at the heads of chapters will be found in proper context in the chapters. In general they are identified where they appear below the chapter headings; the words quoted here occurred in an army order.

past the Army of the Potomac had ventured to cross the Rapidan, and the lower Rappahannock. Twice it had returned after suffering defeats; once it had marched back somewhat ingloriously without risking battle. The crossing was made a little above the point where the Rapidan flows into the Rappahannock ten miles from historic Fredericksburg, approximately halfway between Washington and Richmond. Of the fords used by the Federal army, it was Germanna that was on the exposed flank not far from the winter encampments of the Confederates, and for the cavalry division under the command of Brigadier General James H. Wilson, which was to cover the crossing there, the operation order—which began, "The army will move on Wednesday, the 4th of May, 1864"—gave the following direction:

At midnight on the 3d of May, the Third Cavalry Division, with one-half the canvas pontoon bridge train, which will join it after dark, will move to Germanna Ford, taking the plank road, and cross the Rapidan as soon as the bridge is laid, if the river is not fordable, and hold the crossing until the infantry of the Fifth Corps is up. It will then move to Parker's Store on the Orange Court-House plank road, or that vicinity, sending out strong reconnaissances on the Orange pike and plank roads and the Catharpin and Pamunkey roads, until they feel the enemy, and at least as far as Robertson's Tavern, the New Hope Church, and Almond's or Robinson's.[1]

One can imagine Wilson's troopers, as the hour of midnight approached, standing to horse with all equipment in good order, carbines and revolvers inspected, sabers checked, saddle bags packed, canteens and cartridge boxes filled, forage on their saddles, wagons gone to the assembly point of the army quartermaster—completely mobile and quietly waiting. The two six-gun batteries of regular horse artillery, Pennington's and Fitzhugh's, which had been given to Wilson to add more substance to his fire power, had recently reported "in splendid condition." Now they waited with horses well groomed, leather cleaned and oiled, carriages immaculate, as if for a holiday parade; but with caissons and limbers filled for the grim business ahead. Probably there were no trumpet calls to break the quiet of the night, for this was enemy country and every inhabitant was a potential intelligence agent. The march order had provided for this fact by sending cavalry guards the day before to all the houses "in advance toward the Rapidan, so as to prevent any communication with the enemy by the inhabitants." In-

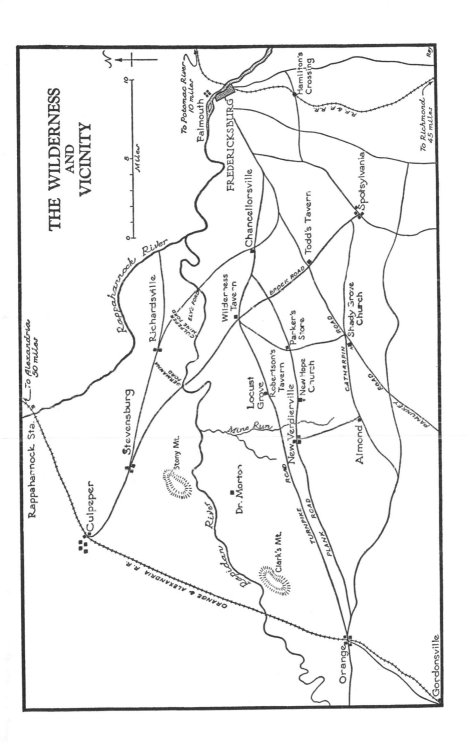

THE WILDERNESS
AND
VICINITY

Miles

To Alexandria
50 miles

Rappahannock Sta.

Culpeper

ORANGE & ALEXANDRIA R.R.

Stevensburg

Richardsville

Rappahannock River

Stony Mt.

Dr. Morton

Rapidan River

Clark's Mt.

Mine Run

Locust Grove

New Verdierville

Robertson's Tavern

New Hope Church

PLANK ROAD

TURNPIKE ROAD

ROAD

Almond

Orange

Gordonsville

GERMANNA ROAD

CULPEPER MINE FORD

ELY'S FORD

Wilderness Tavern

Parker's Store

BROCK ROAD

PLANK ROAD

CATHARPIN ROAD

Shady Grove Church

PAMUNKEY ROAD

Chancellorsville

Todd's Tavern

Spotsylvania

FREDERICKSBURG

Falmouth

To Potomac River
10 miles

Hamilton's Crossing

R. F. & P. R.R.

To Richmond
45 miles

stead of bugle calls, "Prepare to Mount—Mount," in low voices, but voices used to command, passed from unit to unit as the moment came for each to take its place in column. Wilson's Second Brigade, Colonel George H. Chapman, Third Indiana Cavalry, commanding, led the way from the camp at Stevensburg to the river. Soon from out the darkness over the plank road came the inimitable sound of mounted troops, the rumble of the guns, and the rattle of the engineer vehicles with the pontoons. But a listener by the road would have heard little conversation; it was a column of seasoned, disciplined troops, who did not need to reassure themselves with talk.

When he reached the Rapidan, Chapman at once placed his brigade —Third Indiana, First Vermont, Eighth New York, Eighth Illinois— so as to force a crossing, in case his passage should be disputed. But the advance guard, after crossing the river, found only a small enemy cavalry patrol, which it easily drove back. Then Chapman crossed, moved down the plank road toward Old Wilderness Tavern for a distance of two or three miles, and halted.

It was not a cheerful place to wait. This was the Wilderness.

Just one year before—almost to the day—this forest had echoed with the deadly and unexpected volleys of Stonewall Jackson's infantry, as it fell with customary fury upon the flank of the Army of the Potomac. About four miles from here Jackson himself was on that night mortally wounded.

Chapman covered himself with dismounted detachments. The carbines of his troopers were good weapons for close-in work. Still it was not a cheerful place; green men could have heard many unfriendly sounds; their fingers would have been nervous on their triggers. The troopers holding the horses—so vulnerable—must have been pleased to think that their comrades among the trees had done much night picket duty, were schooled in forest sounds, were alert but not too imaginative, and had careful fingers.

At 4:40 A.M., Wilson, remaining at the river until his division was entirely over, but with ears attentive to the dark forest to the south, and with frequent thoughts of Chapman, wrote to General Warren, whose head of column—veteran infantry—was not far away, that the last of his brigades would soon be crossing.[2] No force of the enemy had, he said, been found at the ford, and the brigade that had crossed had not encountered any resistance. An hour passed and Wilson sent this message:

ARMY OF THE POTOMAC
Germanna Ford, May 4, 1864—5.50 a.m.
Major-General Warren, Comdg. Fifth Army Corps:
General:
    The last regiment of my command is crossing. My advance is well out. No resistance shown as yet. The bridge is nearly completed.
Yours respectfully,
J. H. Wilson,
Brigadier-General, Commanding Division [3]

The young brigadier of twenty-six had written the first field messages of the great campaign, clear notes and much to the point.

As he waited and watched, Wilson—who was the scourge of everything lazy—probably observed with special interest the handling of the artillery teams, noted whether the lead and swing drivers got their pairs into draft where the pulling was bad, and whether the wheel drivers could make the "off" horses throw themselves properly into their harness. Guns are grim-looking things, especially in the half-light of dawn as they come up from a river, well handled by skillful drivers, and vanish into shadowy woods. The six two-gun sections with their capable-looking cannoneers must have given the experienced Wilson a feeling of reassurance as he left the river and rode to the head of his column. It was probably well for him that these woods were unfamiliar and did not evoke memories. Though a newcomer to the Army of the Potomac, he had known hard campaigning and bitter fighting in the West, at Vicksburg and Chattanooga, where woods had been as dark and roads as difficult; but his mind was not preyed upon nor dulled by the recollection of past defeat.

By early afternoon the situation had assumed some order and Wilson reported to the chief of staff of his own immediate commander, Major General Philip H. Sheridan, who had set up his headquarters near the Old Wilderness Tavern:

HDQRS. THIRD CAV. DIV., ARMY OF THE POTOMAC
Parker's Store, Va., May 4, 1864—2.10 p.m.
Lieutenant-Colonel Forsyth, Chief of Staff, Cavalry Corps:
    Chapman's brigade is now here; Bryan close up. Only a few men seen; 1 rebel captured on his way from Gordonsville to Hamilton's Cross-Roads, where his regiment is lying. I send herewith a civilian, Mr. Sime, a citizen of Great Britain. He says he left Orange yesterday 2 p.m. Longstreet's corps lies between there and Gordonsville, part at the latter place; Ewell

and Hill about Orange Court-House. Troops well down toward Mine Run, on all the roads, except this one; none on this road nearer than 7 miles to this place. He seems well disposed, and if properly rewarded may give other valuable information. I have sent patrols well out in all directions, but as yet hear of nothing, except few light parties scattered through the by-roads. Mr. Sime thinks no re-enforcements received by Lee since Longstreet's arrival. Beauregard not here. The roads from Old Wilderness Tavern very narrow and sometimes obscure. Distance about 5 miles. Plank road in fine condition. My position a very good one. Will report again soon.

J. H. Wilson,
Brigadier-General, Commanding [4]

Lieutenant Generals James Longstreet, Richard Ewell, and A. P. Hill commanded the three infantry corps of Lee's Army of Northern Virginia. Knowledge of the location of their troops was of course of much importance to the commander of the Army of the Potomac, and new reports were valuable, even though they might merely confirm older intelligence. General Pierre Gustave Toutant Beauregard—whose impressive name seemed intended for the pages of history—was the Confederate commander who had started the war by opening fire upon Fort Sumter in Charleston harbor, on April 12, 1861, in accordance with a telegram from the Confederate Secretary of War. In the spring of 1864 it was known by the Federal High Command that Beauregard was in command of Confederate forces south of Richmond in the vicinity of Petersburg; but as he had moved about considerably in the course of the war a fresh check upon him, even though negative, was important. After mention of personalities—of which soldiers think much—Wilson had reported on topography—of which they think equally much. Sheridan and the army commander would be glad indeed to have late information about roads, and Sheridan—not many years the senior of Wilson—knew exactly what he meant when he said, "My position a very good one"—cover, a stream to the rear where he could water his horses, and a field of fire to the front.

Wilson's troopers and their mounts had a chance to rest that afternoon, except those on patrol. To draw an assignment to Robertson's Tavern doubtless seemed preferable to spending the afternoon and night at New Hope Church; but Almond's or Robinson's might have been the choicest of any of the places the army order had mentioned. Veteran troopers may take a clash with a hostile patrol as merely part of the day's work; but they do not become casual about the possibility of a home-cooked meal or pleasant smiles, and they button their jackets and polish their leather with something more in mind than the approval of their officers. At least one of Sheridan's troopers who had recently been a sentinel at the home of a stanch Southern family just north of the Rapidan returned when the war was over to marry the daughter of the household.[5]

At 5:30 P.M. Wilson directed, "All horses will be saddled and bridled by 8 o'clock to-night, and the command be ready for any emergency, at a minute's notice."[6] He added that there might be small fires for cooking, but these only inside the brush. The instructions may not have reached all elements of Wilson's command, for so close were enemy detachments that a copy of them was captured.[7] A little later Wilson reported to Sheridan that a patrol had been within a mile of Mine Run on the pike, skirmishing with small detachments of the enemy.[8] The situation at Robertson's Tavern was not certain, but Wilson believed that he had executed all orders to date, for patrols were out as directed and had "felt the enemy"; and he asked for new orders for the next day, saying politely, "Be good enough to send instructions for to-morrow." He again assured his commander that he was strongly posted, and stated that he would be ready to move the next morning at 3:30.

The good work which Wilson had already done on his first day of field command was only the beginning of the fulfillment of a prophecy which had been put in writing by no less a person than Charles A. Dana. When, in the spring of 1863, there had been questions and gossip about General U. S. Grant, and doubt among politicians and the people as to the outcome of his operations around Vicksburg, the Secretary of War, Edwin M. Stanton, had sent Dana as his personal emissary to report confidentially about the state of affairs. Dana had remained for months and had become one of Grant's loyal supporters and admirers. All the members of Grant's staff naturally were made the objects of Dana's frank and able pen, in his reports to his chief. Of Wilson, then a lieutenant colonel and Grant's inspector general, he had written:

He is a captain of engineers in the regular army, and has rendered valuable services in that capacity. The fortifications of Haynes's Bluff were designed by him and executed under his direction. His leading idea is the idea of duty, and he applies it vigorously and often impatiently to others. In consequence he is unpopular among all who like to live with little work.

But he has remarkable talents and uncommon executive powers, and will be heard from hereafter.[9]

Now, James Wilson, wearing a star on each shoulder when only in the mid-twenties, was receiving the supreme test of a soldier, the test which would determine whether there beat in his breast the heart of a commanding general. An active mind, study, and a high sense of duty had enabled him to design good fortifications and reveal executive ability; but something quite different was needed in the very first assignment given him as a field commander—the qualities of not only physical but also high moral courage. As darkness settled over the forest, he certainly was aware of the grave responsibility resting upon him; he was in close proximity to the army of General Robert E. Lee, whose cavalry was led by the famous Jeb Stuart. He would indeed have been content could he have been sure that morning would come without his being attacked in a forest unknown to him, but familiar to the enemy perhaps in its every bypath. He could take heart in the fact that the regiments he commanded had fine battle records, would respond quickly to his orders, and would behave well even in tough positions. But for him the test was still ahead, and he must have known it was not far off, even though it might not come during the hours of night. And he knew that far more was involved than his own career. How did it happen that he, untried before by command, was in this post of special responsibility? There were three divisions in the cavalry corps, and the commanders of both the others were old to their commands and familiar with this region; but one of them was covering the unexposed column of infantry on the left, and the other was guarding the rear of the army—easy tasks compared with Wilson's. The young general knew full well why his division and not that of Gregg or Torbert was thrown out toward Parker's Store and had its detachments extended westward on the plank road and the pike until they felt the enemy. Of the many general officers leading commands across the river, only he and Sheridan were personally well known to Grant, the new Federal General in Chief, on whose orders the Army of the Potomac had been thrust again across the Rapidan into the tangled Wilderness. Toward them alone could the new chief have the feeling of certainty and confidence that a superior has for a subordinate who has executed his orders before, who has stood beside him in moments of uncertainty and doubt, and who understands and anticipates the workings of his mind. Probably Wilson's selection of 3:30 A.M. as the hour he would be ready to move reflected a little of his understanding of the farm-reared Grant.

The three infantry corps of the army (Second, Fifth, Sixth) executed their march orders perfectly. At 9:50 A.M., Major General Winfield Scott Hancock reported from Chancellorsville that the leading division of the Second Corps, which had crossed the Rapidan below Germanna at Ely's Ford, was going into camp.[10] The left column of infantry had been covered by the cavalry division of Brigadier General David Gregg, and Hancock passed on to army headquarters a report he had received from Gregg, which stated that there was no hostile infantry near Fredericksburg, but that the enemy cavalry was scheduled for a review in the afternoon at Hamilton's Crossing, four miles below Fredericksburg. Again at 11:05 Hancock reported,[11] and at 1:00 P.M. Major General Andrew A. Humphreys, the army's able chief of staff, acknowledged the two reports and informed Hancock: "Warren is getting up to his position and Sedgwick is now crossing to his. Some few shots have been fired toward Robertson's Tavern. Enemy moving; some force coming out toward New Verdierville." [12] Major General John Sedgwick commanded the Sixth Corps, which had followed behind the Fifth Corps of Major General Gouverneur K. Warren. At 3:05 P.M. Warren sent word that his whole corps was in the vicinity of Old Wilderness Tavern, and added, "The men are almost all in camp washing their feet, and with a good night's rest will feel fine." [13]

There is more to an army than combat troops. Without good supply organizations a great army cannot keep up a campaign for long. On May 4, 1864, a very fine field quartermaster was having the satisfaction of seeing the results of months of worry and hard work. In his subsequent report Brigadier General Rufus Ingalls wrote: "Probably no army on the earth ever before was in better condition in every respect than was the Army of the Potomac on the 4th of May, 1864." [14] The people of the North were supporting their armies generously; the factories had produced ample equipments, and the farms abundant food. But it was the quartermaster who saw that the shoes got to the feet of the soldiers, the rations to their haversacks, and the harness and saddles to the animals.

With the troops went "50 rounds of ammunition upon the person; three days' full rations in their haversacks; three days' bread and small rations in their knapsacks, and three days' beef on the hoof." In the wagons was ten days' subsistence for the men, and ten days' grain for the animals. In one column Ingalls's great train would have reached almost seventy miles, and it would have taken about four days of good marching to pass one point. He had "4,300 wagons, 835 ambulances, 29,945 artillery, cavalry, ambulance, and team horses; 4,046 private horses, 22,528 mules; making an aggregate of 56,499 animals." [15] (Accurate counting and punctilious arithmetic make the basis of good quartermastering.) The army order put the trains across the Rapidan at Ely's and Culpeper fords, covered by the First Cavalry Division under Brigadier General A. T. A. Torbert, and infantry details. Ingalls himself issued a circular that gave pertinent instructions for the coming movement and outlined what would now be called the Quartermaster SOP—Standing Operating Procedure.[16] After crossing the river, the trains moved by roads for the most part poor—or worse —to parks in the vicinity of Chancellorsville.

By noon the Headquarters, Army of the Potomac, Major General George G. Meade commanding, were established on the south side of the Rapidan overlooking the two bridges—one canvas pontoon, one heavy wooden pontoon—across which moved the long columns of blue infantry and artillery. Some tents had been pitched, and necessary facilities established for the work that had to be done. Messages were coming in and going out, and Humphreys was beginning to plan the field order that would have to be issued that evening with assignments of missions for the different corps for the next day.

Not far away from Meade's headquarters was another very important establishment: the Headquarters of the Armies of the United States, Lieutenant General Ulysses S. Grant, commanding. It was something novel indeed, for until recently the headquarters of all the Federal armies had been in Washington. Amazingly modest it also was, when one considers that Grant was directing the operations of upward of one million men, organized into a number of armies and operating in a vast theater of war. Although many heavy administrative matters had been left in Washington under the direction of Major General Henry W. Halleck—Grant's predecessor as General in Chief —strategical direction of all forces was to be in the field with Grant. The supreme headquarters staff was small, and consisted largely of officers who had served in the West with the new three-starred general.

The chief of staff was Brigadier General John A. Rawlins, a civilian who had learned much about war from his chief and was greatly devoted to him. He could supply richly colorful and sharp language, a matter in which the General in Chief was himself somewhat deficient, though he could express himself very clearly in dictionary words. In addition there were a half-dozen lieutenant colonels, and about the same number of captains, including a full-blooded Indian who was the reigning chief of the tribes called the Six Nations. On the afternoon in question a few tents were up, but the General in Chief preferred the porch of a near-by deserted house, where he sat smoking and conversing with his staff, who had little to do at the time although they probably expected activity soon. A newspaper correspondent appeared and manifested the customary eagerness of the profession for a story. As "public relations" officers had not yet been invented, the general had to handle the matter himself. When the reporter inquired how long it would take the army to reach Richmond, he was told by the man who had grown up on an Ohio farm, "I will agree to be there in about four days—that is, if General Lee becomes a party to the agreement; but if he objects, the trip will undoubtedly be prolonged." [17]

Grant must have been much pleased with the scene below him; any soldier would have been stirred with the smooth and tight marching of the infantry of Warren's Fifth and Sedgwick's Sixth Corps, and the steady flow of battery after battery of field artillery. Never before had the quiet general from the West seen the Army of the Potomac march to battle. During the few weeks that he had been East, Grant had reviewed parts of the army, and had commended its fine bearing, its discipline, and its excellent appointments. But impressive as the events about him were on the afternoon of May 4, 1864, Grant could not give all his thoughts to them, or think much of his young friend Wilson, to whom had fallen an assignment of so much importance. Other armies were about to take the field in accordance with Grant's great coordinated plan. Major General William Tecumseh Sherman, trusted lieutenant and devoted friend of the General in Chief, had his orders to strike south from Chattanooga toward Atlanta with his three armies, the Army of the Tennessee, the Army of the Ohio, and the Army of the Cumberland. Major General Franz Sigel with a small army was to move up the Shenandoah Valley in the direction of Lynchburg, and Major General Benjamin F. Butler with the Army of the James was to move from Fortress Monroe on the rear of Richmond. The signal for Butler to be on his way had been given in Grant's first field telegram as General in Chief:

> Germanna Ford, May 4, 1864
>
> Maj. Gen. H. W. Halleck, Chief of Staff:
> The crossing of the Rapidan effected. Forty-eight hours now will demonstrate whether the enemy intends giving battle this side of Richmond. Telegraph Butler that we have crossed the Rapidan.
>
> *U. S. Grant,*
> Lieutenant-General [18]

Information of the enemy had been coming from other than cavalry sources and the mounted patrols. At 9:30 A.M., Captain P. A. Taylor, the Federal signal officer on Stony Mountain, had reported an enemy message which he had intercepted and decoded, and which had been flashed from the Confederate signal station on Clark's Mountain to General Ewell, commanding the Third Corps of Lee's army. It read, "From present indications everything seems to be moving to the right, on Germanna and Ely's Ford roads, leaving cavalry in our front." [19] That daylight would reveal the march of the Federal columns to the enemy observers, advantageously situated to watch the area north of the Rapidan, had of course been foreseen; but it was very important to be in possession of their messages. Early in the afternoon another message to Ewell seized and decoded by Taylor had found its way into Grant's hands. This read: "We are moving. Had I not better move D. and D. towards New Verdierville?" [20]

Grant had already directed Major General Ambrose E. Burnside, who was at Rappahannock Station with the Ninth Corps, to march as soon as he was relieved by new troops presently to arrive.[21] (Burnside's command at the time was not a part of the Army of the Potomac, but an independent, though supporting force, and so was subject to Grant's orders, and not Meade's.) After reading the message that Taylor had intercepted, Grant telegraphed:

> Germanna Ford, May 4, 1864—1.15 p.m.
>
> Major-General Burnside:
> Make forced marches until you reach this place. Start your troops now in the rear, the moment they can be got off, and require them to make a night march. Answer.
>
> *U. S. Grant,*
> Lieutenant-General [22]

Burnside, in no doubt whatever as to what was wanted, replied at 3:58 P.M., "Dispatch received; will start column at once." [23] Captain Taylor continued to observe the country to the south of the Rapidan from his post of vantage on Stony Mountain, and at 3:00 he reported:

Enemy moving infantry and trains toward Verdierville. Two brigades gone from this front. Camps on Clark's Mountain breaking up. Battery still in position behind Dr. Morton's house, and infantry pickets on the river.[24]

The Confederates were on the move, but where to? Would Lee return to his old position along Mine Run, where he had defied the Army of the Potomac the preceding November, and where Meade had feared to attack him? Would he move past Mine Run and strike the Federal column as it sought to get through the Wilderness into the more open country beyond? Or, instead of doing either, would he swing southward and interpose between the Federals and the Confederate capital, which had been so successfully defended for three years? There was no way whatever to answer the questions, and the Army of the Potomac would have to continue its advance until the situation cleared. Humphreys accordingly wrote his field order.[25] It put the army in motion at five o'clock the next morning; infantry corps would have cover from their own security detachments; Sheridan would move his first and second divisions of cavalry against the enemy cavalry, which had been located at Hamilton's Crossing; Wilson would cover the right of the army with his division.

Lee, whose headquarters had been at Orange,* only twenty miles from those of Grant and Meade at Culpeper, had of course been giving much thought to the probable operations of the Federal army under the command of the new General in Chief, who had come East in the last of March. Though he had been a careful reader of Northern newspapers, which throughout the war printed information of value to the Southern leaders, Lee's biographers say little as to the care with which he had studied Grant's operations in the West. He must have realized that aggressiveness and persistence were leading characteristics of the new Federal commander who was to take the field with the Army of the Potomac while directing from a distance his

---

* Modern spellings and place names are used. Thus the words Court House and Station are dropped in the text, though they appear often in quotations.

other armies. From his opinion of the new commander and from the Federal dispositions, he had concluded that the Army of the Potomac would again cross the Rapidan below his forces, as it had done six months before, and he had put his command on the alert several days before. Thus his corps were ready to move promptly when the long columns of Federal troops were reported by his observers on Clark's Mountain. Lee issued nothing like a formal field order, but by 8:00 P.M. his general plan for the next day was formulated, and was announced in the following message:

> Rodes', near New Verdierville,
> May 4, 1864—8 p.m.

Lieutenant-General Ewell:
General:

General Lee directs me to inform you that he will be found in the woods opposite this house to-night. He wishes you to be ready to move on early in the morning. If the enemy moves down the river, he wishes to push on after him. If he comes this way, we will take our old line. The general's desire is to bring him to battle as soon now as possible. General Hill is on this road. Heth has passed this place. Wilcox near here. Longstreet is on our right, moving up. The cavalry in your front has been instructed to keep you informed of all movements of the enemy.

> Respectfully,
> *W. H. Taylor,*
> Assistant Adjutant-General [26]

Here is war with great courtliness and some indefiniteness. Grant's blunt telegram to Burnside, written by himself, and Lee's polite note to Ewell, written and signed by an adjutant, reveal some of the difference between the two great captains. Battle had not yet been joined; there had been only very light and intermittent contact; not a soldier may have fallen. Nevertheless, the two great generals revealed themselves in a small but highly important matter in the business of war, in their orders.

Although Burnside had caught completely the spirit of urgency from Grant's telegram—as shown by the precision with which he set down the time of his reply—Ewell may have been somewhat perplexed by the note he received from Taylor, and may have wondered how accurately it reflected his commander's ideas. A Federal movement "down the river" must have seemed to him quite unthinkable, however advantageous it would have been for the Confederate commander. As a matter of fact, the order which had already gone out from Meade's headquarters directed neither of the alternative moves which Lee had indicated.

When he bivouacked his corps on the night of the 4th, General Longstreet was perhaps soberly reflective. He had been a cadet with Grant at West Point for three years; had served with him in Mexico; had been at his wedding; and had studied his campaigns in the West. Several years after the war he told General Horace Porter, who was a lieutenant colonel on Grant's staff on the night of May 4, 1864, that upon learning that Grant was to take personal direction in the East he had said to officers at Lee's headquarters, "We must make up our minds to get into line of battle and to stay there; for that man will fight us every day and every hour till the end of the war." [27] Prophetic words indeed. So it was to be!

In order to comprehend the year of bitter fighting that still was necessary before the armies of the South laid down their arms, it is essential to understand the character, the minds, and the generalship of Grant and Lee, as well as their chief subordinates. It is also important, before one sees the clashes of 1864, to appreciate fully the valor of the armies that wore the blue and those that wore the gray.

Accordingly we shall leave Grant in his unpretentious headquarters on the bluff overlooking famous Germanna Ford, as darkness settles over the woods, the thickets, the few small clearings, the streams, the roads, and the trails of the eerie Wilderness, wherein he knows that his bold enemy is already moving, though with an as yet undiscovered purpose. We leave Grant there with thoughts we do not know, with an army he has never seen in battle, and a small staff that is at perfect ease with the friendly imperturbable general, while we turn back and review the three preceding years of war.

CHAPTER II

THE FORT THAT WAS A SYMBOL

Nearing the bar it was observed that war had commenced, and therefore, the peaceful offer of provisions was void.

Report of Captain G. V. Fox

THE first seven states to declare that they had withdrawn from the United States of America sent delegates to Montgomery, Alabama, early in February, 1861, and within a few days these representatives announced the formation of the Confederate States of America. The final constitution for the new government, which was adopted on March 11, differed in significant ways from that of the United States, as was quite natural, since the Southerners had found the old document so unsatisfactory. The rights of the individual states were emphasized, and significant reference was made to the "delegation of powers" to the central government by the "Sovereign and Independent States" of the Confederation. There were no scruples about naming slavery, and the South's "peculiar institution" was given explicit protection, not only in all states of the Confederacy, but in any territories it might hold.

Secession had in all instances been accomplished through special conventions called by the legislatures of the states. South Carolina had been the first to act, on December 20, 1860, and Texas the last, on February 1, 1861. Unanimity had marked the course of South Carolina, which had long meditated and threatened secession; in all the other states there had been opposing votes. It was not until the North, under the leadership of Abraham Lincoln, had shown that it

intended to treat secession as nothing more and nothing less than rebellion, and had begun measures to suppress it by force of arms, that
the four remaining states—Virginia, Arkansas, North Carolina, and
Tennessee—joined the original group of South Carolina, Mississippi,
Alabama, Florida, Georgia, Louisiana, and Texas.

The South Carolinians naturally felt a certain impatience for the
rapid prospering of secession, for they had fretted many years at the
shortcomings of the Union. Now they were irked by the presence of
three forts of the United States in the harbor of Charleston, their
largest and much cherished city. Though it may have been suspected
that the recent census would show that Charleston was no longer
fifteenth in population in the United States, South Carolinians could
well say that size alone is not a proper measure of a city's true worth.
But the city's imposing list of cultural possessions made only more
oppressive the thought of the three forts—Castle Pinckney, Fort
Moultrie, and Fort Sumter—in the possession of Yankee soldiers and
Yankee workmen. In many ways the Yankees were more objectionable than the pirates of olden days, for they were actually inside the
harbor, whereas the less impertinent pirates had been content to have
their haunts on islands outside the port.
Much more was involved than wounded pride and unwanted
Yankees. Charleston was a great port: from the excellent landlocked
harbor, there was a heavy export of rice, indigo, tobacco, lumber,
and cotton. Independence should greatly increase this commerce. But
so long as the Stars and Stripes flew from the staff of a single fort it
was unlikely that any foreign country of consequence would accept
South Carolina into the community of sovereign nations. Palmetto
flags within the city would be of no avail; the flag of the United States
above a fort whose guns could smash all shipping in the harbor would
be what counted. "We must have the forts" had been the earnest cry
of the enthusiastic Charlestonians as they eagerly awaited the meeting
of the convention which was to vote their deliverance from the op-
pressor. After the Ordinance of Secession had been passed, the words
expressed an objective immediately to be achieved, and the convention selected three commissioners, who solemnly set out for Washington with a copy of the Ordinance, duly attested by witnessing hands
as "true and correct" to the last comma and period, and bearing the
great seal of South Carolina. In addition the commissioners carried

an impressive document that gave them power to negotiate with the United States "for the delivery of the forts, magazines, lighthouses, and other real estate, with their appurtenances, within the limits of South Carolina . . . and for the division of all other property held by the Government of the United States as agent of the Confederated States, of which South Carolina was recently a member."

Probably the commissioners were very hopeful about their reception in Washington, whose fifth column of Secessionists, extensive and well organized, had been active since the election of Abraham Lincoln on November 6, 1860. The column's roster had been headed by three members of President Buchanan's cabinet: John B. Floyd of Virginia, Secretary of War; Howell Cobb of Georgia, Secretary of the Treasury; and Jacob Thompson of Mississippi, Secretary of the Interior. The President himself probably never entertained any disloyal purpose, but he was, without question, much influenced in his positions by the schemers close to him. His message to Congress on December 3, 1860, admitted that "the state of the Union" was bad indeed, and said that Southern discontent was caused by "long-continued and intemperate interference of the Northern people with the question of slavery in the Southern states." Because the bitter controversy then raging had arisen chiefly from the question of the status of slavery in new states and in territories, the falsification by Buchanan could do no good, and must do harm. The right of a state to secede from the Union was clearly denied by Buchanan, but the right of the Federal government to coerce a seceding state was equally denied. Although the Buchanan doctrine might not give the secessionists all they wished, it did not fall far short of doing so. Secession might cause recriminations and de- nunciations, but it would cause no gunfire. Though seceding states might not go with blessings and good wishes, they at least could go. Such was what Buchanan's statement appeared to mean. Cobb left the cabinet on December 8 in order to actively engage in secession; Floyd remained, for evidently he could serve "the cause" excellently in the War Department; Thompson stayed so as to help keep the "workers" well informed.

Expecting much, the commissioners from South Carolina arrived in Washington on December 26. They at once made their presence known to President Buchanan, and an appointment was made for one o'clock the next day. But before the meeting took place word came from Charleston that changed the entire situation.

The United States commander at Charleston was Major Robert Anderson, First U.S. Artillery. His command of nine officers and about seventy men comprising Battery E, First Artillery, occupied Fort Moultrie, which was situated on a large island—Sullivan's Island —near the mouth of the harbor. Castle Pinckney, on a small island

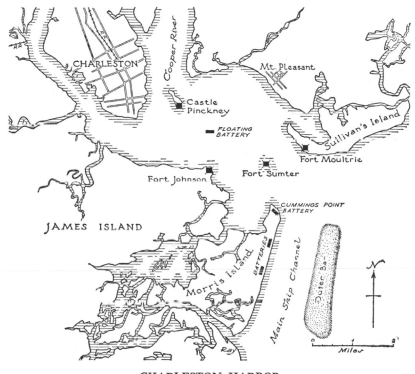

CHARLESTON HARBOR

close to the city, was occupied by one caretaker and family; Fort Sumter, on a small artificial island near mid-channel, and advanced toward the harbor's entrance, was in the hands of engineer officers and workmen who were engaged in completing installations and mounting guns. Moultrie was very vulnerable to land assault, whereas Sumter was not. In addition, Sumter's heavy masonry walls, forty feet high and five feet thick, could have withstood bombardment by the customary naval guns of the day, while its own intended armament of 140 guns, provided they were served by the proper garrison of 650 men, could have dealt heavy punishment to attacking ships. Realizing that he could not defend Moultrie, Anderson decided to move to Sumter. On December 26, he quietly and secretly made preparations, and at dusk that evening very skillfully executed the transfer. Earlier in the afternoon, the families of the garrison with their baggage were moved in a schooner to the vicinity of Fort Johnson, another post on the south side of the harbor, as though they were to be transferred to the barracks there. When the troops had reached Sumter, a signal gun brought the schooner to its wharf, and the women and children entered the dark and heavy gates of the island fortress.

His delicate task completed, the good soldier at once—at eight o'clock in the same evening—sat down and wrote a report of his action in a letter to the Adjutant General of the Army. This letter is the first entry in the many volumes of the great Official Records of the war. With thankful heart Anderson began: "I have the honor to report that I have just completed, by the blessing of God, the removal to this fort of all my garrison, except the surgeon, four non-commissioned officers, and seven men." [1] Anderson's letter was not received in Washington until the 29th; but the secession underground worked rapidly and on the 27th Anderson received the following telegram from the Secretary of War:

Intelligence has reached here this morning that you have abandoned Fort Moultrie, spiked your guns, burned the carriages, and gone to Fort Sumter. It is not believed, because there is no order for any such movement. Explain the meaning of this report.[2]

Anderson's reply to the telegram was as forthright as his action had been:

The telegram is correct. I abandoned Fort Moultrie because I was certain that if attacked my men must have been sacrificed, and the command of the harbor lost. I spiked the guns and destroyed the carriages to keep the guns from being used against us.

If attacked, the garrison would never have surrendered without a fight.[3]

"Command of the harbor" expressed the military necessity simply and clearly. Robert Anderson, Major of Artillery, would keep such command, in spite of treason in high places. His move to Sumter had said one simple but very elemental thing: Do not have me swear to "bear true allegiance to the United States of America, and . . . serve them honestly and faithfully against all their enemies or opposers whatsoever" unless you expect me so to do.

Floyd denounced Anderson's move as a violation of orders, although the latter had received considerable discretionary power on December 11 from Major D. C. Buell, Assistant Adjutant General, on a visit to Fort Moultrie, in a memorandum which ended:

The smallness of your force will not permit you, perhaps, to occupy more than one of the three forts, but an attack or an attempt to take possession of any one of them will be regarded as an act of hostility, and you may then put your command into either of them which you may deem most proper to increase its power of resistance. You are also authorized to take similar steps whenever you have tangible evidence of a design to proceed to a hostile act.[4]

Although Buchanan may for a while have considered ordering Anderson back to Moultrie, in the end he suspended judgment.

On the 28th, the President received the commissioners, and was handed not only their documents but also a covering letter that should have angered him. In bitter language the South Carolinians charged that Anderson's move to Sumter was a direct violation of a personal pledge by Buchanan, upon whose "honor" they had counted. The weak reply that Buchanan submitted to his cabinet for approval caused some of its members to threaten to resign, and he turned over to Secretary of State Jeremiah Black and Attorney General Edwin M. Stanton [5] the drafting of the momentous document dated December 31,[6] which reflected the enthusiastic approval of Anderson's move that had been shown in the North. In the words of the two ghost writers the President stated that he had no power to negotiate as the commissioners wished, and went on to say, "I could therefore meet you only as private gentlemen of the highest character." This was very deflationary for three men sent as commissioners of a sovereign state who were eager to divide the effects and the assets of a great nation. (The assets of the United States included a large area held as territory.) The document weakened Buchanan's position by a lengthy defense. Quoting in full Buell's memorandum of instructions to Anderson, it admitted ignorance as to whether Anderson had had "tangible evidence of . . . a hostile act," but stated, "Still, he is a brave and

honorable officer, and justice requires that he should not be condemned without a fair hearing." [7] It noted that South Carolina troops
had seized Castle Pinckney and Fort Moultrie on the 27th and had
raised the palmetto flag. Refusing to withdraw Major Anderson, the
President stated manfully in the words of Secretaries Black and Stanton, "This I cannot do; this I will not do." There was one serious error
in the long communication, for the two cabinet members caused him
to say that, although he was himself unauthorized to negotiate, he was
willing to communicate "propositions" to Congress. Here was recognition of a sort; and, if the offer had been accepted, Buchanan would
have been prevented from taking action of any kind while debate
followed debate. But the advantageous opening was not seen by the
South Carolinians, who apparently were so angered that they had lost
all judgment.

The commissioners were not to be outdone by the President in letter
writing, and on January 1, 1861, they presented him a document that
fills more than four large printed pages.[8] Very appropriately it bears
the indorsement, "Executive Mansion, 3½ o'clock, Wednesday. This
paper, just presented to the President, is of such a character that he
declines to receive it." In spite of his justified official action, it is to be
hoped that Buchanan peeped at the paper just a little, for it contained
some very notable statements, among which are:

> Scarcely had their [South Carolina's] commissioners left, than Major
> Anderson waged war. No other words will describe his action. It was not
> a peaceful change from one fort to another; it was a hostile act in the
> highest sense—one only justified in the presence of a superior enemy, and
> in imminent peril. He abandoned his position, spiked his guns, burned his
> gun carriages, made preparations for the destruction of his post, and
> withdrew, under cover of the night, to a safer position. This was war . . .
> By your course you have probably rendered civil war inevitable. Be it
> so. If you choose to force this issue upon us, the State of South Carolina
> will accept it, and relying upon Him who is the God of Justice as well as
> the God of Hosts, will endeavor to perform the great duty which lies
> before her, hopefully, bravely, and thoroughly.

The theory that a hostile àct is committed by a man who prepares
to defend himself against attack is rather striking.

On the 29th Floyd offered his resignation, and on the 31st the
President accepted it. Floyd's statement as to his reason for resigning

does not survive; the only information we have is: "No record of Mr. Floyd's letter of resignation can be found in the War Department." [9] There was more reason for his hasty departure from Washington than the government's disapproval of events at Charleston, for on the 30th he had been indicted by a Federal grand jury in Washington for malfeasance and conspiracy to defraud the government in a bond issue.[10] Although the indictments were quashed about three months later because of a technicality in one instance and lack of evidence in the other, Floyd's position would have been one of embarrassment. The office of Secretary of War was filled by the appointment of Joseph Holt, a Kentuckian by birth and an able lawyer, until then Postmaster General. His views were so opposed to those of Floyd that his enemies called him a Coercionist, but the Senate confirmed the appointment on January 18, 1861, in a 38-to-13 vote. He warmly commended Major Anderson for his move to Sumter in a letter that closed: "The movement, therefore, was in every way admirable, alike for its humanity, as for its soldiership." [11] This message was not sent until January 10—an unfortunate delay, for prompt and warm official endorsement of the move to Sumter would have meant much to Anderson and might have influenced his decision at a very critical moment.

Two of South Carolina's congressmen, William Porcher Miles and Lawrence M. Keitt, wrote to the State Convention, which was still in session, a letter that made Floyd a hero and martyr and Buchanan a villain of the blackest kind.[12] Had their minds not been filled with consuming rage, they would have seen that Floyd himself should have been held responsible for Anderson's move to Sumter. The important thing was not what Buchanan had said or promised, but what instructions had actually gone to Anderson. Floyd, the Secretary of War, held the key post, because instructions would go through him and the conspirators had direct access to him, an arch conspirator. Floyd made the mistake of sending Major Buell, a very loyal officer, with *verbal* instructions to Anderson. Shrewdly enough, Buell left a written memorandum; but it was probably only one-half Floyd and one-half Buell. The injunction about carefully avoiding acts "which would needlessly tend to provoke aggression" sounds much like the scheming Floyd; the fine closing sentence, "You are also authorized to take similar steps whenever you have tangible evidence of a design to proceed to a hostile act," sounds much like Buell, the honest soldier.

A plotter should never allow one loyal officer to write the last sentence in a directive to another loyal officer.

Anderson certainly repeated to Buell accounts of the many ominous events and of threats which he had already reported to the War Department. His own dispatches would indeed have been grounds for charging he had not obeyed the instructions in Buell's memorandum, if he had not moved to Sumter. Though Floyd was not honest enough to refer in his telegram to the Buell memorandum, President Buchanan very effectively made his stand upon its concluding sentence. It was that sentence, which the scheming Secretary had hesitated to alter, not President Buchanan, that proved the undoing of the commissioners.

The person who suffered most during the trying days of December was Winfield Scott, General in Chief of the Army. His seventy-four years rested heavily upon him and he was quite ill when, on December 12, he came from his regular headquarters in New York to Washington at Floyd's suggestion. He was a Virginian, but his reaction to the South Carolina crisis was not what Floyd wished. For years the old soldier had had an oath registered in Heaven, an oath he would never violate. As soon as the situation was explained to him, he supported the position of Lewis Cass of Michigan, Secretary of State, that adequate reenforcements be sent at once to Anderson, at that time in Fort Moultrie. Cass resigned on the 14th because nothing was done, and on the 22nd Anderson wrote: "I do not think that we can rely upon any assurances, and wish to God I only had men enough here to man fully my guns." [13]

The old general, though sick, never forgot Anderson, parading his small command in salute as he lowered his flag each night at retreat, looking at his slender stores—and the many unmanned guns. On December 28, he wrote to Floyd:

Lieutenant-General Scott, who has had a bad night, and can scarcely hold up his head this morning, begs to express the hope to the Secretary of War—

1. That orders may not be given for the evacuation of Fort Sumter;

2. That one hundred and fifty recruits may instantly be sent from Governor's Island to re-enforce the garrison, with ample supplies of ammunition, subsistence, including fresh vegetables, as potatoes, onions, turnips; and

LIEUTENANT GENERAL WINFIELD SCOTT

3. That one or two armed vessels be sent to support the said fort.[14]

Two days later the general, still harried with thoughts of Sumter's cannons without cannoneers, very reluctantly appealed directly to the President, over the head of the Secretary:

Lieutenant-General Scott begs the President of the United States to pardon the irregularity of this communication.

It is Sunday; the weather is bad, and General Scott is not well enough to go to church. But matters of the highest national importance seem to forbid a moment's delay, and if misled by zeal, he hopes for the President's forgiveness.

Will the President permit General Scott, without reference to the War Department and otherwise, as secretly as possible, to send two hundred and fifty recruits from New York Harbor to re-enforce Fort Sumter, together with some extra muskets or rifles, ammunition, and subsistence stores?

It is hoped that a sloop of war and cutter may be ordered for the same purpose as early as to-morrow.

General Scott will wait upon the President at any moment he may be called for.[15]

Scott on December 31 again wrote to the President, calling attention to Anderson's isolation and saying, "It is just possible in his state of isolation a system of forged telegrams from this place may be played off so successfully as to betray him into some false movement." [16] On the same day, anticipating that something would be done after the resignation of Floyd, General Scott sent to the commanding officer at Fort Monroe directions to prepare a relief expedition, adding as a postscript: "Manage everything as secretly and confidentially as possible. *Look to this.*" [17] Such was the man that Floyd thought might be made an agent of conspiracy!

The hour was very late. On December 30 Anderson had written:

I have the honor to report that the South Carolinians have established a post at Fort Johnson. . . . I saw that there was a party yesterday on Morris Island. . . . The governor was called upon by a friend of mine in reference to his decision, by which all communication between us and the city (except the sending for our mails) was cut off, and he refuses to modify or recall his order. We are pushing forward our work here very vigorously, and if we have a week longer, shall, by the blessing of God, be fully prepared for any attack they may make.[18]

The ominous fact was that the battery being built on Morris Island, like the battery being repaired at Fort Moultrie, could fire on ships seeking to enter the harbor: the time for sending reenforcements or supplies was running out.

Anderson's letter reached the Adjutant General's office on January 2, 1861, and a memorandum of that date, in General Scott's handwriting, gives instructions for a relief expedition of "two hundred well instructed men" and provisions, to go from New York instead of from Fort Monroe as previously contemplated. Foreseeing the possibilities, the General in Chief wrote significantly:

> Instructions to be sent by Colonel Thomas [Lorenzo Thomas, Assistant Adjutant General] in writing to Major Anderson that should a fire likely to prove injurious be opened upon any vessel bringing re-enforcements or supplies, or upon her boats, from any battery in the harbor, the guns of Fort Sumter may be employed to silence such fire, and the same in case of like firing upon Fort Sumter itself.[19]

At last things were working as they should: the General in Chief was giving orders. But with matters in its hands, the army bungled. A warning order should have gone to Anderson at once, since communication with him was somewhat precarious. Though such orders are an essential part of good staff work, they are often forgotten: failure of the present relief expedition was due to the omission of just such an order. It constitutes one of the most important purely military lessons in the entire story of Fort Sumter. Intrigue and political considerations fill many of the pages about Sumter, but here was a simple staff problem that required careful handling.

Utmost secrecy was needed in the preparation of the expedition. A private vessel had to be chartered; in his memorandum, General Scott directed Colonel Thomas to conclude arrangements already begun with a Mr. Schultz in New York, after satisfying himself that the latter was reliable, and provided the terms were reasonable. On account of the wording of Scott's memorandum, Thomas went to New York himself, an act which both delayed his letter to Anderson—perhaps needlessly —and very likely aroused suspicion in the many watchful agents of secession in Washington. The assistant adjutant general does not go about on minor matters, and it would have been better if Thomas had remained at his desk in Washington with the customary weekday look of an adjutant annoyed because somebody's strength report does not balance. An aide to General Scott might have gone to New York without exciting suspicion, for the general's habitual headquarters were in that city. On the 4th, Thomas wrote Scott an interesting letter from New York about arrangements [20] and, perhaps unwisely, wired him: "Arrangements made as proposed; to leave tomorrow evening; send map." The men, arms, and supplies were to be put on the vessel —the *Star of the West*—after dark at Governor's Island, and Thomas stated, combining optimism and caution, "I shall cut off all communication between the island and the cities until Tuesday morning, when I expect the steamer will be safely moored at Fort Sumter."

On the 5th, Thomas, still in New York, wrote a very careful letter to Major Anderson.[21] The thing that should have been done first was done last. Thomas had waited until he could give full details of the expedition, which were of minor importance. What counted was that Anderson knew that he could use the guns of Sumter to aid the expedition. That fact, and the following sentence were the really significant parts of Thomas's letter: "The General in Chief desires me to communicate the fact that your conduct meets with the emphatic approbation of the highest in authority." The General in Chief! That was Winfield Scott! *Emphatic approbation of the highest in authority.* What a phrase! The old general still knew what to tell soldiers as well as what to send them. Floyd's telegram, which was the last communication Anderson had received from the government, would have been forgotten, and the major's determination would have been rekindled by those words. Not later than January 3, a messenger should have been sent to Anderson bearing the instructions and commendation of General Scott. Hearing nothing, Anderson grew somewhat discouraged as well as uncertain or distrustful of his government's position. On the 6th he wrote:

At present, it would be dangerous and difficult for a vessel from without to enter the harbor, in consequence of the batteries which are already erected and being erected. I shall not ask for any increase of my command, because I do not know what the ulterior views of the Government are. We are now, or soon will be, cut off from all communication, unless by means of a powerful fleet, which shall have the ability to carry the batteries at the mouth of this harbor.[22]

It was not that bad yet, and Anderson would have felt differently if, on the 6th, he could have laid the guns of Sumter on their probable target, and posted a watch for the expected ship.

In the early light of January 9, the *Star of the West,* with troops concealed below decks, started into Charleston harbor, flying the American ensign from her flagstaff. Fearing attack from Fort Moultrie, she laid her course close to Morris Island, and was fired on at close range by a masked battery located there. Promptly she broke a full-sized United States garrison flag from her fore, but the firing continued, and she received hits. Officers on her deck, seeing the United States flag above Sumter, confidently expected Anderson's guns to silence the battery that was attacking her.[23] But those guns gave no aid to the vessel trying to bring assistance. From the vicinity of Fort Moultrie vessels appeared, evidently intending to cut off the *Star of the West.* The master of the ship, fearing this, and believing he could never pass Moultrie without the assistance of the guns of Sumter, put about and left the harbor. As long as the ship was within range it was fired on.[24]

Anderson had not received the letter which stated that he might use his guns to aid the succoring ship, and which also gave him the cue by praising him for past bold action. Uninformed and perplexed, he witnessed from the ramparts of Fort Sumter the attack upon the *Star of the West.* For years at evening he had stood at attention as his flag was lowered; day after day he had heard the morning gun salute the flag's return to the top of the mast. A subtle effect of this had taken hold of him: an effect that cynics and certain "intellectuals" do not and never will understand—though they may be the first to call for men like Anderson when they are in trouble. There was the battery firing on a ship that flew the same flag that was above his fort. Sumter's guns were quickly ready: an eight-inch howitzer was laid on the battery on Morris Island, the lanyard in an impatient but disciplined hand; lighter guns in the casemate were trained on Fort Moultrie, with cannoneers ready for the duties they knew so well. The command "Commence firing" must have been very close to Anderson's lips. Has any officer in our history been in a more trying position than Major Robert Anderson, First Artillery, on Wednesday morning January 9, 1861? He was in the dilemma of seeing his flag disgraced —when he could prevent it—and of acting without proper instructions and perhaps contrary to the wishes of his government. He withheld his fire. He turned to letter writing, as others in much higher place have done since that day in order to avoid war. He wrote at once to Governor Pickens of South Carolina:

Two of your batteries fired this morning upon an unarmed vessel bearing the flag of my Government. As I have not been notified that war has been declared by South Carolina against the Government of the United States, I cannot but think this hostile act was committed without your sanction or authority. Under that hope, and that hope alone, did I refrain from opening fire upon your batteries. I have the honor, therefore, respectfully to ask whether the above mentioned act . . . was committed in obedience to your instructions, and to notify you, if it be not disclaimed, that I must regard it as an act of war, and that I shall not, after a reasonable time for the return of my messenger, permit any vessels to pass within range of the guns of my fort.[25]

Major Anderson's letter could have been answered in one brief sentence. But Governor Pickens replied voluminously and deceptively. The pertinent part of the long letter was:

Special agents, therefore, have been off the bar to warn all approaching vessels, if armed or unarmed, and having troops to re-enforce the forts on board, not to enter the harbor of Charleston, and special orders have been given to the commanders of all forts and batteries not to fire at such vessels until a shot fired across their bows would warn them of the prohibition of the State. Under these circumstances, the Star of the West, it is understood, this morning attempted to enter this harbor, with troops on board, and having been notified she could not enter, was fired into. The act is perfectly justified by me.[26]

Though the governor justified the firing, he neither disclaimed nor avowed giving an order. The inference that the *Star of the West* had been stopped by agents and notified not to enter the port was false. She had been off the harbor with no lights showing from midnight, but had not been hailed. A steamer that saw her in the early morning preceded her into the harbor, burning lights and firing rockets quite obviously as a warning. Governor Pickens had been directly advised of the coming of the *Star of the West,* so it was not necessary to have her hailed and interrogated as to cargo. His suggestion that this had been done was mere dissimulation. On the morning of January 8, Louis T. Wigfall, a senator from Texas and a most industrious agent of secession, sent the following telegram from Washington to Governor Pickens:

The Star of the West sailed from New York on Sunday with Government troops and provisions. It is said her destination is Charleston. If so, she may be hourly expected off the harbor of Charleston.[27]

South Carolina had won no mean victory, and the incident aroused enthusiasm at a very opportune time for secession. Mississippi's Convention voted on the very day that the *Star of the West* somewhat ignominiously was returning to Fort Monroe with her object completely unaccomplished; and five other states soon followed. The Charlestonians had not a single wound to lick; theirs was a complete and almost unequaled victory. Amateur artillerymen and schoolboy soldiers had turned back a ship under the very muzzles of guns commanded by a professional officer and served by regular soldiers. Only a very unimaginative people would have failed to be aroused by the amazing success that they had achieved. Now the persons who had proclaimed the weakness of the Federal government were fully vindicated; the doubters fell jubilantly in line. Well could the delegates from all seven of the seceding states convene in Montgomery feeling confidence mixed with a little disdain or even contempt for the administration in Washington.

But secession would not have looked so easy if Sumter's guns had replied. Artillery in the sixties, though far less terrible than today, was nevertheless a powerful arm. Fort Sumter itself was reduced to a great heap of brick and dust before the end of the war by heavy Federal guns that had been brought ashore. Only a few of Sumter's guns were mounted, but they should have been effective against the lightly protected batteries of the South Carolinians. The guns in Moultrie could have been taken in enfilade, and at a range of only 1,900 yards, so that Anderson could easily have neutralized or silenced them. Had that happened, the South Carolina delegates would have boarded the train for Montgomery with quite a different story.

The people of the North were stunned by the *Star of the West* incident. The friends of the apparently helpless Union had to seek a measure of comfort in a candid recognition of gallantry on the part of the seceding South Carolinians. The very loyal *Harper's Weekly* carried a full-page picture of the battery with its stern commanding officer and the sober cannoneers firing like steady veterans upon the unhappy ship, a picture that would have made an excellent recruiting poster—on the streets of Charleston. More damaging than such a picture was the dismal account of the correspondent aboard the *Star of the West*. Probably he had anticipated writing a stirring report of a dramatic scene—but this is what, unhampered by censorship, he substituted:

Why does not Major Anderson open fire on the battery and save us? We look in vain for help; the American flag flies from Fort Sumter, and the American flag at our bow and stern is fired upon, yet there is not the slightest recognition of our presence from the fort from [to] which we look for protection.[28]

The South Carolinians had ready answers for the distressed reporter and his unhappy Northern readers. Their own newspapers, as well as letters sent North and published, asserted that Major Anderson's men had refused to fire, and that he had put many of them in irons.[29] The source of the information was naturally said to be a deserter from his command. Other papers recalled the fact that the major was from the border state of Kentucky while his wife was from Georgia; and they suggested very strongly that at heart he was in favor of the Southern cause.[30] It made no difference that stories contradicted each other; each found believers, and all were hard to deny. Thus the hero of a few days before became the object of malicious rumor and undeserved doubt.

The incident of the *Star of the West* was inexplicable: it was like Pearl Harbor. Both the disgrace of January 8, 1861, and the catastrophe of December 7, 1941, came after decisions in high places that involved warnings to subordinates. But it was much to the credit of President Buchanan and General Scott that Major Anderson was not made a scapegoat. Complete candor in regard to Washington's failure to give warning was not achieved, but Secretary Holt wrote to Anderson on January 16:

Unfortunately, the Government had not been able to make known to you that the Star of the West had sailed from New York for your relief, and hence, when she made her appearance in the harbor of Charleston, you did not feel the force of the obligation to protect her approach as you would naturally have done had this information reached you.[31]

No carelessness of the government or higher military headquarters is here implied, but the tone of Holt's letter was kindness itself, and there was no suggestion of fault on Major Anderson's part, though the disappointment of the Secretary was clear.

The siege of the island fortress, with its small garrison and its band of workmen, had begun. When Major Anderson read Governor Pickens's reply to his note of the morning of January 9, he pereceived that his threat to allow no ships to pass within range of his guns had been very unwise. The honest soldier was not a match in the art of letter writing for the wily governor, who, evading a categorical answer to the pointed question, slipped neatly out of the corner in which he appeared to have been placed and deftly put the major himself into a very bad position by saying, "In regard to your threat in regard to vessels in the harbor, it is only necessary to say that you must judge of your own responsibility." This masterful thrust might well be compared with the famous stroke that Charles Francis Adams, as Minister to Great Britain, later delivered to Earl Russell, which kept two ironclad vessels from being delivered to the Confederates.[32] Anderson got out of his predicament with a second note to the governor that afternoon, in which he said he was referring the entire question to his government, and would defer action until instructions were received. At the same time he sent an officer to the War Department to make a full report.

That day Pickens had won two victories: the one-sided firing affair, and the two-sided letter-writing engagement. But he was far from being in a comfortable position, and he shortly took up a policy of bluff and appeasement. On the 11th two of his cabinet ministers demanded the surrender of the fort. On Anderson's refusal, they stated they would be satisfied if the *status quo* were maintained. The major made no commitment on this point but suggested referring it to Washington—a proposition the secretaries took back to Pickens.

In spite of a stiffening attitude of the Buchanan administration that must have indicated the futility of the enterprise, Governor Pickens sent his attorney general, I. W. Hayne, to Washington; and Anderson availed himself of the opportunity of further communication with the government by dispatching another of his officers. Hayne could find no one who would listen to his demand for Sumter, and the situation had something of a comic aspect. Someone certainly owned Sumter, for there was Anderson with his cannons and his seventy professional cannoneers; but no one could be located who could give it up. Hayne soon modified his demand for surrender to a request for the preservation of the *status quo*. In this also he was rebuffed on February 6, when Secretary Holt terminated the matter in a letter stating emphatically that President Buchanan considered the right to reenforce Sumter rested on the same unquestionable foundation as the right to occupy it.[33]

Major Anderson felt a natural relief when all the persons for whom he was responsible had been brought within the thick walls of Sumter, surrounded on all sides by water. But the fort was far from ready for either defense or offensive action, and he and Captain John G. Foster, his energetic and resourceful engineer officer, at once began to put everything in order. Embrasures that might be entered and that could not be easily defended were closed with shutters or masonry. The main gates were walled up except for a narrow passage which was guarded by three guns. Arrangements were made to bring effective fire of canister upon the landing wharf, which was mined. The room above the gate was carefully stocked with hand grenades, and openings were made for throwing them. By January 21 Anderson could report a total of fifty-one guns in position: 22-pounders, 32's, 42's, 8-inch columbiads, 8-inch seacoast howitzers, and 10-inch columbiads.[34] Men who knew their business were at work, men of stout heart. "We can hold our own as long as it is necessary to do so," wrote Captain Foster on January 14,[35] repeating to the chief of engineers what Anderson had already reported. Although he well knew that Sumter would eventually have to be given up if the whole South seceded, Foster added, "We are, however, all prepared to go all lengths in its defense if the Government requires it."

On February 3, after two weeks of negotiations between Anderson and Pickens, the women (about twenty in number) and the children were evacuated from Sumter, and sent to New York. About the same time Anderson was allowed to resume buying beef and some other supplies from a contractor in Charleston, so that in one respect the life of the garrison was improved, for its chief diet had been pork and bread; but there was a shortage of certain items, notably candles, soap, and coal, which caused discomfort and inconvenience, and unusually bad and stormy weather increased the gloom of the situation. Nevertheless, both Anderson and Foster wrote of the good health and the excellent spirits and morale of the command.[36]

A more important shortage which in the end proved to be crucial was that of cartridges for the guns. There were many barrels of powder in the magazines, but only a few hundred cartridges, and there was no cloth for making more powder bags. When Lieutenant Norman J. Hall went north on January 12 with Attorney General Hayne, he took a memorandum covering the deficiencies in supplies, and powder bags and cloth to make them must have been among the principal items. Later Major Anderson wrote that he had had powder bags made out of the surplus flannel shirts that the quartermaster had on hand.[37] Although he did not have sufficient ammunition to engage in target practice, which he much regretted,[38] he was not parsimonious on Washington's birthday. Unable completely to forget the great Virginian, the South Carolinians fired thirteen guns in his honor at sunrise. A foreign minister or a major general is entitled to that much gunpowder, and Major Anderson made up for the affront by giving the first President a national salute at high noon—a gun for each state, including South Carolina.[39]

On February 12, the Provisional Congress of the newly formed Confederate States adopted a resolution asserting that the Montgomery government was taking over the questions and difficulties existing between states of the Confederacy and the United States, relative to forts, arsenals, and navy yards. The respective governors were notified,[40] and the next day Governor Pickens wrote a long and intricate letter on the Sumter situation to Howell Cobb, President of the Provisional Congress, stating "I am perfectly satisfied that the welfare of the new confederation and the necessities of the state require that Fort Sumter should be reduced before the close of the present administration at Washington." [41]

Although time was short the new government at Montgomery did not act quickly. It was on February 23 that Jefferson Davis—the new Provisional President—dispatched Major W. H. C. Whiting, formerly of the United States Army, to Charleston with orders to report upon the situation. Pickens evidently was somewhat displeased by the delay, and wrote President Davis asking which of them should make the demand for the surrender of Fort Sumter.[42] On March 1, L. P. Walker, Secretary of War for the Confederate States, telegraphed as follows:

Your letter to President received. This Government assumes the control of military operations at Charleston, and will make demand of the fort when fully advised. An officer goes to-night to take charge.[43]

The officer referred to was Brigadier General Pierre G. T. Beauregard, recently in the United States Army. At Charleston he found no Confederate troops, but only state units—a peculiar mixture of South Carolina army, militia, and volunteers. The difficulty of command was solved by a prompt order from South Carolina's Secretary of War, enjoining all officers and men of the state forces to obey orders emanating from General Beauregard.[44] Beauregard, free of all worries about paymasters and quartermasters, set to work in a competent professional way to make an effective and disciplined military force out of the somewhat lax but enthusiastic companies and regiments that had been put at his disposal.

On March 4 Lincoln was inaugurated. North and South alike had waited for this event, uncertain, doubtful, and apprehensive. Although his general views were well known from his debates with Douglas, his campaign speeches, and the addresses he had made on his trip to Washington from Springfield, nothing he had previously said compared in importance with the pronouncement he made after taking the solemn oath of office.

Lincoln's entire inaugural address was devoted to the momentous crisis facing the country, and to an explanation of his general policy. A few sentences bore specifically on the situation at Charleston and the similar one in Pensacola Harbor. Without naming them, the new President said: "The power confided to me will be used to hold, occupy, and possess the property and places belonging to the Government." He indicated very clearly that his course would be subject to modification in accordance with current events and the results of experience. Near the end he spoke with candor directly to the dissatisfied people of the South, and made these specific promises: "The Government will not assail you. You can have no conflict without being yourself the aggressor."

By many persons in the North Lincoln's address was regarded as not merely conciliatory, but weak. The Southern agents in Washington, however, viewed the words of the new President quite otherwise. Busy former Senator Wigfall, still in Washington though both his native and his adopted state were in the Confederacy, at once telegraphed Governor Pickens that the inaugural meant war, and that reenforcements would probably be sent at once to Sumter.[45] In the evening of the same day some five or six Southerners met to study the address. One of them, L. Q. Washington, reported at length the next day to Confederate Secretary of War Walker that the group agreed unanimously that Lincoln intended "to re-enforce and hold Fort Sumter and Pickens, and to retake the other places." [46] Washington described Lincoln as "a man of will and determination," and predicted that "his Cabinet will yield to him with alacrity."

Probably at the very hour when the Southern agent was writing that reenforcement of Sumter was certain, Lincoln was reading disturbing letters just received from Major Anderson. Although prior to his inauguration he had received some significant letters from army officers, as well as views of General Scott communicated through friends in Washington, he could not have known the exact situation in the Charleston fort. Anderson had written February 28:

> I confess that I would not be willing to risk my reputation on an attempt to throw re-enforcements into this harbor within the time for our relief rendered necessary by the limited supply of our provisions, and with a view of holding possession of the same with a force of less than twenty thousand good and well disciplined men.[47]

Most of Anderson's officers indicated a force of some 4,000 regular troops as necessary, together with four to six war vessels, but Captain Foster was in close agreement with Anderson. General Scott presently also assured the President that, as a practical military question, the time of succoring Sumter with any means at hand had passed a month before.[48]

The first meeting of Lincoln's cabinet was held on Saturday night March 9, and the question of Fort Sumter was taken up, with something like a decision favoring evacuation. The leak in information was prompt, and on the 11th Wigfall, recently so sure that reenforcements would be sent, wired both Beauregard and Jefferson Davis that evacuation had certainly been decided upon informally at the cabinet meeting on Saturday.[49] To Davis he said: "It is believed here in Black Republican circles that Anderson will be ordered to vacate Fort Sumter in five days." Two days later H. P. Brewster, substitute observer and telegrapher for Wigfall, wired Governor Pickens that the evacuation of Sumter was probable, but not certain.[50] On the 14th, John Forsyth—one of the three commissioners of the Confederacy who were trying to get recognition and the forts from the Lincoln administration—optimistically telegraphed the South Carolina governor: "I confidently believe Sumter will be evacuated, and think a Government messenger left here yesterday with orders to that effect for Anderson." [51] Rumor and counter rumor prevailed, and the high-placed "contacts" seemed either to be playing tricks upon the distressed commissioners from Montgomery, or to be themselves receiving inaccurate and misleading tips. Finally the perplexed commissioners—Martin J. Crawford, John Forsyth, and André B. Roman

—actually tried to find out what was happening by turning to Charleston itself, and wired Beauregard: "Has Sumter been evacuated? Any action by Anderson indicating it?" [52] But no help could come from Charleston, for that city like Washington was filled with false reports and uncertain rumors, which, however, favored evacuation. On the 19th, a Charleston correspondent had telegraphed *Harper's Weekly* that the garrison was to leave on the 23rd on the steamship *Columbia,* and that the abandoning of the fort was hourly expected. But still it was not reported that there was baggage piled on Sumter's wharf. The belief that the fort was to be given up was general in North and South alike. The Washington correspondent of *Harper's Weekly* reported on March 23: "The question as to the evacuation or reinforcement of Fort Sumter has been decided by the Cabinet. The fort is to be evacuated, and peace will thus be preserved. The order for the evacuation has not as yet been dispatched, but will be. The abandonment of the fort is a military necessity, and the President and Cabinet, in coming to a conclusion on the subject, are said to have been governed by the opinions of the chiefs of the army."

In spite of the fact that the cabinet had been almost unanimous for abandonment of Sumter on March 15, Lincoln had not decided.[53] The man who had split rails would not give up quickly. He had told the country he would hold the forts, and, though he had very definitely left the way open for a change of course in accordance with events, he intended to fulfill the pledge. On March 19 the Secretary of War wrote to General Scott:

The President requires accurate information in regard to the command of Major Anderson in Fort Sumter, and wishes a competent person sent for that purpose. You will therefore direct some suitable person to proceed there immediately, and report the result of the information obtained by him.[54]

What could possibly be found out that had not been duly reported in the many letters of Major Anderson and Captain Foster? Nevertheless, the tenacious spirit and the forthright integrity of the new President rekindled a spark of hope in the old general, and he wrote the indorsement: "The within may do good and can do no harm. It commits no one." *May do good and can do no harm.* Those were strange words for Winfield Scott, and they show how low the national spirit had fallen. The note received another endorsement by the new Secretary of War, Simon Cameron, equally significant: "G. V. Fox, formerly of the Navy, was selected by General Scott as the messenger, and approved by the President." Pessimistic advisers may have had their influence on General Scott, but he selected one of the few men who would not have reported unfavorably on the problem of succoring Sumter with means available.

Gustavus V. Fox, former Navy officer, brother-in-law of Montgomery Blair, the new Postmaster General, who alone in the cabinet had strongly opposed evacuation of Sumter, had for some time urged a plan for getting into Sumter a limited number of men and supplies. He proposed to make use of three large and powerful tugboats that were in New York Harbor, and already had tentative contracts for them. Fox had no faith in the feasibility of using open whaleboats, a proposal which had been often discussed in Northern papers, and which the Confederate authorities were expecting might be used. Such boats would have to be rowed in from a considerable distance, and they would be slow and very vulnerable. The tugs, on the other hand, would come on their own power and at a speed of fourteen knots; they could have their vital parts protected by bales of cotton, and they would be more than a match for the inferior tugs the Charlestonians had at their command for defense. General Scott had not accepted the plan when it was first proposed by Fox, in large part because it could be used only once, so that the date of necessary evacuation of Sumter would be merely postponed.[55] But he now selected Fox as the special agent of the President, so that the mission was weighted for rather than against a favorable report.

Fox could not reach Sumter without the permission of Governor Pickens, and the Governor later wrote that he exacted the pledge that the visit be "pacific"—a rather indefinite term. It has been stated that the escort furnished Fox—Captain H. J. Harstene of the Confederate Navy, formerly of the United States Navy—kept within earshot during the conversation between Fox and Anderson.[56] Captain Foster's letter written the next day, March 22, contradicts this assertion, referring to the "confidential interview" between the two officers;[57] furthermore, Anderson later criticized Fox for failure to be altogether frank with him—which he could not have fairly done if their conversation had been restricted by the presence of an unfriendly third person.[58] Fox merely "hinted" at the idea of relief, according to

Anderson, and apparently did not refer to any pledge he had given Pickens as to topics he would discuss. On his part, Anderson left with Fox the belief that Sumter's provisions would last longer than they did.[59] The interview was a draw: the sailor confused the soldier, and the soldier confused the sailor. The statements of both Anderson and Foster place Fox in Sumter at night, so that as an actual reconnaissance of the harbor, the surrounding batteries, the obstructed channel, and the landing wharf, the visit must have been disappointing. But though he had seen little and had been told little, Fox reported to the President that his plan was feasible.

Just a few days after Fox's visit there arrived in Charleston an important two-man mission whose observations were to have a determining effect on the events that were rapidly developing. Lincoln wished a personal report as to the temper and feeling in Charleston made by men whose loyalty was beyond question and whose judgment he trusted; he wanted no war if honorable reconciliation were possible. For the very delicate errand he chose men who were Southerners by birth, Stephen A. Hurlbut, a native of Charleston itself, and Ward H. Lamon, from Berkeley County, Virginia. Both Hurlbut and Lamon had removed to Illinois, where they practiced law, the latter having been Lincoln's partner at Danville and at Bloomington. Lamon was among the party that had set out with the President-elect from 'Springfield on February 11, and he remained in Washington as one of Lincoln's closest friends and advisers; but accidental presence in the Capital was entirely responsible for Hurlbut's sharing one of the most important tasks that Lincoln ever gave to anyone.

The Lincoln Papers contain a long report that Hurlbut wrote on the 27th,[60] clearly proving that he was indeed the "shrewd and sagacious judge of human nature" Nicolay and Hay proclaim him to be.[61] In detail Hurlbut recorded the events of the two days—Sunday and Monday, March 24 and 25—that he had spent with his sister and acquaintances of former days. He passed on to the President the distressing fact that, while foreign ships showed their colors and flags of South Carolina were everywhere displayed, "the tall masts of Northern owned ships were bare and shewed no colors whatever." Only over Fort Sumter was the flag of the United States to be seen. In all of Charleston there remained but one avowed adherent of the Union, and that was the distinguished jurist James L. Petigru. Other men who a few years before would have been "ready to draw the sword in civil war for the Nation" had been won over to the South and were "ready to take arms if necessary for the Southern Confederacy." Not only Petigru, but also some of those who had recently turned against the North, assured Hurlbut that the "whole matter of Secession could have been stopped in the bud by prompt and gallant action on the part of the late Administration," but the Union men had not been supported and "Rebellion had assumed the stature and dignity of Revolution fulfilled and accomplished." Sparing in no way the Buchanan administration, Hurlbut continued: "Treason was abetted by our own high functionaries and every impediment sedulously removed from its path. It is impossible to expect from this Administration that they can restore at will the lost habit of obedience, the patriotism worn out, the power whose prestige over the minds of men had been willfully thrown away and abandoned by its immediate predecessor." Conflict was inevitable in the view of the native son of Charleston who viewed the amazing transformation that had taken place in the city of his birth. He said: "I solemnly believe that the Seven States are irrevocably gone—except perhaps Texas and Louisiana, as to which I have no information. . . . Nor do I believe that any policy which may be adopted by this Government will prevent the probability of armed collision."

Though Lamon presented no written report of his Charleston visit, he afterward wrote a somewhat detailed account of the memorable interview with Governor Pickens on the morning after his arrival. He was very courteously received, but was told frankly, "Nothing can prevent war except the acquiescence of the President of the United States in secession, and his unalterable resolve *not* to attempt any reinforcement of the Southern forts. To think of longer remaining in the Union is simply preposterous." [62] Lamon had convincing proof of the feeling in Charleston, for he was almost mobbed, and but for the care taken by the Governor would probably have lost his life.

Part of Lamon's instructions had been to visit Anderson, and for escort he was given a colonel on the Governor's staff, who withdrew during the interview. An authentic record of the conversation is unfortunately lacking. Anderson's subsequent letters clearly indicated that he expected orders to vacate Sumter upon the return of Colonel Lamon to Washington; but one must be cautious in drawing a conclusion as to what Lamon really said. Anderson may have been influenced too much by a letter from General Beauregard, dated

March 26, which stated that Lamon had told Governor Pickens that "yourself and command would be transferred to another post in a few days." [63] Then followed a beguiling offer to help Anderson in the matter of evacuation. A definitely successful effort to trick Anderson occurred later, on April 3, when Pickens slyly got before him, along with some truthful matters, a badly distorted version of a telegram that had been received from one of the Confederate commissioners in Washington. Though reluctant to believe part of it, Anderson was influenced by the statement.[64]

None of the many crucial decisions that Lincoln had to make as President could have been harder than that when he read the careful report of Hurlbut, and had direct from Lamon, his trusted and steadfast friend, the final word: there could not be peace except on the terms of the South.

After a sleepless night [65] the President received his cabinet on the 29th and presented to them formally a plan on which he had already received their written views. William H. Seward, the Secretary of State, who since his 1858 address referring to an "irrepressible conflict" had become a strong advocate in the Senate of compromise and appeasement in the early months of 1861,[66] advised against the Sumter expedition that Lincoln proposed.[67] Likewise Caleb B. Smith, the Secretary of the Interior, opposed such a move and advised that Anderson and his little force be "unconditionally withdrawn," since Sumter could not be defended.[68] Edward Bates, Attorney General and the oldest of the presidential advisers, stood for evacuation or relief of the garrison.[69] Salmon P. Chase, Secretary of the Treasury, was of a very different mind. Said he: "I am clearly in favor of maintaining Fort Pickens and just as clearly in favor of provisioning Fort Sumter. If that attempt be resisted by military force Fort Sumter should, in my judgment, be reinforced." [70] Similar views were expressed by Gideon Welles, the Secretary of the Navy, whose reply is especially valuable because it leaves no doubt of the fullness with which Lincoln had explained his plan.[71] It was hardly necessary for Lincoln to ask the views of Montgomery Blair, who from the start, in accordance with his outspoken nature, had denounced anything that resembled voluntary withdrawal of Anderson's force. Cameron, the Secretary of War, was not at the cabinet meeting; [72] but on March 15 he had submitted a long document reviewing the Sumter situation and recommending abandonment of the fort on the ground that any relief would be for only a few weeks.[73]

Lincoln's friend Hurlbut had not hesitated to place in his report on the situation in Charleston his own views as to what should be done. He wrote:

If Sumpter [*sic*] is abandoned it is to a certain extent a concession of jurisdiction which cannot fail to have its effect at home and abroad. Undoubtedly this will be followed by a demand for Pickens and the Keys of the Gulf. To surrender these if Pickens has been or can be reinforced tarnishes the National honor and the U. States ceases to be a respectable Nation. At all hazards and under all circumstances during this stage of proceedings any Fortress accessible by the Sea, over which we still have dominion should be held. If war comes, let it come.[74]

Thus wrote a man whose childhood memories were memories of Charleston with the flag of the United States flying above its forts.

Though the stanch support of Chase, Welles, and Blair and the milder endorsement of Bates must have been gratifying, nothing could have given pleasure to the decision they led to. Immediately, however, the decision was carried into action, and on the same day this directive was written:

Executive Mansion, March 29, 1861

Honorable Secretary of War:
Sir:

I desire that an expedition, to move by sea, be got ready to sail as early as the 6th of April next, the whole according to memorandum attached, and that you cooperate with the Secretary of the Navy for that object.

Your obedient servant,
A. Lincoln [75]

Such is the first note in the Official Records signed [76] by the man who was to take the nation through the great crisis.

Preliminary directions by both the Navy Department and the War Department were attached to Lincoln's note. On April 4, one month to the day after the inaugural, final orders were issued. Lincoln himself wrote a characteristic letter to Major Anderson, which was, however, sent over the signature of the Secretary of War.[77] It announced the relief expedition, and closed as follows:

You will therefore hold out, if possible till the arrival of the expedition. It is not, however, the intention of the President to subject your command to any danger or hardship beyond what, in your judgment, would be usual in military life; and he has entire confidence that you will act as becomes a patriot and soldier, under all circumstances.

Whenever, if at all, in your judgment, to save yourself and command, a capitulation becomes a necessity, you are authorized to make it.[78]

The letter was received on April 7, and Anderson's letter of April 8 to the Adjutant General contained the following very frank sentence:

I had the honor to receive by yesterday's mail the letter of the honorable Secretary of War, dated April 4, and confess that what he there states surprises me very greatly, following as it does and contradicting so positively the assurance Mr. Crawford telegraphed he was authorized to make.[79]

Anderson was clearly at fault in basing his opinion as to what was planned upon a written message from a Confederate commissioner to Governor Pickens, which he had never seen, and which reached him distorted by the governor, whose trickery he had every reason to suspect. His letter closed with sentences sometimes unjustly used to impugn his loyalty; he stated that his heart was not in the war which he saw was about to begin. The letter did not reach the War Department, for it was seized and sent to Montgomery.

To Fox, Cameron sent on April 4 a brief note [80] which gave him much pleasure, though it might have meant his death. It was indeed something to cherish if one had the proper stoutness of heart, for it was a commission to lead a military expedition where coolheadedness, skill, knowledge, great daring, and ability to command would all be needed. Fox also received a note that would assure the chartering of the boats and ships he wished. To General Scott's aide in New York went full instructions as to details, and authority to give all necessary orders in the general's name.[81] It was an occasion when blank checks were needed, and the new government did not hesitate to write them.

The scene now shifts to the office of Governor Pickens, for one of the gravest and most humorous events in history. President Lincoln's plan was unfolding, and it differed as much from previous suggestions as Fox's plan to use tugboats differed from proposals to employ whaleboats. Lincoln would first offer to put only supplies into Sumter. If this move were opposed he would try to force in both men and supplies, and, most important, he would notify the Charleston authorities of his intention. He would have no truck with the Confederate officials; he would deal solely with the duly elected constitutional executive of the offending state. But Lincoln sent no document bearing an impressive seal, and no note with his brief but finely written signature. A young man from the State Department, Robert S. Chew, presented himself to Governor Pickens on the evening of Monday April 8, and read from a paper these thoughtfully written and well rehearsed lines:

I am directed by the President of the United States to notify you to expect an attempt will be made to supply Fort Sumter with provisions only, and that if such attempt be not resisted no effort to throw in men, arms, or ammunition will be made without further notice, or in case of an attack upon the fort.[82]

After reading the message, Chew handed to Pickens an unaddressed, unsigned copy of it. Beauregard was sent for, and it was read to him by Pickens—not by Chew. Chew had done what he had been told to do, and like Viola, would do nothing outside his part. Naturally the thought of a hoax occurred to the Southerners. Well, with Chew had come Captain Talbot, stalwart soldier of Anderson's garrison, known personally to both Pickens and Beauregard; and Talbot confirmed that the President of the United States had in very truth ordered the delivery of the message. An endorsement to this effect was placed by Pickens and Beauregard upon the copy, which was thus made a record with signatures—but no Washington signatures.[83] When Pickens spoke of an answer, Chew replied that it was beyond his instructions to receive one. Apparently the man who was now President of the United States did not care what the Governor of South Carolina thought—which must have been a blow to the self-esteem of Pickens.

Lincoln had placed the pompous governor and the chesty general in an actually comical position. He handled them as readily as he had handled a flatboat on the Mississippi, or the suave and polished Douglas. Throughout his career Lincoln could find relief at the most tragic moments in rare and genuine humor. But no one except Shakespeare has mixed tragedy and comedy as Lincoln combined them in the scene at Charleston on the evening of April 8, 1861.

Talbot was not allowed to communicate with Fort Sumter. He accompanied Chew to Washington, where he ended his report very significantly: "I brought back with me the sealed dispatch, intrusted to my care by the President." [84] No revelation as to the message was apparently ever made. Perhaps there were no further instructions for Major Anderson, but merely the statement that the Confederates were being informed of the expedition.

Beauregard at once telegraphed to Secretary Walker: "Authorized messenger from Lincoln just informed Governor Pickens and myself that provisions would be sent to Sumter peaceably, otherwise by force." However momentous the message was, it could not have been unexpected by the Montgomery authorities. Walker replied, still under date of April 8: "Under no circumstances are you to allow provisions to be sent to Fort Sumter." [85] He had directed Beauregard on April 2 to stop all supplies from Charleston and to prevent reenforcements reaching Sumter; [86] but these instructions did not cover the situation that had arisen, because no one in Montgomery had seen the real weakness of the Confederate position, which Lincoln perceived and used with the peaceful offer of food only. On the 9th he telegraphed: "Major Anderson's mails must be stopped. The fort must be completely isolated." Beauregard had asked about the mails on April 4, but took action before a reply was received. Now he wired Walker, "The mails have already been stopped" [87] a very inadequate description of an episode that was quite discreditable.

On April 7, when informing Anderson that he was cutting off supplies from Charleston, Beauregard wrote, "The mails, however, will continue to be transmitted as heretofore, until further instructions from the Confederate Government." [88] On the morning of the 9th Pickens—to use his own language—"took possession of the mails." [89] Anderson remonstrated and requested that they be returned to him, but was told: "The private letters . . . were sent to their destination, but the public ones were sent to the Confederate Government at Montgomery, in return for the treachery of Mr. Fox, who has been reported to have violated his word given to Governor Pickens before visiting Sumter." [90] Beauregard had not a bit of respectable evidence of treachery, and well knew the charge was utterly false. The explanation was fabricated after the seizure; and the stolen letters actually disproved the charge, for in one of them Anderson complained of both Fox and Lamon and said bitterly: "I ought to have been informed that this expedition was to come." [91] Beauregard had doubtless read the letter, though he concealed the fact, so that Anderson could not be positive that the general was aware of the injustice of his accusation. The only promise clearly violated was Beauregard's—to allow mail to pass until the Confederate Government directed the contrary. Whether he remonstrated when Pickens nullified it, is uncertain; but one very manly and soldierly thing was to his credit: his letter to Anderson did not shift to the governor the responsibility for what had happened.

The instructions not to allow provisions to be taken to Sumter meant war; but if the Montgomery authorities had gone no further, and had been content to repel efforts to supply and reenforce, they might have argued that they were not the aggressors. They made the much more critical and significant decision to start unqualified offensive action. The order that began the great conflict was this:

Montgomery, April 10, 1861

General Beauregard, Charleston:

If you have no doubt of the authorized character of the agent who communicated to you the intention of the Washington Government to supply Fort Sumter by force you will at once demand its evacuation, and if this is refused proceed, in such manner as you may determine, to reduce it. Answer.

L. P. Walker [92]

In spite of the long and extensive preparations and the impatient waiting, optimism did not prevail at Charleston. Captain Harstene, in charge of naval operations, wrote to General Beauregard on the 10th:

It is my opinion that Sumter can be relieved, by boats from vessels outside of the bars, on any night that is as dark as last. . . . If a vessel of war is placed off each bar, when Sumter opens I will lose all my steamers for there will be no escape for me. Therefore, before firing, these steamers should be called in.

Soldiers as well as sailors were in something of a panic. Major Whiting, in command of strategic Morris Island, where a landing was expected, was unhinged by the confusion of his command, and at four o'clock on April 11 wrote to Beauregard:

For God's sake have this post inspected by yourself, or some one else competent, before you open fire . . . De Saussure complains that he has not men enough to work his guns for any length of time, and Kershaw's force is "helter-skelter," having just arrived. Cunningham's is but little better. Both are badly supplied with cartridges.

By way of encouragement and cheer, Beauregard told Whiting, "Remember New Orleans," and gave him the assurance that he would be present himself when the fighting commenced.[93]

Although he tried to stiffen his subordinates, Beauregard himself weakened. On Monday April 1, he had telegraphed Walker: "Batteries here ready to open Wednesday or Thursday. What instructions?" But nine days later, when he received instructions, he was not yet ready and had to delay making a demand on Anderson, to the expressed displeasure of Secretary Walker. Then as the fateful hour approached he weakened again: he did not want the sole responsibility for the act that had to be committed. Perhaps after all it was not such a great honor to demand the surrender of a fort of the United States. He wired: "Ought not demand of Sumter be made also by the Commissioners at Washington for its evacuation?" Walker answered briefly: "No. Yours is the only demand to be made." Beauregard replied: "Demand sent at 2. Allowed until 6 to answer." [94]

At last the issue lay squarely between two soldiers. General Beauregard, writing to Major Anderson, recited how the Confederate Government had foreborne and refrained. This was really a political question outside a soldier's concern. But there was no nonsense in his third paragraph: "I am ordered by the Government of the Confederate States to demand the evacuation of Fort Sumter. My aides, Colonel Chesnut and Captain Lee, are authorized to make such demand of you." Major Anderson, expressing the unanimous view of his officers, replied that his sense of honor and his obligations to his Government prevented compliance. There was a sentence of courtesies in reply to those that Beauregard had placed in his letter; but there was no politics.[95]

In conversation at the exchange of notes, Anderson commented that the garrison would be starved out in a few days, if the fort was not battered to pieces. The remark was reported to Secretary Walker, and the Confederate authorities were quick to grasp the hope that they might get the fort undamaged and without war. They directed further communication with Anderson, and after midnight Beauregard sent a boatload of aides with the message: "If you will state the time at which you will evacuate Fort Sumter and agree that in the meantime you will not use your guns against us unless ours are employed against Fort Sumter, we will abstain from opening fire against you." Anderson, well prepared now for trickery, saw the trap; they were seeking to bind him so he would not be able to use his guns to aid a relief expedition unless Sumter itself were fired upon. He replied that he would evacuate Fort Sumter by noon on the 15th, and that he would agree not to use his guns

unless compelled to do so by some hostile act against this fort or the flag of my Government by the forces under your command, or by some portion of them, or by the perpetration of some act showing a hostile intention on your part against this fort or the flag it bears, should I not receive prior to that time controlling instructions from my Government or additional supplies.

The trick having failed, Beauregard's aides wrote a note which they handed to Anderson at 3:20, stating that General Beauregard would "open the fire of his batteries on Fort Sumter in one hour from this time." [96]

H-hour thus was set for 4:20 A.M., Friday April 12, 1861; but the signal gun, a mortar whose shell burst neatly above Sumter, was ten minutes late, so that the war started at 4:30. Twenty or thirty minutes later all the Confederate batteries were engaged, but no answering flashes came from Sumter's guns. To all appearances the little garrison had slipped away into the night after the gate had closed upon the departing Confederate messengers. Some of Anderson's men had been up and knew that unusual things were astir; but they had been sent back to their beds, moved two days before to the casemates. Anderson had given new instructions to the officer of the guard, but directed reveille to be sounded at the usual time. However, there was one very important change in routine: the flag was raised to the top of the mast at once, without waiting for the light of morning. The very signal shell that opened the tumult of attacking guns showed the flag, and made the record straight. For two hours no answer was made to the Confederate fire, at first quite inaccurate.

Anderson had difficult decisions to make, but for a while at least they would be entirely military. The enemy had a great advantage, for his batteries brought converging fire from different directions upon an easy target, whereas Anderson's fire would be against scattered targets, some of which were concealed, and others well protected by earth, heavy timbers, and railroad iron. Beauregard with 4,000 men, largely infantry, had had time to train an abundance of battery personnel for the continuous service of all of his guns. Anderson had fewer than 70 artillerymen and the 43 workmen in Foster's engineer force. On April 2, Foster had asked permission to send away all the mechanics and the laborers, but the Confederate authorities had refused.[97] Almost without exception the workmen volunteered to serve as cannoneers, or in other capacities, so that they more than made up for the food that they had been consuming.

Because of his limited personnel, which had to be divided into reliefs, Anderson could man only part of his guns. He had a surgeon on his staff and had arranged facilities for caring for the wounded, but was not in a position to stand many casualties. He decided to start the action with only the guns in the casemate, where there was complete all-around and overhead cover for the gun crews. Unfortunately the guns in the casemate were light, seventeen 32-pounders and four 42's, and could fire only solid shot. The powerful part of Sumter's armament, the eight-inch howitzers and the ten-inch columbiads, could not be used in the casemate on account of their high angle of fire, and accordingly they had all been mounted on the terreplein and the parade. This situation would have been satisfactory against attack by naval vessels, for which Sumter had been intended, but land batteries firing high-angle mortars presented a different threat. Shells from mortars would burst among the exposed personnel manning the barbette guns on the terreplein, and casualties might be heavy, although traverses had been built to give some protection—an element of defense especially attended to after the receipt of Lincoln's letter of April 4.[98]

It is possible that Anderson's decision not to use the barbette guns came from a much more studied purpose than the avoidance of casualties. The most valuable use he could make of his fire power would be to aid the relief expedition, which would be subjected to heavy attack when it was landing; if he could smash the enemy batteries at that time, or drive the hostile gunners from their pieces he would achieve the utmost possible. There was a strong chance that if he did not use the barbette guns during the day the enemy would not destroy them by direct hits, and he could open them with a burst of unexpected fire. Clever arrangements had been made to lay Sumter's guns on all the hostile targets at night,[99] and Anderson's cannoneers could have brought much succor with the potent fire of their howitzers and columbiads to those who were succoring them.

It was not an easy artillery problem, but Anderson had ingenious and experienced officers who well knew the gunner's trade.

At seven o'clock Sumter opened fire, the first shot coming from a gun under the command of Captain Abner Doubleday. Captain Foster's careful journal records that 30 guns and 17 mortars were firing on Sumter.[100] As anticipated, the ten-inch mortar shells burst quite effectively above the fort or parade, although poor or badly cut fuses caused them to burst at varying heights.[101] By the middle of the day, because of lack of cartridges, Sumter's reply was reduced to six guns. The effect of the light metal they were throwing disappointed the men in the fort, but the Confederate reports speak well of the accuracy of the fire. Foster reported that a shot was put through a little schooner that incautiously got out from cover, the shell causing "her to haul down her colors, the flag of the so-called Confederate States, to hoist her anchor and sails, and get out of range as soon as possible." Many shots were fired with precision against the floating battery near Fort Moultrie, but its armor and the light weight of the projectiles saved it from damage. Foster recorded: "At 1 o'clock two United States men-of-war were seen off the bar, and soon after a third appeared." Three times during the day the barracks caught fire from a hot shot fired from Moultrie, but the flames were extinguished.

Sumter stopped its fire when darkness came, but the work of making cartridges out of heavy paper as well as from extra clothing continued until midnight. The night was very stormy, with heavy rain, a high wind and tide. Foster made a close examination of the exterior of the fort, which he found little damaged; he inspected means and arrangements for taking in any reenforcements and supplies from the ships off the bar, and found them satisfactory. It was a night of tension, a careful watch being kept for a relief, and for a landing attack by the enemy, masquerading as a friendly force. The Confederates stopped the fire of their guns, but continued that of the mortars at reduced intervals throughout the night. They were on the alert for an attempted relief of Sumter, with enfilading guns at Moultrie in readiness to sweep faces and landings at the fortress. One false alarm was sounded, which caused an increase of the Confederate fire.[102]

When morning came "the three U.S. men-of-war were still off the bar," though so far as the garrison could tell there had been no attempt at relief, while the Confederates suspected that some men and supplies had been put in.[103] For breakfast the last of the rice was cooked with pork—after that meals would be just pork and water. The increased supply of cartridges made it possible for Sumter to fire briskly for a while, paying special attention to Moultrie; the pork-filled cannoneers did good shooting, "almost every shot grazing the crest of the parapet, and crashing through the quarters," according to the Confederate commander.[104] But the solid shot were too light to do any real damage to the greatly increased defenses at Moultrie, although they demolished parts of the quarters and damaged the hot-shot furnace, which received three direct hits. On their part, the besiegers increased their rate of fire above that of the day before, and improved its quality. Hot shot, a somewhat delicate matter to handle, was used in greater number, and by eight o'clock fires broke out in the barracks at Sumter. They could not be controlled, for after the flames appeared the attackers poured in a still greater deluge of bursting shells. Fifty barrels of powder were removed from the magazine before its doors had to be closed, but the flying embers and intense heat soon made it necessary to throw most of this out the embrasures for fear of explosions. Heat, smoke, and the shortage of cartridges soon reduced the reply of Sumter to a mere token fire, one shot every ten minutes. At one o'clock the flagstaff, hit twice during the morning and seven times the preceding day, was shot down; but a temporary staff was at once put up, and the flag was again raised.

Trickery, which had been attempted at the beginning of the battle, was to mark its end. Soon after Anderson's flag had been hoisted on the temporary staff, Louis T. Wigfall, missing from the Washington scene for a number of days, appeared at one of the lower embrasures. The accomplished duelist and former senator crawled through the opening, resplendent in a colonel's uniform, sword in hand, white cloth on the weapon's point. He asserted that he was General Beauregard's aide and had come from him, and answered Major Anderson's question as to the terms of surrender offered, according to Captain Foster, who was present, "Any terms you may desire—your own terms—the precise nature of which General Beauregard will arrange with you." Anderson said he would accept the terms offered him on the 11th, whereupon Wigfall left and Anderson took down the United States flag and raised a white flag. Firing, which had begun again after a brief pause while Anderson's flag was down, ceased. The guns were silent; the first battle of the Civil War was over.

Presently other messengers arrived, and Anderson learned that

Wigfall was on duty at Morris Island and had not been at headquarters for two days. Actually he had set out for Sumter entirely on his own responsibility, during the period Anderson's flag was down. The Federal commander felt he had been victimized, and the report of Beauregard's aides states:

> Major Anderson then declared that he would immediately run up his flag; that he regretted it had ever been taken down, and that it would not have been lowered if he had not understood Colonel Wigfall to come directly from General Beauregard to treat. We requested that, under the peculiar circumstances, he would not raise his flag until we could communicate to General Beauregard the terms of evacuation with which he had furnished us; he assented to the proposition, and we left the fort.[105]

To the aides Anderson gave a note, written at 2:20 P.M. and addressed to Beauregard. After referring to the embarrassing situation in which he had been placed, he stated that he would accept the conditions offered him on the 11th, and would abandon the fort at any hour on the 14th that the general would set. But Wigfall had not finished with his knavery. He arrived at Beauregard's headquarters with the statement that Anderson had surrendered unconditionally. There should have been no question on Beauregard's part as to whom he should believe—though to dispute a great dueler was somewhat hazardous. In his written report, the general frankly recorded the disagreement between Wigfall and Anderson, but he marred his record of the 13th by wiring Walker: "Anderson surrenders to the Confederate Government unconditionally, but I have granted him the same terms as on the 11th instant." [106]

When Major Anderson was firing a salute to his flag—which Beauregard had generously allowed him to do—there was an accidental explosion due to a heated ember and a soldier was killed. It was the only fatality of the battle. Anderson closed his final report with the statement that he "marched out of the fort Sunday afternoon, the 14th instant, with colors flying and drums beating, bringing away company and private property, and saluting my flag with fifty guns." [107] He and his men of Battery E, First United States Artillery, were taken to the steamship *Baltic;* and, as they passed, the Confederate soldiers lined the beaches with heads uncovered in silent salute.

The fury of the storm of the night of the 11th–12th was greater on the sea than on the land, and as the final interview between Anderson and Beauregard's aides came to an end, the steamer *Baltic* arrived off Charleston and found the *Harriet Lane*. Captain G. V. Fox was somewhat reassured, for he had been anxious about the other units of his task force as the sturdy *Baltic* drove through the gale. Punctually in the morning the *Pawnee* anchored some way out, to await the other ships-of-war, *Powhatan* and *Pocahontas,* and the tugboats *Uncle Ben, Yankee,* and *Freeborn*. One week later Fox wrote in his report:

> I stood in with the Baltic to execute my orders by offering, in the first place, to carry provisions to Fort Sumter. Nearing the bar it was observed that war had commenced, and, therefore, the peaceful offer of provisions was void.[108]

With difficulty the ships kept station in the storm, looking anxiously for *Powhatan, Pocahontas*, and the tugs. Fox made plans to send in during the night a couple of boats with provisions for Sumter's gunners, but he could report only failure:

> All night and the morning of the 13th instant it blew strong, with a heavy sea. The Baltic stood off and on, looking for the Powhatan, and running in during the thick weather struck on Rattlesnake Shoal, but soon got off. The heavy sea, and not having the sailors (three hundred) asked for, rendered any attempt from the Baltic absurd. I only felt anxious to get in a few days' provisions to last the fort until the Powhatan's arrival. The Pawnee and Lane were both short of men, and were only intended to afford a base of operations whilst the tugs and three hundred sailors fought their way in.

The *Powhatan* and tugs not coming, a schooner engaged in the ice trade was seized on the 13th and plenty of officers and men volunteered to go in with Fox that night. But in the afternoon the white flag went up above Sumter, and the guns became silent. It was too late. A relief could have been made if things had gone as Fox had planned, for he wrote: "As I anticipated, the guns from Sumter dispersed their naval preparations excepting small guard-boats, so that with the Powhatan a re-enforcement would have been easy."

For a second time in the story of Fort Sumter everything depended upon communication. Again a ship at the harbor's entrance could send no message to Sumter, nor receive any from the fort.[109] Anderson did not know that the most important elements of Fox's task force had not arrived, and Fox could not explain why he had not sent in relief the first night, or flash the assurance that he would be in on the night of the 13th with at least token help. And Anderson could not tell Fox that cartridge bags or cloth and more needles—Sumter had only six—to make bags, were needed as sorely as bread. But Anderson had foreseen the bitter moment that had come. On January 22, in a letter to Adjutant General Cooper he had written: "Lieutenant Hall may bring on a copy of the private Navy Signal Book with the signals, and also the designation of the key (or number) agreed upon in concert with the Navy Department. This may be of service." [110] The request may never have passed beyond Cooper's desk, for early in March this Northern-born admirer of Jefferson Davis resigned,[111] and within two weeks he was signing orders for the Confederate President.

With a touch of bitterness Fox closed his report:

I learned on the 13th instant that the Powhatan was withdrawn from duty off Charleston on the 7th instant, yet I was permitted to sail on the 9th, the Pawnee on the 9th, and the Pocahontas on the 10th, without any intimation that the main portion—the fighting portion—of our expedition was taken away. In justice to itself as well as an acknowledgment of my earnest efforts, I trust the Government has sufficient reasons for putting me in the position they have placed me.

Again there had been errors and also meddling in high places. The intricate story of what had happened has been told by several writers, including Lincoln's secretaries, and the details are apparently well cleared up.[112] The ultimate cause of the trouble was unquestionably the Secretary of State, William H. Seward, who by presenting the President with a mass of papers, obtained his signature to one that had nothing whatever to do with the State Department, and which he would not have signed if he had read it carefully and understood its import.

Seward, senator from New York and formerly governor, had been perfectly confident that he would be nominated by the Republicans at the national convention in the Chicago "Wigwam" in June, 1860. Only temporarily humbled by the outcome, he thought that he alone could rescue the country in the rapidly developing crisis of the next winter. After consenting in December to enter Lincoln's cabinet, he devised with his devoted friend, the superpolitician Thurlow Weed, the "Albany plan," which contemplated nothing less than his becoming the "Premier," the real President, and Lincoln's surrender of constitutional responsibilities. His attitude changed rapidly, and in early June, 1861, he wrote to his wife about Lincoln's "rare . . . executive skill and vigor" and commented on the cabinet—which contained strong though discordant men—"The President is the best of us." [113] Though his conduct of foreign affairs in the difficult months ahead has generally been pronounced skillful, Seward's talking and meddling for the first weeks after March 4 caused the new President much embarrassment and trouble.

In his efforts to all but "take over" the government, Seward conspired with an ambitious and very competent naval officer, David D. Porter—then lieutenant, later admiral—to send a relief expedition to Fort Pickens at Pensacola. Among the papers he presented to Lincoln for signature on the evening of April 1—the very day the President had signed the order for the Sumter expedition—was one directing that the strong and well gunned ship *Powhatan* should be turned over to Lieutenant Porter. When the vessel was about to leave New York under Captain Samuel Mercer on the evening of April 6, with orders from Secretary of the Navy Gideon Welles to rendezvous off Charleston harbor for duty under Fox, Lieutenant Porter presented himself and took over the ship from his superior, on the ground that his order was signed by the higher authority. A report from Mercer naturally amazed the Navy Secretary, and in a midnight conference at the White House the strange sequence of events came to light. Lincoln directed that the *Powhatan* should be restored to Mercer and that nothing should be done to compromise the Sumter expedition. Then Seward slipped in the clever stroke that is the most unforgivable. Dutifully, he sent an order to Porter to give up the *Powhatan* to Captain Mercer, but signed his own name instead of the President's. It is hard not to believe that he was well aware that he was nullifying the order; in the sequel the order was not obeyed precisely because it bore the signature of the Secretary of State. When the telegram arrived at the Brooklyn Navy Yard the *Powhatan* had already departed; but she was overtaken by a speedy vessel, and the order to surrender the ship to Mercer was handed to Porter. Now Porter presumptuously refused to obey the Secretary's telegram because he had taken command on an order signed by Lincoln—though concocted by himself and Seward; so he continued on his way to Fort Pickens, where his supplies were not needed and were not landed, and whence he returned somewhat crestfallen.

In spite of the bungling and the trickery no one was punished. Manfully Lincoln shouldered more than his share of blame. On May 1, when he must have been overwhelmed with the difficulties of the first days of the war, as well as harassed by the office seekers, he wrote to Captain Fox:

The practicability of your plan was not, in fact, brought to a test. By reason of a gale, well known in advance to be possible, and not improbable, the tugs, an essential part of the plan, never reached the ground; while, by an accident, for which you were in no wise responsible, and possibly I to some extent was, you were deprived of a war vessel, with her men, which you deemed of great importance to the enterprise.[114]

Lincoln went further, terminating his letter with a statement which revealed the honesty of his nature:

You and I both anticipated that the cause of the country would be advanced by making the attempt to provision Fort Sumpter [sic], even if it should fall; and it is no small consolation now to feel that our anticipation is justified by the result.

The war which he had come to believe was inevitable unless secession were acquiesced in, had been begun by the South firing on Sumter when he offered to supply its little garrison with "bread"—as he said with considerable effect. Well could he feel that the cause of the North had been advanced both at home and abroad by such an action. Governor Pickens never saw the note that Fox had prepared for the pilot who was to start into Charleston harbor, announcing that boat and crew were unarmed and the sole cargo was provisions; but the note is in the record.[115] Whether Lincoln was right in believing that the conflict was inevitable is still debated; but the President who had to make the awful decision, in the light of what he saw and knew, would certainly have felt vindicated by the weighty judgment of John Morley, the English historian and biographer and a leading pacifist, who some fifty years later pronounced the Civil War "the only war in modern times as to which we can be sure, first, that no skill or patience of diplomacy could have avoided it, and second, that preservation of the American Union and abolition of negro slavery were two vast triumphs of good by which even the inferno of war was justified." [116]

There is not sufficient reason to believe that Lincoln knew after the visit of Hurlbut and Lamon to Charleston that the offer merely to provision Fort Sumter would result in its being attacked, though this has recently been asserted.[117] Sending supplies but not men to Sumter had certainly been discussed, though the actual procedure, which was a crucial part of the plan, may not have been developed until it appeared fully in Lincoln's proposal to the cabinet on March 29. Hurlbut had written in his report of the 27th, "I have no doubt that a ship known to contain *only provisions* for Sumpter would be stopped and refused admittance." To refuse admittance to a ship, even by firing upon her, would be one thing; to open fire on Sumter before the arrival of an expected ship would be something very different. Hurlbut did not predict that the latter action would be taken by the Southerners; nor did Lamon. Lamon merely reported that Governor Pickens had said in effect that an effort at "reinforcement" would certainly cause war; but this did not imply that an attack would be launched if it were learned that at some future date a ship would start into Charleston harbor conveying food only. Actually of course Pickens was in no position to tell authoritatively what would or would not be done; for the decision lay with the officials at Montgomery, to whom he could do no more than transmit information. Lincoln's prompt order to have the *Powhatan* returned to the command of Fox shows that the Sumter expedition was something more than a gesture, and that the continued holding of the fort was a primary object. On March 4, he had said very plainly that he would hold the forts; on that promise he still was standing. In offering to hold Sumter with the small garrison that it contained, and promising that the status quo would not be changed without further notice, Lincoln in fact gave the men of Montgomery the opportunity to keep things quite as they were, with the chance that it might be Lincoln who would fire the first shot—in spite of the last sentence of his inaugural. His strategy placed Jefferson Davis in a difficult position; and, feeling that the war was inevitable, he may have experienced a sense of relief when the Confederacy's Provisional President failed to use the remaining chance of escape and opened his batteries upon the fort in an outright shooting war.

There were brave men in Sumter. For them a "cold war" had indeed become "hot." As the barracks burned, the heat within the casemate became intense; the smoke was stifling; flying embers threatened every minute to explode the cartridges and barrels of powder that the men sought to protect with wet blankets. There was constant danger that the fire might reach the magazines. But the guns never quite stopped, and General Beauregard reported with pride that his soldiers cheered the courage of their enemies as the defiant shots rang out from the flames and smoke of Sumter. The fire was nearly out, and as soon as the walls cooled sufficiently to reopen the magazines the guns could have again been used, except for the shortage of cartridges. Foster wrote: "The want of provisions would soon have caused the surrender of the fort, but with plenty of cartridges the men would have cheerfully fought five or six days, and if necessary much longer, on pork alone, of which we had a sufficient supply." [118] Apparently there was only one point at which the wall of the fort could have been breached, and a week to ten days would have been required. Even with the wall opened up, he believed the small garrison could have defended itself against assault by vastly superior numbers. It was not the lack of food that was Sumter's undoing, but lack of cloth for cartridges and lack of cannoneers. Foster stated that, if there had been sufficient personnel to man the barbette guns and accept the resulting casualties, they could have "smashed" the besiegers' ironclad batteries, and have "destroyed the cannoneers" in his open batteries.

The fort could not have held long even if the relief expedition had been a success. But if Fox had forced his way in, and if Sumter's howitzers and columbiads, served by trained men eager to pay back for suffering endured, had then smashed some of the Southern batteries and destroyed the gunners or driven them from their posts, it would not have looked as if the United States was militarily inept.

It had been a gala time in Charleston, where the people joyfully watched from the housetops the agonies of Sumter. Not often are there such convenient places from which to view a battle that goes well. They saw 4,000 shells from their batteries bring flames to the fort, which then raised the white flag; and practically no damage had been done to them. In comparison, the *Star of the West* incident, which they had thought was very good, was hardly a curtain raiser. It was not strange that the Charlestonians were delirious, that Pickens and Beauregard swelled with pride, and that the Confederate leaders were unbalanced.

The South indeed had Sumter and its guns. The people were too happy to reflect upon where those guns had been made, as well as the guns they themselves had fired. Before long they would often have occasion to think of such unpleasant things.

The North had the men, the shipyards, the factories, and the farms. Not always would the roster of cannoneers be so short; not always would it be necessary to send a chartered, unarmed merchant ship on a warlike errand; not always would there be a shortage of cartridge bags; not always would there be nothing to eat but pork.

The North also had the President: a man who then knew almost nothing about war, but who had toiled hard and was familiar with adversity; a man with an indomitable will, a splendid mind, and a great heart: and, over and above all that, a man who was habitually very honest and truthful.

And after a while, after many months of dark discouragement and repeated failures, the North also would have the General.

CHAPTER III

A DAY TOO LATE

But the hour, the day, the night pass'd, and whatever returns,
an hour, a day, a night like that can never again return.

Whitman

N ews of events at Charleston came to the North a little slowly; but the papers of Saturday April 13 told of Beauregard's demand, Anderson's refusal, and the bombardment.[1] There was no excitement in the Executive Office, and only minor departure from daily routine occurred. The next morning Lincoln himself wrote the historic proclamation; after approval by the cabinet he signed it and sent it to the State Department, which published it the following day. The proclamation commanded treasonable combinations to disperse within twenty days, called into service 75,000 militia for three months, and convened Congress in extra session on the coming 4th of July. The fact that troops were called for only ninety days did not mean that it was confidently believed that the issue would be settled that soon. The call was made under the act of February 28, 1795, which authorized use of the militia only "until the expiration of thirty days after the commencement of the then next session of Congress."

Telegrams from the Secretary of War to the governors of all states—including the recently admitted Oregon and Kansas—except the seven in rebellion, at once assigned their quotas of troops under the call. The messages had hardly been dispatched before replies came.[2] On April 15 eight governors gave warm assurance of compliance and support; others soon followed. The reply from Massachusetts was very brief: "Dispatch received. By what route shall we send?" Ohio's governor could not wait for instructions from the War Department, and impatiently wired the President:

What portion of the 75,000 militia you call for do you give to Ohio? We will furnish the largest number you will receive. Great rejoicing here over your proclamation. Answer immediately by telegraph. I await your answer to issue my proclamation.

There were also blunt refusals, which showed the depth of the division in the country. On the day of the call Governor Beriah Magoffin wired the Secretary of War: "Your dispatch is received. In answer I say emphatically Kentucky will furnish no troops for the wicked purpose of subduing her sister Southern States." North Carolina also refused the same day. Two days later Missouri's governor, C. F. Jackson, replied: "Your requisition, in my judgment, is illegal, unconstitutional, and revolutionary in its object, inhuman and diabolical, and cannot be complied with. Not one man will the State of Missouri furnish to carry on any such unholy crusade." A week after the call the governor of Arkansas, H. M. Rector, replied: "The people of this Commonwealth are freemen, not slaves, and will defend to the last extremity their honor, lives, and property against Northern mendacity and usurpation."

The loyal governors offered to oversubscribe. Indiana offered 10,000 men, and the governor said the six regiments allotted would be full in three days. Michigan soon had a second regiment ready in addition to the one asked for; the governor of Wisconsin said that the people would not be content with only one regiment and requested that two additional regiments be accepted. Missouri repudiated her bragging governor, and sent 10,591 men instead of the 3,123 that had been requested. The original call for 73,391 men had been made upon twenty-four states; actually 91,816 men were furnished by twenty states and the District of Columbia.[8]

In addition to sending men, the legislatures, cities, and towns voted to contribute money and to aid in defraying expense of equipment and mobilization, which was most helpful because the federal treasury was not in good condition. In New York City there was formed the Union Defense Committee, which gave great assistance to the government in many ways. Philadelphia, with a strong tradition for peaceful adjustment of disputes, was no less aroused; on April 19, a

Committee of Public Safety was formed, and it was determined to raise ten regiments of 800 men each for home defense.[4] Believing that the expense "should be borne by the citizens and institutions whose lives and property it will be the object of this organization to protect," the committee voted to raise $250,000 for the purpose of arming and equipping the regiments. A friend of the Secretary of War, reporting on the general situation, wrote:

> You have no conception of the depth of the feeling universal in the Northern mind for the prosecution of this war until the flag floats from every spot on which it had a right to float a year ago. . . . I saw many of the solid men in New York, and they have embarked their all in this contest, provided the Administration will prosecute it to the bitter end . . . so that no madcaps will ever try the experiment again.[5]

The magnitude of the task ahead was not appreciated, and the response by the North deceived people into thinking the war would be short. Thus the editor of *Harper's Weekly* wrote: "With such support, and such resources, if this war is not brought to a speedy close, and the supremacy of the Government asserted throughout the country, it will be the fault of ABRAHAM LINCOLN." [6]

The safety of Washington had been a grave concern to the President, who received almost daily reports from General Scott. On April 5 the strength of the regular army was 17,113 officers and men, of whom only 3,894 were in the Department of the East.[7] General Scott had been almost stripping forts, arsenals, etc., in order to bring available men and units into Washington, and volunteer militia organizations had been formed within the city. On April 13 the general reported that there were present six companies of regulars, the marines in the navy yard, and fifteen companies of volunteers. Of trained soldiers there were not so many as one small regiment. Other regular units, including both horse and foot artillery, were expected within five to seven days. But no organization as large as a regiment could be obtained except from the states.

The condition of the state forces varied greatly. Some were mere paper organizations with neither arms nor uniforms, and some had not only these essentials but also some equipment for field service, and were trained in basic drill. On January 16, General Charles W. Sandford of the New York militia had written to General Scott:

And should it be necessary (as I trust it will not) to sustain the Government and keep the peace at Washington by a larger force than you can concentrate from the U.S. Army, I can send you, at short notice, five or six good regiments, upon which you could rely with confidence.[8]

Massachusetts, whose minutemen had been first to answer roll calls in 1775, had again looked ahead. Her governor, John A. Andrew, began early in the year to prepare her troops; men who could serve quickly had been enlisted, and new arms and uniforms had been procured.[9] The Sixth Massachusetts regiment began to muster on Boston Common the morning after the call, and entrained the next night with new rifles and ammunition ready for distribution. A change of railroad stations, involving a movement of about a mile, was necessary at Baltimore. Part of the regiment was moved in cars and reached the Washington station after receiving nothing worse than taunts and jeers from a hostile crowd; the companies that marched had to use the new rifles when they were attacked: four soldiers were killed and thirty-six were wounded, while the toll of the mob was two to three times as great. When the regiment reached Washington about five o'clock on April 19 and marched to its quarters in the senate chamber, it was greeted with cheers.

After the attack on the Sixth Massachusetts, the mayor and the chief of police, who had done much to restrain the mob, destroyed the railroad bridges connecting Baltimore with Harrisburg and Philadelphia so as to prevent further movement of troops through the city. Thus was Washington isolated. But the Eighth Massachusetts, following promptly after the Sixth, and New York's famous Seventh, were moved partly by water to Annapolis, where they arrived on the 21st and 22nd. The railroad out of Annapolis to the junction with the Baltimore-Washington line had been torn up, and the troops had to rebuild it. One enthusiastic reporter wrote that a locomotive had been dismantled, but that one of the Massachusetts men stepped forward with the assertion that he had built the engine and could put it together again—which he proceeded to do.[10] There was also trouble about rations, for the delay had not been foreseen; some of the men got very hungry and felt that they had had a real campaign when they reached Washington on Thursday, the 25th. First to arrive were the New Yorkers. Though the Seventh was not battle-toughened, it had laid rails and rebuilt bridges in order to reach the capital; and it was well accoutered, and marched smartly with straight ranks and well carried muskets. Its parade up Pennsylvania Avenue to the White House, behind a very good band, was one of the important incidents in the city's life. On the preceding Sunday night the Washington telegraph instruments had stopped their clicking, with the wires cut. The government did not even know what was taking place in the country, and, as wild rumor followed wild rumor, the states were frightened by lack of news about the government. Then came the march of the New Yorkers; presently there passed a second regiment from the state that had taken such toll from British regulars on Bunker Hill. The capital was reassured, and reopened wires informed the country and dispelled alarm. From the West, too, men were moving to defend the capital. On April 19, Ohio's governor had wired: "I have ordered the two regiments en route to Washington to proceed to Harrisburg to await orders." [11] The man who had requested his quota before it was announced had again anticipated.

Mustering officers were promptly sent to rendezvous points, where they worked long hours giving oaths to men, supervised physical examinations, and made careful records of the important act of entry into the United States service. There were plenty of arms in the arsenals for new units, though they were not of the latest patterns: 422,325 percussion muskets (smoothbore shoulder arms) and rifles—chiefly with a caliber .69 of an inch—"recognized as suitable for the service," and, in addition, 35,335 rifled muskets (muskets altered to rifles) and rifles, caliber .58, model 1855, called "the latest improved arms." [12] The artillery situation was not so good, for though the arsenal inventory showed 4,167 pieces, there were only 163 field guns and howitzers. Time of course was needed for shipping and distributing weapons and other equipment, and governors and men, as well as the public, became impatient. Advertisements of military books promptly appeared, among them Hardee's *Tactics*, two volumes, and Scott's *Tactics*, three volumes; but a shortage of training manuals was to handicap instruction in various camps.

The last days of April saw important acts and decisions in Washington. On the 25th Secretary Cameron wrote "Accepted" on the tender of resignation which Colonel Robert E. Lee had presented on the 20th, probably not suspecting that meanwhile, in an impressive ceremony, Lee had accepted the commission of major general in the Virginia forces. On the 27th Cameron wrote to a Philadelphia friend that the President had that day ordered the erection of a manufactory for arms at Rock Island, Illinois; and he asserted, as an assurance of the government's attitude in all war matters, "If the officers now in command will not act with energy, General Scott shall be authorized to find others that will." On the same day the superintendent of the census sent Lincoln some very important man-power data from the unpublished figures of 1860.[13] The order for the new arsenal certainly showed that the Executive was not expecting a short war, because it could not produce weapons for many months. (Construction waited in fact until 1863, first efforts being given to increasing the output of the famous Springfield establishment.) A by no means minor point in Cameron's letter was the indication that the appointment of officers to posts of special responsibility was entrusted to the General in Chief. The data from the census head revealed that there were 3,778,000 white males between the ages of eighteen and forty-five in the nineteen free states; also, that the eleven states that were to join in the Confederacy would have 1,116,000 such men. One cannot tell how Lincoln appraised the slaves as a Southern agricultural and industrial asset; but his conviction of the importance of Maryland, Kentucky, and Missouri must have been strengthened by learning that together they had 517,000 white males of military age.

The original call had hardly been sent out when first steps were taken to increase the armed force in an entirely different way; and on May 3, before the mustering of the three-months men had been completed, the President called for 42,034 volunteers to serve for three years, unless sooner discharged. At the same time he increased the strength of the regular army by 22,714 men, and directed the enlistment of 18,000 more men by the Navy.[14] For these acts he had no legal authority; but the temper of the country had become clear, and Congress was certain to approve at its forthcoming special session. The call for three-year men met with the same response as the shorter call. The governor of Iowa wired: "I am overwhelmed with applications." Governor Andrew asked: "How many regiments will you take? I want to give all six now." [15] Whatever the country generally might have thought of the probable length of the war, the administration was questioning the value of the ninety-day men, and on May 6 the Secretary of War suggested to the governors that all regiments be mustered for three years unless they had been sent forward.[16] He asked if it would not be possible to replace men not willing to serve three years by others who would accept the longer period.

In the proclamation of April 15 it was stated that the first service assigned the force to be raised "will probably be to repossess the forts, places, and property which have been seized from the Union." It was soon realized that this natural desire was quite out of the question, and would, furthermore, be of little value. Accordingly new war plans had to be matured. After Washington had been made secure, it was necessary to hold Baltimore in force; this was done on May 13. On May 22 Fort Monroe was occupied by a command of 15,000 men, an act of great strategic value because of the location of the post at the mouth of the James River. But in spite of such diversions of regiments, a large force accumulated in the vicinity of Washington.

Shortly after midnight on May 24, with the full moon illuminating the martial spectacle, about ten regiments were moved across the Potomac to Virginia—an event dramatically described by correspondents and pictured by the artist as the crossing of the "Advance Guard of the Grand Army of the United States." [17] The movement had been delayed partly at least because the Ordinance of Secession passed by the Virginia Convention on April 17 was subject to ratification or rejection by the people on the 23rd. Though there was no doubt about the outcome of the balloting, Lincoln preferred to make no specifically hostile act before the votes were cast. Four days later Irvin McDowell, promoted shortly before from major to brigadier general in the regular army, was appointed to command the Department of Northeastern Virginia, and he established his headquarters in Arlington. Then began the formation of the first considerable field force of the war. Few American officers had ever seen such an army; none had ever commanded one.

A primary requisite was an adequate staff. Suitable material was meager, because of the small number of regular officers, and the many uses to which they would have to be put. The return for December 31, 1860, showed a total of 1,108 officers in the army; but of these more than 300 joined the Confederate forces. Among those who went South were such officers of high rank as Brigadier General Joseph E. Johnston and the previously mentioned Robert Lee—who had accepted promotion to regimental command after Lincoln had declared he

MAJOR GENERAL IRVIN McDOWELL

would hold the forts, but refused an unofficial tender of the Federal high command,[18] and tendered his resignation when the President showed he was in earnest after Sumter had been fired upon and captured. Many others, of lower grades, who resigned also had high military capacity. The places of departing officers were in part made good by the return to service of officers who had previously left the army for private life, some of whom achieved high rank. But it was not merely a question of an inadequate number of trained officers to fill the places where they were needed. There were few if any of the regular officers who had more than a rudimentary understanding of the staff work needed for the successful conduct of extensive operations and the skillful handling of even moderate-sized commands. No staff school existed for the training of officers in the problems of command and logistics, and because the army itself was so small as to give no experience worthy of the name there had been little real professional growth among regular officers. American military literature was at the time not very impressive, and foreign writings were generally inaccessible because of the language deficiencies of officers. General McDowell was definitely an exception to the rule, and selection of him for the command of the field force forming near Washington must have been prompted in part by his special qualifications. He had attended school in France and had spent the year 1859 on leave of absence in that country. As he was familiar with their language, contact with French officers should have broadened his knowledge beyond what his own field service in the Mexican War had taught him.

McDowell secured an adequate "special staff" group: adjutants, engineers, signal officer, quartermasters, commissary officers, medical officer, ordnance officer, inspector-general. But he had on his staff no one to help with the adequate planning and conduct of a battle, or even a troop movement in enemy country: he had no semblance of a "general staff." The staff included a chief of artillery—an important position—and four aides-de-camp (two regular lieutenants and two volunteer majors), who could do little more than deliver messages more or less accurately. McDowell had no chief of staff who could formulate orders, take responsibility, and in an emergency serve as a second in command. Practically alone, McDowell was going to try to direct a large force in battle when he had never commanded even a small one.

The deficiency in McDowell's staff revealed itself in the inadequate training of his troops. As soon as the new regiments were mustered, they ceased being "militia"; they were completely under Federal control. A carefully prepared program of instruction should have been devised for officers and men, and this program should have been carefully supervised by a member of the staff who had no other function. It is true that at that time the idea of a "general staff" had not been evolved, but it seems a little strange that that particular need was not provided for. Ultimately, McDowell's command was formed into brigades, all but a few of which were commanded by regular officers or former regulars; but even if such officers had been assigned earlier, training should not have been left entirely to them, for it was essential that it be thorough and uniform throughout the command, a desideratum to be achieved only if well supervised by a competent officer. When McDowell in his report on Bull Run complained that his men were "not used to carrying even the load of 'light marching order,' " he was merely writing an indictment of himself. Washington, the "city of magnificent distances," afforded ample opportunity for drilling and marching men with both light and heavy equipment. It is true that after the regiments reached Virginia they were called on to furnish men to help build fortifications; though this complicated the matter of training, it hardly seems an adequate reason for neglecting a very important element in conditioning soldiers.

Another force was mobilizing in the vicinity of Chambersburg, Pennsylvania, which, because of failure to fulfill a promise Scott made to McDowell, has been too much blamed for the defeat at Bull Run. It was commanded by Robert Patterson, who had served in both the War of 1812 and the Mexican War, and who had returned to service as one of Pennsylvania's two major generals under the call of April 15. Patterson was highly regarded by Scott, and his letters dealing with organization and mobilization problems indicate a thoroughness that supports Scott's good estimate. Aware of the rigors of field service, Patterson wrote picturesquely on May 24 that he was "disposing of troops unserviceable for marching purposes, so as to untie the legs of good regiments." [19]

It was Patterson's intention to move through Hagerstown, Maryland, where the railroad from Harrisburg ended, cross the Potomac at Williamsport, and attack Harpers Ferry, the uniquely situated and in-

teresting village that had been made famous by John Brown. The place
had been rather precipitately abandoned on April 18 by the lieutenant

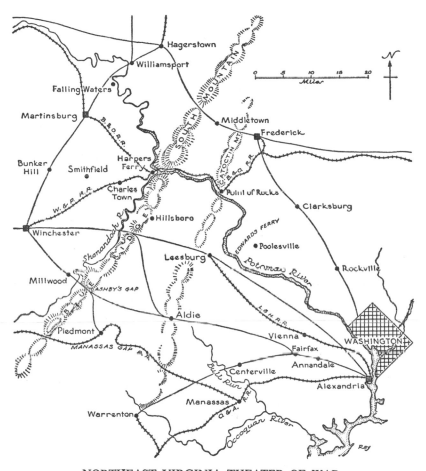

NORTHEAST VIRGINIA THEATER OF WAR
The railroads shown by abbreviations were: Winchester and Potomac; Baltimore and Ohio; Loudoun and Hampshire; Orange and Alexandria. An important artery of communication not shown on the map was the Chesapeake and
Ohio Canal, which followed the north bank of the Potomac River.

commanding at the United States arsenal, who burned considerable
property, but failed to damage the valuable rifle-making machinery,
which was moved to Richmond. On April 26 Colonel Thomas J.

Jackson—the future Stonewall—was placed in command of some 4,500 Virginia troops in the vicinity, and he quickly began a serious training program. On May 24 he was superseded by Brigadier General Joseph E. Johnston, who reported that Harpers Ferry was untenable, because it could "be turned easily and effectively above and below." On May 31 Johnston suggested that the place be at once given up, and that his command be joined to one of the other Confederate forces, though he stated that his troops were not equipped for field service.[20] President Davis, now in Richmond, the new seat of the Confederate Government, thought Harpers Ferry had much political value, and since it gave access to the rich Shenandoah Valley, wished to deny it to the Northern forces. General Robert E. Lee, who held the rather strange position of "military advisor" to Davis, was also reluctant to give up Harpers Ferry.[21] Whatever its permanent value might be, there was at the time quite a flow of supplies from Baltimore through the village and across the river by the wagon and railroad bridges.

Patterson believed the Confederates would defend Harpers Ferry to the last, a view shared by both Scott and McDowell.[22] He intended to move slowly but surely, and Scott approved in a letter piling caution on caution: "I have said that we must sustain no reverse; but this is not enough, a check or a drawn battle would be a victory to the enemy." He further enjoined Patterson to "attempt nothing without a clear prospect of success, as you will find the enemy strongly posted and not inferior to you in numbers."[23] In view of what later happened, it may be that Scott forgot he had so strongly prescribed circumspection.

After a great deal of difficulty in matters of equipment, especially transport—wagons, horses, mules—Patterson's leading division under Major General George C. Cadwalader, Pennsylvania Volunteers, took the road from Hagerstown to Williamsport on June 15, and on the same day it was definitely learned that Harpers Ferry had been abandoned.[24] Patterson suspected that Johnston was decoying him,[25] and Cadwalader stated, "The whole affair is a riddle to me." The General in Chief must have been equally bewildered, for his adjutant, Colonel E. D. Townsend, wrote to Patterson on June 13, the very day that Johnston started to move, "Indications received from this side confirm the impression you seem to have that a desperate stand will be made at Harpers Ferry by the rebels."[26]

The enemy, however, was practicing no sly stratagem, and what had happened is a good example of the unexpected repercussion that a small event can have. At historic Cumberland on the Potomac, sixty miles by the National Road above Hagerstown, was Colonel Lewis Wallace with the Eleventh Indiana Volunteers. Colonel and men alike were eager to remove a stain left on their state by the report of General Zachary Taylor about the behavior of the Second Indiana Volunteers at Buena Vista in the Mexican War. Wallace knew that his regiment was in the theater of operations because his governor had pleaded, "All we ask is a chance—is a chance," [27] and then had loaned $20,000 from the state treasury to pay for troop movements. Hearing that a Confederate force of about 400 was assembling at Romney, Virginia, Wallace saw the chance. With no direction from higher authority, he entrained about 500 of his men at ten o'clock on the night of June 12, and moved twenty miles by rail to near Piedmont, Virginia, then marched thirteen miles over a dangerous mountain road. The enemy, informed of his approach an hour before his arrival, had mostly withdrawn. Nevertheless, Wallace showed himself a good troop commander in the dispositions he made to cross a long covered bridge over the South Branch of the Potomac, the exit of which was covered by musketry from a masonry building as well as by the fire of two guns, on a ridge beyond. After destroying the property the enemy had left, Wallace returned to Cumberland. In less than twenty-four hours the Hoosiers had marched forty-six miles over mountains and won no mean skirmish.[28] Nothing Stonewall Jackson's famous "foot-cavalry" ever did was much better than that.

Wallace's bold move did more than liquidate the Buena Vista account. Johnston was informed on the morning of the 13th that 2,000 Federals had seized and occupied Romney.[29] Believing this indicated the advance of Major General George B. McClellan's force from the West, Johnston at once sent two regiments by rail to Winchester, where they picked up a third regiment and marched forty miles over indifferent and bad roads to Romney, with instructions to prevent further Federal advance. Then Johnston began at once to move all his equipment and stores by railroad to Winchester, partially destroyed the bridges over the Potomac on the 14th, and marched his troops off on the 15th. By a rear attack seventy miles away, Wallace had pulled Johnston out of Harpers Ferry. Johnston already had received considerable discretionary power to move when necessary, but a clearer authorization was written on the 13th,[30] which he did not receive until he reached Winchester, when he also learned the truth about Romney, and knew he had precipitately abandoned a place his superiors wished held.

On the 16th Scott was seized with fear for the safety of Washington and ordered Patterson to send all regular units he had and the Rhode Island infantry and artillery. A few hours later he repeated the order and stated: "The enemy is concentrating upon Arlington and Alexandria, and this is the line first to be looked to." On the 17th he telegraphed Patterson: "We are pressed here. Send the troops I have twice called for without delay." The troops were actually on the way, after some excellent work by Patterson and his staff—perhaps as good logistical work on a small scale as was done in the entire war.[31] The Rhode Island regiment of Colonel Ambrose E. Burnside marched all day and until after midnight, crossing South Mountain and Catoctin Mountain, and making a total of thirty-three miles, in order to reach Frederick, where it entrained.[32]

Washington was under no threat at all, and the Rhode Islanders would have been disgusted when they bivouacked with weary feet and aching backs if they had known the truth. For on that very day, McDowell's regiments, after probable hours spent in polishing equipment, were passing in review before the Secretary of War, behind floating colors and cheerful bands, serenely unaware of any danger. Also on the 17th McDowell wrote to Scott about a reconnaissance toward Vienna, in the most casual way, "It is reported re-enforcements have been sent from Manassas to Fairfax Court-House." [33] An examination of the letters of Davis, Lee, Beauregard, and Johnston shows that a move towards Washington at this time was merely a mild wish, and was not even in the planning stage.[34] Yet on the 17th Scott said the Capital was actually "pressed," and the next day the Secretary of War, Simon Cameron, wired to rush troops from New York, using freight cars if there was a dearth of passenger equipment.[35] Evidently the Secretary had been infected by the General's fear—unless he was merely in a great hurry for another and larger review than the one he had witnessed the day before.

In addition to Patterson's command, the force which Scott had started on June 8 to act as the other half of the pincers on Harpers

Ferry, was also paralyzed. It was commanded by Colonel Charles P. Stone, Fourteenth United States Infantry, and consisted of three infantry regiments, a few "District" troops, a section of regular artillery, and a few cavalrymen. Stone was to seize Edwards Ferry, "and, if practicable, cross the river and continue on to Leesburg," but caution was strongly prescribed to him too in the admonition: "The General has left much to your well-known discretion, but he enjoins upon you to proceed with caution, and by no means hazard the safety of your expedition." [36]

Stone handled his column well, and on June 15, after having already strongly commended the marching performance of his three militia regiments, wrote from Poolesville, "The command is well and doing well." But though he had been directed to cross the river and take Leesburg, "if practicable," he did not cross. On the 18th he wrote: "I can now at any time, with very small loss, occupy Leesburg, but can see no advantage which would justify even the small loss which would be sustained, and the slight risk to my line which would necessarily result." [37]

Caution and hesitation everywhere in this theater—except with the volunteer colonel! Fortunately Wallace did not ask for permission from Washington, or he would not have attacked Romney, and Johnston would have remained in Harpers Ferry. Perhaps Providence was acting in its strange way when it caused General Taylor to make a distorted report about the Second Indiana at Buena Vista, for because of the charges he had made, there was in 1861 a regimental commander eager to fulfill the promise of his governor: "All we ask is a chance—is a chance."

Scott's fear may have been due to exhaustion. His years, the recent illness, the weeks of heavy strain, and the constantly mounting responsibility, told heavily upon him; he must often have been near the breaking point. But the old general never conceded that he had been wrong: to the end he had the Confederates all but in the White House grounds and the Capitol rotunda during those days of mid-June. On March 31, 1862, five months after he had retired, he wrote to the Committee on the Conduct of the War in reply to statements by Patterson, relative to the recall of troops from the latter, "But the recall was necessary to prevent the Government and Capital from falling into enemy's hands." [38] The hero of the Mexican War was as unswerving in his opinion as he was in his loyalty. If Scott had had a competent staff to sift and weigh the many reports that must have come to his headquarters, the error would probably never have been committed.

The three-months men, who would soon be going home, had served well as an Initial Protective Force. But the North clamored insistently for the war to move on in a more decisive way, and the administration could not ignore the demands of public opinion, even though it was not able fully to appraise the complex military situation. How to get some significant offensive achievement before the end of July was no simple problem: but it was exactly the question that Scott had to face. Since Harpers Ferry had fallen without the heavy fighting that had been anticipated, the next logical thing was to move against the Confederate force near Manassas under General Beauregard.

On June 24, General McDowell presented to General Scott a lengthy and able discussion of the proposed operation, followed the next day by an intelligence summary of the enemy situation at and in front of Manassas.[39] He estimated the enemy strength at 25,000 and thought that an additional 10,000 men might be brought up after he himself started to move. He was careful to stipulate that such enemy reenforcements should not be the force under General Johnston at Winchester, which was to be held fast by Patterson. But McDowell accepted a possible enemy force of 35,000, and he added significantly: "They have, moreover, been expecting us to attack their position and have been preparing for it."

As to his own attacking force McDowell said: "Leaving small garrisons in the defensive works, I propose to move against Manassas with a force of thirty thousand of all arms, organized into three columns, with a reserve of ten thousand." The balance in his favor— if indeed there was a balance—was not sufficient. It would have been adequate only if McDowell's troops had been thoroughly trained or had had combat experience; but he said frankly, "For the most part our regiments are exceedingly raw and the best of them, with few exceptions, not over steady in line." Still he was very hopeful, and he closed his report with the statement that his troops should have every chance of success "if they are well led." This was a brave pronouncement, but it was hardly necessary for the new general to burn his bridges so completely.

On June 29 Lincoln called his cabinet and the principal military officers to discuss the Manassas movement. His private secretaries wrote later:

General Scott took occasion to say that he was not in favor of such a movement. "He did not believe in a little war by piecemeal. But he believed in a war of large bodies." He adhered to the "Anaconda" policy, and a decisive campaign down the Mississippi in the autumn and winter. . . . But, being overruled . . . the old soldier gracefully yielded his preference, and gave his best counsel and coöperation to the new enterprise. He caused to be read the plan matured by General Irvin McDowell and approved by himself.[40]

Whether Lincoln and his cabinet saw at this date that the war would be long, is not the question; a big war is won little bit by little bit. The overruling of the old General in Chief, whose very presence inspired respect if not awe, could not have been agreeable for either President or cabinet. The administration had had almost unlimited confidence in Scott, as shown by a remarkable unfinished and unsigned War Department letter to John Sherman, dated June 20, which ended with this sentence about the Mexican War hero:

He has superior military knowledge, experience, wisdom, and patriotism over any other member of the administration, and enjoys the unlimited confidence of the people, as well as the President and his advisers.[41]

Why was this reply to a letter from John Sherman,[42] questioning Scott's action in calling troops from Patterson when the former was in the panic about Washington, never sent? It seems very probable that Cameron realized the futility of what he had written, though every word was true, as an answer to the letter he had received from Sherman. The groundless fear for the safety of Washington that had gripped Scott must have been duly appreciated and appraised, and some of the "unlimited confidence" probably had begun to disappear. It is also possible that Scott contradicted himself with regard to the possibility of effective action with the three-months men. At least on July 18 he thundered in a letter to Patterson, "A week is enough to win victories," [43] which was an emphatic endorsement of the contention of the President and the cabinet. Everything considered—including the optimistic concluding sentence in General McDowell's letter—little can be said against the decision of June 29.

McDowell's operation was originally scheduled to start on Monday July 8, which would have given almost two weeks before the expiration of the enlistments of any of his regiments.[44] But a delay arose because of the lack of transportation, and some regiments did not join his command until a week before he marched. Whether every possible effort had been made by the Quartermaster General to get wagons, horses, mules, and harness, it is impossible to say; but in the situation that existed a delay was serious—even days counted.

The field force was composed of fifty regiments of infantry, two regular infantry battalions—one marine, one army—ten batteries, and one battalion of regular cavalry. Nine of the batteries were regular, mostly six-gun; there were twenty-nine rifled, and twenty-six smooth-bore pieces.[45] In artillery McDowell had a marked superiority over the enemy. The lack of engineer troops is notable. None had been provided for in the call; but as troops had been engaged in fortification work, some experience in pioneer and engineer activities had been acquired.· Medical troops also did not exist, though provision for medical service existed within the regiments. The complete command was organized into five divisions, and all except the Fourth were divided into brigades. The Fourth Division was held as reserve and did not make the march toward Manassas. Probably for some good reason the First Division had four brigades, which left only two each for the Second and the Fifth. All division commanders and eight of the eleven brigade commanders were either active or former regular army officers, most of them with the rank of colonel.[46]

The most serious deficiency in McDowell's organization—one for which he paid very quickly—was in the disposition of his cavalry. His mounted strength was not great, but his eight companies of regular horse made a fair cavalry regiment, though called only a battalion. It should have been kept under his own control; instead it was made a part of the Second Division.

A great deal of very hard work had been required to make in some ten weeks an army such as McDowell commanded. There were grave shortcomings, but with the small attention the country had given to military education, and the careless, wasteful tendency of the people, it had in it a touch of the unbelievable.

By no means all of the available troops in and about Washington were in McDowell's force, according to *Harper's Weekly,* which listed sixty-four regiments by states, with a total of about 60,000 men. On July 4, twenty-three New York regiments passed in review before the President, the cabinet, and General Scott, and only fourteen of them were among the nineteen New York regiments in McDowell's army. Perhaps shortage of wagons, horses, and mules would have prevented McDowell's army from being increased, even if the state of training of troops and his ability to command a larger force had justified it. At Baltimore, still unsettled and restless, eleven regiments acted essentially as an army of occupation.[47]

McDowell's field order,[48] issued on July 16, began: "The troops will march to the front this afternoon in the following order." The contents must have been already well known to regimental and higher commanders, or there would not have been time to carry it out. The formal document should be carefully searched for possible causes of the lost battle. There were two chief—and somewhat related—faults. No mission whatever was given to the cavalry: a person reading the order would not have known that McDowell had a single cavalryman. The omission resulted from the fact that McDowell had strangely surrendered his eight companies of excellent horsemen to a division commander. The other error was the inclusion of something that should have been omitted. McDowell threatened and enjoined as follows:

The three following things will not be pardonable in any commander: 1st. To come upon a battery or breastwork without a knowledge of its position. 2d. To be surprised. 3d. To fall back. Advanced guards, with vedettes well in front and flankers and vigilance, will guard against the first and second.

Such instructions do not belong in a field order, and the fact that troops were new did not justify their inclusion in the present case, for all but two of McDowell's division and brigade commanders were or had been regular officers. March security must have been discussed in conferences preceding the operation; but even there it should not have been overemphasized. The explicit threat in McDowell's order was responsible for slowing down his march, and caused some of his soldiers to pick blackberries, as has been charged.

No clear-cut objective for the operation was stated, other than that of marching to the front; but it must have been known to all sub-ordinate commanders that the purpose was to defeat the enemy and drive him from his positions about Manassas and Manassas Junction. The order specified: "Troops will march without their tents, and wagons will only be taken with them for ammunition, the medical department, and for intrenching tools." Small field trains—twelve to fifteen wagons per brigade—were allowed for camp kettles, mess pans, and mess kits, and essential personal baggage. Instructions were given for army subsistence trains, each of which was to be accom-panied by a herd of beef cattle. The order included the ominous warning: "There is on many of our regiments nothing to distinguish them from those of the enemy, and great care must be taken to avoid firing into each other." Actually some of McDowell's regiments were in gray, while some of the Confederate organizations were in blue; and there was the inevitable and tragic result in spite of the caution in the order. "Light marching order" was carefully specified for each division.

The immediate march objective was Fairfax, only thirteen miles from Arlington. Four of the divisions were put on the road in three columns, two divisions on the inner road, one each on the flank roads. The Fourth Division was left in reserve in its camps, its commander taking command also of all fortress and other remaining troops. The marching column consisted of approximately 1,450 officers and 30,000 men.

The first day's march was very short, probably because the start was to be made late. On the second day the divisions were to move early and reach Fairfax (Third Division, Sangster's) by 8:00 A.M. Then it was evidently intended to issue new orders for a farther advance, if the enemy were not seriously encountered. But the faulty assignment of the cavalry caused an undue amount of time to be consumed in a short move of about six miles. The First Division had to execute a flank march directly across the enemy's front from Vienna to Fairfax, and succeeding divisions had to regulate on it. If the cavalry had been employed to reconnoiter with some boldness both ahead of and toward the badly exposed flank of the First Division, the march could have been easily made by the hour specified, and without too much fatigue. Though the country was somewhat wooded, cavalry reconnaissance was entirely possible. But instead of being where it could be of great service, the cavalry was with the Second Division, which was marching safely on an interior road.

When McDowell—at an hour he does not state—found the First Division a little beyond Fairfax, and tried to get it on to Centerville, he was told it was not possible for the men to go farther. After the battle he wrote frankly and somewhat ruefully:

They had only come from Vienna, about six miles, and it was not more than six and one-half miles farther to Centreville, in all a march of twelve and one-half miles; but the men were foot-weary, not so much, I was told, by the distance marched, as by the time they had been on foot, caused by the obstructions in the road and the slow pace we had to move to avoid ambuscades.[49]

The regiments of the First Division could in all probability have marched just as well as Wallace's Hoosiers, or Burnside's Rhode Islanders, or Stone's three regiments from New York, Pennsylvania, and New Hampshire, or the regiments from Ohio and Indiana that McClellan praised for their "long and arduous marches, often with insufficient food, frequently exposed to the inclemency of the weather," in a congratulatory order issued the very day McDowell marched out of his camps.[50] McDowell's men had been worn out starting and stopping, falling in and falling out, while a search was made for masked batteries. Nothing so tires and exasperates a command as a constantly interrupted march. It is likely to make berry pickers out of any regiment of recently enlisted volunteers.

Whatever he might have thought in retrospect, there was cheerfulness in the report that McDowell made on the evening of July 17:

We have occupied Fairfax Court-House, and driven the enemy towards Centreville and Manassas. We have an officer and three men slightly wounded. The enemy's flight was so precipitate that he left in our hands a quantity of flour, fresh beef, intrenching tools, hospital furniture, and baggage. I endeavored to pursue beyond Centreville, but the men were too much exhausted to do so.[51]

By night of the 18th, after two and a half days on the road, McDowell's troops were in the vicinity of Centreville, twenty miles from their starting point, and five to ten miles from the enemy: but they did not have the two days' cooked rations in their haversacks which his order of the morning said "they must have." [52] One ration train with its ninety beef cattle arrived punctually at 7:00 A.M. at Fairfax, and it contained enough rations for the entire army for two days, but the other two trains did not arrive until evening. On this delay McDowell very unfairly put responsibility for his defeat.

As McDowell, near Centerville, pondered what he should do, Patterson was at Charles Town, seven miles southwest of Harpers Ferry, on the railroad to Winchester, disturbed about the past as well as uncertain of the future. July 18 had been a very rough day for him, a day he would remember unhappily. It virtually marked the close of his campaign in Virginia, which had begun auspiciously enough on July 2, when his command of some 14,000 men forded the Potomac at Williamsport.[53] About five miles south of the river, at a place called Falling Waters, the enemy was encountered, strongly posted. After being dislodged he retreated toward Winchester. Colonel George H. Thomas, a regular army officer—who afterwards became famous at Chickamauga—said that his brigade "behaved with the ultmost coolness and precision during the engagement," and Colonel John J. Abercrombie spoke favorably of his brigade, which bore the brunt of the action.[54] Though they did not know it at the time, the Federals had been opposed by the future very famous "Stonewall Brigade," under Colonel T. J. Jackson, which was in action for the first time.[55] Losses in killed and wounded were low; the Federals lost about a company as prisoners, and Jackson had to leave many tents, other equipage, as well as provisions. Officially the records classify Falling Waters as an "engagement"—the second land contact of the war to be so dignified. (The first was at Big Bethel, near Fort Monroe, where the Federals were defeated on June 10.)

Martinsburg gave Patterson an ovation when he arrived on the 3rd, for there was strong Union sentiment in the community. But troubles were near at hand: supply, transportation, expiration of enlistments, contradictory reports as to enemy strength, and—worst of all—an indefinite mission. On July 4 an officer delivered to Patterson a note from Townsend written on July 1, that told him "in confidence" of the intended movement within about a week of a column of 35,000 men towards Manassas "for aggressive purposes." But not a word was said about the cooperation that was expected of him. The next night Scott wrote the first of three directions that went from bad to worse.[56] Although Patterson had informed him that the enemy had merely retired on Winchester as a result of the action at Falling Waters, the General in Chief evidently believed that Johnston would retreat to Manassas. Accordingly he instructed Patterson to pursue Johnston via Strasburg or move through Leesburg to Alexandria, but in so confused a manner that it was difficult to tell just what he wished. Since the enemy remained at Winchester, Patterson sensibly ignored the instructions and stayed at Martinsburg. On July 12, in accordance with the unanimous vote of his staff and higher commanders, he repeated a request he had made on the 9th for permission to move to Charles Town, and shift his base from Hagerstown to Harpers Ferry, so that he would have the great advantage of the railroad; he could then move towards Winchester, or "march to Leesburg when necessary." [57] To this request the following reply was received:

> Go to where you propose in your letter of the 9th instant. Should that movement cause the enemy to retreat upon Manassas via Strasburg, to follow him would seem at this distance hazardous, whereas the route from Charlestown, via Key's Ferry, Hillsborough, and Leesburg, towards Alexandria, with the use of the canal on the other side of the river for heavy transportation, may be practicable. . . .
> Let me hear of you on Tuesday. Write often when *en route.*

Here the move to Charles Town was unconditionally approved, even though it might cause Johnston to go to Manassas: Scott in fact was as unconcerned on July 12 about keeping Johnston at Winchester as he had been a week before, on July 5. The thought of following through Winchester on Johnston's heels was also virtually ruled out; it is amazing that it was ever entertained. Then some one on Scott's staff must have reminded him that McDowell expected that Johnston would be kept at Winchester. Instead of revoking the order of the 12th and giving a new one, Scott disingenuously wired Patterson on July 13:

> I telegraphed to you yesterday, if not strong enough to beat the enemy early next week, make demonstrations so as to detain him in the valley of Winchester; but if he retreats in force towards Manassas, and it be too hazardous to follow him, then consider the route via Key's Ferry, Leesburg, etc.[58]

A totally new mission is here adroitly slipped in as if it had been previously directed, and the old thought of following on Johnston's heels is revived. The order abounds with *if*'s. *If* Patterson cannot "beat" the enemy, he is to detain him; *if* he cannot detain him, he is to follow him; *if* he cannot follow him, he is to move through Leesburg. A plan with three *if*'s is not simple: and simplicity is the first principle for military plans.[59] The thought of following Johnston should never have been revived; and the thought of moving through Leesburg should also have been abandoned. Although the Leesburg route was not dangerous, it would put Patterson at Manassas three or four days after Johnston, for the latter had the railroad from Strasburg, while the rail line from Leesburg to Alexandria had been torn up and the rolling stock burned. The closing sentence of Scott's dispatch of July 12 showed he knew the move would take several days, and it would require Patterson about two days to learn that Johnston had left Winchester and to start moving in a new direction. The General in Chief should have made up his mind as to what he really wanted done. If he wished Johnston immobilized at Winchester, he should have so directed unequivocally, and he should have annulled all previous instructions, except permission for Patterson to change his base to Harpers Ferry, and operate through Charles Town. What was to happen was a good illustration of Moltke's doctrine: "If an order can be misunderstood, it will be misunderstood."

On Monday July 15, which was certainly "early next week," Patterson, whose command had been increased by the arrival of Colonel Stone's force as well as some New York regiments under Major General Sandford, marched to Bunker Hill, nine miles on the direct road to Winchester from Martinsburg, and made demonstrations that day and the next. Scott probably wanted Patterson to read his telegram as if the word "indefinitely" followed Winchester; but Patterson did not so read it and, the first of the week being over, moved to Charles Town on Wednesday the 17th, with the intention of carrying out the last part of Scott's order of the 13th, in case Johnston went to Manassas. While en route to Charles Town, he sent a brigade from Smithfield a short distance on the road to Winchester, by way of further demonstration as well as a protection to his column.

Patterson and his staff—partly at least regular officers—continued to exaggerate Johnston's strength. At Martinsburg they put it at from 25,000 to 30,000,[60] though D. H. Strother, who joined them there, insisted the Confederate commander did not have over 15,000 effectives.[61] At Bunker Hill, Strother, now a part of Patterson's topographical force, presented new evidence that Johnston had about 17,000

men and thirty-one light guns, and ten heavy guns in emplace-
ments [62]—approximately the same as Patterson at the time. But the
intelligence officers on the staff very knowingly rejected his information and insisted on putting Johnston's force at 42,000 men and
seventy guns. Naturally Johnston's lines were somewhat cautiously
approached.

Troubles from approaching expiration of enlistments now began to
present themselves. On June 18 Patterson had reminded Scott that
all his regiments save one were three-months men, expressing the
belief that all except possibly one regiment would claim discharge
without delay. From Bunker Hill he reported that the enlistments of
a "very large portion" of his force would expire within a few days,
and that from an undercurrent of feeling he was confident the men
would be "inclined to lay down their arms the day the term expires. . . . With such a feeling existing any active operations towards
Winchester cannot be thought of until they are replaced by three
years' men." [63] He would hold himself at Charles Town prepared to
move with the remainder of his force through Leesburg, "provided
the force under Johnston does not remain at Winchester, after the
success which I anticipate from General McDowell." He asked to be
advised if the General in Chief approved his plans, and he closed in a
way that showed he had an important element of a good commander:
"Telegrams will reach me via Hagerstown and also via Point of
Rocks."

After he reached Charles Town on the 17th Patterson telegraphed
that the term of service of his eighteen Pennsylvania regiments
would expire within eight days.[64] He stated that unless given some
three-year men at once he would have to retire to Harpers Ferry,
where he had already begun to set up a base. As a result of his
earlier request, seven three-year regiments had already been ordered
to Harpers Ferry for him,[65] though he may not have known it yet.
At 9:30 P.M. on the 17th Scott sent Patterson one of the most crucial
dispatches of the campaign. "Do not let the enemy amuse and delay
you with a small force in front whilst he re-enforces the Junction with
his main body. McDowell's first day's work has driven the enemy
beyond Fairfax Court-House. The Junction will probably be carried
to-morrow." [66]

The word "amuse" was a little unbecoming to the General in Chief,
but "delay" was the word that continued the state of uncertainty

created by his order of the 13th. Was Scott anxious that Johnston be *held* at Winchester, or merely that he *not get too great a start in a race for Manassas*? The message also closed on the wrong note, for the optimistic prediction could only confirm Patterson's belief that he had held Johnston at Winchester long enough for McDowell's operation to succeed. Scott should have wired: "In his first day's work McDowell has driven the enemy beyond Fairfax Court-House. It is essential that you continue to hold Johnston at Winchester by such means as are necessary."

Scott's message reached Charles Town promptly, and Patterson replied at 1:30 A.M. on July 18 referring to his telegram of the previous day (which he had repeated) and to his letter of the 16th about the state of his command, and asking categorically, "Shall I attack?"— a question very pertinent in view of Scott's closing sentence. The General in Chief avoided a direct answer and equivocated: "I have certainly been expecting you to beat the enemy. If not, to hear that you had felt him strongly, or, at least, had occupied him by threats and demonstrations." [67] He gave no instructions about further pressure on Johnston, but asked: "Has he not stolen a march and sent re-enforcements toward Manassas Junction?"

In the important matter of information about the enemy, Scott had done badly with Patterson. On July 6 the latter stated that the enemy in his front had received large reenforcements and was said to have 26,000 men. [68] Instead of questioning the accuracy of the figure, Scott tended to confirm and strengthen Patterson's apprehension that there might be a combination against him, by sending on July 11 a memorandum that outlined a plan to reenforce Johnston, defeat Patterson after luring him away from the Potomac, attack McClellan farther west, and after that have Johnston's augmented force return and join Beauregard. [69] This plan contemplated the use of all the Confederate forces, so that it was of primary concern to Scott and should have been evaluated at his headquarters. But he contented himself with stating that the author of the memorandum, who believed it authentic, was known—a skillful dodging of his own responsibility. With a shrug of his massive shoulders the General in Chief passed the whole matter off on a subordinate, and forgot about it. But Patterson could not forget, for he certainly received confirmatory rumors that were deliberately issued at Winchester and were brought to him by persons who feigned sympathy with the North. There is no way to tell when

Scott arrived at an accurate appraisal of Johnston's force, but it was not until July 18 that he said to Patterson: "You have been at least his equal, and, I suppose, superior, in numbers." [70] This was a rather casual and blunt way to correct an exaggerated idea that he had helped to confirm. It was, furthermore, altogether too late: something should have been said on the subject on July 13, and again in the message of July 17.

It would have been easy for Patterson to clear himself and put the General in Chief in an embarrassing position. He had merely to invite attention to the second half of Scott's telegram of the 13th, and to his own letter of the 16th stating that he intended to move through Leesburg if Johnston did not remain at Winchester. But he was deeply stung by Scott's tone, and he replied: "The enemy has stolen no march on me. I have kept him actively employed, and by threats and reconnaissances in force caused him to be re-enforced." [71] There was exaggeration in this statement, but Johnston may have received some reenforcements, and another regiment was definitely on the way to him.[72] Though he was still in Winchester the place was astir with his preparations for departure. But Scott as well as Johnston got away from Patterson, who wrote into the record the rather weak dispatches of July 18, instead of a very brief one that would have put responsibility where it belonged: on Scott and the order of July 13.

Patterson appealed almost in vain to his regiments "to stand by the country for a week or ten days," but some agreed to remain.[73] As McDowell studied his situation at Centerville, Patterson at Charles Town recorded the unheroic verdict: "The men are longing for their homes, and nothing can detain them."

On the 20th—at an unstated hour—Patterson wired Townsend: "With a portion of his force Johnston left Winchester by the road to Millwood on the afternoon of the 18th." [74] Strother, the civilian topographer with Patterson's staff whose accurate estimates of Johnston's strength had been rejected since the 9th, furnished information early on the 19th of Johnston's departure from Winchester; but the "intelligence section" of the staff again rebuffed him.[75] It was already too late to follow Johnston effectively.

On the evening of July 16, General Beauregard—of Sumter fame—commanding the Confederate forces at Manassas, received from Rose Greenhow, socially prominent Washington spy, a message stating that orders had gone to McDowell to march that night.[76] Word that the Federals were already on the road should of course have been received directly from patrols, and Beauregard apparently withdrew his advanced brigade from Fairfax that night. The next morning he telegraphed to President Davis: "The enemy has assailed my outposts in heavy force. I have fallen back on the line of Bull Run, and will make a stand at Mitchell's ford." The hero of Charleston was anything but cheerful; after speaking of the possibility of retiring to the Rappahannock he asked that Johnston be informed of his plight via Staunton, and he ended with an earnest plea that reenforcements be sent at the earliest moment and by every possible means. Although Mrs. Greenhow was to mitigate the tedium of her coming imprisonment with the thought that her act caused the sending of more troops to Manassas, it was McDowell's actual advance that made Beauregard cry for help.

Beauregard's command, the Army of the Potomac, consisted of seven brigades of infantry, a separate regiment, three cavalry regiments, a battalion and four separate batteries of artillery. There was a total of twenty-nine infantry regiments; nine of the twenty-nine guns were rifled. The effective strength was about 24,000 men.[77] Neither Beauregard nor Johnston had to face the serious problem of expiring enlistments which confronted McDowell and Patterson. Their men could be counted upon to see the campaign through, for the first Confederate regiments had been enlisted for a year, and from early May regiments had been accepted only for the duration of the war.

Bull Run, behind which Beauregard had taken position, was a narrow stream, but its steep wooded banks made it a military obstacle of considerable defensive value. There were few bridges, but numerous fords which varied in the facility they offered for troop movement. Beauregard held all crossings from the stone bridge that became historic on the Alexandria-Warrenton Turnpike southeast to Union Mills (on the railroad just east of Bull Run), a distance of about twelve miles. The entire Confederate force was apparently deployed along the excessive distance, so that there was no large mobile reserve—a bad arrangement.

President Davis acted promptly to provide reenforcements, for the contingency had been expected. Three regiments and a battery were ordered from Fredericksburg,[78] and Johnston was directed to go to Beauregard's assistance "if practicable." [79] In addition, the assurance was given that more troops were expected in Richmond and would be pushed on promptly. Beauregard, not foreseeing the extreme caution with which McDowell would advance, expected him to get his force to Centerville or beyond on the 17th. Afraid that succor would not reach him in time, he wired Richmond that day: "I believe this proposed movement of General Johnston is too late. Enemy will attack me in force tomorrow morning." [80] This was the same prediction that Scott had made in his telegram to Patterson.

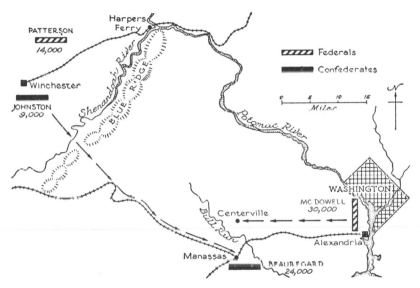

MARCHES TO FIRST BULL RUN

Johnston's force consisted of four brigades, a separate infantry regiment, a cavalry regiment, and a battery with each brigade.[81] There were in all eighteen infantry regiments, and twenty smooth-bore guns: the total strength was about 11,000. He received Davis's dispatch about 1:00 A.M. of the 18th. Though not yet certain as to the meaning of Patterson's recent move to Charles Town,[82] he must have known of the near expiration of the enlistments of many of the Federal soldiers, which, added to the natural caution of a seventy-year-old general, newly recalled to service, might well prevent any boldness. He promptly decided to support Beauregard; but he had something of a problem in getting away, for 1,700 of his men—the equivalent of two regiments—were sick, mostly with measles. He moved them into Winchester, to be cared for by the inhabitants, and left two brigades of Virginia militia to hold the town. With a cavalry regiment commanded by Colonel J. E. B. Stuart screening his movement from Patterson, he took such baggage and rations as his deficient trains could carry and marched about noon for Ashby's Gap in the Blue Ridge Mountains, entraining his foot troops at the village of Piedmont and finishing the movement by rail.[83] Leading the column was the brigade of Thomas Jackson, headed for battlefield rechristening.

McDowell had set out on his campaign with the intention of turning the enemy's right flank.[84] But a reconnaissance he himself had made, and an action by Colonel Israel B. Richardson's Fourth Brigade of the First Division at Blackburn's Ford, on the afternoon of the 18th, convinced him that such a plan was not feasible. The engagement had not been contemplated by the army commander; it developed out of a reconnaissance carried farther than he wished.

Maps were then scrutinized and inquiries made to discover a place to get around the enemy's left flank above the stone bridge, which was the highest up the stream that he was believed to hold in force. At Sudley Springs, two to three miles above the bridge, there was a good ford, where for a considerable distance the stream could be crossed by wheeled vehicles. Midway between this place and the bridge the maps indicated another ford, likewise reported as good. Although the fords were accepted as suitable for crossing, the maps showed no road to them from Centerville; but information was obtained "that a road branched from the Warrenton turnpike a short distance beyond Cub Run, by which, opening gates and passing through private grounds," the fords could be reached.[85] There was time to look over the ground and be sure, but not too much time, since it was necessary to cook more food and refill haversacks, which had not been done on the 18th as McDowell had ordered. He had started from the Potomac with three days' cooked meals for the men, which should have lasted until the afternoon of July 19; but many of them had already consumed all they carried, and were beginning to experience disagreeable but instructive hunger. By reconnoitering and cooking on the 19th, McDowell was giving Beauregard his first clear day of grace.

The next day Major John G. Barnard and Captain Daniel P. Woodbury, Engineer Corps, accompanied by William Sprague, the thirty-year-old governor of Rhode Island, and—what was far more important—a troop of regular cavalry, reconnoitered the route. After following Cub Run valley to a point about four miles in a direct line from Centerville, they found a road which was "believed to lead to the fords." But enemy patrols were encountered before the Sudley Springs ford was reached; and as Barnard did not wish to arouse enemy suspicion, the party returned.

Then the almost unbelievable mistake was made. Of the road they had followed Barnard wrote: "We had seen enough to be convinced of the perfect practicability of the route." The presence of the enemy patrol certainly indicated it led to the ford. But in order to be more certain than plain certain, it was decided to try to get to the stream at night by stealth and the help of Michigan woodsmen. This decision was to keep the army idle another day—except for further unnecessary cooking—and gave Beauregard his second clear day of grace. And all the time the brigades of Johnston were moving toward Manassas! Though McDowell did not know that at the moment, he had definitely expected that reenforcements would be brought to Beauregard. The discharge dates of his own regiments were also fast approaching. And the sacrifice of precious time was all for nought; enemy pickets drove back the engineers and the woodsmen, so that Barnard had to be content to be just certain—not doubly certain.

Then on Saturday July 20, with no more information than was possessed on Friday, it was decided to make on Sunday the movement that could easily have been made a day earlier. In his report McDowell said that it was cooking on the 20th that made "it necessary to make on Sunday the attack we should have made on Saturday." [86] But that was not the case. In a dispatch sent Saturday morning, he spoke of making further reconnaissance, but not one word about the necessity of cooking. [87] His claim is further contradicted by the reports of four commissary officers, which show that two days' rations for his whole army were issued on July 18. [88] The next day more rations were issued, so that the army had five days' food, more than should have been in the hands of troops, who always waste it. McDowell did not go on the reconnaissance on the 19th; he should have given personal attention to seeing that the two days' rations which he had ordered cooked on July 18 were prepared and put into the haversacks on the 19th without fail; and he should have directed that the food that came on the two late trains should not be issued to the men, but should be properly stored under army control.

By the morning of the 20th an alarming rumor had come in: Johnston had joined Beauregard. Dutifully and ominously McDowell reported the bad news to Scott in the dispatch previously referred to. Secretary Cameron doubtless received the information directly, for he was among the officials who inopportunely visited McDowell's headquarters.[89]

The plan for the battle was this:

Richardson's brigade, temporarily attached to the Fourth Division (Colonel Dixon S. Miles) would make a "false attack" on Blackburn's Ford. The rest of the Fourth Division to be in reserve at Centerville.

The First Division (Brigadier General Daniel Tyler) to move at 3:00 A.M. on the 21st "towards the stone bridge of the Warrenton turnpike, to feint the main attack upon this point."

The Second Division (Colonel David Hunter) and the Third Division (Colonel S. P. Heintzelman) to make the main effort by a turning movement that would envelop the enemy left flank. These divisions in the order named were to move at 2:30 A.M., and, following the First Division—encamped three miles west of them—were to diverge from the turnpike onto the road to Sudley Springs. It was expected that the head of Hunter's column would reach Sudley at 7:00 A.M. at the latest—with luck, an hour before that time.

Though the formal order did not so stipulate, the First Division was probably intended to force the stone bridge as soon as the Second Division should "clear away the enemy who may be guarding the lower ford and bridge."

It has been universally said that McDowell's plan was good. It was, but it was also complicated: two feints, and an envelopment by two divisions that had to advance in one column. Furthermore, the main effort was at right angles to the army's route of advance. If the movement were successful, this would make control difficult, and the presence of Bull Run would magnify the problem.

But the fatal error lay in timing. Night movements of troops are unbelievably difficult, and will run smoothly and according to schedule only when units have had adequate training, and when there is good staff work and good troop leading. The two divisions that were to make the envelopment should have been moved the night before to bivouacs as near the Sudley Springs ford as possible. There they could have rested, eaten their breakfasts, crossed the stream early, and been on with the heavy work of the day relatively unfatigued. And this was what McDowell himself wanted to do, for he wrote in his report:

> It had been my intention to move the several columns out on the road a few miles on the evening of the 20th, so that they would have a shorter march in the morning; but I deferred to those who had the greatest distance to go, and who preferred starting early in the morning and making but one move.[90]

McDowell could not quite realize that he had stars on his shoulders and not only maple leaves; it was a time when he needed a good chief of staff or operations officer to give him confidence in his decisions and to help him remember he was a general. The officers who tricked the new brigadier were not militiamen, but regulars.

Very early on the morning of the 21st, ranks were formed of unrested men: some had not slept at all, some had just begun to sleep, none had slept adequately. Before them was a march—and battle. Time was lost in forming units; time was lost in reporting to higher commanders that units were ready to move—if indeed the effort were made. Men stumbled over roots and logs in the woods, or fell in ditches; artillery teams were as ill-humored as their drivers. At last organizations started to move, slowly, and only for a short distance. The unit ahead had halted—or had not yet started. A regiment or a brigade would move again—and halt again. And so it went. A column of 18,000 men, infantry and artillery, bravely on their way to battle, moving along at night, a jerk at a time, wearing themselves out, and dissipating the strength they would need for combat: it was an agonizing sight for their general, who must have regretted the unwise advice he had taken. And presently he was also to regret an unwise supper, and the physical misery of an upset stomach was to be added to the mental misery of upset plans.

About 9:30 A.M. the head of the Second Division reached the Sudley Springs ford, where a halt was made to let the men rest and drink. From a commanding position, which gave a view along the road toward Manassas, McDowell made a disturbing discovery: it would be necessary to emerge from something like a defile into the face of a waiting enemy. In such a situation a general has to think as fast as an admiral. His decision must be immediate—and it must be right. McDowell made the correct decision; he ordered his organizations to double on each other, so as to get away from the evils of the fatal

FIRST BATTLE OF BULL RUN, JULY 21, 1861

single column. He also sent orders to Tyler to force the stone bridge. More he could not have done.

On the Confederate side alertness and an excellent battlefield decision were responsible for McDowell's predicament. The stone bridge position was being held by Brigadier General Nathan G. Evans [91] with two regiments of infantry, a squadron of cavalry, and two guns.

At about 5:15 Tyler had opened on the bridge with some artillery, to which Evans made no reply. A little later Tyler pushed up a considerable force of skirmishers; but the skirmishers did not show much conviction or resolution, and Evans divined that it was only a feint—quite as if he had read McDowell's order. Telltale dust clouds confirmed his suspicion that the Federals meant to cross above the bridge; and, courageously accepting responsibility, the young brigadier left the post where orders had placed him, and moved most of his force to where he could intercept the turning column. As if seasoned by many battles, he remembered to report his action to the neighboring brigade commander on his right, so that support might be brought to the weakened force he had left at the bridge.

Thus soldiership of the highest order on both sides marked the beginning of the first real battle of the Civil War: the quick clear thinking and prompt action of Evans, the equally quick thinking and correct counter orders of McDowell. The columns approached each other with the promise that in this war there would be not only hard-fighting soldiers, but also some excellent generals.

The Federal column was led by the Second Rhode Island Regiment of the Second Brigade—Colonel Burnside commanding—of the Second Division. As the regiment emerged from a wood about a mile south of Sudley Springs, on the road to Manassas, it received the sharp fire of the Fourth South Carolina and the First Louisiana, as well as the two guns that Evans had put in position. Hunter, forgetting that he was a division commander, began to take steps to get the battery belonging to the Second Rhode Island into position, and Fate exacted prompt payment for the error, as if impatient to teach commanders to keep to their proper duties and not to interfere with those of subordinates. Hunter fell badly wounded, and for a while there was confusion and uncertainty in the division command. Colonel John S. Slocum, at the head of the Second Rhode Island where he belonged, soon fell with mortal wounds, but there was no confusion, for the command at once devolved on an able lieutenant colonel. Evans's men had the advantage of steadying themselves by opening fire—no small matter. But the Rhode Islanders took their harsh reception well enough, and they soon were in action, and, much reassured by their battery, which was served "with great coolness, precision, and skill," [92] they covered the deployment of their brigade.

The action now became virtually a "meeting engagement," McDowell striving to develop the power of his superior attacking column, and Johnston and Beauregard marching their brigades in haste to their left. Johnston had reached Manassas at noon on the 20th, having been preceded by Jackson's brigade of five regiments; by morning of the 21st all but one of his brigades were on hand.[93] He had just been made a full general, and, his four stars exceeding Beauregard's one, he assumed command. By nine o'clock word of the Federal turning movement had been received, and it was presently seen to be so strong as to cause Johnston and Beauregard to abandon an attack that they had planned against McDowell's left in the direction of Centerville. After considerable confusion due to change of orders (which had originally been poorly drawn up), troops were pressed towards the badly threatened region west of the stone bridge. Johnston set up a general headquarters where he remained, and Beauregard hurried on to take command on the field. This was an excellent arrangement, which, with the union of their staffs, gave them an advantage over McDowell that played no small part in the battle's outcome.

At first the superior Federal forces and the excellent batteries of rifled guns with well trained regular soldiers swept the Confederate lines out of the way, and McDowell's men pushed on with a victorious feeling. The Henry House hill, just south of the turnpike, was carried, and batteries were advanced to new positions to carry on their effective attacks. But McDowell was without a second in command and a chief of staff; and soon he lost effective control of the battle. The error of Hunter constantly reappeared. The army commander himself forgot he was a general, and thought he was a colonel or a major again. Attacks were piecemeal. Colonel William T. Sherman—who later well knew how to run a battle—on this day could not get his brigade of Tyler's division into action except regiment by regiment.

At a very critical time a single bad decision had a terrible consequence. The batteries of Captains Charles Griffin and James R. Ricketts were in action side by side, a powerful mass of eleven good guns—one of Griffin's had been damaged and had been left in an earlier position—doing heavy damage to the Confederates, but insufficiently supported by infantry. A regiment in blue approached from a woods. It came from a suspicious direction—though lines had badly lost their original orientation—and in the still air its flag drooped unrecognizable about the staff. It was an awful moment—already there had been firing into friendly troops by both sides. Griffin thought the regiment was Confederate and was about to change the direction of his guns and open on it.[94] Major William F. Barry, McDowell's chief of artillery, said it was a Union regiment coming to support the guns. Suddenly the blue-clad regiment halted and at about seventy yards poured in its deadly fire: it was the Thirty-third Virginia of Jackson's brigade. Every cannoneer went down, and many horses were killed. The destruction was so overwhelming that the supporting battalion of marines and regiment of Zouaves broke. The enemy seized the guns, though they subsequently lost them.

On the Confederate side regiments had also broken and left in disorder, but there had been a good deal of success in re-forming them, probably because more Southern officers had had battle experience in the Mexican War. Jackson's brigade stood firm against the Federal attack, which had been weakened by the loss of Griffin's and Rickett's batteries, as well as by extensive disorganization. At about 3:30 P.M., Jackson with two of his regiments made a charge that had great effect,[95] and at about the same time Kirby Smith's brigade, just arrived from Winchester, and Jubal Early's brigade of Beauregard's command, fresh to the battle, delivered telling attacks against the Union right flank.

At 5:45 McDowell, back at Centerville, sent a dispatch to Colonel Townsend that quite fairly described the rapidly changing fortunes of the battle:

We passed Bull Run. Engaged the enemy, who, it seems, had just been re-enforced by General Johnston. We drove them for several hours, and finally routed them.

They rallied and repulsed us, but only to give us again the victory, which seemed complete. But our men, exhausted with fatigue and thirst and confused by firing into each other, were attacked by the enemy's reserves, and driven from the position we had gained, overlooking Manassas. After this the men could not be rallied, but slowly left the field.[96]

Having put the bad news on the wire to Washington, where early favorable reports had sent the President out for his customary Sunday drive, with his anxiety pleasingly replaced by confidence, McDowell had next to save his army from destruction, rather than from mere defeat. For the purpose he had three brigades, one of which had spent the day languidly at Centerville, while the other two, after a demonstration at Blackburn's Ford, had retired on an order from Miles, and had been cautiously followed toward Centerville by two Confederate brigades. These three brigades, together with some regiments of the Fourth Division that had arrived from Alexandria, were put in position covering Centerville; and behind this protection of almost fresh soldiers it was thought the army might be re-formed. Just what unused troops Johnston had that he might have used in launching an attack, McDowell did not know; such forces as appeared were not impressive and were duly cautious. At nine P.M. Scott wired that he supposed McDowell would rally at Centerville, "or at the worst at Fairfax Court-House and Fairfax Station." [97] He stated that additional reenforcements would be sent next day, and ended cheerfully: "We are not discouraged." It was soon seen, however, that the defeated men were headed for the Potomac, with no intention of stopping at any way station.[98] They wanted to get to their tents and their letters from home. At about ten the order for retreat was given, and the covering brigades took up an orderly march, with the Second Michigan of Richardson's Fourth Brigade of the First Division as the final rear guard.[99]

That historic day saw a strange flow of traffic between Centerville and the Potomac. In the morning there had been a regiment of infantry and the personnel of a battery, whose periods of enlistment had expired, and who were returning to Washington for discharge.[100] They would stay no longer, and were marching away at the moment McDowell's column began to cross at Sudley Springs to engage the enemy. After that there was the customary flow of army wagons in both directions, and the dusty, thirsty march of a few additional regiments toward the front to help exploit the expected victory. Also there were carriage loads of politicians and society people from Washington, coming to see the Federals triumph and the "Rebels" destroyed. Presently the stragglers from the battle appeared, then the defeated army: individuals, small groups of weary disheartened men, and broken mixed units with officers striving to re-form them. Here and there was a well formed organization—such as Sykes's regulars— tired, too, and thirsty like the others, but still marching steadily with precision, and attracting frightened men to fall in behind, where there was such an air of perfect safety. Also there were little mobs, where officers too had thrown in the sponge. Interspersed with the men were wagons with swearing drivers, the few guns that had been saved, and the carriages with the salvaged congressmen and ladies. After a break of empty road came the three well formed brigades, untouched by battle, with cartridge boxes full and pieces ready, and batteries at hand with caissons filled. On the whole scene the moon shone, just as it had shone two months before upon the advance of the Grand Army across the Potomac. But this night clouds of heavy dust increased the thirst of the weary soldiers, the unimpressive congressmen, and the now unlovely ladies. Probably some of the men, haunted by the specter of attacking cavalry, thought the moon unfriendly, and would have preferred the greater security of total darkness, even though it made them stumble. So it was throughout the long night, and throughout the next day until the Second Michigan reached its camp at four P.M. Some men had been on their feet for thirty-six hours, marching or in battle. It was a day none would forget.

But not all the men went back through the clouds of dust, thirsty and tired toward Washington; many remained on the field, for Bull Run was a *battle,* not just an action, an affair, a skirmish, or an engagement, as previous clashes had been. Scattered through the woods and over the rolling fields lay 481 dead in the Union blue: men from Connecticut, Maine, New York, Ohio, Wisconsin, New Hampshire, Rhode Island, Massachusetts, Minnesota, Michigan, and Vermont.[101] And there were 387 in the Confederate gray, from Louisiana, Mississippi, North Carolina, South Carolina, Virginia, Alabama, Georgia, Maryland, and Tennessee.[102] About half of those who were to be buried in Virginia graves were from New York and the Old Dominion itself. Never on the Western Hemisphere had so many men fallen on a field of battle. The Federals reported 1,011 wounded, and the Confederates 1,582. In missing, which included many wounded, the Federal loss was 1,200, the Confederate negligible. Though the policing of the battlefield gave the Confederates unpleasant duties, it also gave them a rich harvest of needed armament and equipment, including twenty-eight pieces of artillery, seventeen of which were good rifled guns.[103] It is difficult to say just how many troops actually opposed each other in the major battle. Johnston made the preposterous statement in his report that 6,000 men of his army and 2,000 from Beauregard's had successfully resisted 35,000 Federals.[104] McDowell stated officially that he had crossed Bull Run with 18,000 men, and very modestly added: "The numbers opposed to us have been variously estimated. I may safely say, and avoid even the appearance of exaggeration, that the enemy brought up all he could." [105] Never was anything said much truer than that. About thirty-three regiments on each side had casualties, and about twenty-two regiments in each army had as many as 20 wounded. Of about 30,000 men available for combat in each force, Federals and Confederates alike had about 18,000 engaged.[106]

Without question the Confederates had many significant points of advantage, which weigh even heavier when one remembers that this was the first battle. They were on the defensive, they had had a better night's rest; and Beauregard did not have the difficult problem of feeding inexperienced men upon a march, a problem that McDowell handled badly, and that had so much bearing on the outcome of the battle. But in spite of the fact that the Federals were the attackers—after an exhausting march—they did the better work with their weapons, as is shown by an analysis of the casualties. Each 1,000 Union soldiers had 80 men hit, but hit in return 100 of their enemy; but 1,000 Confederates sustained 100 casualties, while inflicting only 80 on the Federals.[107] It is often said that the Southerners were the better soldiers in the early days of the war because more of them were habituated to the use of weapons; but at Bull Run the Northern "shop-keepers" outshot them—though they seemed to be killed more easily. (How much allowance should be made for quality of weapons is impossible to say.)

Though Jackson's brigade was the only organization that received a new designation because of valor, there were many cases of bravery and hard, steady, courageous fighting. The palm should go—as should be expected—to Major George Sykes's battalion of eight companies of regular United States infantry. They were in the hottest of the battle, and though regiments broke around them they were as steady and unshakable as on the drill field. The fire of their rifles broke several enemy regiments and drove back others. They also served well in covering the withdrawal and the flight from the actual battlefield, and the mere order and regularity of their march sufficed to keep threatening enemy cavalry at a very respectful distance from their accurate gunfire. No one could read with real comprehension Sykes's modest but significant report without being touched by the soldiership of the fine companies he commanded.[108] When the sequence of the phrases is changed, so as to shift the emphasis, the last sentence reads eloquently: "My men are destitute of blankets, and in want of necessary clothing; but the arms and equipment of my command are in good condition."

The striking performance of Sykes's men has led some critics to observe that McDowell would have won his battle if he had had twenty such battalions, or perhaps only a dozen of them. Assuredly he would. But Sykes also revealed this important fact in his report: though his men were not just new volunteers, still they were not men with a great deal of service, and most of his officers were fresh from civil life or the Military Academy. The difference between them and the volunteers was not after all so very great.

McDowell, conscientious and modest to a fault, closed his report frankly: ". . . and could we have fought a day—yes, a few hours—sooner, there is everything to show that we should have continued successful, even against the odds with which we contended." [109]

McDowell could have started across the ford four hours earlier than he did, and with much fresher men, if he had but followed his own judgment and had not deferred to his subordinate commanders: then he would not have encountered the last of Johnston's brigades, whose flank attack was final. He could have fought the day before, by getting all his reconnaissance and all his cooking done on the 19th: then he would have had to fight less than half of Johnston's force, and that general would not have been on the field at first. He could have attacked on July 19 if he had reached Centerville—as he could have done—on the evening of the 17th, and made his reconnaissance on the 18th while the 65,000 rations that arrived at Fairfax at seven A.M. were being distributed, cooked, and put into the haversacks: then he would not have had to fight any of Johnston's good brigades. And if he had attacked on July 19 he still would have been one day later than Scott had confidently expected him to carry Manassas.

McDowell's delay of a week in starting the operation was disastrous; he lost a regiment of infantry and a battery of artillery on the very day of battle, and Patterson could list on July 21 only a few regiments of "active troops," because many of his organizations had departed.[110] Ironically enough McDowell stated in his report that sending reenforcements to Patterson "by drawing off the wagons" had been an "unavoidable cause of delay." [111] Peter had been robbed to pay Paul, and Paul need not actually have been paid, if Patterson's suggestions had been followed. On June 17 he had proposed that he move at once from Hagerstown and Williamsport to Harpers Ferry and rebuild the bridge. The next day he repeated the suggestion and described the rebuilding of the bridge as "a military necessity," calling attention to the fact that with the railroad opened he could operate toward Winchester and could easily maintain himself.[112] But the suggestion was not accepted by Scott, and toward the end of the month Johnston sent back a force that completed the destruction of the bridge at Harpers Ferry, did other damage, and removed stores and property that he had left when he evacuated the place. If Patterson's proposal had been followed, he would not have needed a large wagon train, for he could have advanced on Winchester by the railroad; he might even have sent some wagons to McDowell.[113] Patterson may have grasped both the strategic and the supply value of railroads better than Scott, who toyed with the idea of having Patterson join McDowell, even though the latter already had a larger force than he could command well. So, to keep Patterson mobile with a train of dust-raising mules and wagons, McDowell was robbed of some of his transport, and precious days were lost. And in the end Patterson did change his base to Harpers Ferry and in the end Scott saw it was futile for him to attempt to reach Manassas in time to aid McDowell.

When reasons for the Federal defeat at Bull Run are looked for, it also should be remembered that on the Southern side that day were no fewer than seven officers who were destined to attain high distinction: Johnston, Beauregard, Jackson, Longstreet, Ewell, Early, and Stuart (the latter two only colonels at the time). Not often is there so much talent among 30,000 men. On the Northern side were several officers who later became division or corps commanders (one, Burnside, briefly an army commander); but the units some of them commanded at Bull Run were only a regiment, a battalion, or even a battery. Among the commanders on July 21 of brigades or larger units, only Colonels William Tecumseh Sherman and Oliver Otis Howard held prominent positions when the war closed.

Such an unexpected defeat usually requires that there be a victim to take the blame; and Patterson seemed almost sent by Heaven for the purpose. His failure to immobilize Johnston was apparent and undeniable, while all the instructions given to him were not known. On

July 19 the order had been issued for his discharge on July 27,[114] as well as that of Cadwalader, who had commanded a brigade in Scott's army in Mexico. Of course McDowell had to be saved, because he was potentially worth many Pattersons, as were also the officers who had misled McDowell, and those who had advised Patterson badly. Probably not many persons knew that McDowell had attacked three full days after Scott expected him to; safe in the files was the telegram that the General in Chief had sent McClellan on July 21 containing the sentence, "You will soon redeem blunders, and so will McDowell," [115] which showed that he was aware of the gravity of McDowell's delay. Less charitable to Patterson, Scott stated: "Johnston has amused Patterson and reenforced Beauregard." He would have been nearer the full truth if he had said that Johnston had deceived Patterson, and he himself had confused him by a careless order. Just a few weeks before, Scott had subscribed himself in a letter to Patterson, "Your brother soldier." [116] In the grim business of war the long friendship was forgotten, and Patterson was tossed disheartened and bewildered to the condemning public.[117] Perhaps there was no other way, but some aspects of the affair tarnished somewhat the fine record of Winfield Scott.

On the day after the first real battle of the war the people of the North had a taste of bitter disillusionment, for early papers proclaimed a great Union victory. Horace Greeley's influential *New York Tribune* carried a two-column account of the engagement, which ended with a condemnation of Patterson and the statement that there was no doubt that Johnston had joined Beauregard. Above the story there was a short dispatch sent from Fairfax Station at 5:30 P.M. and cleared from Washington at nine o'clock. The news still was good: "The day is ours. The enemy totally routed." Headlines went still further and proclaimed: "A Death Blow to Secession." Spirits elevated by such words were soon cast down by news of the sudden reversal and retreat. Contradictory accounts of the battle followed, and arm chair strategists took over the field. General Colin Ballard states: "Perhaps more nonsense has been written about First Bull Run than about any other battle in history." [118] His brief appraisal may be as balanced as any that has appeared. Only one phase of the battle and its aftermath has been adequately described. Of the Washington scene Walt Whitman wrote:

Amid the deep excitement, crowds and motion, and desperate eagerness, it seems strange to see many, very many, of the soldiers sleeping— in the midst of all, sleeping sound. They drop down anywhere, on the steps of houses, up close by the basements or fences, on the sidewalk, aside on some vacant lot, and deeply sleep. A poor seventeen or eighteen year old boy lies there, on the stoop of a grand house; he sleeps so calmly, so profoundly. Some clutch their muskets firmly even in sleep. Some in squads; comrades, brothers, close together—and on them, as they lay, sulkily drips the rain. . . .

But the hour, the day, the night pass'd, and whatever returns, an hour, a day, a night like that can never again return. The President, recovering himself, begins that very night—sternly, rapidly sets about the task of reorganizing his forces, and placing himself in positions for future and surer work. If there were nothing else of Abraham Lincoln for history to stamp him with, it is enough to send him with his wreath to the memory of all future time, that he endured that hour, that day, bitter than gall— indeed a crucifixion day—that it did not conquer him—that he unflinch-ingly stemm'd it, and resolv'd to lift himself and the Union out of it.[119]

CHAPTER IV

THE ADVENT OF McCLELLAN

One of the greatest perplexities of the Government is to avoid
receiving troops faster than it can provide for them.
Lincoln to Congress

GENERAL SCOTT HAD BEEN so confident of victory that he forgot
arithmetic and believed in miracles. In the dispatch to McClellan in
which he referred to McDowell's blunders and revealed that Johnston
had reenforced Beauregard, he nevertheless confidently predicted
victory, saying: "McDowell is this forenoon forcing the passage of
Bull Run. In two hours he will turn the Manassas Junction and storm
it to-day with superior force." The General in Chief evidently could
not add the strengths of Beauregard and Johnston and get the correct
sum; it was not strange, therefore, that he found it impossible to accept the first tidings of disaster. At seven P.M., July 21, he wired the
commanding general at Baltimore, "Bad news from McDowell's army
not credited by me." Nevertheless the old general's instinct had him
say, "Put your troops on the alert." An hour later he turned a wish
into a fact and said to Brigadier General Theodore Runyon, commanding McDowell's Fourth Division which had been left at Alexandria, "It is now known that McDowell has rallied his army at or
about Centerville." At the same hour he telegraphed McClellan, "Mc-
Dowell has been checked." This restrained sentence would have been
appropriate about twelve hours later—as an expression of ironical
thankfulness that McDowell was stopping his retreat at the Potomac.[1]
By midnight Scott no longer denied the distasteful facts, but groping

somewhat vainly for an explanation, he wired McClellan at one o'clock: "After fairly beating the enemy, and taking three of his batteries, a panic seized McDowell's army, and it is in full retreat on the Potomac. A most unaccountable transformation into a mob of a finely-appointed and admirably-led army."

On the 22nd, Lincoln, with his mind upon the future and not on the cruel defeat of the day before, had the following telegram sent to General McClellan: "Circumstances make your presence here necessary. Charge Rosecrans or some other general with your present department and come hither without delay." [2]

And so George B. McClellan came to Washington with the idea that he was a savior. This very mischievous thought was worse than mischievous in a man disposed toward vanity and arrogance, who had risen rapidly, without the chastening and tempering benefit of tough experience.

McClellan, now only thirty-four years old, had graduated high in his class at West Point and had served with credit on Scott's staff in the Mexican War, where he was brevetted for bravery. After a tour of duty as instructor in practical engineering at West Point, he became an engineer officer in the West. In January, 1857, while captain in the First Cavalry, he resigned from the army to become chief engineer of the Illinois Central Railroad, and he was successively vice president and president of the Ohio and Mississippi Railroad, residing in Cincinnati. He entered the service as major general of volunteers, filling the position to which Ohio was entitled by her quota of thirteen regiments. He was presently appointed major general in the United States Army, with rank from May 14 and seniority next to Scott, and commanding the Department of the Ohio, which included the states of Ohio, Indiana, and Illinois, as well as parts of western Virginia and Pennsylvania.

The good repute in which McClellan had been held was shown in 1855, when Jefferson Davis, as Secretary of War, appointed him with Majors Richard Delafield and Alfred Mordecai to a commission for the study of European armies. The Crimean War was then being fought, and American preparedness was arousing more than usual interest. In Paris permission to visit the French army in the Crimea was refused to the commissioners unless they engaged themselves not to go to any other part of the active theater—a promise they would not make; in Russia they were allowed to see some military posts and

MAJOR GENERAL AND MRS. GEORGE B. McCLELLAN

establishments, and also troops in review, but not to go to the Russian army in the Crimea. However, they visited the British field forces, and received every courtesy and consideration while with the active army. Afterward they saw many European fortifications, barracks, hospitals, and other military installations in France, Prussia, and Austria, in some places having full, unrestricted opportunity to study details with the help of plans, and in other places seeing no more than would be revealed to any person with a printed ticket of admission.

Probably European travel gave McClellan the ideas he subsequently incorporated in the "McClellan saddle," which was adopted soon after its recommendation in 1856. The saddle had a rather grim and businesslike appearance, was durable, and packed well; and the army retained it as long as it retained horses.

Before the end of April, McClellan had devised a plan of campaign which included not only ambitious operations in the West but also a march upon Richmond through the valley of the Great Kanawha River. He officially submitted his ideas in a long letter to General Scott, who forwarded a copy to the President after adding an indorsement setting forth faults and weaknesses in the proposals.[3] But by the time of the Bull Run defeat McClellan had achieved success in western Virginia, and it was on that account that he received the rather spectacular summons to repair to Washington. As a military operation the Virginian exploit was a minor matter; but the Confederates were nevertheless driven out of the western anti-secession counties with a considerable loss in killed, wounded, and prisoners, as well as property, while McClellan's losses were only nominal. There was only one contact worthy of being called a battle; and careful study of McClellan's operations and his telegrams and letters fully reveals the characteristics that were so pronounced later—characteristics that led to his failure in the Peninsular and Antietam campaigns, and that completely unfitted him for high field command.

At first McClellan directed his operations from Cincinnati, which was quite proper, for his department was a large one and he had many responsibilities. On June 1 he reported to Colonel Townsend, General Scott's adjutant general, that he had given orders that the "rebels" should be driven from Philippi and beyond Beverly, which place was to be held. "I have already informed you that I have placed the operations in Western Virginia under Brig. Gen. T. A. Morris, of the Indiana Volunteers, a graduate of West Point, and a cool, deliberate man." [4]

The attack that Morris made without delay on Philippi on June 3 was most creditable to himself, his soldiers, and their officers; he successfully converged two columns on the town after "a march of fifteen miles in pitchy darkness, drenching rain, and over a mountainous country." Morris spoke very commendably of "the irresistible attack and hot pursuit of the discomfited enemy." Being a trained soldier, he knew that uniting two columns at an objective point is one of the most difficult feats in war and he justly added, in view of the terrain and the weather: "I regard it as remarkable that under such circumstances the two columns were but fifteen minutes apart at the time assigned for their meeting." Men who had been in service about five weeks were indeed doing well! The enemy's killed were estimated at from fifteen to forty, and "a large amount of camp equipage, provisions, arms, wagons, horses, and medical stores were captured." Morris had no men killed.[5]

Such was McClellan's first victory in western Virginia. Miles away, he himself heard no discharge of cannon, no roll of musketry.

He reached Parkersburg on June 21, and reported to Townsend the next day that he doubted that the enemy had as great a force as Morris and others believed. "I have, I think, a force enough to fight them wherever I find them." This statement indeed promised well; but the letter also contained the boast: "I will, without delay, beat them up in their quarters." The bombastic note that McClellan too quickly sounded was continued in a proclamation to his command on the 25th: "Soldiers! I have heard that there was danger here. I have come to place myself at your head and to share it with you." [6]

The main enemy force under Brigadier General R. S. Garnett was in position on Laurel Hill between Philippi and Beverly. McClellan gave Morris the smaller half of his force to detain Garnett, while he took the larger half to Buckhannon, with the intention of seizing Beverly and cutting Garnett's communications through that place and Huttonsville with Staunton.

On July 2 Morris asked for reenforcements in a letter unfortunately not in the Official Records; but the next day McClellan replied in a letter officially preserved. After lecturing his subordinate in a lofty tone, the man who had not yet heard the noise of battle said to the man who had:

I propose taking the really difficult and dangerous part of this work on my own hands. I will not ask you to do anything I would not be willing to do myself. But let us understand each other. I can give you no more re-enforcements. . . .

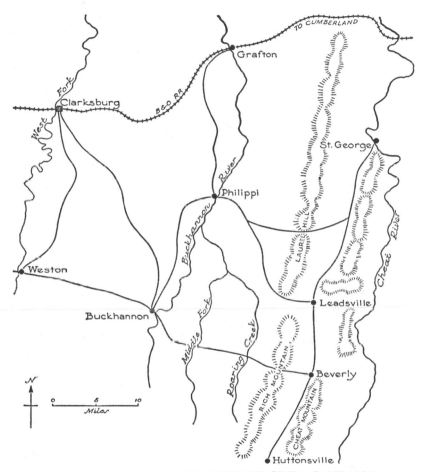

REGION OF McCLELLAN'S WEST VIRGINIA CAMPAIGN

Do not ask for further re-enforcements. If you do, I shall take it as a request to be relieved from your command and to return to Indiana.

I have spoken plainly. I speak officially. The crisis is a grave one, and I must have generals under me who are willing to risk their lives and reputation with such means as I can give them. Let this be the last of it.[7]

So wrote the general who a few months later began continually pressing his own superiors for reenforcements. A man who could write like that, who had no military achievement to his credit—except the invention of an uncomfortable saddle—was not likely to prove fit for high command. As to the forces involved: McClellan with about 8,000 men was faced by 1,300 astride the good highway from Buckhannon to Beverly; Morris with 4,000 men was opposed by 4,000 to 5,000. Ironically, after the contest was over McClellan stated in his report to Washington that Garnett, who faced Morris, had had 10,000 men.

On July 5 McClellan wrote to Townsend a long letter that began with a characteristic apology for delay and revealed the traits that afterward became so prominent—the traits that brought to naught all his promises and plans. He had the "intention of gaining success by maneuvering rather than by fighting," and he proposed "not to move until I know that everything is ready, and then to move with the utmost rapidity and energy." Somewhat boastfully he said, "The delays that I have met with have been irksome to me in the extreme," but still he could assure Townsend that he had not given way to impatience, which would have been foolish.[8] Although he had hoped to move on the 6th, McClellan still was in Buckhannon on the 7th, making more promises: "I will be prepared to fight whatever is in front of me. . . . The men are in magnificent spirits for a battle. The only trouble will be to restrain them. . . . If the Government will give me ten thousand arms for distribution in Eastern Tennessee, I think I can break the backbone of secession." A few days later another apology for delay was made that sounds much indeed like the Peninsula: "I have great difficulties to meet." Though he had previously reported that there were good roads in the region, McClellan now stated: "This country exceedingly difficult to operate in."

On the 6th Morris was directed—in a courteous letter written by Major Seth Williams of McClellan's staff—to start "amusing" operations against Garnett the next day, and was told that the general with the main force expected to occupy Beverly by the 9th at latest, probably by the 8th.[9] Actually McClellan arrived at Beverly on the 12th.

Having reached Roaring Creek, ten miles from Buckhannon, on the 10th, McClellan determined to follow his plan to turn the force under Lieutenant Colonel John Pegram at the base of Rich Mountain, rather than attack it.[10] A suitable route was not known, but at ten o'clock that night Brigadier General Rosecrans suggested a very difficult operation which was accepted by McClellan, and on which Rosecrans set out at five o'clock the next morning with a force of about 2,000 men.[11] Through rain and thick woods, by poor roads, paths, and no roads at all, he led his column around the left of Pegram's position and up Rich Mountain to the rear of the enemy. About 350 of the enemy were waiting behind log intrenchments with two six-pounders, but Rosecrans carried the position with a charge at the loss of twelve killed and forty-nine wounded.

McClellan's main force with the general "in person just in rear of the advance pickets" was drawn up ready to assault the enemy position west of Rich Mountain when Rosecrans should attack it from the rear.[12] Lieutenant Colonel John Beatty, waiting with the Third Ohio Infantry to make the assault, wrote in his diary under date of the 11th:

Between two and three o'clock we heard shots in the rear of the fortifications; then volleys of musketry, and the roar of artillery. Every man sprang to his feet, assured that the moment for making the attack had arrived. General McClellan and staff came galloping up, and a thousand faces turned to hear the order to advance; but no order was given. The general halted a few paces from our line and sat on his horse listening to the guns, apparently in doubt as to what to do; and as he sat there with indecision stamped on every line of his countenance, the battle grew fiercer in the enemy's rear. Every volley could be heard distinctly. There would occasionally be a lull for a moment, and then the uproar would break out again with increased violence. If the enemy is too strong for us to attack, what must be the fate of Rosecrans' four regiments, cut off from us and struggling against such odds? [13]

Finally the noise of battle completely died away, and the Ohio officer recorded that "the belief grew strong that Rosecrans had been defeated and his brigade cut to pieces or captured." When shout after shout went up from the enemy position in their front the fear in the hearts of the Federals was changed to certainty. Late in the afternoon McClellan had begun to prepare to put his twelve guns into position so as to give Rosecrans a little assistance; but darkness came on and sent him back to his main camp with the intention of moving the guns and all available infantry into position at daybreak. But there was delay, and as the guns were about to take the position completed for them during the night "intelligence was received that the enemy had evacuated their works and fled over the mountains, leaving all their guns, means of transportation, ammunition, tents, and baggage behind." [14]

At nine o'clock General McClellan sped the news of victory to Washington, stating that his success was complete and almost bloodless, and that he was pushing on to Beverly, from which Rosecrans's troops were said to be only three miles distant. After some detail of the operations, he closed with a tribute to his soldiers, "Behavior of troops in action and towards prisoners admirable." At eight P.M. a rather long dispatch from Beverly stated, "I hope to be able to give you to-morrow full details of the transactions of the last few days. I advanced so rapidly to this place that it is not now in my power." He had a strong defensive position and was, moreover, "constantly picking up more prisoners." The next day's work was set forth in the statement, "I shall move on Huttonsville to-morrow morning, and endeavor to seize the Cheat Mountain pass before the enemy can occupy it in any strength." [15]

Again, however, McClellan failed to carry out his announced plan; he remained at Beverly and allowed the enemy to escape with valuable supplies. Apparently fearing that Washington had not appreciated just how speedily he had moved to Beverly, McClellan said in the telegram of the 13th, "Occupied Beverly by a rapid march," and he closed the dispatch, "I hope the general will approve my operation." [16]

Washington was more than ready to commend, and General Scott telegraphed: "The General-in-Chief, and what is more, the Cabinet, including the President are charmed with your activity, valor and consequent success of Rich Mountain on the 11th, and of Beverly this morning. We do not doubt that you will in due time sweep the rebels from Western Virginia, but we do not mean to precipitate you, as you are fast enough." [17]

On the 14th McClellan, now near Huttonsville, wrote a long report noting for the third time that he had "made a rapid march and occupied Beverly." He contended that Morris had not followed Garnett vigorously; "and had it not been for the rapid and well-directed march of the advance, conducted by Captain Benham, it is believed that the rebel general would have escaped unharmed. Captain Benham is entitled to great praise for his prompt and energetic movement up Garnett's rear, the result of which will be seen from his report inclosed." This looks like an effort to hit Morris below the belt. Benham commanded the pursuing part of Morris's force, and his report was forwarded to McClellan by Morris, who could claim credit for anything that he did with quite as much propriety as McClellan could for Rosecrans's fine operation. As a matter of fact, Morris pursued Garnett quite effectively over difficult roads toward St. George, through rain and with little food for his men. Though most of the enemy escaped, General Garnett was killed and his command lost heavily in both equipment and supplies.[18]

On August 26 Colonel Beatty wrote in his diary that McClellan had not properly followed up the defeats of Pegram and Garnett; the Southern force was completely demoralized and the "men composing it, who were not captured, fled, terror-stricken, to their homes. We could have marched to Staunton without opposition and taken possession of the very strongholds the enemy is now fortifying against us." Remembering that troops need subsistence, he asserted that food could have been procured locally. Actually McClellan telegraphed Scott on July 17 that he could probably take Staunton and asked if a movement against it were desired; but though Scott replied the next day that the move would be "admirable" he prepared for a longer and harder march westward because a Federal force had been "checked" on the Kanawha.[19] The general's dispatch certainly proves, however, that Beatty had more than afterknowledge; and even a threat toward Staunton close after the capture of Beverly would have puzzled the Richmond authorities and made them doubtful as to what to do with Joe Johnston when McDowell marched on Centerville.

As one studies McClellan's future career it is to be remembered that he was completely unseated, and that he abandoned an apparent purpose, when he learned—in his own words—that one of his commanders had "fought something between a victory and a defeat." Forgetting what Morris and Rosecrans had done, he asked Scott "in Heaven's name" to give him general officers who understood their profession; and he wrote the untrue and ungracious sentence, "Unless I command every picket and lead every column I cannot be sure of success." [20] With no delay the western commander, Brigadier General Jacob D. Cox, turned the position of his opponent, Brigadier General Henry A. Wise, throwing him into such a panic that he retreated through Charleston. Cox pursued him closely, and was in that city on July 25, occupying the strong defile at Gauley Bridge on the 29th; he was in no need whatever of assistance, and an excellent way to loosen up Wise would have been for McClellan to make his contemplated move on Staunton. Though the railroad through that place terminated ten miles short of Covington, a main wagon road from Covington afforded the usual communication with the Charleston area.

Confederate Colonel W. C. Scott, who commanded the Forty-fourth Virginia and was in position near Beverly on the 11th with very inadequate instructions, made an amusing comment on McClellan's failure to follow up his success. Scott had loaded the large accumulation of supplies at Beverly into all the wagons he could find, and retreated through Huttonsville. He was criticized for retiring too far, and in his long account of the day's events he justified his action by the statement: "General Morris pursued General Garnett; why should not McClellan pursue me, as I was encumbered by a long train of wagons conveying our commissary and quartermaster's stores, etc.?" [21]

That is the brief story of the victories that McClellan won in western Virginia. He deserves full credit for the plan of the operations; but they succeeded because of good troop leading by brigadiers he officially disparaged or openly affronted.[22] In his memoirs McClellan seems to make a point of the fact that he carried out his operations without specific directions from Washington; he forgets, however, a significant telegram that Townsend sent to him on May 20 and a long letter that Scott wrote the next day.[23] Replying to the general's complaints that he did not know the views of the administration and lacked authority, Townsend called attention to the fact that McClellan's department had recently been enlarged by the addition of western Pennsylvania and Virginia. "Your authority is ample within your command." Scott reproved his subordinate for repeatedly giving advice about Cumberland, Maryland, which was outside his department, and expressed surprise that he had complained directly to the Secretary of War about having "his hands tied up." He listed eleven facts that disproved his subordinate's allegation, told him that he had "full sway" within his wide department, and expressed a general policy by saying that he was expected to defend his department "against all enemies of the United States." Scott even said that permission would readily be given for McClellan to march into other states "to protect the friends of the Union," in case he made a reasonable case for such action. This correspondence, which plainly shows that aggressiveness on his own initiative was expected of McClellan, had been lost at the time of the publication—five years before McClellan's death—of the volume of the records covering the West Virginia campaign; and it appeared only years later with other supplementary material.

In spite of McClellan's success, a competent high command weighing his dispatches would not have called him to a more responsible position, unless—as was the case—there was an emergency and almost no one else to choose. If Scott in the weeks ahead recalled his letter of May 21 he may have regretted that he had not terminated it with the reproof administered, instead of tossing in at the end an expression of his great confidence in the ex-captain's "intelligence, zeal, science, and energy."

McClellan was not entirely truthful about the situation when he took over command of troops in the vicinity of Washington on July 27, six days after Bull Run. Six months later, February 3, 1862, he wrote to the new Secretary of War, Edwin M. Stanton:

> I found no army to command—a mere collection of regiments cowering on the banks of the Potomac, some perfectly raw, others dispirited by the recent defeat. . . . The city was almost in condition to have been taken by a dash of a regiment of cavalry.[24]

The first six words were true enough; but the rest of the charge was a deliberate reflection upon officers with more combat experience than himself, who were better able to evaluate the gravity of the situation. Washington never for a moment was in any peril, although civilians were in a panic and some politicians were alarmed because of the sleepy, hungry, and apparently helpless soldiers on the streets.

The army command had not been disturbed for long. Colonel T. A. Scott of the War Department, who at 2:30 A.M., July 22, showed some signs of alarm,[25] a few hours later relaxed the censorship on news and wrote:

> Our loss, by officers from rear of column, is estimated at from 2,500 to 3,000. All beyond that we believe to be exaggeration. The retreat was covered by a good steady column, and the forts on the south bank of the Potomac are all strongly reenforced with fresh troops.[26]

"Covered by a good steady column." A professional soldier—which Colonel Scott was not—could not have made a more appropriate statement. It was very significant that the division in position at Centerville had been entirely unaffected by the retreating men that passed through its ranks. Ballard knew whereof he spoke when he referred to the nonsense that has been written about Bull Run, though some writers have enjoyed speaking of an "armed mob," getting the cue perhaps from the telegram that the General in Chief—completely tired out—sent to McClellan at 1:00 A.M., after a day that would have been hard on a much younger man, and before all the facts were in. Later on the 22nd General Scott had the situation well in hand, and he even directed that McDowell's force west of the Potomac should be reduced to fifteen regiments with appropriate field batteries as rapidly as possible, all retained regiments being three-year organizations (which continued to arrive in impressive numbers); he also directed McClellan, "Bring no troops with you." [27] On July 22 Congress went calmly about the business on its calendar, the Senate beginning with a tariff bill and the House with a measure to provide for the payment to the widow of Senator Stephen A. Douglas of the money due at the time of his sudden death. A resolution mentioning the reverse of the day before and calling on the people for their support which was read in the House was immediately tabled. But unanimous consent was given to the first and second readings of a bill about a Pacific railroad. Taken all in all, July 22 was a day much to the credit of the nation.

Lincoln's call of May 3 had asked for only 42,000 volunteers for three years, but far more were accepted. Secretary of War Cameron carefully surveyed the military situation as of July 1 in a long report to the President which was published in full in the Official Records, but which has been overlooked by some historians.[28] He stated clearly that under the call of May 3 a total of 208 regiments had already been accepted—although the call had been for only 40 regiments. "Of the 208 regiments accepted for three years, there are now 153 in active service, and the remaining 55 are mostly ready, and all of them will be in the field within the next twenty days." [29] Then he gave figures showing that after withdrawal of three-months men there would still be a total of 230,000 soldiers.

Congress soon authorized 500,000 volunteers in response to the President's request for "at least 400,000 men." On the day after Bull Run a bill was introduced in the Senate to allow the President as many volunteers as he deemed necessary; as amended it granted authority for an additional 500,000 men to "be mustered into the service for 'during the war.' " [30] Under the two acts 700,000 men were enlisted and officially credited to the call of May 3; [31] most of the enlistments were for three years; none were "for the war" in spite of the reading of the last act passed.

Three-year men had, in reality, been raised as fast as they could be equipped and otherwise provided for; and the achievement was nothing less than remarkable. In 1940–1941 when the National Guard of some 400,000 men was mobilized, it was done in successive increments over a period of four months, although very extensive plans and preparations had been previously made. Some writers who have overlooked the problems involved have severely criticized Lincoln for not calling Congress into session immediately after Fort Sumter, so as to secure authorization for a large volunteer force.[32] When the pertinent facts are noted and understood, it is seen that Lincoln acted with great wisdom. By calling first for *militia*, he secured the regiments that the states already had organized and equipped; by deferring the meeting of Congress, he could call such regiments for ninety days—as previously noted—and thus secure protection for the capital and other vital points, while the situation was developing and broader war plans were being matured. Lincoln observed with all his acumen the reaction of both North and South to his initial step, and without hesitation he increased the regular army and the navy, and also called for volunteers, though he did not yet have the legal basis for either step. It is true that he called volunteers very modestly; but he accepted very liberally.

When Congress met on July 4 the situation was much clarified. There was already an army of 310,000—according to the Secretary of War—of whom 80,000 were soon to be disbanded, after having performed no mean service. By that date Lincoln knew more what he wanted to ask for, and the public generally was in less doubt and perplexity than in the last days of April. As a result, the meeting of Congress was very harmonious, and after about a month it adjourned and went home, with a fine record of efficiency and accomplishment. What Lincoln needed immediately after Sumter was the chance to think and study, unhampered by legislators suffering from excitement, confusion, and uncertainty. When he asked in July for at least 400,000 men, he could say he already had over half of them, and he could assert as an established fact, "One of the greatest perplexities of the Government is to avoid receiving troops faster than it can provide for them." [33] In view of what had been achieved by July, it meant something to speak of 500,000 volunteers. It was characteristic of Lincoln to admit candidly that he might have overstepped his legal authority; but he added significantly, "It is believed that nothing has been done beyond the constitutional competency of Congress." Although it would have been possible to authorize a large volunteer force in April if Congress had been in session, it would not have been possible to make laws providing for the necessary changes in the army. By July the War Department, which was badly overworked, had prepared legislation that could not have been ready two months before—a fact sometimes forgotten. Before adjournment Congress passed a bill validating "all the acts, proclamations, and orders of the President of the United States" since the 4th of March, and giving them the same intent and "the same effect as if they had been issued and done under the previous express authority and direction of the Congress of the United States."

Nor is it to be forgotten that Congress could have extended the call of the ninety-day militiamen, and held them in service. Less than a year later, the Confederate Congress was to do a far more extreme thing: it voted a conscription act that held men who had volunteered for one year's service to a service for three years. Although the words "militia of your State" were carefully used in the letters to the various governors on April 15, it is likely that Lincoln did not wish to raise any distinction between the status of such men and "volunteers." But the militia at that time had a somewhat ill defined status—like the National Guard of our time, as every officer well knows who has sought to understand the distinction between a "call" and a "draft" of the Guard by the President.

Secretary Cameron did much more than inform the President as to the number of men he had in service: he reported in addition upon steps taken to assure the health and morale of the armies being raised. He touched upon subsistence as particularly important: "It is desirable, therefore, that the quality of rations distributed to the troops should as far as possible, be adapted to their previous dietary habits." Already a commission of prominent scientists and doctors, appointed by the President, was cooperating with the Medical Bureau of the army, on "the best means of guarding and restoring" the soldiers' health "and of securing the general comfort and efficiency of the troops, the proper provisions of hospitals, nurses, cooks, etc." The Secretary's prediction that tangible results would soon be forthcoming was justified with the publication of "Rules for Preserving the Health of the Soldier," [34] as drawn up by the United States Sanitary Commission, addressed to officers and men alike; it constituted something quite new for the guidance of an army. On June 9 a general order of the War Department had made provision for women nurses in military hospitals, but not in camps or with regiments on the march; the necessary credentials would be furnished upon sending to Miss D. L. Dix, Washington, applications accompanied by "certificates from two Physicians, and two Clergymen of standing." No real battle had been fought, but the worst was evidently expected; and, although in the nature of things there could not be a declaration of war, there was a frank recognition of conditions when on June 15 the War Department ordered, "From the date of this order Officers entitled to Forage, will receive the amount authorized during a state of War."

Major Delafield's report of 1860 on the "Art of War in Europe" stated that the electric telegraph, a novelty first employed at the siege of Sebastopol, had been "unquestionably useful" for quick communication between the armies and the respective governments though it strengthened the impulse of officials distant from the scene to give ill advised instructions. He also stated that it had been "successfully used between the English trenches, headquarters, and depots." [35] It was not strange that use of a field telegraph should be attempted in a city that had been a terminal of the first telegraph line in the world and was then the home of Joseph Henry, who had done so much to make electric telegraphy possible. On June 27, Albert J. Myer, Signal Officer for the United States Army, submitted an estimate for $10,-000 "to be expended in the construction of movable (portable and flying) electric telegraphs," which Secretary Cameron did not recommend to Congress. The persistent Myer, regretting that there had been "no portable or flying telegraphs" at the battle of Manassas, wrote to Cameron on August 1 outlining the development of the signal corps for an army of 500,000 in such a way as to enable each division to have "suitable apparatus and the appurtenancies for both fixed and movable field telegraph and for the use of aerial and electric signals." He went so far as to write a law that Congress might pass in order to carry his plan into operation. The recommendations were approved by both McDowell and McClellan, but were not presented to Congress. Still, on August 17 Myer was authorized "to purchase a small telegraphic train." Though embarrassed by want of explicit funds, he had model reels and specimens of portable telegraphs made, and by November 30 he had convinced himself that it was possible to have movable electric apparatus that was simple and reasonable in cost; at that time he made a long report and further recommendations.[36]

The rapid growth of the army continued after the date of Cameron's report, and a War Department memorandum of August 3 informed McClellan that up to that time 418 regiments of infantry, 31 regiments of cavalry, and 10 regiments of artillery had been accepted.[37] The army strength stood at 485,640 three-year men. It was natural that numerous changes in the service should be put into effect, either by act of Congress or by order of the War Department; and among them were the abolition of flogging as a punishment, and the increase of a private's pay to thirteen dollars a month.[38] Even before Bull Run the elimination of unfit officers was being considered, and on July 25 an order directed that all officers of volunteer regiments must appear before a board appointed by the department commander and the General in Chief.[39] Those who were found incompetent were to be replaced by men who had passed the examinations. After that time frequent lists in the papers of officers who had "resigned" showed that the order was correcting much of the looseness in the original method of appointment by the governors of the states. The temper of the country was revealed by a telegram of August 5 sent by Governor Dennison of Ohio to Secretary Cameron, who had just authorized that five Ohio regiments be sent to Major General John C. Frémont in Missouri: "Will you name and give leave of absence to five Army officers whom I may appoint as colonels of these regiments? I want energetic men, graduates of West Point. Under their auspices the regiments can be organized in short time. The country demands educated military men at the head of regiments and I fully concur." [40]

In truth, McClellan did not find "regiments cowering on the banks of the Potomac," as he afterward scornfully asserted, though many men were absent from their organizations. Actually he found already laid the basis for substantial reform and improvement; but he does not appear to have given proper credit to the work of the War Department or the army command.

McClellan did, however have a part in the very important decision to arm the Federal infantry with a muzzle-loading rifle and make no effort to supply a breech-loader. The Delafield Report, which he signed, stated, "It is a remarkable fact that notwithstanding a knowledge of breech-loading small arms for at least two centuries, and that every museum of arms in Europe has numerous specimens, no satisfactory weapon for war purposes has as yet been invented." [41] The difficulty was largely one of ammunition. Metallic cartridges were only in an experimental stage, and when paper cartridges were used in breech-loaders there was much escape of gas with a resulting decrease of range. The heavy residue from the black powder of the day also caused breeches to stick or not to close completely, and in some cases a soldier could not raise his gun to his shoulder after he had fired a few rounds. But in addition to the adverse report of the Delafield Commission the ordnance department had to take into account another important fact. The army that was to be raised would have to be supplied in large part with weapons purchased abroad, and breech-loaders were simply not on the market. But the entire question has been badly misunderstood, and one historian, after asserting that the famous Prussian needlegun used a metallic cartridge—although the encyclopedia he cited as authority stated clearly that it used a paper cartridge—is strong in his denunciation of the ordnance department, speaking contemptuously of "stereotyped automatons" and suggesting that the officers in authority in 1861 lacked "brains." [42] He goes so far as to assert that the converting of muzzle-loaders to breech-loaders that was started in 1865 could equally well have been begun in 1861, without supporting the strong assertion in any way. Nowhere in his long chapter is it pointed out that a firearm that is very satisfactory for a hunter or a sportsman may be totally unfit as a military weapon. A soldier's rifle must work reliably when dirty and when it is hot. That fact is crucial, and the Delafield Commission must have had it in mind when it referred to a breech-loader satisfactory for war purposes. Questions of manufacture were also involved, and only a person with much knowledge of the manufacturing practices and capacities of the day as well as expert understanding of military ordnance could say that it was not a wise decision to have private firms make breech-loading carbines for the cavalry—where range and sustained fire were not so important— while the national armory stepped up greatly its capacity to make muzzle-loaders for the infantry. All the time the master armorer at Springfield worked on the problem of conversion; the United States was to have a breech-loading rifle that used a safe center-fire metallic cartridge before any European nation, and it was an American who showed the British how to convert their Enfield rifles into breechloaders.

It was indeed with a motley array of weapons that the Civil War was begun. The variety of ammunition for the different calibers and models must have driven ordnance officers almost crazy in the effort to requisition proper proportions of the different types and have them ready to issue to the ordnance wagons of the various organizations. During the Second Battle of Bull Run General Pope's ordnance officer asked on one requisition for eleven different kinds of ammunition for carbines, rifles, and muskets.[43]

Such was the army of 1861. On August 1 its strength was twenty-seven times what it had been on the day that Sumter fell.[44] The growth had been accomplished without previous preparation, under the handicap of many resignations of officers from regiments and important offices in the War Department alike, with the city of Washington itself insecure and isolated for a while, and with near-by Baltimore almost a hostile stronghold. The increase had been effected in the only way possible, the states undertaking to raise regiments and appoint officers, and the War Department stipulating merely the composition of the different units and relying upon subsequent efforts to eliminate unfit officers. Admittedly there was confusion, and there were counter orders, and some governors felt that they were slighted or believed that the War Department did not know what it was doing (which, of course, was the case at times).

No one who has had anything to do with a mobilization will be surprised either at the confusion or at what seemed at the time to be agonizing delays.

A comparison may be made with the mobilization of 1917. In 1917 officers were not asking to walk out on the government; Washington was serenely safe; for a number of years there had been a General Staff and an Army War College; plans had been made for mobilization; the summer before, there had been a mobilization of the National Guard (attended with plenty of confusion) for service on the Mexican border, from which much had been learned. In spite of all these favorable circumstances, and with the draft act passed on May 18 the army grew to less than three times its original strength in 1917 [45] during a time equal to that in which it had increased twenty-seven times in 1861.

There has been frequent failure to see the real problems that existed in 1861 as well as lack of appreciation of the great accomplishment. One historian goes so far as to speak of the "blundering incompetence of politicians" and the "haphazard method of raising the emergency force"; but he does not compare the results with those of World War I, and he does not explain the yardstick by which he is measuring. It seems also to be overlooked that the officers who resigned in 1861 could have been held to their oaths of service. The Army Regulations of 1857 made it clear that an officer was not out of service merely upon the "tender of his resignation"; he was not out until the tender was duly accepted. The revision of August 10, 1861, added the statement that an officer would be regarded as a deserter if he quit his post of duty without leave, intending to remain permanently away, before his tender of resignation was accepted. On April 1 Lincoln directed that all officers except those who had entered the service since the beginning of the month should take anew the oath prescribed by the Articles of War; in July Congress wrote a new oath for the cadets at West Point.[40]

Little appears to have been said about Lincoln's policy of accepting the resignations of Southern officers without even requiring a "cooling off" period; and it is a question one hesitates to touch. The man who loved the Union above all things, who saw in its preservation the sole hope of perpetuating the liberties of men and popular government, continued to allow the departure of officers who had made solemn oaths to defend the Union, and who were leaving with the unmistakable purpose of destroying it. He probably did so not only because it seemed to be the one practicable course, but because he believed it wise and right.

CHAPTER V

QUAKER GUNS AND BIG REVIEWS

The bottom is out of the tub. Lineoln to Meigs

Although the Confederates were in no condition on July 21 to pursue McDowell, General Joseph Johnston moved his force up to Fairfax, in order to show the greatest boldness that his strength and equipment allowed. Slight reenforcements had been received since the recent battle, and his Army of the Potomac was divided into two corps: the First Corps under Beauregard, now wearing the four stars of a full general; and the Second Corps under Major General G. W. Smith. (The corps organization had in fact no basis in Confederate law at that time.) Sickness—measles and other camp afflictions—and short rations were causing serious trouble. It was not that Johnston's men were sitting down three times a day to just "hog and hominy"; they were not sitting down to much of anything. The decrees of an incompetent commissary department in Richmond combined with railroad inefficiency to make Confederate soldiers go hungry in a harvest season near the rich Shenandoah Valley.[1] Johnston could not be reenforced by new regiments, for the chief of ordnance on August 12 had only 3,500 muskets, chiefly antique flintlocks that would have to be reworked before they were issued, and the states had no more firearms on hand.[2] Southern factories and arsenals had produced few rifles, and Captain Caleb Huse, sent to England on April 15 to purchase arms, reported that Northern agents with more money in their pockets had anticipated him.[3]

The gloomy prospect that was settling on the Confederacy so quickly after Bull Run is revealed in a letter of September 5 from President Davis to General Johnston: "One ship load of small-arms would enable me to answer all demands, but vainly have I hoped and waited." Unable to give his general more weapons, he closed, "May God protect and guide you." In a later letter he impressed on Johnston the responsibility imposed upon him, writing, "The cause of the Confederacy is staked upon your army." [4]

The former quartermaster general of the United States Army, lacking even food for the stomachs of his men, proceeded to build boldness into their very marrow, with the aid of unusual officers whose talents he appreciated, as shown by his report on Stuart:

He is a rare man, wonderfully endowed by nature with the qualities necessary for an officer of light cavalry. Calm, firm, acute, active, and enterprising, I know no one more competent than he to estimate the occurrences before him at their true value. [5]

Ten miles east of Fairfax, and less than that distance from the Capitol in Washington was Munson's Hill, just outside the part of Virginia originally in the District of Columbia. Its summit was 150 feet above Bailey's Cross Roads, distant one mile. On the hill Johnston put an outpost which could control the good road coming from McClellan's front yard. There was more than impudence in the arrangement, for the enemy pickets proved downright annoying to the Third New Jersey Volunteers commanded by Colonel George W. Taylor. Probably because no orders had been given to eject the Confederates, Taylor called for volunteers from his regiment; and he set out at three A.M. on August 31 to do something on his own initiative in the business of saving the Union. The "Rebs" seemed to have taken a fancy to the hill and were not inclined to give it up at the mere appearance of the Yankees, and from concealed positions they inflicted several casualties. But according to Colonel Taylor the morale of his men was excellent, for in a little charge each soldier "seemed eager to be foremost." The enemy apparently fell back after some pressure, for their firing ceased; probably the colonel did all that he should have done upon his own responsibility. Taylor's little action—which he officially reported on September 2 [6]—may have been the basis for a Northern correspondent's prediction that the Southerners would soon be ousted from their annoying post of observation; but a Confederate band that was located on the hill had the good taste to add "The Star-Spangled Banner" to the program it rendered on Sunday afternoon, and Johnston's men were not molested any more.

Toward the end of September the Confederate commander withdrew the outpost, for he knew it could be easily captured or destroyed. Then the revelation came, described on the 29th by the *New York Tribune* with full shame for what had occurred:

Munson's Hill will hereafter be the expression and measure of military false pretensions. There were no intrenchments there; there had been no cannon there. In the terrible batteries behind the hill there is but a derisive log, painted black, frowning upon the Federal army.[7]

Sight-seers came from Washington, incredulous, but to be convinced and be amused. Within the Confederate lines there was merriment over the success of the Quaker guns, and Beauregard wrote to Johnston:

To prevent spies and others from communicating to "George" our arrangements, I think it would be advisable to keep in reserve, at some safe place, our "wooden guns," to be put in position only when required.[8]

But those who remembered the stories of Ethan Allen that they had heard in childhood in their New England homes probably were not inclined toward laughter. McClellan's failure to recognize the actual weakness of the position on Munson's Hill and deal with it properly was spot number two on his field record; spot number one had been his cautious inactivity all day July 11 in front of Pegram without even taking steps to put guns in position until late in the afternoon.

Early in June, Johnston had written highly of McClellan to Lee, referring to "the troops from Ohio, who you know are commanded by a man of great ability"; soon, however, the Federal commander was not General McClellan, or McClellan, or even George; he was "George," or the "redoubtable McC." [9] The great force, well equipped and lavishly supplied, which was being mobilized about Washington was causing the Confederates the greatest apprehension; but its commander was a bright spot in the gloomy picture.

Too much credit is sometimes given to McClellan for the fortifying of Washington. Under Scott's direction McDowell had started in June to make the capital secure by an elaborate system of defensive works; but McClellan played down the work that his predecessor had done. Although no fewer than forty forts and some batteries had been constructed in June and July, the report McClellan submitted near the end of the year showed only four of the larger works: Forts Ellsworth, Runyon, Albany, and Corcoran, all of which were on the south of the Potomac.[10] It made the capital look insecure indeed.

On the 4th of August, McClellan submitted a long memorandum on the general military situation, which had been prepared at the President's request. Inasmuch as Scott was General in Chief the request was certainly open to criticism, playing into McClellan's hand and stimulating his natural inclination to by-pass his superior. For his main army of operation, he put down a force of 273,000 men; though he gave no figure for forces to be used in other theaters, his total would have been well within the 500,000 already raised. His price had, however, gone up a good deal since July 7, when he had boasted, "If the Government will give me ten thousand arms for distribution in Eastern Tennessee I think I can break the backbone of secession."

Although McClellan was hesitant in attacking enemy outposts, he was prompt in starting hostilities with Scott, and the war between the two—as he himself called it—can be traced both in his letters to his wife and in official communications. On the day he submitted his long proposal to Lincoln, he wrote to Mrs. McClellan, "It made me feel a little strangely when I went in to the President's last evening with the old general leaning on me; I could see that many marked the contrast." Perhaps some of the forty dinner guests saw a contrast other than that between age and vigor and recalled that Scott's fame rested on a remarkably successful and bold campaign, while McClellan had been nothing more than a captain of cavalry. Even in his infirmity there was something about Winfield Scott that suggested three regiments of infantry, a squadron of horse, and a battery of guns; for McClellan the name Little Mac was inevitable. Three months later McClellan was to tell his wife that every night and every morning he prayed that he would "become neither depressed by disaster nor elated by success." But anyone who knows how easy it is to get soldiers back to their normal mess lines and their proper organizations will think that McClellan had already shown his habit of overcomplimenting himself when he closed his letter of August 4, "I have restored order completely already." [11]

Four days later the real attack was on. After telling his wife of a "row" with the General in Chief, who was always getting in his way, and of his long interview with Secretary Seward about his "pronunci-amiento" against his superior's policy, he said of General Scott, "He understands nothing, appreciates nothing." McClellan defenders are much touched and very eloquent at times over the young military genius—fresh from his triumphant march on Beverly—completely frustrated by an antiquated and perverse superior. A little military perception would put the matter in its proper light, for McClellan revealed to his wife in these extravagant sentences that the dispute was over the security of Washington: "I have scarcely slept one moment for the last three nights, knowing well that the enemy intend some movement and fully recognizing our own weakness. If Beauregard does not attack tonight I shall look upon it as a dispensation of Providence. He ought to do it." [12]

The young general was not just trying to obtain a little domestic hero worship by exaggerating his own view of the situation, for on August 8 he also wrote to Scott about imminence of an attack. The letter and Scott's resulting protest to the Secretary of War were not available when the volume of the Official Records that should have contained them was being compiled. Found and inserted in a later volume, the letters have not received the attention that is their due. Said McClellan to Scott, "I am induced to believe that the enemy has at least 100,000 men in front of us." In order to render Washington "perfectly secure" he urged "that not an hour be lost in carrying" his proposed plans into execution, chief of which was enlarged authority for "the commander of the main army of occupation"—in other words, himself. The letter angered Scott—who after all had fought and won a few battles—and he wrote the next day to the Secretary of War: "Major-General McClellan has propagated in high quarters the idea expressed in his letter before us, that Washington was not only 'insecure' but in 'imminent danger' . . . Relying on our numbers, our forts, and the Potomac River, I am confident in the opposite opinion; and . . . I have not the slightest apprehension for the safety of the Government here." [13] On the issue over which the break between them came, Scott was right and McClellan was wrong, for the Confederates were not contemplating an attack. Nor is the conclusion altered by the fact that Scott himself had been needlessly alarmed about the capital several weeks before.

The old Mexican hero, was, however, worn out and ill, and had no stomach for quarrels with his young subordinate. He told the Secretary, "I feel that I have become an incumbrance to the Army as well as to myself, and that I ought, giving way to a younger Commander, to seek the palliatives of physical pain and exhaustion," and asked earnestly to be put on the list of retired officers at the earliest possible moment. He ended, "But, wherever I may spend my little remainder of life, my frequent and latest prayer will be, 'God save the Union.' "

McClellan's wish for more power was in no way abated, and a month later he requested of Cameron authority not only over the troops in his department—which he already had—but over *all officers* as well.[14] The request looks reasonable until it is remembered that since August 17 the Department of the Potomac had included the District of Columbia, which until that time had comprised the separate military Department of Washington. McClellan was slyly asking for control not only of the officers on duty at the War Department, but also of those on the staff of the General in Chief. But he did more than make a surprising request; he began his intolerable and somewhat childish habit of saying that disaster would not be his fault if his wishes were not granted. Margaret Leech shows moderation as well as insight when she pins on McClellan the label "superman with a mission," and says, "His inflated self-esteem required that he should not be crossed or even questioned." [15] But McClellan's defenders thrill over much of his nonsense, and recently one of them has done more than assert that the request which he made of Cameron was "not remarkable." He claims that the request itself proves poor executive ability or political interference on the part of Lincoln, Cameron, and even Scott.[16] One is reminded of the mother who reported that all the men in the company were out of step but Willie.

Near the end of October, McClellan presented to the Secretary of War a paper designed to show why any offensive action was impossible in the near future, and containing the second of his great overestimations of the enemy strength and the first example of his peculiar arithmetic in dealing with his own numbers.[17] He wrote:

As you are aware, all the information we have from spies, prisoners, etc., agrees in showing that the enemy have a force on the Potomac not less than 150,000 strong, well drilled and equipped, ably commanded, and strongly intrenched.

One had merely to read newspaper reports of Washington correspondents to know that there was much impressive evidence that the enemy's strength on the Potomac was greatly below the number stated by McClellan, that he was anything but well drilled and well equipped, or strongly intrenched. As censorship was not imposed until about October 22,[18] the press had reported freely the statements of "contrabands" (escaped Negro slaves), prisoners, escaped Federal prisoners, and persons of Northern sympathy trapped south of the border who had got through the lines. The courtesy of a visit to Manassas in August was extended by Johnston and Beauregard to Prince Napoleon, a foreign unofficial member of McClellan's staff, and *Harper's Weekly* commented: "With regard to the defenses of Manassas, the suite of the Prince remains silent, but they describe the soldiers, whom they suppose to number sixty thousand, as ragged, dirty, and half starved." [19] "Sea biscuits and poor bacon" was the fare reported by a deserter about September 20. Reports of actual military spies were not available to the public, but there were letters from persons of strong Union sentiments who had been careful observers in Richmond and elsewhere in the South. Thus a letter from Richmond in August stated there were not over 80,000 Confederates in all of Virginia, including 40,000 to 50,000 at Manassas, and 4,000 at Richmond, then completely unfortified.[20] It was probably on extensive information that the Washington *National Republican* stated near the end of September, "That the total force of the enemy in Virginia does not exceed 100,000 men, is as certain as it can be made by anything short of an actual count." [21]

Such an estimate was supported by official figures of the ordnance department. The Confederates had seized approximately 110,000 percussion muskets, caliber .69, and 10,000 rifles, caliber .54, in the United States arsenals located in the South, and the character and number of the weapons in the militia of the states were also known with much accuracy; [22] but as home defense must ever be kept in mind, especially in states with large slave populations, such weapons were not generally available for the Confederate government. The hurried efforts that Southern states had made to buy arms in the North had netted small results; and the State Department could inform McClellan about the success and failure of Confederate agents in Europe.[23] Implacable arithmetic showed that the Confederates could not have had more than 175,000 well armed infantry in all their armies.[24] McClellan knew all these things, but he coolly dismissed them and accepted instead the deductions and estimates of Allan Pinkerton, the Chicago detective whom he had placed in charge of intelligence work. Perhaps it was some such appointment that he had in mind when he wrote from West Virginia on June 23: "It seems to be a peculiar characteristic of the information obtained here that it is exceedingly vague and unreliable. I hope to inaugurate a better system." [25] On the whole, Pinkerton and his band turned out to be a great asset to Jefferson Davis, on account of the exaggerated reports that they made of the Confederate strength. The first Pinkerton report—over the signature of E. J. Allen—that appears in the Official Records is dated March 18, 1862; [26] but many previous reports had gone to McClellan. Although in his memoirs the general set forth at considerable length the reforms and reorganization he made in the army, he did not mention the great detective; eventually he must have realized the fantastic deception that had been perpetrated by his "better system" for enemy intelligence. It was his most original military contribution, and his failure to refer to it shows that it was not McClellan's purpose to make a full and correct record of what he had done.

McClellan's figure of 150,000 for the enemy on the Potomac, put down with perfect confidence, was actually two and a half times the "aggregate present" shown by official Confederate returns, and nearly four times the 41,000 men "capable of going into battle," which Johnston gave, using returns in his possession.[27]

With the figures for his own forces McClellan could also do amazing things; here his forte was subtraction. For a "column of active operations" he wished 150,000 with 400 guns; and he wanted 58,000 men with 88 guns to garrison Washington and Baltimore and guard the upper and lower Potomac.[28] As it is not likely that he expected to encounter more than 100,000 enemy in any one position, his mobile column of 150,000 with superior artillery should have been sufficient. He should also have questioned his own ability to handle so large a force, for he had had little or no field experience as a commanding officer and had passed through no severe command training. He set his over-all strength at 168,318 as of September 27, and then began deductions, some of which were legitimate while others savored of trickery. First, he dropped off the sick, absent, etc.—a somewhat dubious procedure, because they are a normal part of any command—and had 147,695 men remaining; then he dropped off the unarmed or otherwise unequipped—perhaps fairly enough, though their lack might be quickly remedied—and had left 134,285. Then he subtracted the 58,000 men he wanted for garrison and guard duty, and so whittled himself down to 76,285 men "disposable for an advance." Now when McClellan said he wanted 58,000 men for garrison and guard work he should have assumed that there would be in this force the normal sick, the normal absent on leave or without leave, and the normal number in the guard house; for every military command has men so classified every day, cannot help it and expects it. But McClellan subtracted all the ineffectives, and then deducted all the 58,000. If, working with his figures differently, we drop the unequipped and the 58,000 for garrison and guard, we find that the general had practically 100,000 men for his field force, of whom some 15,000 were not effective for duty October 27, the other 5,000 ineffectives being in the garrison and guard components. Thus McClellan had 85,000 effectives for a march column, as contrasted with the 30,000 effective infantry, artillery, and cavalry that Johnston stated he had at that time at Centerville.

McClellan felt unable to take the field at the end of October. But what were his plans for the future? He recommended that preference in arms and men be given to the Army of the Potomac, "to enable it to assume the offensive." Also he urged "no further outside expeditions be attempted until we have fought the great battle in front of us." *The great battle in front of us.* Those were his words, voluntarily written to the Chief Executive of the United States. If the words of McClellan were worth anything, his statement meant that he intended to move against Johnston's army when he felt able, and—by implication—as soon as feasible. It was known that President Lincoln favored a move upon Manassas; and he should have been able to accept his general's statement as an indication of purpose, not to be altered without consultation with the President. McClellan, if he had had even a moderate realization of Lincoln's great responsibility, would have so regarded it himself.

On October 31 General Scott again requested that the Secretary of War place him upon the list of inactive officers, although he regretted to withdraw at such momentous times "from the orders of a President who has treated me with distinguished kindness and courtesy, whom I know among [from?] much personal intercourse to be patriotic, without sectional partialities or prejudices, to be highly conscientious in the performance of every duty, and of unrivalled activity and perse-verance." [29] Though the old general had sometimes written poorly to Patterson, his last official letter had a little of the ring of his mes-sage to Robert Anderson; and his entire life was a testimony to his sincerity.

Promptly on November 1, in the order that retired Winfield Scott with a fitting tribute, President Lincoln placed McClellan in "command of the Army of the United States." It had been rumored in Washington that Major General Henry W. Halleck, recently returned to service from civil life in California, would be given the Army of the Poto-mac; [30] but he was assigned to command at St. Louis, and McClellan continued to fill his old position as well as the new one. It was a bad thing to have the General in Chief also serve as the commander of a field army; but when Lincoln spoke of the dual and heavy responsi-bility McClellan replied cheerfully, "I can do it all." From army headquarters the new General in Chief at once issued a general order narrating Scott's great exploits, which ended with the words, "Beyond all that, let us do nothing that can cause him to blush for us; let no defeat of the Army he has so long commanded embitter his last years, but let our victories illuminate the close of a life so grand." [31] How-ever fine the sentiment, the words came with poor grace from a man who, by studied disregard and slighting remarks, had done much to make bitter Scott's last weeks in Washington. Two days later he wrote to his wife:

I have already been up once this morning—that was at four o'clock to escort Gen. Scott to the depot. It was pitch dark and a pouring rain; but with most of my staff and a squadron of cavalry I saw the old man off. He was very polite to me; sent various kind messages to you and the baby; so we parted. . . . The sight of this morning was a lesson to me which I hope not soon to forget. I saw there the end of a long, active, and ambitious life, the end of the career of the first soldier of his nation; and it was a feeble old man scarce able to walk; hardly any one there to see him off but his successor. Should I ever become vainglorious and ambitious, re-mind me of that spectacle.[32]

Though age should have taken Scott out of his high office years before, it was a very great American soldier who, avoiding ceremony, left the capital that dismal morning, and two years and more were to pass before another soldier of great military stature appeared in Wash-ington. He would come with as little show: there would be no flashing of sabers in salute as he descended from the train with his hand clasping that of his little boy; there would not be a single trooper to escort his carriage from the station.

McClellan had chafed at having Scott between himself and the constitutional Commander in Chief, and—with some unfortunate encouragement from Lincoln and Cameron—he had tried to ignore his superior. But, once General in Chief, he found that rank insufficient, being apparently irked by the receipt of orders from the Secretary of War. Scott very properly had been issuing a series of general orders from the Headquarters of the Army; but the order which retired him and appointed his successor had come from the War Department, ending "By order of the Secretary of War." McClellan managed very quickly to do away with the two sets of orders, and took over the War Department series. Orders dealing with administrative questions, such as the recruiting service, the forms to be used in mustering volunteers, and promotions of officers, now came from the Headquarters of the Army and ended "By command of Major General McClellan." [33] That was a good beginning for a man who ten days before his little coup had written, "I pray every night and every morning that I may become neither vain nor ambitious." [34] With the War Department no longer issuing orders, it looked as if McClellan's future was assured as General in Chief: he could not be removed unless he issued the order himself.

The country was beginning to want action, or at least some promise or indication of action. For a few weeks after Bull Run the phrase "All's quiet on the Potomac" was one of deep relief; then it began to provoke a smile; eventually it was spoken with derision and humiliation by the people of the North. As a whole they were not unreasonably impatient, but they did want to be on with the war. They wished some assurance that the regiments that were arriving day after day in Washington would be used as soon as reasonable. And there were reasons to grow dubious.

People noted that McClellan had taken quarters in a house in Washington and was not living in the field like a soldier. He could constantly be seen riding through the streets from here to there with an impressive cavalry escort. Did he like the trappings and the show of war, and view field service reluctantly? It was anything but a foolish question. The truth about the West Virginia campaign soon came out; the papers printed it, and the people talked about it. It was learned that McClellan had been miles away in comfortable Cincinnati when Morris was marching over mountain roads through heavy rains at night and seizing Philippi so neatly. On August 3 *Harper's Weekly* referred to Rosecrans "who so gallantly won the battle of Rich Mountain" without mentioning McClellan's "rapid march to Beverly," which apparently was recorded only in his own dispatches. Even before the end of July the general's friends found it necessary to give assurance that "within two months he will establish his fame upon a broader basis of achievement than that on which it now rests." [35]

Joe Johnston, who had given up all thought of an offensive after a visit from President Davis on September 30,[36] received many warnings from spies in Washington, increasing in number as October gave way to November, that McClellan would move against them soon.[37] The Northern press assured eager readers of the imminence of active operations by the Army of the Potomac. Very knowingly *Harper's Weekly* had discussed on September 28 the plan of the fall campaign: a movement on Manassas by McClellan, flanking columns under Sickles and Banks, and a thrust from the lower Potomac by Burnside against Johnston's communications. A month later the editor found it necessary to indite an editorial, "Why the War Moves Slowly." In a learned and impressive way he pointed out that the theater of operations was great and there were many difficulties; but he did not put forward any story of large, well equipped enemy forces   probably he had read his own columns, and had no stomach for such an explanation. Still hopeful, he wrote, "Signs indicate that the impatient among our fellow citizens will very soon be gratified by the occurrence of startling events." [38]

Reconnaissances by detachments of McClellan's army were faithfully reported by correspondents, who dwelt with relish upon anything that savored of aggressiveness or getting the better of the "Rebels." On September 25 a demonstration was made against Lewinsville— four miles east by north of Vienna—by 5,000 men; McClellan was represented by a staff officer. On October 11 it was stated that the general had spent the day looking at the outposts, and the belief was expressed that he would soon transfer his headquarters to the west side of the Potomac. Occasionally it was announced that McClellan had spent the night with one of his generals, which indicated an encouraging intimacy with his army. About October 16 Johnston had abandoned his position at Fairfax and established himself at Centerville; and the name of an escaped civilian who brought the word was printed as a voucher for the accuracy of the news welcome to many readers. Very cautiously McClellan's soldiers approached Fairfax from three sides; but the easy prize was not taken, for the patrols had been specifically instructed not to risk entering.[39]

Reviews of increasing size were held, until on November 20 seven divisions numbering 70,000 men, infantry, artillery, and cavalry, were drawn up near Bailey's Cross Roads.[40] But the smart marching of the well turned-out regiments brought little cheer to the Northern people, when the enemy had just closed the lower Potomac to navigation by means of their batteries, and had recently won the victory of Ball's Bluff—on the Potomac three miles from Leesburg—over badly managed Federal troops. Everywhere, except about Washington, Northern armies were on the stir with a measure of success. But nothing had been done to atone for Bull Run; nothing had even been done to make up for the humiliation of Munson's Hill.

On December 11 word came from Washington that the army was making itself comfortable for the winter in log huts.[41] As if to excuse inaction it was announced at the same time that it was believed at army headquarters that the Confederates were stronger than the Federals, 75,000 fresh troops having reportedly been sent by Richmond to the line of the Occoquan River. It was even stated that General McClellan believed an attack upon his army was very probable and might take place momentarily. Careful readers of the papers could not have been deceived, and must have been further discouraged by the new report.

Though no news of an attack was to come, a dispatch two days later told of a grim incident, the execution of Private William H. Johnson of the First New York Cavalry for desertion. According to Johnson's story, the wish to have a drink of milk while on outpost duty led to his undoing. After asking vainly at the first house he had continued toward Centerville on the old Braddock Road when the thought came to him that he might easily go on, pretend to be a deserter, make a little visit to his mother in New Orleans, then come back and rejoin the Yankees in plenty of time to help save the Union. Presently he encountered a patrol of the Third New Jersey. Though their uniforms should have revealed their identity, he stupidly took them for the

Confederates he wished to find, explained that he was eager to join them, and, upon being questioned, described accurately the location of the Federal pickets. Three days after Christmas readers of *Harper's Weekly* saw a full-page picture of the blindfolded man, the firing squad, and the division of General Franklin drawn up to witness the execution.[42]

While correspondents reported that too much caution had been instilled into patrols, they also wrote that too abundant supplies were being given to the army. On December 26 honest General McDowell told the Congressional Committee on the Conduct of the War:

> There never was an army in the world that began to be supplied as well as ours is. I believe a French army of half the size as ours could be supplied with what we waste. The amount of the waste is fearful. I am ashamed of the amount of scolding I have to do on the subject of the waste of bread. I have seen loaves of bread thrown away that had not even been broken open. Our men will not use it if it is a little stale. I have begged them not to draw it, if they cannot eat it. They get large pay, and when the sutlers come around with their pies, tarts, and cakes, the men stuff themselves with those things and waste the rations drawn from the government. It is a waste that comes out of the country at large. But I believe we ought to supply twice the force we do with what it costs us to supply this force.[43]

Years later an English soldier wrote:

> To feed, clothe, and equip the Union armies no expenditure was deemed extravagant. For the comfort and well-being of the individual soldier the pursestrings of the nation were freely loosed. No demand, however preposterous, was disregarded. The markets of Europe were called upon to supply the deficiencies of the States; and if money could have effected the reestablishment of the Union, the war would have already reached a triumphant issue.[44]

Some gestures toward economy had been made by the War Department in late summer. On September 7 an order stated that officers were telegraphing matter that could go by mail; in the future they would have to pay out of their own pockets for unnecessary telegrams. On September 23 an order sought to encourage an economical use of rations. However, minor efforts were futile when they encountered the impetuous generosity and extravagance that the people of the United States show in a time of crisis. The illustrations in pictorial magazines suggest lavishness in the uniforms and equipment of the Federals; even in the picture of the death of Johnson one is so impressed with the nattily dressed officers and men that one almost forgets the man seated upon the box with hat and overcoat laid upon the ground. For the four million yards of blue cloth required to fit out the 550,000 men in service the resources of the country had been strained, and at the end of October Quartermaster General Meigs had written to the Secretary of War, "I fear that there is neither the wool nor the indigo in this country to make the cloth we need." [45]

During the fall plans were matured for a great naval and military operation against New Orleans. To David Farragut, the sailor from Tennessee, was given the command of the ships that were to force their way up the Mississippi past the forts that the Confederates had seized and strengthened. On December 21 he wrote to his wife, a Virginian: "Keep your lips closed and burn my letters; for perfect silence is to be observed—the first injunction of the Secretary. I am to have a flag in the Gulf, and the rest depends upon myself. Keep calm and silent; I shall sail in three weeks." It was not strange that a man who wrote like that would later order: "Damn the torpedoes. Go ahead."

But in Washington things were to go from bad to worse. On the same day near the end of December both McClellan, the General in Chief, and McClellan, the commanding general of the Army of the Potomac, became sick. His chief of staff, Brigadier General R. B. Marcy—who was no other than his father-in-law—was also sick,[46] so that no well person knew what his plans were, and things were at a standstill. Though it was announced that McClellan had only a cold, rumors of typhoid fever were being passed about. President Lincoln was much disturbed, and made his first call on McClellan since the deliberate slight given him a few weeks before by his young general; but he was not allowed to see the sick man. In his distress Lincoln went to see Brigadier General Montgomery C. Meigs, the able quartermaster general, to whom he said: "General, what shall I do? The people are impatient; Chase has no money, and he tells me he can raise no more; the General of the Army has typhoid fever. The bottom is out of the tub. What shall I do?" [47]

John Codman Ropes has severely criticized Lincoln for being disturbed about the military situation, pointing to the large army about Washington as an indication that all was well. General Ballard effectively blasts his criticisms by remarking that it was precisely the large army with not a single accomplishment to its credit and with no plans known to its staff that was causing the bottom to fall out of the tub.[48] In addition, relations with England were in a "deteriorated" state, because of the Mason-Slidell incident.

Meigs advised consultation with some of McClellan's subordinates, and so the President invited Major General McDowell and Brigadier General William B. Franklin—division commanders—to the White House on the night of January 10, 1862. McDowell's full notes on this meeting and its continuation on three subsequent days form an important and interesting document.[49] Some critics have said it was irregular for the President to consult with McClellan's subordinates. This contention is groundless: Lincoln was Commander in Chief under the Constitution, and his course was not only reasonable but necessary. As President he could have designated a temporary commander; therefore he certainly could consult with officers, while exercising his constitutional position.

The conferences were the most fortunate event that had taken place, being a medicine that speeded the recovery of McClellan. He was present at the final meeting on January 13, and so were several cabinet members. In the second meeting it was brought out—largely through Postmaster General Blair—that McClellan had given up the idea of an attack on Manassas in favor of a movement down the Potomac River and the Chesapeake Bay, thence up the Rappahannock to Urbanna, or up the York River toward Richmond. McDowell knew nothing of this plan, believing that a movement upon Manassas was still intended as soon as roads permitted; and McClellan does very poorly explaining the period between November 1 and the middle of January in his final report.[50] Although the President was not impressed by the new plan of operation, believing with McDowell that all the difficulties attending a movement against Manassas would be found, together with many new ones, in the Urbanna or the peninsula venture, he directed Meigs in the second meeting to study the necessary water transportation problem.

McClellan quite properly was cautious in discussing his plans before some of his division commanders and several cabinet members; but it is amusing to note that Mrs. Rose Greenhow, who had communicated to Beauregard when McDowell was about to march in the preceding July, later boasted that she obtained not only reports of cabinet meetings, but *"minutes* of McClellan's private consultations, and often extracts from his notes." [51]

On January 31 Lincoln issued the President's Special War Order No. 1, which directed a movement toward Manassas, details being left to the Commander in Chief (General in Chief), the expedition to move on or before February 22. McClellan asked if the order were final or if he might prepare his objections to the operation in writing and give his reasons for preferring his own project; and permission was at once accorded.

On February 3 Lincoln wrote a letter to McClellan, and McClellan in turn wrote to Edwin M. Stanton, who had replaced the discredited Cameron as Secretary of War and was himself to be a controversial figure. The two documents are entirely characteristic of the two men. Lincoln's letter is remarkable for its directness and should be looked at in full just as he wrote it:

You and I have distinct and different plans for a movement of the Army of the Potomac—yours to be down the Chesapeake, up the Rappahannock to Urbana, and across land to the terminus of the railroad on the York River; mine to move directly to a point on the railroads southwest of Manassas.

If you will give me satisfactory answers to the following questions, I shall gladly yield my plan to yours:

1st. Does not your plan involve a greatly larger expenditure of *time* and money than *mine*?

2nd. Wherein is a victory *more certain* by your plan than mine?

3rd. Wherein is a victory *more valuable* by your plan than mine?

4th. In fact, would it not be *less* valuable in this, that it would break no great line of the enemy's communication, while mine would?

5th. In case of disaster, would not a retreat be more difficult by your plan than mine? [52]

It is unfortunate that Lincoln wrote "my plan," as if he had conceived it, and did not merely refer to the "Manassas plan," which was essentially the one that had been followed by McDowell in the preceding July, and that McClellan had himself formerly accepted. Maurice writes bluntly, "It was no part of Lincoln's business to have a military plan of his own"; instead he should have had "wishes and policy" [53]—a distinction hard to maintain. Lincoln might, for example,

have said that it was a policy or a wish of the government not to uncover Washington except by an operation that had very great advantages over the Manassas plan; then he could have asked McClellan
virtually the same questions that he did ask him.

Few military writers have put in a more striking way the points
to be kept in mind in forming an "Estimate of the Situation" than
Lincoln did in his letter to McClellan. In the pages of history it would
be difficult to find an illustration that could more appropriately go into
a textbook on strategy. The suggestion that soldiers might even consider the question of money when they weigh plan against plan, is not
to be overlooked.

Any contention that Lincoln should not have insisted upon very
good reasons for adopting a new plan in place of one previously accepted looks foolish at the present time, when it is taken for granted
that it was proper for the President of the United States and the Prime
Minister of Great Britain to sit with the Chiefs of Staff of the two
countries and together make the great decisions regarding theaters of
operation and the critical "second front" in World War II. General
Marshall, Chief of Staff of the United States Army, and General
Eisenhower, American commander in Europe and later Supreme Allied
Commander, both favored the earliest possible direct attack across the
English Channel over a roundabout attack against a deceptive "soft
under-belly of Europe." [54] Thus they held in 1942 views similar to
those of Lincoln and unlike those of McClellan. It was the impossibility
of even a safe diversionary cross-Channel attack in 1942, and a direct
Presidential order, that led to the African landing that November and
the postponement until 1944 of the landing on the French coast and
offensive against the German armies that the American generals were
planning for 1943.

The danger of inopportune and damaging interference by political
leaders in military operations is so great as to be frightening. The
trained, competent soldier who also has high intelligence and a clear
courageous mind should always be trusted to choose operations and
carry them through. Lincoln was not a trained soldier. But he was a
political leader of great intelligence, who saw things clearly and was
courageous. The first step is always to formulate a problem and remove irrelevancies and the deceiving incidentals. "Well, what's it all
about?" was a favorite question of Foch. Lincoln's letter of February 3

formulated the issue with remarkable clarity, just as his sentence "The bottom is out of the tub" had pointed up the situation at the beginning of the year.

The letter of February 3 was not the only thing that Lincoln wrote which forms excellent material for military study. British soldiers with vision and frankness admitting the remarkable judgments he uttered on various occasions have demolished a criticism by Ropes more distorted and false than the one already discussed, as spokesman for a committee of three:

> Few men at the head of affairs during a great war have ever given such evidence of an entire unfitness to have any general direction over military men as Mr. Lincoln and Mr. Stanton. And this inaptitude for war the former retained to the end of his life.[55]

At the time Ropes made the charge against Lincoln there were in the records facts that disproved it. There was the spontaneous tribute in the last official communication from General Scott, who had served under many Presidents. The more than remarkable and harmonious relations between Lincoln and Grant have often been commented upon, and the charge would certainly have been repudiated by many other Federal generals who had contact with Lincoln. Maurice has described the relationship of Lincoln and Grant as almost ideal for the conduct of war by a democracy and he set it up as a standard.[56] General Ballard, in the very title of his book on the Civil War—*The Military Genius of Abraham Lincoln*—repudiates Ropes's charge. General Fuller quotes the damaging sentence of Ropes, apparently accepts it, but then destroys it by the recognition and approval he gives to some of Lincoln's statements to General Hooker.[57]

It will be seen in this narrative that frankness, honesty, and sincerity made the basis of Lincoln's dealing with his generals, and that he exhibited great understanding and patience. It would be a reflection upon soldiers to say that as a class they cannot be dealt with upon such a basis.

McClellan's letter—four pages of small type in the Official Records [58]—contained much irrelevant material that must have annoyed both Lincoln and Stanton in their wish to get on with the question at issue. The general took occasion to defend his months of inactivity, going back to the badly distorted picture of regiments "cowering on the banks of the Potomac." He had asked permission to submit a memorandum on a specific question, but he could not keep to the point which was up for decision. After he had terminated his wanderings, he dwelt at great length upon the difficulties of an operation against Manassas; but he did not reveal when it was that he had given up all idea of "the great battle in front of us," of which he had spoken in October, and which was in the nature of a compact with the President. Following the long list of faults of Manassas, McClellan took up the military virtues of the lower Chesapeake Bay and put down as specific merit number one: "The roads in that region are passable at all seasons." Then he stated that the terrain generally was more favorable for offensive action than that about Manassas, the land being more level, the soil more sandy, the woods less dense.

The engineer—the expert—was as inaccurate in matters where he should have been professionally competent as he had been in his estimation of the enemy strength. In a few weeks he would be applying to the roads of the peninsula every unkind adjective that he could think of: horrid, horrible, execrable, impassable. He also would learn something about the swamps of the Chickahominy—about which either his ignorance was inexcusable or his silence unpardonable.

Continuing, McClellan wrote: "It is by no means certain that we can beat them at Manassas. On the other line, I regard success as certain by all the chances of war." An operation through Urbanna promised the "most brilliant result," but, "the worst coming to the worst, we can take Fort Monroe as a base, and operate with complete security, although with less celerity and brilliancy of results, up the Peninsula." He then got entirely outside of his province, concluding with condescension to both Secretary and President: "I believe that the mass of the people have entire confidence in us. I am sure of it. Let us then look only to the great result to be accomplished and disregard everything else."

Instead of well digested and soldierly answers to five clear-cut questions, the general gave a long-winded anthology of excuses, fables, and military judgments, topped off with a preachment.

The document must have increased rather than lessened the President's doubts; but there was only one thing for him to do after his general's statement that it was "by no means certain" that he could win at Manassas, while success of the other operation was nearly certain: the plan of battle that the actual commander believes offers the most chances of success is to be preferred. McClellan was allowed to proceed with at least tacit approval, although the President's order of January 31 was not formally revoked. On February 27 an order was given to collect the necessary water transportation with all promptness. Meantime, however, another incident almost ended the career of George McClellan.

The closing of the Potomac to navigation annoyed the President, for it complicated the supply problem further, with traffic on the impor-

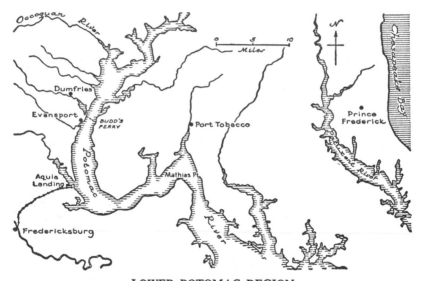

LOWER POTOMAC REGION

tant Baltimore and Ohio Railroad already interrupted west of Harpers Ferry. McClellan had seemed provokingly indifferent to the enemy batteries on the river, although the press had early suggested that he would do something about it.[59] Unquestionably they presented no simple problem; but a General in Chief whose mind is disposed toward "brilliant" operations should not expect only easy tasks. One division of McClellan's army was in fact well situated to do something, for in the last of October the command of Brigadier General Joseph Hooker was sent to lower Maryland and was disposed in the area of Budd's Ferry, opposite Evansport, where some of the offending batteries were located. Hooker was an energetic officer, and from the first he had a lively ambition to advance. Nothing could have advanced his cause more than a valuable and bold stroke under the very eyes of the administration, as well as the rest of the army, and circumstances seemed designed to give him an unusual opportunity. Hooker thought it impossible to destroy the enemy works by gunfire, for the "Rebels" seemed very thorough in their construction and could be heard sawing and hammering all night when contented people should be asleep. Therefore he proposed that he take his division across the river by night in scows, and seize an unguarded high point above the enemy's position which he thought he could quickly put in condition for defense against a force three times his strength. Field guns introduced into this position would command the enemy batteries and render them untenable. In spite of the boldness of his plan he stated, "I write of this with great confidence, for the reason that I feel no doubt of its absolute and complete success." [60]

McClellan disapproved of the proposal, and the ambitious division commander settled down to suppressing secession activities, and court-martialing misbehaving soldiers who amused themselves as best they could in a region not without opportunities for the more enterprising.

One of Hooker's colonels, however, did not take well to military inactivity, and had feet that itched to explore the other side of the river. The officer was Charles K. Graham of the Seventy-fourth New York Infantry, who on November 10 carried out a raid on the enemy that caused his superiors a little embarrassment. Graham had made friends of some equally enterprising gunboat and cutter commanders, and on that Sunday night he loaded 400 picked men on the *Island Belle* and the *Dana* and descended on Mathias Point on the right bank of the Potomac. He landed without opposition and proceeded some four miles inland with a command ready for whatever might turn up in the way of adventure. He found nothing but a few pickets and battery positions without guns, though he learned that there was an enemy camp with three guns some nine miles away. Destroying a large amount of forage and grain, he carried away some horses and two suspicious armed citizens who he thought might give valuable information, withdrew his men in good order, and was back in camp at one o'clock the next afternoon.

Graham immediately wrote a full report on his little project, about which he had neglected to inform his superiors in advance. His immediate superior, Brigadier General Daniel E. Sickles, seemed much pleased, and Hooker wrote to McClellan, "as it appears to have had no unfortunate sequence so far as I have learned, I shall not censure him." But McClellan ordered that the too enterprising colonel be put in arrest.[61]

Although McClellan did not want the enemy molested, he did want him observed, so he sent Professor T. S. C. Lowe with his balloon to Hooker, and Lowe proceeded to watch the Confederates carefully with spyglasses.[62] This may have been more of an advantage than a misfortune to the enemy, for it gave them an excellent chance to practice deceptions. A balloonist cannot tell a wooden gun from a real one or a pile of dirt from an earthwork. A regiment marched judiciously in a rear area would very likely be reported by the observer as a new division just arriving. So Professor Lowe may have performed a service about as valuable as Detective Pinkerton's.

In February, 1862, after having again rejected other plans for operations against the Potomac batteries, McClellan gave his attention to opening the Baltimore and Ohio Railroad by throwing a protective force across the Potomac and carrying out certain constructions. He was more than hopeful, and gave the annoyed President the firm assurance that the operation would be successful; then it failed dismally because some canal boats were six inches too wide for the locks. This was almost too much for Mr. Lincoln, who had been giving his general a good deal of public support, whatever his private doubts might have been.

For months, the President had urged McClellan to organize the Army of the Potomac into corps, because of its unwieldy size and because a corps organization was at that time the approved larger basic unit. McClellan did not wish to do so, although he had been reported in October as urging it,[63] and stated that he wanted to pick corps commanders after his officers had been tried in battle. In spite of any seeming plausibility, such an idea was unsound; the President was correct, and the general was wrong. Lincoln knew that some of McClellan's generals were more qualified by experience to be commanders of corps than McClellan was to be the commander of a large army. The generals who looked most promising and who had the best records should have been appointed; the assignment need not involve a promotion in rank, and so any error would be remediable. In its subsequent wars the United States has followed Lincoln's idea, and has filled the various echelons of command with appropriate officers. When McClellan refused to take the suggestion, the President on March 8 ordered the Army of the Potomac to be organized into four corps under the command of Major General McDowell and Brigadier Generals E. V. Sumner, S. P. Heintzelman, and E. D. Keyes.

With the rank and file of the army, as well as with many of the officers, McClellan was unquestionably very popular. No one should discount the desirability of an army's having faith in its leader; but soldier esteem is difficult to appraise, and a study of many great commanders shows that at first they were not "popular." Nothing could come nearer making soldiers invincible than the kind of faith the Stonewall Brigade grew to have in Jackson; but at first his heavy exactions and hard discipline almost caused mutiny in the ranks. It was the victories he won after the hard marches he forced from them that built the esteem of the Valley soldiers for Old Jack. Examining the basis of the affection for McClellan, General Peter S. Michie—himself an excellent soldier and scholar—could put down only this:

His engaging manner, as exhibited in his personal intercourse with his troops, his martial bearing and skillful horsemanship as he rode the lines of the army, added their influence in sowing the seeds of affection in the hearts of his soldiers that made them trust him, believe in him, and love him.[64]

A captain of Jeb Stuart's staff has left a contrasting description of Jackson's appearance the first time he saw him after his fame had become great.[65] Stonewall was riding at the head of the "Valley army" —road- and battle-toughened infantry and artillery. Mounted on a cob of sorry appearance and wearing a threadbare, faded semimilitary suit with a disreputable cap, he made a great contrast with the plumed and gaudy Stuart, who had ridden out from Richmond on a striking thoroughbred to meet him. Before long Jackson began to preen a little, and his soldiers loved it; but they knew that the stern, quiet, praying Presbyterian, who almost marched their legs off, was every inch a soldier.

Spring was coming after a winter of turmoil in the capital. Elsewhere restless generals were showing some of the spirit that Farragut had put in the words "the rest depends upon myself." On February 6 Grant took Fort Henry, in northwest Tennessee, and a week later the North was thrilled by his capture of near-by Fort Donelson with most of its garrison. About the same time news came of the successful combined operations under Commodore Goldsborough and General Burnside at Roanoke Island. Before long word would be received of the victory at Pea Ridge, Arkansas, atoning for the defeat at Wilson's Creek near Springfield, Missouri, so soon after Bull Run. But nothing had been done by the main army before Washington, and many persons had come to think that McClellan was an impractical perfectionist who never would be quite ready: if he were not waiting for longer shoe-strings, he would be hunting about for smaller canal boats. The excuses of his contemporary defenders, however resourceful, were beginning to wear a little thin. Perplexed editors had to parade the same old alibis touched up a little differently. On March 8, *Harper's Weekly,* which had put itself in an embarrassing position in October by forecasting prompt action, was again discussing "The Wisdom of Delay"; but still it referred to "the army that McClellan will shortly lead to battle." The latter-day defenders have sometimes sought sup-port from Henderson, without always citing the page. Although this fine soldier hedged a little about an early operation against Manassas —because of McClellan's bad intelligence reports—he wrote:

> But for all this there was no reason whatever for absolute inactivity. The capture of the batteries which barred the entrance to the Potomac, the defeat of the Confederate detachments along the river, the occupation of Winchester or of Leesburg, were all feasible operations. By such means the impatience of the Northern people might have been assuaged. A few successes, even on a small scale, would have raised the *moral* of the troops and have trained them to offensive movements. The general would have retained the confidence of the Administration, and have secured the re-spect of his opponents.[66]

In the words "respect of his opponents," Henderson put his finger on an important consideration. If McClellan had promptly cut off and captured or destroyed the outpost the enemy put on Munson's Hill, Beauregard would not have written laughingly of "George" or John-ston of "the redoubtable McC." Leaving out this consideration, Margaret Leech put the matter thus: "Even a small success would have appeased the politicians and delighted the country." [67] Never had a general a chance to achieve so much by doing just a little.

On November 14 McClellan had issued an order informing the army of successes by Brigadier Generals T. W. Sherman, William Nelson, and U. S. Grant, on the coast of South Carolina, at Pikeville,

Kentucky, and at Belmont, Missouri. The order ended: "The Major General Commanding cannot too highly extol the steadiness, courage, and admirable conduct, displayed by officers, sailors, and soldiers, alike, in these several engagements. He commends them to the imitation of the whole army." Apparently McClellan, the commander of the Army of the Potomac, did not read the orders of McClellan, the General in Chief.

Since World War I there has been some effort to justify McClellan's eight months of preparation by pointing to the length of time it took both Britain and the United States to train their new armies.[68] But a careful comparison harms rather than helps McClellan, for the training needed for the warfare of the sixties in comparison with that needed today is like a mathematical education that stops at algebra against one that requires mastery of the calculus.

McClellan's army had few specialists; in a modern army they are very numerous. Present-day weapons—the machine gun, for example —are complicated in comparison with the muzzle-loading rifle. In addition, there is much complex technical equipment that must be kept in order in difficult situations and must be used expertly. Tactics are also very different. In the sixties, hostile infantry formed in ranks, shoulder to shoulder, and shot at each other. It was forthright, and it required good stout hearts to stand the ordeal; but an exacting training of the individual or of small groups was not required. "Steadiness in ranks" was then a phrase that was very important, and steadiness in ranks was undoubtedly helped by drill and length of training—at least, up to a certain point. But just as regiments broke under fire at Bull Run, so units with much longer training broke in later battles. Paradoxically, new troops have sometimes been amazingly steady, which led one of Jackson's staff officers—a veteran of many battles— to remark, "More than once have battles, nearly lost by veterans, been restored by the intrepid obstinacy of new soldiers." [69]

Even the individual infantryman must now be imbued with the idea of maneuver; and it would hardly be an exaggeration to say that an infantry platoon leader sometimes has a more difficult task than a regimental commander had in 1861, or that a battalion commander, with his various weapons, his intricate communication apparatus, and his highly dispersed units, has in many ways a harder problem of leadership than a division commander had in McClellan's army. All these considerations greatly influence the time needed for training, because knowledge and experience are needed—not raw bravery. Nor is it to be overlooked that in both world wars the newly trained forces of Britain and the United States had to be pitted against well trained, combat-hardened troops, while in the Civil War the soldiers on both sides were inexperienced. But in spite of the great complexity of modern combat the basic training period in World War II consisted of thirteen weeks—three months—ending with some instruction in advanced maneuver. Upon this basis there was afterward built training for special operations—complicated landing procedures, jungle fighting, etc., as well as maneuvers of the larger units. Nothing resembling this advanced instruction faced McClellan, and one can well wonder how many weeks of the training of his day, troops could take without getting a little stale. The analogue of the present-day supplementary training would have been precisely such minor operations as Henderson spoke of. And in that connection one can recall the great importance of the seizing of Guadalcanal and the stand at Port Moresby. Both operations were hazardous, and both hung in the balance for many days.

To the distrust caused by McClellan's inaction there was added suspicion because of his political affiliations. Washington naturally buzzed with politics after Congress assembled in regular session in December, and the opposition party was properly scrutinizing Lincoln's conduct of the war. Although McClellan carefully avoided contacts with those in arms against the United States, he sought the company of the enemies of the President. Of the elaborate dinners in which the General in Chief showed a little of his aversion to the soldier's fare, Margaret Leech writes, "There would be twenty guests at least, and they were not friends of the administration, either." [70] The result was inevitable; McClellan began to be looked to by the opposition as the hope of their party, and his special friends began to claim that he was made to suffer militarily for his political beliefs. More was involved in the arguments in Washington than the natural opposition of the old Democratic party to the new Republicans. By winter the question of "war aims" was becoming prominent. Was it just a war to restore the Union with perhaps a little chastening of the offending states? Or was the old slavery question to be permanently disposed of now that armed conflict had broken out? Lincoln was adamant on the restitution of the Union; never would he stop fighting until that was accomplished, unless his armies were completely defeated or authority to raise them was taken from him. But he held moderate views as to his constitutional power to interfere with slavery, differing on that issue not only with strong elements within his own party but even with some of his cabinet.

Nothing revealed more clearly how mixed up matters were than the relation of Stanton and McClellan. Both were Democrats, and when the general made his first appearance at Washington, Stanton was a loud critic of the administration. McClellan took up with him quickly, and sought refuge in his house from "browsing Presidents." After he became Secretary of War, Stanton more than cooled toward McClellan; he became in time a leader of the opposition to the general. Out of the Secretary's change of attitude comes one of the debated questions of the Civil War. Anything that McClellan said in explanation can have little weight, and one must constantly remember that Stanton, who must have known McClellan's very conservative views on war aims from the first, began by being well disposed toward him. The reader must judge whether there were grounds for loss of confidence in McClellan's ability as a field commander, and also whether or not Stanton sought to encourage and aid McClellan as long as he was at the head of the Army of the Potomac, even after he had ceased to be his advocate and champion.

There was lack of harmony south of the Potomac also, and the Confederate councils in Richmond were vexed with problems in many ways more overwhelming. Here also there had been a change of war secretaries, Judah P. Benjamin taking over from Secretary Walker. From the time of Bull Run there had been something of a feud between Davis and Johnston, and Benjamin soon did things that touched off tempers. But great progress had been made, especially in equipment and supply. Johnston's soldiers at Manassas were getting enough to eat, though they had neither the variety nor the abundance of the Federals. A meat-packing plant had been built at Thoroughfare Gap, and unwisely—and contrary to the recommendations of Johnston—Manassas was made a depot for supplies. Much progress had been made in construction of factories to manufacture articles never made before in the South or made only in small numbers. Powder mills were under construction, and Richmond and Atlanta were becoming centers for the manufacture of ordnance. Blockade running was carried on with considerable success, for the Federal fleet, large as it was growing to be, could not patrol the long coast line and the many harbors effectively in all kinds of weather and at all hours of the day and night. Precious commodities were also coming in by way of Mexico, though this meant a long wagon haul across Texas.

Though the crisis in ordnance, food, and other supplies had eased somewhat, man power for the army became a grave problem during the fall and winter. Regiments had been enlisted in the early months of the war for a year, then for the period of the war, and finally, under an act passed by the Provisional Confederate Congress in August, they were enlisted for three years. Lincoln's ninety-day men were all gone, and—though short-term men would reappear from time to time —he stood firmly on a growing army of three-year regiments. But Davis faced the loss of a large part of his smaller army, for at least a third of his regiments were made up of the one-year men. On December 11, 1861, an act of the Confederate Congress sought to induce reenlistments as well as new enlistments. A bounty of $50 and a furlough of sixty days with transportation to and from their homes— or the money value of the trip if they did not go—were offered to men in the service who would sign for two years in addition to the one for which they had contracted. But the men were also tempted by something very unwise militarily. Upon the expiration of their original terms they were to have the right to reorganize themselves into new companies and regiments, and—what was worse—to elect their officers. It is bad for military units to begin by electing their officers; it is much worse to compel officers who may have learned their jobs to campaign for reelection in the midst of a military campaign.

Bounties were used also to encourage the formation of new units, and an act of December 19 aimed to entice volunteers to fill the depleted ranks of the regiments enlisted for the period of the war. Early in 1862 it became clear that the new measures were inadequate, and that the Confederate army was in danger of melting away before the Yankees. Only one measure, conscription, would keep the 148 one-year regiments from being lost and fill depleted regiments. Some of the Southern *states* already had conscription laws to raise the men *requested* of them by President Davis. That was proper, for it was good states' rights. But it was quite another matter for the Confederate Government to lay hold by conscription of men from South Carolina, North Carolina, Georgia, and the eight other states.

On February 18 the Provisional Congress of the Confederate States passed quietly into history and the first regular Congress took over. The provisional body had had the heavy burden of all the initial war acts, but the new Congress was soon forced to give history one of its greatest paradoxes: the acceptance of a conscription act by a people in rebellion against centralization of authority and vociferous in its attachment to state rights. Certainly it was a determined people and a people more than a little put out with the Yankees, or it would never have carried inconsistency that far. It had indeed made up its mind to break the Union and take from the flag of the United States eleven of its respected stars.

And so by early March things were shaping for an eventful year.

CHAPTER VI

YORKTOWN TO FAIR OAKS

Good for the first lick! Hurrah for Smith and the one-gun battery!
Stanton to McClellan

THROUGHOUT SUNDAY MARCH 9, there were conferences at the White House of alarmed, if not somewhat terrified, officials called on account of bad news from Hampton Roads.[1] The day before, the Confederate ironclad ship *Merrimac* had wrought havoc upon the Union naval vessels in the mouth of the James River, destroying two wooden ships with no damage to herself. President and cabinet members were viewing an ominous situation and a future full of unpredictable possibilities, caused by a new instrument of warfare. There was one hope. It was known that the *Monitor*—that strange ship designed by John Ericsson and sponsored by Gustavus V. Fox, now Assistant Secretary of the Navy, who again had had faith when others doubted or even laughed—had been expected to arrive during the night. Toward noon word came that the little craft had come in the darkness and had silently taken her place beside the ships that the *Merrimac* had left over for destruction the next day. And so they waited, and tempers rose and fell in disputes over the outcome of the seeming unequal contest. Not until evening did the wire from Hampton Roads bring word about the historic battle that had raged throughout the morning. The little *Monitor,* Lieutenant John L. Worden commanding, her machinery secure from shot and shell beneath her low-lying deck, had stood up with her two guns to the ten-gunned *Merrimac* and had driven her back to the safety of her harbor. "The Monitor is uninjured, and ready at any moment to repel another attack," was the way that Fox terminated the dispatch which told of the great event in world history.

But the day, after the hours of dread and fear, was to be more than a day of happy exultation. Word less fateful, but perhaps more amazing than the message from Fox, soon came. First, it was learned that the enemy batteries on the Potomac had been withdrawn; and the tale of surprises was completed by the information that the Confederates had abandoned Centerville and Manassas, and also Leesburg. McClellan at once went to the other side of the river, ostensibly to verify the information; but while there he issued an order for an immediate advance of the army upon Centerville and Manassas.

Just as the general made a "rapid march" on Beverly as soon as Rosecrans had dislodged the enemy, so with comparable boldness and promptness he descended upon Manassas—after Johnston had marched away. In his report McClellan stated that the march to Manassas "afforded a good intermediate step between the quiet and comparative comfort of the camps around Washington and the rigors of active operations." [2] Much more aptly Margaret Leech writes: "The march of the Federals was no more than a promenade, an exercise in the neglected business of making an advance." [3]

The stories that the correspondents who were with the army on the "promenade" sent back did not make cheerful reading, for again Quaker guns were found. One reporter wrote: "The fancied impregnability of the position turns out to be a sham. There are three or four light earthworks, and a fortified camp at the Junction. Between Manassas and Bull Run there was no fortification of any kind. The position at Centerville is very strong, but some of the forts have maple logs painted to resemble guns." By this time correspondents could look at fortifications with a comprehending eye, and one of them, not deceived merely by embrasures, wrote, "There were no platforms on which to work guns, nor any appearance of there having been any." [4] Stories that soldiers burst into tears when they saw the defenses will hardly be believed by any who know the ways of soldiers; but that they burst into swearing is most likely.

The Federal soldiers—master wasters though they were—were appalled at the destruction of stores and property that had been carried out at Manassas by the Confederates, and they began to realize what the destructiveness of war meant. The great stock of meat that had been unwisely accumulated at so exposed a place could not be transported to a safer locality, and after the inhabitants of the region had been invited to help themselves the remainder was given over to flames. Great clouds of a strange yellow and bluish smoke filled the air, and the burning bacon could be smelled for twenty miles, according to a cavalryman who himself helped apply the torch to great cribs of corn.[5] Bad as was the destruction of food and forage, the burning of the extra clothing of the soldiers was in many ways a worse misfortune for the Confederates. Nearly every man had a little trunk or a box of personal effects that had done much to add both comfort and cheer to a soldier's very drab life in winter quarters. Such things could not go into the field, and Johnston had the trunks piled and burned. Wise foresight would have obviated such destruction, which was soon to be felt, for by fall many of the soldiers from Manassas had tattered clothing and were marching barefoot.

Estimates of Johnston's strength as derived from the Centerville-Manassas scene varied. One writer stated: "It is supposed from what could be gathered, making a fair average for the number the huts could contain, that the Rebel troops at Manassas, including Centerville, did not at any time exceed 60,000 men, and that no more than 30,000 have occupied that section within two months." A contraband from Manassas stated that during the winter there had been 12,000 men at that place and 14,000 at Centerville; another native in giving 60,000 as the number of Confederates added, "At least they said so."[6]

The revelations were embarrassing to McClellan, and in his report he referred to "the ignorance which led some journals at that time, and persons in high office, unwittingly to trifle with the reputation of an army, and to delude the country with Quaker-gun stories of the defenses and gross understatements of the number of the enemy."[7] He remained faithful to Pinkerton's March 8 report of 80,000 men about Manassas, and asserted that there had been about 300 field guns and 26 to 30 siege guns in front of Washington. The correspondents came much nearer to the truth than the general.

Originally the Confederate Secretary of War had planned to have housing of sawed lumber made for about 40,000 men; but Johnston apparently got the plan bungled and was finally embarrassed, not only by the lack of sawmills, but of logs with which troops could make huts where he wished them.[8] The amount of shelter originally intended, however, remains significant. The Confederate strength return for February, 1862, gave Johnston and the Potomac District (including Leesburg) 42,860 men present, and 60,062 present and absent.[9] The number of guns was not given, but the 2,104 artillerymen would indicate not over 200 guns at the outside. Perhaps McClellan's enumerators counted embrasures and neglected to check on platforms or the evidence of occupation. Even such signs would not be conclusive, for a gun may be in one place today and in another tomorrow, leaving tracks in both. Generals who put wooden guns in position and who write of "George" may think of many tricks.

It was not long before McClellan sought to turn Johnston's retirement to his own advantage by saying that it was due to his own intended movement down the Chesapeake, word of which he claimed had leaked out through administration indiscretion.[10] This was merely another misrepresentation and an effort to place guilt upon the innocent. Johnston relates that at a meeting in Richmond, on February 22, with President Davis and his cabinet it was decided that he should retire to the line of the Rappahannock as soon as the condition of the roads allowed [11] and the date was five days before Lincoln gave tentative approval to McClellan's plan by ordering that shipping should be assembled. Freeman in his interesting chapter "Johnston Passes a Dark Winter" sums up the situation as follows: "Against that amply equipped and numerically superior Army [McClellan's] Johnston believed it impossible to hold his lines in Northern Virginia." [12] The truth was that the plans for the Potomac-Chesapeake operation were kept secret very successfully in spite of the extensive preparations that the War Department had to make.

Mr. Lincoln's secretaries described the receipt of the momentous news about the evacuation of Manassas thus: "General McClellan was with the President and the Secretary of War when the message arrived . . ." In his report McClellan wrote, "The President and Secretary of War were present when the most positive information reached me . . ." [13] Lincoln and Stanton were with him, not he with his superiors. One would imagine from McClellan's version that the conference had been at his headquarters and not at the White House. It is upon such statements, quite as much as upon his letters to his wife, that the charge of McClellan's great vanity has been based, though some writers either imply or assert the contrary.[14]

Lincoln had given an explicit order that McClellan should decide in consultation with his corps commanders how large a force should be left for the protection of Washington,[15] and on March 13 McClellan held a council of war at Fairfax to decide this and other questions. It was agreed by the generals that a covering force of 25,000 men should be left in addition to a full garrison for the defenses on the right bank of the Potomac and some occupying forces in the forts on the left. This decision was to have much influence on the course of events, and from it there grew a bitter dispute. The council also voted that the water movement should be down the Potomac and Chesapeake to the vicinity of Hampton Roads, provided that the *Merrimac* could be held in check. The operation by way of Urbanna that McClellan had favored in February was not endorsed by his subordinates, and it was decided that the alternative to the movement to the peninsula between the James and York rivers should be a direct move against Johnston's force in its new position in the vicinity of Gordonsville behind the Rappahannock and Rapidan rivers.

Things now began to move rapidly. The decisions of the corps commanders were at once communicated to the President, and a reply from him written the same day by Stanton was sent to McClellan.[16] The vote of the corps commanders, which had been assented to by McClellan, received the President's approval. Lincoln stipulated, however, that a force must be left at Manassas sufficient to prevent the enemy from easily repossessing that strategic railroad junction. With Washington and Manassas provided for, McClellan was left as free as an army commander could hope to be, for the Secretary told him:

Move the remainder of the force down the Potomac, choosing a new base at Fortress Monroe, or anywhere between here and there, or, at all events, move such remainder of the army at once in pursuit of the enemy by some route.

There was a note of impatience that seemed to say: Get on with the war. Do something!

On the 13th McClellan also received a reply from Fox to an inquiry he had sent about the prospects of keeping the *Merrimac* neutralized. The good sailor could guarantee nothing; but he said that the *Monitor* was more than a match for the Confederate craft, and he thought (or at least hoped) the *Merrimac* might be destroyed if she ventured to engage in a second fight. Positively enough he said, "The Merrimac must dock for repairs." [17] Thus assured, McClellan decided to go ahead with moving the army to Fort Monroe.

In his memoirs McClellan sought to shift to Lincoln the responsibility for the failure of his campaign by asserting that the administration forced Fort Monroe on him as a base instead of Urbanna: "The fears of the administration and their inability to comprehend the merits of the scheme, or else the determination that I should not succeed in the approaching campaign, induced them to prohibit me from carrying out the Urbanna movement. They gave me the choice between the direct overland route *via* Manassas and the route with Fort Monroe as base. Of course I selected the latter." [18] The phrases in Stanton's instructions "or anywhere between here and there" and "some route" show how completely McClellan's memoirs distorted the facts as he had himself recorded them officially in his report. It has already been noted that the corps commanders voted for Fort Monroe rather than Urbanna as the base of operations; and General Michie shows that McClellan himself had come to prefer it a short time after he wrote his letter of February 3.[19] The insinuation that the administration wanted McClellan to fail led General Ballard to comment, "Wellington was often at loggerheads with the Cabinet, but bitterly as he complained, he never accused a fellow countryman of deliberate intention to ruin his campaign." [20]

McClellan had completely won his point with the administration. But with the full liberty of action that was given him there came a clear reproof in the vexed tone of the Secretary's words. McClellan was to start his campaign with some distrust on the part of the administration, but that should have been an incentive to redeem himself and not an excuse for failure, as some writers—following his own lead— have asserted.[21] There have been few soldiers who have not been conscious at some time of a loss of confidence in them by their superiors, and among them few generals who have never felt such a loss by their government or their people. It is an inescapable attribute of the soldier's life, and to the extent that a man cannot accept it, he is no soldier. With regard to the cabinet distrust of McClellan, Ballard states bluntly, "It was his duty to satisfy them, and apart from all duty it was only common sense to satisfy them before he went away." [22]

While on his "promenade" McClellan received word that he had been relieved of the duties of General in Chief. The proper place for the announcement of the change would, of course, have been in a War Department general order; but McClellan had taken over that series, so that Lincoln took care of the matter in a President's War Order saying simply, "Major General McClellan having personally taken the field at the head of the Army of the Potomac, until otherwise ordered he is relieved from the command of the other military departments, he retaining command of the Department of the Potomac." [23] The news was a surprise to the general, and much has been made by some writers of the fact that he had not been informed of the impending change; but in his report McClellan stated that he "cheerfully acceded" to the order. Lincoln's action was of course necessary, for McClellan's dual position, undesirable even while he was in Washington, would have been impossible once he was in the field with the impossibility of prompt communication and full information about all the theaters of war. Over and above that, no one but the most tried and experienced general, engrossed with the details and uncertainties of one campaign, should be either allowed or compelled to make decisions relative to armies far removed from his own. Coordination of different forces should be in the hands of a man not in direct command of any one of them; when such a commander weakens one army to strengthen another, the personal element is not so strongly present as it is when an army commander is also the General in Chief.

With McClellan out of the top command the War Department resumed its proper function of issuing general orders and the war orders by the President ceased to appear. These have been the object of considerable criticism; but they were no more anomalous than McClellan's issuance of orders that should have come from the Secretary of War, and it was fortunate that a vehicle was at hand for the necessary removal of McClellan. Lincoln, in fact, had two vehicles standing by, a series of general war orders and one of plain war orders. It is hard to see just why one of the latter was chosen on March 11 to combine termination of McClellan's career as General in Chief with instructions to all department commanders. Perhaps A. Lincoln merely had a sense of numerical balance as well as general equipoise, and accordingly wished to "sign off" with three orders in each of the series that have annoyed some writers so much.

A new General in Chief was not appointed, and Lincoln and Stanton took over the direction of the armies, with assistance from Major General Ethan Allen Hitchcock, a veteran with forty years of service, including some valuable experience in Mexico, but whose interest in military matters had waned considerably. Though the effort was not too successful, the Lincoln-Stanton record compares quite favorably with some of the months of true professional command and would have succeeded if McClellan had been a steady field general. The venture was not at all the result of desire; it was caused by the great dearth of good officers with which the President was confronted in the defection of many of the army's best officers to the South. For this situation the blame certainly did not lie with Abraham Lincoln.

Men worked hard and late under the efficient and exacting Stanton to assemble the shipping needed to move the great army with all its equipment: 113 steamers, 188 schooners, and 88 barges. Embarkation started on March 17, General McClellan himself giving careful supervision, and General Wool cooperating in the debarkation and the assignment of troops to temporary camping areas in the vicinity of Fort Monroe. McClellan, prone to be unbalanced by a minor success as well as by a minor difficulty, wrote jubilantly to Stanton after the first division of 10,000 men had been loaded: "The worst is over. Rely upon it that I will carry this thing through handsomely." [24]

It was well for the country that the President and the Secretary were keeping a close eye on the young general, who not only lacked balance but who had also shown by his repeated disregard of orders from General Scott that he was not above one of the worst of all military offenses. From the steamer that was to take him to Fort Monroe, McClellan on April 1 addressed a note to the adjutant general of the army, giving the number of troops left at Manassas and Warrenton, in the Shenandoah, on the lower Potomac, and at Washington.[25] His figure was 73,456, but Lincoln and Stanton may have suspected it was another case of McClellan's peculiar arithmetic.

Brigadier General James S. Wadsworth, in command of troops left at Washington, reported at once that he would have only 13,000 men, of whom many were undisciplined. On April 2 Stanton submitted to the adjutant general of the army and to General Hitchcock all pertinent papers, and directed that they determine whether the President's orders relative to the protection of Washington and Manassas had been complied with. They reported promptly that the President's orders had not been obeyed, and any careful investigation of McClellan's figures shows that this was the case.[26] General Ballard states, "On this Lincoln would have been warranted in recalling McClellan for disobedience of orders." [27] There can be no question about that.

Not a few writers have derived "cheap fun"—as Ballard puts it— from the concern that the President felt for the safety of Washington.

Certainly he was much concerned that Washington should not fall. Foreign recognition of the Confederacy was a very real danger; and the Southerners had confidently expected that it would come shortly after February, 1862, when they believed that Europe's supply of cotton would be exhausted.[28] Lincoln was aware of this, and he realized that the capture of the city might well be the determining influence in favor of the South. The military importance of the city was small; its political importance was great. Henderson used the strongest comparison he could think of when he wrote, "The Capitol, the White House, the Treasury, were symbols as sacred to the States, as the colours to a regiment." [29] It will be recalled that in the preceding October, when McClellan was considering an operation against Manassas, his first charge against his total strength was 35,000 men as a garrison for Washington, although the movement he was contemplating at the time would not have uncovered the city. General Ballard, with a full appreciation of political problems and responsibilities, as well as military understanding and vision, states that Lincoln "was responsible to the country for the safety of Washington, and that must be his first consideration." In this he concurred with the judgment of Michie.[30]

The upshot of McClellan's disobedience of an explicit order was that the President himself provided for the security of the capital by directing that either the corps of General McDowell or that of General Sumner should be retained. As McDowell's troops were to be the last to embark, they were the ones kept at Alexandria, presently to march to Fredericksburg, so that they could join McClellan in case the Confederates staged no threat against Washington.

A close surveillance of McClellan was to continue, and very properly, for nothing less than the fate of a nation was in the hands of an inexperienced and unstable general. The untried commander was to be watched closely by a veteran, full of years, full of experience, and full of wisdom—Major General John E. Wool. Wool was seventy-eight years old, but as a soldier he had been everything that McClellan was not: bold, unhesitating, and rapid in movement. (His father had been with Anthony Wayne at the storming of Stony Point.) After starting life as a lawyer he had joined the army in 1812. Before long he commanded a regiment; and at Queenston he was badly wounded. Then he had studied military science for a year in Europe and had been inspector general of the army for about twenty-five years. One of his exploits in the Mexican War has been compared with that of Xenophon; his promptness and efficiency were largely responsible for the victory at Buena Vista. After the Mexican War he had commanded both the Department of the Pacific and the Eastern Department. McClellan was operating in Wool's department, and very properly Stanton asked the veteran for reports as to how things were proceeding. Wool's soldierly, discerning, but very fair dispatches must have been a great satisfaction to the President and the Secretary of War, contrasting greatly with the reports of McClellan, which sometimes suggested a hysterical, emotional schoolgirl rather than a major general commanding a great army.

Wool, commanding the Department of Virginia, had about 15,000 troops, including seventeen infantry regiments and a little more than a regiment of cavalry. In addition to permanent forts armed with 223 pieces of heavy artillery, he had mobile troops and 44 field guns; but he had few gun teams. In reply to a note of March 18 from Stanton that put forth the great importance of the impending movement Wool expressed hearty willingness not to be bound by technicalities or regulations in cooperating with McClellan. McClellan, however, on March 19, asked to have some of Wool's regiments formed into a division under General Mansfield. The next day this was directed by Stanton, and on March 21 Wool wrote to the Secretary, "I repeat, nothing will be wanting on my part to organize in the most efficient manner the forces designed for the command of General McClellan." Then on March 26 McClellan was given complete command over Fort Monroe and all of Wool's forces. Very significantly, and probably very fortunately, this order was annulled on April 3 by an order which said, "General Wool will continue in command of Fort Monroe and the troops heretofore assigned to the Department of Virginia, and General McClellan will command the troops constituting the Army of the Potomac." [31] The President and the Secretary had set up something that somewhat resembled the present conception of a Zone of Communications, with its independent commander and independent troops.

The cooperation and assistance which the fine old veteran gave were outstanding, and McClellan seemed very appreciative in spite of a mild rebuke that Wool promptly administered when he questioned some of the arrangements made for arriving troops.[32] Wool's staff made up for some of the incapacities in that of the young general, and he informed Stanton that he and the younger man were getting along quietly and harmoniously.[33] As McClellan advanced, Wool not only looked out for his flank and rear, but also picked up after him. "I find that the troops have an immense quantity of useless baggage," the old campaigner wrote.[34] Nothing would hurt a former inspector general quite so much as to see troops abandon property without a guard, so Wool told his men to gather up what McClellan's soldiers left behind. And nothing would so worry an old veteran who knew what mobility was, and who had set some speed records himself, as to see a green army marching to battle encumbered by useless baggage and unneeded luxuries, even if it were not moving into a region of swamps.

On the morning of April 4 McClellan had two columns moving toward Yorktown. The short marches and the simple tasks set for the day were readily accomplished, but prospects were not so good for the next day, and at 5:50 P.M. McClellan wired Stanton: "I expect to fight to-morrow, as I shall endeavor to cut the communication between Yorktown and Richmond." A few hours later he put the forecast in a slightly more doleful key: "The enemy evince determination to hold Yorktown. In that case we shall have fighting to-morrow." [35] The next morning the rain began to fall, and the good roads that McClellan had told Lincoln about with so much confidence became very difficult for infantry and, in places, impossible for artillery and wagons. In addition, the left column under General Keyes encountered the enemy behind the Warwick River, and the right column, Fitz-John Porter's division leading, was brought to a halt by some of the outer defenses of Yorktown. There was the enemy quite as McClellan had prophesied, waiting for him—but not quietly. The enemy, in fact, "evinced" his determination to hold Yorktown by opening with some guns upon the Federal column, and McClellan was not only in the rain and in the mud; he was finally in the war.

General Michie says, "General McClellan had now arrived at the most critical point of his career as a commander of an army in the presence of an enemy." [36] It was even worse than that. The four things that give a soldier most trouble are acknowledged to be rain, roads, the enemy, and his *superiors*, though there is dispute as to the order in which the handicaps should be listed. Perhaps just as the enemy's guns started booming at him and his own guns were found to be stuck in the mud, just to make difficulties complete, a telegram from the adjutant general informed McClellan that McDowell's corps had been detained upon the order of the President. The brief wire stated that a letter was following, but he must have suspected the reason for Lincoln's action. The act was perhaps the most fortunate thing that

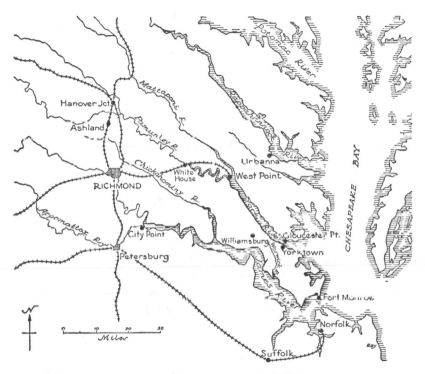

THE YORKTOWN PENINSULA

ever happened to McClellan, for it gave him another excuse for failure. But that evening in the rain and the mud he did not see it.

At seven o'clock McClellan addressed to "Abraham Lincoln, President," a dispatch that showed a rather new and unusual tone of humility. In it he stated: "I am now of the opinion that I shall have to fight all the available force of the rebels not far from here. Do not force me to do so with diminished numbers. . . . If you cannot leave me the whole of the First Corps, I urgently ask that I may not lose Franklin * and his division." [37] It would have been fitting if there could have been read to McClellan at that moment of humility the biting and scornful reprimand which he had sent ten months before when General Morris—an older man than himself—asked for reenforcements.

At 10:30 P.M. McClellan wrote to Commodore L. M. Goldsborough, naval commander in the vicinity, showing clearly that all resolution had about left him when he heard the first enemy gun: "The rebels are close in my front. . . . I can not turn Yorktown without a battle, in which I must use heavy artillery and go through the preliminary operations of a siege." [38] Although practically no reconnaissance of the enemy position had been made, he had already made up his mind that it was strong, and that siege operations were necessary. The next morning the sun was out; yet everything was not encouraging, for he wrote to the adjutant general, "I see the secession colors as I write." [39] That indeed settled it—the enemy intended to fight. He was already a defeated general.

By evening of that day, April 6, McClellan had formulated his excuse. In his dispatch of 1:35 P.M., just quoted, he had said, "I will take Yorktown, but it may be a slow process." At eight o'clock he sent another dispatch with a significantly altered ending, "The affair will be protracted in consequence of my diminished force." [40] Thereafter he talked and wrote about the detention of McDowell persistently. Michie, in his mild but thorough way, has exposed the disingenuousness of his pretending that the withholding of McDowell's corps could have been in any way responsible for delay in taking Yorktown.

A bold reconnaissance pushed with some vigor would have shown that from Yorktown to the Warwick River the Confederate line was everywhere weak, with no parapet at all for 500 yards; [41] furthermore there were suitable approaches for attacking columns. Major General J. Bankhead Magruder was holding fourteen miles with 23,000 men— perhaps fewer before April 11. He had few field guns outside the Yorktown lines and was almost destitute of tools for preparing defenses. On April 11 he issued an appeal to the citizens: "Without the most liberal assistance in axes, spades, and hands to work we cannot

* Brigadier General William B. Franklin commanded one of the divisions in McDowell's corps, which Lincoln had detained.

hope to succeed, and the Northern army will be in possession of your farms in a few days." [42]

Lincoln grasped the situation accurately, and on the evening of April 6 he wired McClellan, "I think you better break the enemy line from Yorktown to Warwick River at once." [43] (Michie states that for at least four days "McClellan had the golden opportunity of a magnificent success within his grasp.") But McClellan contented himself with rather timid investigations and some observations from Lowe's balloon. In a note of April 7 to General Wool, signed "Your anxious and obliged friend," he wrote, "The Warwick River grows worse the more you look at it." [44] In that sentence he bared himself: the more he contemplated a present difficulty, the more he magnified it. He had learned nothing from Munson's Hill, and nothing from Manassas.

Both Lincoln and Stanton wished McClellan to have all the force they could give him that he needed and could use effectively. The President promptly directed that Woodbury's good two-regiment brigade of engineers, which was part of McDowell's corps, should go forward as planned. By April 10 orders had also been given for Franklin's division to proceed,[45] in accordance with McClellan's urgent request. Though it arrived on April 22, it was allowed to remain on the transports for two weeks, which disproved some of McClellan's claims and excuses. On April 6 the Secretary asked Wool if McClellan would need a stronger force for the work before him. As usual, however, there was mystery about McClellan's strength. General Wool had asked commanding officers of the Army of the Potomac to give him strength returns for arriving units, to which he was entitled as the department commander. But they had refused to comply, so that he could only report that McClellan had said he would have over 100,000 men and a large artillery train after the arrival of Sumner's corps. This was entirely adequate, Wool thought, for the work at Yorktown.

The President did not relax his pressure. On April 9 he wrote, "There is a curious mystery about the number of troops now with you," and asked McClellan to explain the discrepancy between the 85,000 men he said he had, and the 108,000 the adjutant general reported as having gone forward according to McClellan's own returns. He concluded in memorable sentences:

The country will not fail to note, is now noting, that the present hesitation to move upon an entrenched enemy is but the story of Manassas repeated. I beg to assure you that I have never written you or spoken to you in greater kindness of feeling than now, nor with a fuller purpose to sustain you, so far as, in my judgment, I consistently can. But you must act.[46]

Of Lincoln's letter General Ballard says:

The unexperienced lawyer summed up in three lines the situation which the professional soldier was constitutionally incapable of realizing. "By delay the enemy will relatively gain on you—that is he will gain faster by fortifications and reinforcements than you will by reinforcements alone." [47]

Lincoln also probably realized that the Confederates would note the added proof of McClellan's supercaution and would duly capitalize upon it. But he could not have foreseen that on April 22 Joe Johnston, after an inspection of Magruder's lines, would write to Lee, "No one but McClellan could have hesitated to attack." [48] In military history it would be difficult to find a more crushing judgment than that.

Lincoln carefully read every line that McClellan wrote, as he later read the reports of his other generals—including Grant. After repeated reports of progress with his extensive siege work, the general—always wanting something he did not have—wired on April 28: "Would be glad to have the 30-pounder Parrotts in the works around Washington at once. Am very short of that excellent gun." Lincoln replied on May 1, "Your call for Parrott guns from Washington alarms me, chiefly because it argues indefinite procrastination. Is anything to be done?" [49]

Secretary Stanton too was keeping on the pressure, but with a touch of indirection. On April 6 he telegraphed, "Your advance on Yorktown gratified me very much, and I hope you will press forward and carry the enemy's works and soon be at Richmond." Two days later he told the general that official information confirmed General Pope's capture of Island No. 10 in the Mississippi River, with rich military booty, and broke the news of a "brilliant victory" of General Grant and General Buell's advance corps over Beauregard at Shiloh. "Brilliant" was one of McClellan's favorite words; maybe Stanton had learned it from him, and used it advisedly. He concluded: "We hope for even greater results from your operations, and are longing to send the shout of victory from the Chesapeake to the Mississippi!" [50]

While he was waiting to send up a shout of triumph so loud that it would be heard by the soldiers of Pope and Grant, Stanton did not delay commending the least success. On April 10 McClellan telegraphed that General Smith had just "handsomely silenced" the fire of a one-gun battery, and had compelled the enemy to suspend some work. It is almost easier to forgive McClellan for disobeying a direct order of the President than for telegraphing quite trivial information to Washington. A general who would report that he had silenced a one-gun battery showed that he did not have the great sense of balance needed by a commander, and Stanton may have felt it was indeed time to have a new man even if it were necessary to choose him by drawing a name from a hat. The Secretary was definitely on the "tough" side of center, and it is not recorded that anyone ever slapped him on the back and called him "Ed" or "Stan"—even if he smiled. Nevertheless, Stanton tried to be cheerful and he telegraphed the jubilant general, "Good for the first lick! Hurrah for Smith and the one-gun battery!" [51]

When morning broke on May 4 the "secession flag" that McClellan had first reported seeing just one month before was gone, for the Confederates had evacuated the Yorktown lines during the night, before he opened with his field guns and the heavy artillery so laboriously put in place. On the same field Washington had captured Lord Cornwallis and his men, and from that achievement had come the fine heritage that was in Lincoln's keeping, a heritage now in grave peril. Lincoln had not read many books, but he had read and thought much about the General who had also been first President. He knew of his bold and rapid move from New York to Yorktown with 4,000 French troops and 2,000 Continentals—heroes of hard service and privation. He knew there had been an investment of the British lines, but he also knew that in the dim light of dawn on October 15, 1781, there had been an assault with unloaded muskets—the Americans led by twenty-four-year-old Alexander Hamilton, the French by Lieutenant Colonel G. de Deux-Points.

Lincoln could well have thought that the honored name of Yorktown had been tarnished.

Two years later a British soldier was to write: "The movement to Fortress Monroe was the stride of a giant. The second, in the direction of Richmond, was that of a dwarf." [52]

When the nature of the Federal spring campaign had become apparent, Johnston's force had been called from the Rapphannock to Richmond and he had been put in direct command of all the troops defending the Confederate capital. Robert E. Lee, now with four stars on his shoulders, was there as director of military operations under President Davis. Though not actually General in Chief he had more authority, as well as more ability, than General Hitchcock, who was advising the Washington administration. However, his career in the war up to the moment had not been such as to increase belief and confidence. Johnston outranked him; but he was happy to have a soldier between himself and President Davis, and also pleased that the objectionable Benjamin had been promoted to be Confederate Secretary of State. George W. Randolph was now Secretary of War; the third man tried in that office, he had been a midshipman before turning lawyer, and was a grandson of Thomas Jefferson. Johnston had made the decision to evacuate Yorktown and retreat toward Richmond, and though badly outnumbered he probably was not too pessimistic about matching generalship with the "redoubtable McC." after the latter had advanced into the woods and swamps east of Richmond.

McClellan soon had troops moving in pursuit of Johnston, and at 9:00 A.M. he wired Secretary Stanton, "I shall push the enemy to the wall." Stanton took the general at his word and concluded his telegram of congratulations, "I hope soon to hail your arrival in Richmond." [53] McClellan, having sent a large force forward, should have been with the advance; instead, he busied himself with things a staff officer should have done. Afterward he explained that he had not supposed that there would be more than a "rear-guard affair," in the casual way of one who had much acquaintance with such minor matters. But Johnston stopped at historic Williamsburg, and the action that took place there the next day was a good-sized battle, fought in a confused way under the direction of General Sumner. Heavy defensive work fell on Hooker's division, but the most outstanding achievement on the Federal side was an attack late in the afternoon by the regiments of Brigadier General Winfield Scott Hancock, who here began to establish a reputation in all ways worthy of his name. McClellan reached the field late in the day, and at 9:40 P.M. he sent a dispatch to Franklin at Yorktown, in which he said, "I found great confusion here, but all is now right. . . . We have now a tangent hit. I arrived in time." [54]

Early on the 6th Johnston again retreated toward Richmond, leaving the Federals in full possession of the old capital of Virginia.

McClellan reported to Stanton (who, accompanied by President Lincoln, arrived that night at Fort Monroe): "The enemy were badly whipped, but will probably fight again. Our men behaved nobly and are in excellent heart and spirits." [55] In his own mind, however, he had increased Johnston's force until it exceeded his own. This fact troubled General Wool at Fort Monroe, who, not knowing that Stanton would soon be with him, wired early on the 6th:

> The desponding tone of Major-General McClellan's dispatch of last evening more than surprises me. He says his entire force is undoubtedly considerably inferior to that of the rebels. If such is the fact I am still more surprised that they should have abandoned Yorktown.[56]

The President and Secretary Stanton did not see McClellan, but they could not have been very optimistic when they returned to Wash ington. They must have believed that he already had many more men than he could manipulate effectively, for, after all, he was practically without experience as a field commander of even a small force, while the country he was entering was very difficult. By this time Lincoln and Stanton also knew that he had the tendency to offset any reenforcements given to him by reporting corresponding or greater increases of the enemy forces. If the commanding general of the Army of the Potomac could not recognize the simple logic that the old soldier of 1812 and Mexico saw, the case was discouraging in the extreme.

By the end of May, McClellan had his army in position only a few miles from Richmond. But he was astride the swampy and treacherous Chickahominy River, which he had overlooked when he wrote to Lincoln so enthusiastically about the offensive merits of the region. After the battle of Williamsburg he had complained about the corps commanders that had been given to him, and the President had given him permission to reorganize his army, though stipulating that corps must be preserved. Accordingly, McClellan created the Fifth (provisional) Corps under Brigadier General Porter, and the Sixth (provisional) Corps under Franklin. These and the Second (Sumner), Third (Heintzelman), and Fourth (Keyes) consisted of two divisions of three brigades each. The divisions were strong, with about 10,000 men and organic artillery (that is, artillery that was an integral part of the division), while the corps had corps artillery or cavalry, or both.

In addition, the army had an engineer brigade, a cavalry division, and extensive medical and quartermaster units; the army staff consisted of fifty-seven officers. More than half of the army was on the left (north) bank of the Chickahominy, covering communications to White House on the Pamunkey, where the base of operations was located on a railroad line from Richmond.

Much time had been spent in building bridges across the treacherous river and long corduroy approaches made necessary by the swampy borders of the stream. It was far from an ideal arrangement, but it was the direct result of McClellan's having placed his base at White House instead of on the James River, which he could have done after the Confederates destroyed the *Merrimac* on May 11 in evacuating Norfolk. With the *Merrimac* gone, the Federal navy was in undisputed control of the James River, and McClellan had to decide between continuing up the tortuous Pamunkey in accordance with his original plan and using the broad expanse of the James to establish a base. Michie states, "It is at such epochs that the governing characteristics of men assert themselves and proclaim their greatness or their mediocrity." McClellan later had to change his base, so that his decision of the 11th was evidently not wise; and again he sought to put the responsibility upon the administration—a claim that Michie tears to shreds, with quotations from the general's own dispatches of the time.[57]

In the meantime McDowell had moved to Fredericksburg, and the division of Brigadier General James Shields, which had been with General Banks in the Shenandoah Valley, had been ordered to join him, replacing Franklin's division, now with McClellan. On May 17 Secretary Stanton ordered McDowell to begin the fifty-five-mile march to Richmond as soon as he was joined by Shields, and to follow in general the route of the railroad. The order was an important one, and in its preparation Stanton consulted not only with the President but with Generals Meigs, Joseph G. Totten, and James W. Ripley and Colonel Joseph P. Taylor.[58] The two civilians who were conducting the war were by no means trying to play things alone; nor were they seeking advice only from the elderly Hitchcock. On the same day McClellan was to receive additional evidence of Stanton's wish to carry out his suggestions in a telegram ending "The instruction you desired respecting the publication of unauthorized official reports has been given." [59]

Lincoln himself made a trip to see McDowell, and on the 24th he reported to McClellan that Shields had joined the First Corps, but his division was somewhat worn out from its long march. He said that McDowell's march would be aided if McClellan should strike in behind the Confederate force (which was small) that seemed ready to oppose his march. This might intercept the retreating Confederates and at the same time save some of the bridges on the railroad. The Commander in Chief could not have been more tactful with a temperamental prima donna, for he asked, "Can you not do this, almost as well as not, while you are building the Chickahominy bridges?" [60] Here is evidence that he kept a good operations map as well as a good intelligence map, and held to the theory that for success in war one should do just as many things as possible at the same time. The 24th was Saturday, and the President wrote that both McDowell and Shields asserted that they could, and positively would, move on Monday. In writing, "I wish you to move cautiously and safely," he was certainly carrying coals to Newcastle. This sentence might have been omitted, but there is no reason whatever to believe it was responsible in the least for what was to take place; and it is equally unquestionable that moves which would have appeared to Lincoln as safe would have been pronounced as hazardous by his general.

After Stanton's telegram of the 17th McClellan had not been certain whether he was to be in full command of McDowell after the latter joined him, since his copy of the order given to McDowell seemed to give the latter the mission of continuing to cover Washington. Accordingly, he had written another long-winded dispatch to Lincoln to clear the matter up. [61] In one sentence of the letter already quoted the President settled the point at issue and got in a hit at the general's tiresome and annoying verbosity: "You will have command of McDowell, after he joins you, precisely as you indicated in your long dispatch of the 21st."

Everything looked very promising except for one matter of which the President informed McClellan on the 24th. The Federal forces in the Shenandoah Valley had been so weakened that when the small garrison at Front Royal was attacked unexpectedly on the 23rd by overwhelming numbers a regiment of infantry and two companies of cavalry had been lost. The result put General Banks (at Strasburg with some 6,000 men) "in some peril." Bad news continued to come in, and May 24 proved to be a day of crucial decisions for Washington. It was clear that Stonewall Jackson had again swung into action. Just two months before, General Shields had harshly dealt with him in the battle of Kernstown, five miles south of Winchester, on which Stonewall, who found it hard to acknowledge defeat, noted in his report to Richmond that he had made the Federals change their plans, ending, "Under these circumstances I feel justified in saying that, though the field is in possession of the enemy, yet the most essential fruits of the battle are ours." [62] Nevertheless, he returned to the upper Valley and spent the next two months in minor operations that wore out shoes but toughened the legs of his troops while netting other results. Receiving reenforcements, he broke loose after Shields had marched away to Fredericksburg, and suddenly appeared at Front Royal. Banks knew that his communications were in jeopardy, and lost not a second in starting a hasty retreat for Winchester, Martinsburg, and the Potomac if need be; but he lost in both supplies and men when Jackson took him in the flank on the 24th.

The question before Lincoln—actually directing armies at the time because of necessity rather than inclination—was clear enough, though arguments could have been made about the answer. What should be done with McDowell? Should his march to join McClellan be continued, or should he be used against Jackson? Lincoln's decision was quick and clean-cut. At 4:00 P.M. he telegraphed McClellan, "In consequence of General Banks' critical position I have been compelled to suspend General McDowell's movements to join you." [63] By itself that looked as if the new events in the Shenandoah were causing serious alarm. But the next and final sentence of the dispatch showed that Lincoln was not starting just a defensive move but one whose main purpose was offensive: "The enemy are making a desperate push upon Harper's Ferry, and we are trying to throw General Frémont's force and part of General McDowell's in their rear." There is only one reason for getting in the enemy's rear, and that is to hurt him badly; and if Major General John Frémont, who was at Franklin (forty miles northwest of Staunton) with some 20,000 men, and some of McDowell's force could seize firm hold of the important Valley turnpike south of Jackson, that annoying general might be dealt a blow more convincing and permanent than Kernstown had been.

The excellent reply that McClellan sent the same evening was perhaps the best of his career; it said merely, "Telegram of 4 P.M. received. I will make my calculations accordingly." [64] The brevity may have been the result of Lincoln's adroit insertion of the word "long" into his telegram of the morning; but the failure to complain in the least at the second retention of McDowell is as pleasing as it is surprising.

Already McDowell's advanced troops were eight miles south of Fredericksburg,[65] and the order stopping his movement on Richmond and sending him to the Valley to deal with Jackson is the military action for which Lincoln has probably been most severely criticized. Of course most of the denunciation grows from the fact that though some heavy casualties were inflicted upon Jackson, he was not destroyed; and not enough insistence has been put upon the fact that the operation might well have completely succeeded if Frémont had not taken great liberties with an order, and if phenomenal rains had not interfered with the Federal concentration. Ballard completely justifies Lincoln, upon what he considers to have been his basic appraisal of McClellan. Certainly on May 24 the President could not have any delusions about what McClellan might do; he had to see the general exactly as the last months had revealed him. Ballard asserts that, if Lincoln could have seen a Grant, a Sherman, or a Sheridan operating against Richmond, McDowell's march would have been allowed to continue, with the knowledge that the troops would be used at once, resolutely, and effectively; "but all he saw was McClellan, sitting in eternal rain, and facing a strong position held by 200,000 of the enemy." That exaggerates a little, for McClellan had not yet reported that the Confederates had 200,000 men. Ballard, however, says much more than that Lincoln was right; he asserts that Lincoln's action gives a perfect example of a true appreciation of Napoleon's maxim: "In war men are nothing; it is the Man who is everything." [66]

The opinion of the eminent British general and military historian quite alone wipes out much superficial criticism. But today we can do more than examine Lincoln in terms of predecessors and contemporaries. We can stand his successors up beside him for a measure of their stature, and we can compare the actions of May 24, 1862, and succeeding days with events of recent time.

There was a real crisis on that Saturday; that of course is the first thing to grasp clearly. Jackson's move, inspired to a certain extent by suggestions from Lee, was one of the best in his career. After doing all that he could by way of deceiving both the Federals and his own subordinate commanders (notably Ewell, who recently had joined him) he had marched his augmented command northward on the east side of the Massanutten Mountains—that for some miles cut the Shenandoah Valley into two parts—and had fallen with overwhelming force upon the unsuspecting Federal garrison at Front Royal. With that little opposition out of the way, Stonewall had moved with customary vigor to cut off Banks, intending next to march for the Potomac. A first-class panic in Washington and alarm throughout the North might not only stop McDowell but bring the recall of McClellan—and so allow the frightened people of Richmond to relax.

There had been no warning that something grave would happen, no chance to put Banks on the alert at Strasburg, or warn Colonel John R. Kenly of the First Maryland at Front Royal.[67] The bolt struck out of the blue sky. Nevertheless, Lincoln immediately sought to turn the Confederate move to advantage. Even before he knew the strength of the enemy column that had completely changed the military situation, he had made his decision; without excitement, and with amazing speed and definiteness, he gave directions for the carrying out of his design. President and Secretary of War were working together smoothly and effectively, and they showed their qualifications for dealing with soldiers. To see this, we must look with some detail at the way the two amateurs carried out the duties of high military command.

First of all, at 11:12 A.M. a message went from Secretary Stanton to McDowell informing him that new events would probably cause a change in his previous orders.[68] Then at one o'clock Lincoln sent a dispatch to Brigadier General Rufus Saxton at Harpers Ferry to straighten out the panicky reports from Brigadier General John W. Geary at Rectortown, twenty-five miles west of Manassas and near the Manassas Gap Railroad:

Geary reports Jackson with 20,000 moving from Ashby's Gap by the Little River turnpike, through Aldie, toward Centreville. This, he says, is reliable. He is also informed of large forces south of him. We know a force of some 15,000 broke up Saturday night from in front of Fredericksburg, and went we know not where. Please inform us, if possible, what has become of the force which pursued Banks yesterday; also any other information you have.

Stanton showed that there was the desire both to help and to trust the decisions of the officers on the spot when he telegraphed to Saxton at 3:41:

A fine battery of artillery will leave Baltimore for you at 4 o'clock. More will leave here this evening. Exercise your own judgment as to your defense. Whatever you do will be cordially approved, be the result what it may.[69]

Whether the situation cleared any in the afternoon is not certain, but at five o'clock Lincoln had new instructions ready for McDowell. After telling him that Frémont had been ordered to march from Franklin to Harrisonburg, he gave him a mission as clearly stated as any well trained commander ever wrote: "Your object will be to capture the forces of Jackson and Ewell, either in co-operation with General Frémont or, in case want of supplies or of transportation interferes with his movements, it is believed that the force with which you move will be sufficient to accomplish this object alone." [70] *Capture* Jackson *and* Ewell: that was the mission. Not a thing was said about relieving a threat to Washington or any other place, but McDowell was told that if Jackson continued to operate against Banks, he—McDowell— might not be able to count upon much assistance from his brother general but might have "to release him." What would happen to Lincoln's dispatch if it passed through the hands of a modern operations officer for correct phrasing would be hard to predict; but all of its charm would certainly be lost, and in spite of the addition of a "not repeat not" it would probably be less understandable.

It might seem that no more was needed than a good telegram to McDowell; but more—much more—was done, for there was a crisis, and there must be complete understanding of instructions and also harmony of minds. So a messenger was sent to McDowell, and the messenger was not a low-ranking officer or even one with stars upon his shoulders. The messenger was none other than the Secretary of the Treasury, solemn, impressive Salmon P. Chase. Chase was contemptuous of Lincoln and already at this time was laying plans to get his place in 1864 [71]—facts which the President knew quite as well as he knew that, the next day being Sunday, the ultra-pious Chase would probably like to go to church. But Stanton and Chase got along well together, and so Lincoln bundled Chase off that Saturday afternoon for Fredericksburg. Remembering that McDowell should be prepared to receive a distinguished messenger, Stanton telegraphed the general at 5:30 that "Governor Chase" was taking the boat, with information that would probably qualify today as "top secret." Stanton did not want the man who held the nation's money bags to be met by a mere aide-de-camp even if he were well turned out in freshly polished boots, and so he told the two-star general, "Meet him there, and have transportation for him to your headquarters."

At six o'clock McDowell telegraphed to Stanton briefly, but fully revealing his great disappointment: "The President's order has been received and is in process of execution. This is a crushing blow to us." With comprehending sympathy Lincoln telegraphed McDowell at eight, "I am highly gratified by your alacrity in obeying my orders. The change was as painful to me as it can possibly be to you or any one. Everything now depends upon the celerity and vigor of your movement." The amateur did not seek to minimize the responsibility that rested upon the man whom he both sincerely thanked and sought to assuage, but chose words that emphasized the great importance of his new task. The disappointment McDowell felt was so deep that in his reply he said he was going beyond what a soldier probably should do—and cast heavy doubt upon both the wisdom and the practicality of the movement which he had already begun to execute. He closed, "I hope to see Governor Chase tonight and express myself more fully to him." Probably about the time Secretary Chase reached Aquia Landing, a telegram arrived from Stanton with the latest information: "General Frémont replied promptly that he would execute his order at once. Nothing heard from Banks since you started." [72] The condition of Frémont's supply and transport was known to be as bad as his previous military record,[73] but it looked as if he would attempt to make good on his part of the program.

Sometime during the day a message from Fort Monroe added more uncertainty to the situation. General Wool telegraphed that deserters and contrabands from Richmond were asserting that the Confederate army was about to leave Richmond.[74] It would be interesting to know whether this was clever enemy deception, or merely a result of natural rumors based on fear that were flying about Richmond; but we can no more tell now which was true than Lincoln and Stanton could at the time. Added, however, to the fact that the enemy force at Fredericksburg had left for an unknown destination, and the rumors that Geary had forwarded, the news from Wool gave some basis for thinking that something more than a raid or a minor diversion was under way in the Valley.

The next day was Sunday, but everyone was apparently at work early. However comfortable the bed McDowell had provided for Chase at Falmouth (across the Rappahannock from Fredericksburg) and however adequate and wholesome the breakfast that may have been set before the robust Secretary of the Treasury, he probably missed his customary leisurely Sunday morning meal with his beautiful daughter Kate, at the time the most courted young woman in Washington as well as the most efficient of presidential campaign managers. Chase knew that even without his stately presence plenty of eyes would be turned upon his pew in case his daughter went to church alone. Perhaps the thought let him concentrate more contentedly upon the matters at hand—matters very remote, it must be noted, from his normal duties in the cabinet—which the President knew he could discharge well because of his great ability and fundamental patriotism. It was an emissary attached to the country, not to himself personally, that Lincoln sent to the headquarters of General McDowell.

Lincoln telegraphed to Chase, "I think it not improbable that Ewell, Jackson, and Johnson [Edward Johnson] are pouring through the gap they made day before yesterday at Front Royal, making a dash northward." Then, revealing again his appreciation of McDowell's feelings, but not wavering in the least from his decision, or his purpose to do more than *check* the enemy foray northward: "It will be a very valuable and very honorable service for General McDowell to cut them off. I hope he will put all possible energy and speed into the effort." Though it was Sunday, Lincoln was wanting and was expecting hard marching that might turn a stroke by the enemy into his own destruction. At 10:15 Chase sent a telegram to Stanton that showed he could understand some military matters, as well as financial affairs, and that he could report accurately. He said that leading the advance toward the Valley was Shields's division—which already had once bested Jackson; and waiting only for it to clear the road was the division of Brigadier General Rufus King. Chase then asked a question which proved the advantage of having dispatched to Fredericksburg a man with rank: "Would not time be saved by bringing General Shields to Washington for consultation? His information and judgment are excellent, and his coming would not delay the movement of his division." Save time! Lincoln and his secretaries knew the value of that commodity even though McClellan did not. They also knew the importance of personal conference. Twenty-five minutes later five words were back from Stanton, "Bring Shields along with you." One must make an adverse entry against the War Secretary for the use of three superfluous words.

Presently Chase sent Stanton another question: "Is it best that General McDowell should command in person or remain here? The considerations on both sides will suggest themselves to you at once." The War Secretary recognized that here was a question on which he should get top agreement; but it was not long before he answered Chase: "Let him remain at Fredericksburg and send forward his best commander. This is also the opinion of the President." Chase's question had been answered, but remembering that he had been met the night before by a two-star general, he repaid courtesy and thoughtfulness in like coin, and replied: "All right. General McDowell remains. We come back immediately." Presently he sent his final message explaining that a brigade was being sent by boat to Alexandria, to go thence by rail so as to speed the movement, and it was added that the recently created division of Major General Edward Ord was being substituted for that of King. Washington could have made out without that last dispatch, but it helped to have the final and complete picture.

While he very appropriately dealt mostly with Stanton, Secretary Chase did not forget the man in the White House, and Lincoln received from him at 12:20 P.M. a telegram with the welcome news that McDowell and other officers were thinking better of the new movement: "General McDowell appreciates, as you do, the importance of the service he is called on to perform. All possible exertion is being made by him and the officers under him to expedite the movement." Chase expected to be back at six o'clock and would have Shields with him.[75]

Lincoln was of course under no necessity of explaining his plans more fully to McClellan; but even on this busy Sunday he took time to send him a comprehensive message. He explained clearly that both the movement of McDowell and that ordered for Frémont were "intended to get in the enemy's rear." Without trace of alarm he spoke of the probability that Banks was "broken up into a total rout" (which turned out not to be the case at all). In language that suffered in no way because it was not professional, he said that "regiments and dribs" were being sent from Washington and Baltimore to Harpers Ferry, and as there was not a single piece of artillery at that place eighteen guns were on the way from the capital. Not one word was said about danger to the capital, and the only hint of such a concern was in Lincoln's concluding sentences: "Apprehensions of something like this, and no unwillingness to sustain you, have always been my reason for withholding McDowell's [corps] from you. Please understand this, and do the best you can with the force you have." It is to be noted that Lincoln did not trouble to recall that one of McDowell's divisions—the one McClellan rated best—had gone to him in early April.

As more news came in, the situation looked worse, for the magnitude of the enemy force striking for the Potomac had not been determined; at two o'clock Lincoln telegraphed McClellan: "I think the movement is a general and concerted one, such as would not be made if [the enemy] was acting upon the purpose of a very desperate defense of Richmond. I think the time is near when you must either attack Richmond or give up the job and come to the defense of Washington. Let me hear from you instantly." [76] The President's momentary belief that the new Confederate operation was not just a diversion was based not merely on what had befallen Kenly and Banks, but upon the disappearance of the force near Fredericksburg, and the message from Wool previously described. The sentence quoted above is the basis for the oft repeated charge that Lincoln ordered McClellan to attack Richmond or come to the defense of Washington; but no order whatever was given, merely a warning of what might result if the procrastination of Yorktown were repeated, and the common accusation is as unfounded as the one that Washington was interfering or meddling when, in exercising the function of high command, the administration gave orders.[77] In his prompt reply McClellan said: "Telegram received. Independently of it, the time is very near when I shall attack Richmond. The object of the movement is probably to prevent reenforcements being sent to me. All the information from balloons, deserters, prisoners, and contrabands agrees in the statement that the mass of the rebel troops are still in the immediate vicinity of Richmond, ready to defend it." [78] The appraisal of the situation was very accurate, but what faith Lincoln put in it cannot be said; McClellan had been wrong very often in his estimates of the enemy's intention. "Very near." One wonders what Lincoln thought that meant. As something to count on in the making of plans it could almost be dismissed.

McDowell came through later in the day with a telegram that showed still more clearly how soldierly he was. He summarized everything that had been done; then the high command would have no misunderstanding. He had, however, done more than execute with complete loyalty an order that he had very regretfully received; he had entered into the spirit of the new enterprise and had himself added something that might aid in bringing it to success. The concluding sentence that Stanton read was, "I am making a strong demonstration to the south over the river with the remaining divisions [McCall's and King's] to mislead the enemy as to our movements and intentions." [79]

Stanton, no less than Lincoln, knew good service when he saw it; and, equally with his chief, he realized the value of a hearty word of commendation, both as a reward and as a spur, especially when it could be given to an officer with no trace of vanity and egotism. Even while he had bad word to send to McDowell, it was natural for Stanton to slip in a sentence that the general could cherish. He telegraphed: "You have properly understood your instructions, and I thank you for their prompt execution. The last intelligence from Banks, he was in full retreat, hotly pressed, and in great danger." [80] The words "have properly understood" not only measure McDowell; they also measure Stanton, for they reveal how carefully he had checked every message from Fredericksburg.

Somewhere on the road the fourteen infantry regiments from Pennsylvania, Ohio, Indiana, Illinois, and West Virginia, the cavalry from Pennsylvania, Maryland, West Virginia, Ohio, and Michigan, and the regular battery and the four from West Virginia and Ohio that made up the road-toughened and battle-tried division of Shields, bivouacked that night. As they countermarched over the route they recently had traveled, the "thinking bayonets" could well have thought that someone had blundered, believing that if they had been left in the Valley Jackson would have been happy to remain close to Staunton. But if they thought of that they also knew full well that they marched for a very appreciative government, because Stanton on March 26 had telegraphed Shields hearty congratulations for their good fighting at Kernstown.[81] He had called them a "brave division," had predicted that wherever their standard was displayed the enemy would "be routed and pursued," and had said to their general, "To you and to the brave officers and soldiers under your command the Department returns thanks." Proudly they had stood at attention and listened to the words of the government, words which would become a part of them and help sustain them on the march and in the bivouac, quite as well as when they faced battle. Edwin Stanton watched for something more than contractors who cheated the government and officers who were incompetent or careless with its property; and he could write something more than tight contracts.

Such was Sunday May 25, 1862. It was a perfect day for the professional soldier, Irvin McDowell, while the amateurs, Lincoln, Stanton, and Chase, made a good record in their prompt and clear messages, fully equal to the occasion, free from technical jargon and marked by a human touch which proves that great men as well as good minds were in charge. Of course, help had come from good assistants, especially perhaps from the great personal secretaries, Nicolay and Hay. It is a proper occasion for contemplating the moral character and the intellectual stature of the two men that Lincoln had as intimates in the White House, who saw him at all times of the day and night, in bright and dark hours alike, the men whose devotion he well knew, and to whom he could go when he felt the need of the comprehending and sustaining sympathy of younger persons.

And if McClellan could only have been resolute and have named his day of attack, May 25, 1862, would also have been a great day for him—provided, of course, he had for once kept a promise.

Late into the night Lincoln worked, completing more perhaps than a circuit of the clock. But good news had begun to arrive. At 12:40 A.M. of the 26th he telegraphed to McClellan: "We have General Banks' official report. He has saved his army and baggage and has made a safe retreat to the river, and is probably safe at Williamsport. He reported the attacking force at 15,000." [82]

Jackson had struck with 16,000 men,[83] and so it is clear that Banks had not been in a panic and had made an excellent record in getting information about the enemy even while he was striving hard to save his men and wagons. Twelve hours later the drummer boy of the First Maryland sent in corroborating information through Brigadier General John W. Geary. The young soldier had been captured on the 23rd (perhaps by the Confederate First Maryland, which fought with the Federal First Maryland at Front Royal) but had contrived to escape to Geary's headquarters at Broad Run near Gainesville. There he stated that Jackson had attacked with 14,000 men on Friday, and that 4,000 more Confederates had pressed through Front Royal the next day for Winchester.[84] When a drummer boy agrees so well with a major general, the case is closed. Thus, Lincoln could cast aside the thought that the enemy operation in the Valley was a major one, unless it developed that other troops were following.

To hold troops in Richmond, it would be well to start operations there; and after asking for McClellan's impression as to the intrenchments he would encounter in an attack Lincoln concluded his midnight dispatch with the interesting query, "Can you get near enough to throw shells into the city?" A few shells dropped into the Southern capital might of course upset Jefferson Davis, but Lincoln's whole line of thought is not very clear.

McClellan's reply of 7.30 P.M. is given in full:

Have arranged to carry out your last orders. We are quietly closing in upon the enemy preparatory to the last struggle. Situated as I am, I feel forced to take every possible precaution against disaster and to secure my flanks against the probable superior force in front of me. My arrangements for to-morrow are very important, and, if successful, will leave me free to strike on the return of the force detached.[85]

Here again was talk about superior enemy forces that the President would probably have put down as merely a relapse by McClellan into his habit of exaggeration of difficulties, even if he had not been in possession of an important estimate by General Wool in his dispatch of the 24th to Stanton: "If I had as many troops as the general [McClellan] I would not ask for more. I would march and take Richmond, which I have no doubt General McClellan will do. The forces of the rebels are by no means equal to his." [86]

The "arrangements" to which McClellan referred rather darkly turned out to be an attack of the 27th by Porter's corps against an enemy force in the vicinity of Hanover (on the railroad east of Ashland). The operation was successful, and it would have been of value —and in accordance with Lincoln's suggestion—if the march of McDowell had not been called off. As it was, however, nothing was accomplished except a waste of time. Not only in his preview did McClellan speak of the affair as "very important"; he subsequently felt somewhat aggrieved because neither Lincoln nor Stanton seemed impressed by it, though Michie confirmed the judgment of the President and Secretary.[87] The weather had improved, and McClellan should have been able to attack Richmond itself by the 27th with a force that was double the one Johnston commanded, and with no danger to his flank from the Confederates at Hanover, that could not have been easily guarded against. Though he thought the movement of McDowell a mistake, he did not see the folly of sending Porter against Hanover. But even after wasting the time he might have done something if he had kept his specific promise "to strike on the return of the force detached." A great opportunity was rapidly slipping away, and Colonel Francis W. Palfrey of the Twentieth Massachusetts, who like Stanton had once been an enthusiastic "McClellan man," [88] later wrote, "In my judgment, there is no room for difference of opinion upon the question whether he ought to have attacked before the 31st of May." [89]

Speed and boldness at Fredericksburg and Washington; slowness and caution at Richmond! The last days of May give a study in contrasts.

As he fell back before McClellan, Johnston had received some new men who had volunteered as a result of the Confederate draft law passed on April 17, as well as some units drawn from other places. Since the new law also held in service the 148 regiments that had volunteered for only one year, his army would not suffer the fatal losses that were in prospect. On May 21 he had a total strength of 53,688 men, his command consisting of the four large divisions of Smith, Longstreet, Magruder, and D. H. Hill, Stuart's small cavalry brigade of 1,289 men, and an artillery reserve of 920 men and fifty-six guns.[90] More additions to his army were expected, but the menace that came from the threatened junction of McDowell and McClellan led Johnston to plan an attack for May 29 upon the right flank of McClellan's superior force. Although such an operation would uncover Richmond, it promised most from the standpoint of interfering with McDowell's march; and Johnston already had had experience of playing upon McClellan's timidity. McDowell's efforts to deceive the enemy about his movements had been as successful as could have been expected, but finally on the evening of the 28th Johnston received word from Stuart that all of the Federal First Corps had returned to Fredericksburg and there were indications that it might move farther north.[91]

Battle plans were then quickly recast, and Johnston prepared to attack on May 31 that part of McClellan's army that had crossed the Chickahominy—Heintzelman's Third Corps and Keyes's Fourth. The Federal commander's great caution and the divided position of his army gave the Confederate general the belief that there was chance for success in spite of disparity of numbers—a disparity which was diminished by the arrival late on May 30 of Major General John Huger with his division of about 10,000 men.[92]

Late in the afternoon of the day before the attack, after Johnston's orders had been issued, there was a storm of unprecedented violence. Some of McClellan's laboriously constructed bridges disappeared in

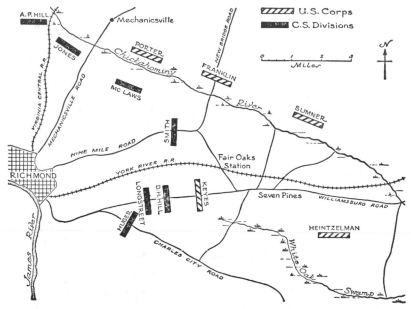

BATTLE OF FAIR OAKS (SEVEN PINES), MAY 31, 1862

the torrent, and the isolation of the two corps south of the Chickahominy was accordingly increased. Johnston knew, however, that the wet fields and heavy roads would make his attack much more difficult so that there was a question whether the rain might not have lessened rather than increased his chances. Nevertheless, he did not call off the attack but continued with his preparations to throw no fewer than twenty-three of his twenty-seven brigades against the two Federal corps.[93]

There was much confusion the next morning not only on account of heavy marching conditions, but because of serious misunderstanding of Johnston's orders. Worse than that, one of the general's aides who was carrying an important message rode into the Federal lines and was captured. As a result, some of McClellan's force was warned and was on the alert, while other units were relaxed or were even doing some "prospecting" when they were struck. Between Johnston's two main columns of attack the coordination was worse than bad. In this battle —as often later—reliance was put upon the sound of gunfire as a signal; but the wind was wrong, or ears were not sufficiently attentive. For the most part, the Federals fought with stubborn valor—even some raw regiments standing steadily to their task against violent assaults. Some regiments, however, broke, and there was some mass movement to the rear; many men were stopped at one of the bridges over the river. There was good troop-leading as well as bad, and late in the day some reenforcements arrived from Sumner's corps, in spite of the difficulty of crossing the Chickahominy. When evening came, the two corps, though driven back, were far from being destroyed. Men and officers alike had had some of the most valuable experience that can come on a field of battle to men of good stout heart, and most of McClellan's officers and soldiers were made of good stuff. About dusk Johnston was severely wounded, and the command of the Confederate force devolved upon Major General G. W. Smith.

During the night troops were shifted, lines were restored, and other matters put in order; thus June 1 broke with the Army of the Potomac ready again to defend itself, but with no intention of launching a counterstrike. Though there was more fighting, Michie says, "During the second day the main struggle had therefore occurred between opposing forces of about five brigades on each side, in a square stand-up fight under no definite plan of battle." With night there came an end of the Battle of Fair Oaks—or Seven Pines, as it is called with about equal frequency. Total Federal casualties were about five thousand, and total Confederate about sixty-one hundred.[94]

McClellan had exercised very little personal influence on the battle, but he was sick and not in good condition to take very active command.[95] It should, however, have been surmised even by a sick man that Johnston had probably thrown most of his army into the fight the first day, and had been held with half of the Federal army. In his first real battle McClellan thus showed that he did not have the ability to estimate the strength of an enemy force by its battle-field behavior—

an essential in a successful commander. While the Federal divisions on the south of the river were readjusting themselves on the night of May 31, two corps on the north bank could have been put in position to develop the enemy force in front of them early the next day. If this had been done, it would have been found that an advance, perhaps even into Richmond, would not have been difficult, for until Smith began to move troops from his right flank there would have been only about four brigades against twelve. At this time there were practically no intrenchments in front of Richmond, and General Barnard, McClellan's own chief engineer, made bold to state in his official report: "The repulse of the rebels at Fair Oaks should have been taken advantage of. It was one of those occasions which if not seized do not repeat themselves." [96]

As was his habit, McClellan was appreciative of the performance of his men in the battle of Fair Oaks and reported enthusiastically about the action, saying that the enemy's losses were certainly heavier than his own—as they should have been, since the Confederates were the attackers. As an effort to destroy part of McClellan's army and liquidate the threat to Richmond, the battle must be called a defeat for the Confederates. But in his failure to make a counterattack, though half of his army was not used,[97] the Federal general had written another page about himself which Lee read carefully and later used to great advantage.

CHAPTER VII

HIGH DRAMA IN THE VALLEY

It is for you a question of legs. Put in all the speed you can.
Lincoln to McDowell

THE order which had gone to Frémont at four o'clock on May 24 noted the importance of immediate relief for Banks and then added:

You are therefore directed by the President to move against Jackson at Harrisonburg, and operate against the enemy in such a way as to relieve Banks. This movement must be made immediately. You will acknowledge the receipt of this order and specify the hour it is received by you.

The inclusion of aid to Banks as part of Frémont's mission was most regrettable, but the second sentence quoted seems to leave little doubt that a movement to Harrisonburg was the first thing wanted—and wanted badly by the High Command. The general's reply was in Washington at 6:35:

Your telegram received at 5 o'clock this afternoon. Will move as ordered, and operate against the enemy in such [a] way [as] to afford prompt relief to General Banks.

Probably the words "Will move as ordered" especially attracted Lincoln's attention and forty minutes later he telegraphed:

Many thanks for the promptness with which you have answered that you will execute the order. Much—perhaps all depends upon the celerity with which you can execute it. Put the utmost speed into it. Do not lose a minute.[1]

In his report written in December, 1865, Frémont stated that the nature of the road from Franklin to Harrisonburg, together with the condition of his troops and considerations of relieving Banks, caused him to follow the spirit rather than the letter of instructions and move to Strasburg instead of Harrisonburg, by way of Petersburg, Moorefield, and Wordensville. "Happily" the next morning, before he left camp, an order from the Secretary of War confirmed his deductions and left him free to choose his own "line of march"; and he quoted a sentence that told him to fall upon the enemy wherever he could find him, and with all speed.[2] But Frémont, who usually quoted dispatches in full, failed to quote the last sentence of Stanton's telegram: "You must not stop for supplies, but seize what you need and push rapidly forward; the object being to cut off and capture this rebel force in the Shenandoah." [3] Here the real mission was stated as clearly as it could have been, and the reason for going to Harrisonburg should have been unmistakable. Frémont made no acknowledgment of the receipt of this message, but there can be no doubt as to when it reached him in spite of what he wrote three years later. However, he had already made up his mind to change his march objective from the one place mentioned in his original order, so that the interpretation he put upon Stanton's telegram is unimportant. To the President, however, he sent the message: "Dispatch received. Our army will do the best to answer your expectations." The heading "On the march" must have made Lincoln believe that Frémont was already on the way to Harrisonburg, only thirty miles away. The rude awakening two days later is shown by a telegram sent by the President to the general at 9:58 P.M.: "I see that you are at Moorefield. You were expressly ordered to march to Harrisonburg. What does this mean?"

At six o'clock the next morning—May 28—Frémont had his reply on the way; and five hours later it was in Washington: His troops had not been in condition to execute the order received in any other way, many men having been reported by the chief surgeon as weak for want of food, and he had thought he was complying with what was broadly intended. He added:

In executing any order received I take it for granted that I am to exercise discretion concerning its literal execution, according to circumstances. If I am to understand that literal obedience to orders is required, please say so. I have no desire to exercise any power which you do not think belongs of necessity to my position in the field.[4]

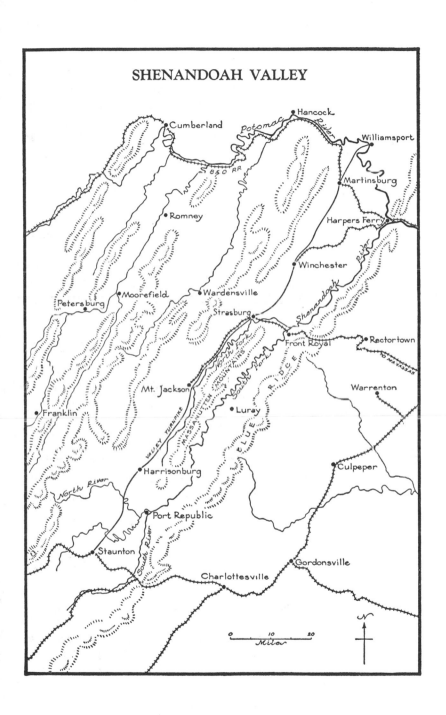

SHENANDOAH VALLEY

Frémont's use of the word "discretion" was a little bad for his case and showed that he had not learned too much from the court-martial that had once dismissed him from the army on three charges, including mutiny. The answer to his question was plainly written in the first sentence of Army Regulations of the time: "All inferiors are required to obey strictly . . ." Lincoln had told him to do this *and* that; Frémont had changed his instructions to read this *or* that. Realizing that his question gave the clear implication that he could have gone to Harrisonburg, he sent a longer dispatch a half-hour later, in which he amplified upon the state of supply of his command—which had in fact been bad—saying that his men had been saved from starvation only because he had marched to Petersburg, where five days' rations were found.[5]

Frémont's move had greatly lessened the chance that he could help in cutting off Jackson, for it was over twice as far to Strasburg as it was to Harrisonburg, and to be effective he would have to be there at least two whole days earlier. The merits of the place to which Lincoln had directed an intercepting force offset many disadvantages. It is altogether likely that he had reason to believe that the road to Harrisonburg was perfectly practicable; furthermore, a map that accompanied Jackson's report of the campaign showed the road to be of the same quality as other roads except the Valley Turnpike.[6] At 1:00 P.M. Stanton telegraphed Frémont that the President directed him to halt at Moorefield and await orders, unless he heard that the enemy was moving on Romney, in which case he should march there. When the directions to remain at Moorefield were received Frémont had already moved ten miles east of the town, and having become very literal-minded, he dutifully telegraphed his intention of returning to that place as soon as morning came. But at 7:00 a dispatch from Stanton indicated that the enemy was in the vicinity of Winchester and Charles Town, adding: "The President directs you to move upon him by the best route you can." Frémont's acknowledgment was in Stanton's hands at 11:00 P.M., but as his dispatch about returning to Moorefield had also arrived, another telegram went from Stanton to make certain that there was no misunderstanding of his order "to move against the enemy without delay."[7] After remarking casually to McDowell, "By the way, I suppose you know Frémont has got up to Moorefield instead of going to Harrisonburg,"[8] Lincoln telegraphed at noon the next day—the 29th—to Frémont:

General McDowell's advance, if not checked by the enemy, should, and probably will, be at Front Royal by 12 (noon) to-morrow. His force, when up, will be about 20,000. Please have your force at Strasburg, or, if the route you are moving on does not lead to that point, as near Strasburg as the enemy may be by the same time. Your dispatch No. 30 received and satisfactory.[9]

Just before noon on the 29th Washington had a message from Frémont stating that scouts and others put the enemy at from 30,000 to 60,000—an idea that Lincoln squelched immediately with a message that said there could not be more than 20,000, and probably not more than 15,000 of the enemy at or about Winchester. He added: "Where is your force? It ought this minute to be near Strasburg. Answer at once." Presently a shock came in the late arrival of a telegram that Frémont had sent the day before. After speaking of the bad marching condition of his command, he said he could not undertake to be at or near Strasburg until five o'clock on Saturday the 31st, but definitely he would be there then. At 2:30 the President replied: "Yours, saying you will reach Strasburg or vicinity at 5 P.M. Saturday, has been received and sent to General McDowell, and he directed to act in view of it. You must be up to time you promised, if possible." Then as if to speed the men over the hard mountain road Lincoln gave the information that the Confederates had evacuated the very important town of Corinth, Mississippi.[10]

McDowell's column was a little ahead of schedule, and at eleven o'clock (instead of the promised noon) on the 30th Brigadier General Nathan Kimball's brigade with four companies of Rhode Island cavalry retook Front Royal,[11] the defending Confederates departing for Winchester in a manner that Jackson described eleven months later, when his temper had cooled, as "hastily and improvidently."[12] The offending colonel was instantly put in arrest, though it is perfectly possible that he had received inadequate instructions. At the cost of eight horsemen killed and five wounded Kimball had achieved much. Not only were some Federals released from capture, but two locomotives, eleven cars, five wagons and teams, as well as much other equipment, were back in the possession of their rightful owners. A quick-witted Confederate captain fired some buildings, but the railroad bridge over the South Fork of the Shenandoah was forgotten—a fact that McDowell reported to Stanton the next day with justifiable satisfaction.[13] The Confederates had hoped for a rich harvest from Front Royal, and Jackson's chief quartermaster had sent directions to Staunton to send forward every possible wagon; but the vehicles were one day's march away when Kimball breezed into town. With melancholy thoughts of what might have been Major John A. Harman wrote ten months later, "With the preparations made as above, had our forces held possession of Front Royal forty-eight hours longer, all the captured property would have been secured, and taken to the rear." [14] At Kernstown, Shields had given Jackson a neat "come-on," only to slap him down the next day; at Front Royal he dealt out another surprise.

As things turned out Jackson would have been better advised to return in force to Front Royal after giving up his pursuit of the skillful and expeditious Banks, instead of moving to Harpers Ferry for some psychological warfare. Then he could have filled his depots; instead he helped fill Lincoln's army. The railroad from Front Royal through Strasburg to Mount Jackson was evidently interrupted, for no use was made of the engines and cars to haul off supplies, and Shields reported that there were no tools for railroad work.[15] Jackson had entertained the thought that Banks might move eastward—a fact that Henderson found hard to explain [16]—and so he may have damaged the railroad between Front Royal and Strasburg to his own disadvantage. In giving thanks for success up to the 26th inclusive and asking further favors from above [17] he evidently did not believe that the Federals might inopportunely appear in force at the very spot where he had surprised them.

Just when the rest of Shields's division closed on its leading brigade is not clear, but it is certain that he had no orders to go beyond Front Royal, and also certain that a railroad accident in Thoroughfare Gap had held up his supply for some hours.[18] In addition to this the great storm which on the 30th washed away some of McClellan's bridges and worried Joe Johnston struck furiously at the two Federal columns hastening toward Strasburg. At 4:40 the next morning Washington had a message from McDowell written after midnight at Rectortown, eighteen miles east of Front Royal, in which the general said, "The rainstorm, which continues violent, may delay us." [19] McDowell tried to look on the bright side of the situation by suggesting that the rain might be worse on the enemy, who had no railroad. But in this he was wrong, for on the afternoon of the 30th Jackson went to Winchester by train, after ordering his troops to retreat from their position in front of Harpers Ferry.[20] McDowell further reported that "the indefatigable Colonel Haupt" had already rebuilt two bridges destroyed by the Confederates and in spite of the rain he would have the line open to Front Royal by morning. Assistant Secretary of War P. H. Watson was on hand to see that all information was moving to the column commanders, and at 1:00 A.M. he telegraphed them that he was just back from Harpers Ferry.[21] For two days Jackson had been threatening the place, and deserters had brought the story that he had been promising his men less hard marching and better food as soon as they entered Maryland. But Watson seemed unimpressed.

The President's main concern that day probably centered about the telegrams that gave news of Johnston's attack upon McClellan at Fair Oaks. But he must have been constantly apprehensive of a message from Frémont, because there could be no doubt as to what the great storm had done to mountain streams. At 8:00 P.M. it came, headed Wardensville, but unfortunately with the hour of sending omitted: "Roads heavy and weather terrible. Heavy storm of rain most of yesterday and all last night." Frémont's cavalry was in sight of that of the enemy on the turnpike, and an engagement was expected; bravely he concluded, "The army is pushing forward and I intend to carry out operations proposed."[22]

So Lincoln went into June 1 anxiously awaiting news from two crucial places. He also had on his hands a somewhat critical Congress.[23] In the morning Frémont telegraphed that he was five miles from Strasburg, that he had been attacked but had a good defensive position, would do more than fight defensively if possible, and that there would probably be a general engagement in the afternoon. A dispatch at the end of the day showed that there had been no real battle: "State of rebels not known. I am now (6 o'clock) about driving in their pickets, and if that does not bring on a general engagement shall close with him early to-morrow morning." [24] Absence of information as to whether he was south or north of Strasburg was an unfortunate feature of his dispatch; but if the President had a good road map he could have feared the latter.

When Shields arrived at Front Royal he picked up the report that there were 20,000 to 40,000 Confederates in the Winchester area; [25] and it would indeed have been possible for troops to join Jackson by way of the turnpike. He also expressed to McDowell doubt as to whether Frémont would arrive on schedule, and urged that Ord be pushed forward as rapidly as possible. But he had to give a word of caution: Ord's division would have to bring supplies, or it would "starve."

Shields has been criticized, sometimes contemptuously, for his failure to push on to Strasburg on the 31st. Although it is not impossible that McDowell had left his division commander some latitude of action, he certainly had not ordered him to march at once to Strasburg. On the 31st McDowell's chief of staff, Lieutenant Colonel Ed. Schriver, sent Shields perhaps as fine a dispatch as any soldier ever put his name to. Schriver began by saying that the corps commander (McDowell) had received with the greatest satisfaction news of his "dash upon the enemy at Front Royal," and that the War Department likewise was much pleased; it was an opportune stroke that would be felt by the enemy and would be "inspiriting" to the Union troops. Then he gave the situation of all the other troops of the corps: Ord's entire division had spent the night five miles west of Rectortown; King's division, which McDowell had brought into the operation, was about to leave Catlett, his infantry by rail; Bayard's brigade of cavalry was at Thoroughfare Gap. Next: "Major-General Frémont telegraphed he will be at Strasburg by 5 o'clock P.M. today. Get your division well in hand to go forward to his support." Schriver closed his message with the big news from the West: Corinth had been evacuated.[26] Thus both the Federal columns had the "inspiriting" intelligence, sent by Lincoln to McDowell on the 30th.

McDowell had seen demonstrated at Bull Run the evils of piecemeal action, and he wanted Shields to have his division well in hand; even then he did not actually direct him to move to Strasburg, for he probably wanted a supporting division at hand.[27]

Shields's intimate knowledge of the country would have been sufficient to hold him back, unless he had received positive orders to proceed. The road to Strasburg, twelve miles away, was only a dirt road,[28] and it crossed the North Fork of the Shenandoah one mile east of the town. The river was high, and if the Confederates were using only ordinary caution they would have taken out not only the wagon bridge but the near-by railroad structure.[29] The ford two miles to the east was probably impractical for infantry, and besides it led straight into twisting Cedar Creek in such a way that troops advancing by it would be struck squarely on the flank by an enemy force coming from

Winchester. Shields had plenty of courage, but he was not a madman; and with his knowledge of the terrain he would have been mad indeed if he had ventured to march a division that day from Front Royal to Strasburg, unless he was positive that the column from the west—which could approach from a favorable direction—would be there promptly on the appointed hour.

Henderson's treatment of the crucial day can be questioned. He does not so much as inquire as to the orders Shields had received from McDowell, and incorrectly has him getting instructions directly from Lincoln and Stanton. Then, having said the President and Secretary of War had urged Shields to Front Royal, he accuses him of irresolution in not going to Strasburg,[30] only to end: "Even had he moved boldly on Strasburg he could hardly have seized the town. The ground was in Jackson's favour." Henderson's assertion that Stonewall had "blinded and bewildered Shields by the rapidity of his movements" is quite unfounded, and he could have saved himself much fine writing by reading the dispatch that Schriver sent to Shields on the 31st. The British soldier notes that there had been a rain, but he does not concede that it may have played a part in the failure of the Federal plans; nor does he observe that Jackson had the good turnpike while the Federals had poor roads. Each Union commander was undoubtedly uncertain of the movements of the other after the rain, knowing it had disarranged a close schedule; but it is going far indeed to claim, as Henderson does, that Jackson had counted precisely upon this uncertainty to save himself at the last minute. Jackson himself tells us about the prayers he pronounced on the 26th, so that it would seem to be at least as good a bet to say he was counting on a hard storm to slow the feet of the converging columns. Finally, it is bewildering to be told first that "the dread of encountering, unsupported, the terrible weight of Jackson's onset had sapped their resolution," and then be reminded presently that, on account of their victory at Kernstown, "neither general nor soldiers had reason to dread the name of Stonewall Jackson." [31]

McDowell personally reached Front Royal after dark on the 31st and was soon planning with Shields action for the next day when Ord's division—now commanded by Brigadier General James Ricketts because Ord was sick—should be up after its hard struggle with bad roads and the gap in the Blue Ridge.[32] The next morning, two of

Shields's officers brought word that the enemy had gone through Strasburg during the night and that his rear guard was passing as they left. Presently the sound of artillery floated in. It looked as if Frémont had arrived and there might be a chance to do something, and so McDowell sent Brigadier General George Bayard with his brigade of cavalry to Strasburg. An abler, braver brigadier was never sent to aid a friendly column or harass a hostile one. His brief report does not give the route he followed or how he crossed the river; [33] but instead of finding the expected chance to fall upon Jackson's trains protected by some cavalry, he found heavy masses of infantry, artillery, and cavalry occupying strong positions. This was nothing for his troopers to meddle with, and after some warning shells had been sent his way he withdrew across the river and put a strong protecting hold on the railroad bridge which Jackson had unaccountably left standing.

By 3:00 P.M. the telegraph had been repaired to within two miles of Front Royal and McDowell had information flowing to Secretary Stanton.[34] The firing that had been heard in the direction of Strasburg in the morning had ceased; Shields was moving toward that place with part of his command; Ricketts was up; though his division was quite broken down from its great exertion, the men were roused by the prospect of battle, and were going forward to support Bayard; the brigade Shields had sent northward the day before had encountered a hostile brigade with considerable cavalry and four guns, had driven them back toward Winchester until after darkness fell, had made some captures of men and equipment, and had released some Federal prisoners.[35] Elzey had been identified by Shields as being with Jackson in addition to Ewell and Ed. Johnson. All this was very positive and encouraging information for Washington but the statement, "Frémont's forces have not yet made their appearance" may have given trouble in interpreting.

Presently the situation became more confused for McDowell; the cannonading he had heard came from north of Strasburg; he thought they were not Frémont's guns, but those of Banks—who was indeed back in the campaign with a small force in the role of pursuer instead of pursued.[36] Realizing that Jackson had made good his escape, McDowell sent four guns to Bayard and ordered him to pursue by the turnpike while he sent Shields southward through Luray as an intercepting force. In taking such quick action the general was exercising a good deal of boldness of decision; but he counted upon Washington's approval and Shields's knowledge of the country. The budget of important information could not go by wire, for the telegraph had ceased to work; the message was forwarded by courier to Rectortown, but did not reach Washington until 10:45 the next night, June 2.[37]

Dispatches from Frémont likewise had to be carried a long distance before they could be telegraphed; but before the delayed message from McDowell was at hand Lincoln doubtless had received one headed, "Strasburg, June 1, via Moorefield, June 2, 1862," which combined in a curious manner bad news with a touch of humor:

> A reconnoitering force just in reports the enemy retreating, but in which direction is not yet known. Our cavalry will occupy Strasburg by midnight. Terrible storm of thunder and hail now passing over. Hailstones as large as hens' eggs.[38]

As an explorer Frémont had been in many places and had seen many things; but the hailstones that afternoon were a novelty even to his eyes. In his lyrical account of Jackson's escape, Henderson recalls a great biblical scene by asserting, "The waters had been held back and the Confederates had passed through them dry-shod." The statement is bewildering because Henderson has previously cast Jackson in the part of Pharaoh over whose "chariots the waters were already closing." [39] Stonewall of course had the baffling habit of disappearing at one place and popping up at another, and so the British colonel may have felt it fitting to have him walk off the stage as the king of the Egyptians and come back presently as the great leader of the fleeing Israelites. Since the Confederate accounts say nothing about hailstones, the imaginative Henderson certainly missed a chance to do something really grand with the seeming meteorological favoritism of that historic day.

On the 2nd Frémont sent a longer message saying that Bayard had joined him. It went by way of Front Royal, and McDowell added the postscript, "General Shields, who advanced for Luray last night, has his whole division on the march to try and intercept Jackson up the valley." (Ricketts's division and the part of King's that had arrived were held at Front Royal.) Confirmation of their action was not long in coming to Frémont and McDowell from the Secretary, who telegraphed:

> Your dispatches received. We are glad to hear you are so close on the enemy. McClellan beat the rebels badly near Richmond yesterday. The

President tells me to say to you do not let the enemy escape from you. Major-General Siegel is advancing with two brigades from Harper's Ferry toward Winchester. Let us hear from you often.[40]

There was not even so much as a hint of disappointment at the failure of the operation upon which so much had been staked. Doubtless Lincoln and Stanton knew that the great storm was largely responsible for the attempt at interception being turned into a pursuit. Just as Henderson repents and has the Yankees entirely unawed by Stonewall Jackson, so too he deflates his account of Jackson's escape by asserting that it "loses something of its extraordinary character" when one notes "the embarrassments under which the Federals laboured" [41]—perhaps a belated recognition of the hailstones. Materials are probably insufficient to afford a basis for sound judgment of Frémont's actions on June 1, though there is no reason to believe that they were what the occasion called for.

Write often Frémont did, and at 6:00 P.M. of the 2nd he sent a long dispatch from near Woodstock—ten miles south of Strasburg—in which he said the woods were full of Confederate stragglers. "Clothing, blankets, muskets, and sabers are strewn also upon the road." [42] It would seem that Jackson was moving a bit "hastily and improvidently."

Though there may be some uncertainty about General Hail, General Rain was again on the side of Stonewall. Heavy roads not only slowed Shields but compelled him to seize two mills, purchase wheat, and grind flour.[43] All the bridges over the brimming South Fork of the Shenandoah were found destroyed, and beyond the uncrossable river there was the additional barrier of the rugged Massanuttens, crossed only at rare intervals and that by poor roads; thus contact with the right column was lost. Though Frémont had the turnpike, Jackson was destroying bridges, and the North Fork of the Shenandoah at Mount Jackson was found in flood. Through forehandedness on the general's part and great labor by his troops while crossing the mountains, a pontoon train was well to the front in his column, but even with it the crossing of the raging stream was difficult,[44] and Jackson had the chance to put a whole day more between himself and his pursuers. What with the flooding rain between Moorefield and Strasburg, the record-breaking hailstones on June 1 that apparently did not hit his enemy, and the river at Mount Jackson rising twelve feet in four hours, the old explorer must have thought that the life of rectitude of his enemy had really lined up the elements on his side. Heroically the two columns of Union troops drove on, each with a faith that the other would persevere.

General Banks was closing up in spite of great difficulties, and he sent messages to Washington from Winchester on the 5th.[45] The Potomac was still impassable at Williamsport for men, horses, and wagons, but one of his brigades was across. Although he probably knew how hard railroaders and soldiers were struggling to preserve the bridge at Harpers Ferry, he was concerned about it. The rails to Winchester from the old ferry town were out of operation and two days later the great bridge was to go in the wash of water, just as its predecessor had gone only six weeks before. Supplies were short, and Banks was having houses searched for stores secreted by Jackson's men. It must have been most distasteful indeed to the people of Winchester to have a Yankee like Banks—a former Speaker of the House and Governor of Massachusetts—prying into their pantries and opening their cupboards in order to replevin the groceries taken from his wagons during his late passage through their town. Probably they reproached Mr. Lincoln for sending a person with such antecedents and record to occupy the Valley, instead of some politically unobjectionable regular officer, forgetting that the President had been left short of regulars after so many prominent ones had "gone over."

Though in addition to his distinguished political career, Banks had had a few months' experience as president of the Illinois Central Railroad, soldiering was new. In Jackson, however, he had an excellent teacher and he was rapidly acquiring knowledge and experience. In addition to indicating that he was recovering his flour and bacon, the general passed on to Washington the news that many men who had been captured from him had escaped from the Confederates at Mount Jackson. Certainly no one could have had more comprehending sympathy for Jackson because of the dither in which the changing fortunes of war had placed him than Nathaniel Prentiss Banks. He revealed this when he wrote in his dispatch to Stanton, "Frémont pursuit close and Jackson much excited." Well might he have added, "And I can assure that I know just how Old Jack feels." Then Lincoln could have derived not only much satisfaction from his telegram but a good chuckle as well.

When Frémont reached Harrisonburg he had covered one hundred twenty miles instead of the thirty that separated Franklin from that point; and he was still behind and not in front of Jackson as he would have been if he had marched directly there. Not far below the town contact was gained with the Confederate rear guard on June 6, and the engagement was a costly one for the Confederates, for the bold leader of cavalry, Brigadier General Turner Ashby, was killed by Frémont's troopers—a loss that Jackson took personally much to heart. The next day the Federal commander reported that the enemy was continuing to leave "wagon loads of blankets, clothing, and other equipments" asserting that they were "piled up in all directions." Frémont knew of his opponent's death, but he showed no jubilation and only respect when he reported it: "General Ashby, who covered the retreat with his whole cavalry force and three regiments of infantry and who exhibited admirable skill and audacity, was among the killed." [46] Two days later the Federal column came up with Ewell's division in position at Cross Keys while the balance of the Confederate command was some four miles away near Port Republic waiting for the advance of Shields.

Stonewall himself spent the night of Saturday June 7 in deserved comfort in the little town at the junction of North River and South River that combine at that place to form the South Fork of the Shenandoah. At 6:00 A.M. of the 8th, Colonel S. S. Carroll, commanding Shields's leading brigade, riding in advance with some 150 troopers and four guns, came within sight of the Confederate trains and lush beef cattle on the north bank of the North River.[47] Quickly posting two guns to cover the bridge that crossed the North Fork and that carried the road from Port Republic to Harrisonburg, Carroll took his troopers and remaining guns through two fords in the South River and squarely into the little town, scattering some much surprised Southern horsemen. First-rate booty quickly fell to the Federals in the form of two of Jackson's staff officers, including a colonel, while the general himself, after mounting a horse with unusual alacrity, narrowly escaped across the bridge to the camp of his army.[48] His total failure to have a covering force east of Port Republic, in spite of the fact that he knew of the approach of the column under Shields, must be put down as a black mark—a very black mark—against Thomas Jonathan Jackson. One wonders if there was any more glaring neglect of obvious security measures in the entire war. Of course it was Sunday; but Jackson did not consider the Yankees as a specially religious people and, having found Shields a good fighter at Kernstown on Monday, he had no reason to believe that the Federal commander's men would not be in their saddles bright and early on a nice June Sunday. Then, too, even generals when in the field often do not know what day of the week it is.

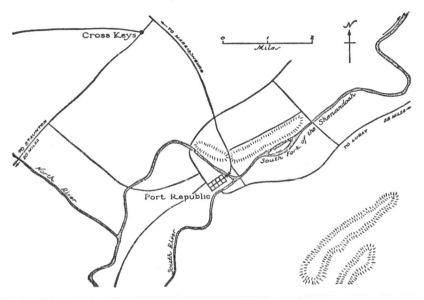

VICINITY OF PORT REPUBLIC

But personal escape from the clutches of blue-clad troopers and escape of his ordnance train were not the only pieces of luck that Jackson had in that early Sunday hour. Carroll—who was to fight skillfully the next day, and who later distinguished himself at Fredericksburg and Gettysburg—thought badly. He gave his attention to devising ways to hold the town until his infantry arrived, but failed to have a big roaring fire built upon the bridge. With the bridge out and the North River in flood Jackson would have had to conduct the concluding phase of his operation very differently than he did. Inability, however, to cross the river at Port Republic would not have put him in jeopardy, for although the North River separated him from Staunton there was apparently a bridge over it, so that he could have continued his retirement to his base. What he would actually have chosen to do cannot of course even be conjectured.

Carroll held Port Republic upwards of an hour; then Confederate infantry drove the cannoneers away from the gun that he had placed near the bridge, crossed over the structure, scattered the blue troopers, liberated Jackson's chagrined and swordless chief of artillery and his fellow staff member, made it safe for the gray troopers to come back into town, and turned the tables by capturing Carroll's two guns. Then well placed batteries drove the two guns away from the position on the hill and turned back Carroll's infantry when it appeared, the Federal commander retiring about three miles north of town where he was joined in the afternoon by the brigade of General E. B. Tyler.[49] Such a Sunday morning Port Republic had never known, and Jackson soon had a brigade of infantry guarding the fords that the irreverent Yankees had found and dashed across in such an unbecoming manner.

It being Sunday, Jackson would doubtless have been willing to call it a day and give his command a third day of rest, while he concocted blows to deal his enemies on the morrow. But Frémont pressed the issue at Cross Keys. In his report the Federal general stated that he had no more than 10,500 men in hand, and that his lowest estimate of Jackson was 18,000 men.[50] Ewell was in a good position which he had had time to study and organize for defense, and Jackson's whole command was within easy supporting distance. Frémont's attack does not appear to have been vigorous enough to reveal how large a force the enemy actually had deployed, and Jackson's biographers have also apparently not been able to uncover the figure. Ewell did so well that Stonewall was able to stay away from the battlefield and give his attention to thoughts for Monday. Lincoln wired his thanks to Frémont, his officers and men for their "gallant battle," [51] a tribute not too strong for men who had recently been hungry, and who had marched many miles and had come upon a rested enemy well posted.

Unquestionably Jackson had a heavy account to settle with Shields, what with the surprise at Front Royal and the fresh indignity; so, bringing Ewell to him and carefully burning the bridge so as to keep Frémont at a distance, he attacked Tyler and Carroll on the 9th. The Union defense was far more remarkable than that of Ewell the day before, for the attack of a Jackson was not the same thing as the attack of a Frémont. Stonewall was goaded badly by fierce counterattacks of the Federals that drove his men back, and he had to throw in troops until he had nearly three to one. After four hours of such stubborn fighting Tyler had the two brigades retire upon a strong position that had been taken by the two remaining brigades of the division, which Shields in person had brought forward. The latter wrote that Jackson feared to attack him and fell back at once.[52] The Confederate commander was not with his pursuing force, and his report,[53] written the next April, tells neither when nor why the pursuit was stopped. He may or may not have known that the whole of Shields's division was now before him. But he did know that he had plenty of wounds to lick. After noting that the Federals who had been in action totaled only 3,000 men and sixteen guns, Freeman says, "A close action this Battle of Port Republic had been, and a costly!" [54]

On the 8th Frémont had received from one of his scouts a note written by Shields at Luray at 9:30 that morning, and he had thus finally learned of the pending operations of the eastern column. Shields had received a report that the bridge at Port Republic had already been destroyed, and, referring to the enemy, he said: "If he attempts to force a passage, as my force is not large there yet, I hope you will thunder down on his rear. Please send back information from time to time. I think Jackson is caught this time." Finding the enemy gone from his front on the 9th, Frémont advanced; but clouds of smoke in the distance soon told him the bridge was burning, and so there could be no "thundering down" upon Jackson's rear.[55] Accordingly he took a position during the afternoon on the bank of the South Fork of the Shenandoah some two miles above Port Republic.

At last the two Union forces that had been put in motion fifteen days before were separated only by a river; and a ferry made contact possible. But now the story becomes a little uncertain because Shields was a character. A veteran of the Black Hawk War and a brigadier in the Mexican War, he had also been a senator from both Illinois and Minnesota—with a senatorship from Missouri still in the future. No one without eloquence and the ability to gild the facts could ever have established such a political record.[56] He wrote to Colonel Schriver on the afternoon of the 10th: "General Frémont and myself were projecting a combined attack upon the enemy this morning, which in all probability must have destroyed him, when peremptory orders reached me, which I did not feel at liberty to disobey." [57] The order in question was to return to Luray at once. A report Shields wrote on the 13th stated that on the evening of the 9th he was actually concerting with Frémont an attack on Jackson for the next morning, he to strike in front, while Frémont crossed the river on his pontoon bridge and took the enemy in the flank. A more restrained report written later in the month indicated that Shields had merely sent a message to Frémont proposing the joint attack.[58] When the order to return to Luray was received he recalled his messenger and informed Frémont of his new order. This version is more in accord with that of Frémont,[59] who received orders to take a defensive position at Harrisonburg, "guarding against a movement of the enemy either back toward Strasburg or toward Franklin," pending further instructions.[60]

Shields, the native of Tyrone County, Ireland, whom Illinois later chose to honor in the National Statuary Hall, was still belligerent on the 12th when he wrote, in a long note to Frémont, "I never obeyed an order with such reluctance, but no option was left me"[61]—an assertion he repeated the next day in his first report. Though angry about the past he was also thinking of future battles, and on the 10th he sent in a long list of what he needed to refit his overworked division for the field.[62] On the 12th he told Colonel Schriver, "I find that half my command are barefoot and foot-sore. Hard bread and salt are indispensable to take us to Catlett's."[63] Then his pride burst forth in the assertion, "Our men fought like devils." He added that the enemy had suffered terribly, and that the odds were overwhelming.

What caused the recall of Shields and Frémont when at last they had joined hands and were in contact with Jackson, though north instead of south of him? In a general way it can be said that it was due to uncertainty in the minds of Lincoln and McDowell about the situation at Cross Keys and Port Republic. McDowell had gone to Washington, leaving his chief of staff, Colonel Ed. Schriver, at Front Royal, and through him messages passed to and from the field commanders. Shields's division looked out of hand, contrary to McDowell's explicit instructions for him to keep his four brigades within close supporting distance of one another.[64] The difficulty of the roads and his state of supply had helped cause dispersion, while the report that the bridge at Port Republic was out had led him to send a brigade forward to that point,[65] in order to make immediate use of a favorable opportunity, following it as quickly as possible with another. President Lincoln knew that Shields was a fighter, and that not only from the military record. James Shields was indeed the very man who twenty years before had almost challenged him to a duel—the duel for which he had specified cavalry broadswords at twelve feet distance, in case a meeting could not be avoided.[66] Recollection of his general's brashness may have occurred to the President as he saw on his map one brigade pushed forward, followed at some distance by another, while the other half of the division was still at Luray. If Carroll had burned the bridge, everything would have been as the eager commander expected; but in the end the brigades were defeated just as Washington feared. Believing that all chance to damage Jackson had vanished, Lincoln ordered the withdrawal,[67] with the intention of sending McDowell's corps with all possible speed to reenforce McClellan in accordance with his previous plan.

In the liquidating of the campaign there is much of interest, and only a little will be noted to show the watchfulness of Stanton in minor details. On June 20 he wired Schriver at Manassas, "Please inform me what is the condition of General McDowell this morning." [68] Equipment quite as much as the health of his generals was in the mind of the man who had once recovered for the government California land worth $150,000,000; [69] and on the 22nd he telegraphed McDowell that he had learned that fifty miles of telegraph wire had been abandoned in the recent operations. After intimating that the enemy would appropriate it, he said, "I think some effort should be made to get it." [70] The general may have wondered how Stanton picked up such curious bits of information, but he certainly had no ground for complaining of harshness in the tone of the man who had so solicitously inquired about him two days before. If it had been one mile of wire and not fifty that had been left for the Confederates, it would have hurt Stanton, for he liked neither the enemies of his country nor wastefulness of its property.

It is not strange that Stanton kept no diary; he worked too much.

A great deal has been made of the panic created in the North by Jackson's descent in the Valley and Banks's hasty retreat from Strasburg to the left bank of the Potomac. Freeman states that the panic in Washington has not been exaggerated by the biographers of Jackson, but he deflates its duration by quoting effectively from several Northern papers.[71] Even the initial panic is hard to gauge with accuracy. Publishers, then as now, liked to sell their papers, and some of the largest and best known Northern papers were not supporting the war and tended to magnify all Northern reverses. How much of the news leaked out on Saturday May 24 cannot be told; but there were not many Sunday papers at the time,[72] and word of the attack on Front

Royal may not have been generally published until accurate accounts were available. A Washington dispatch of that Saturday, appearing in the *New York Tribune* on Monday, stated that the enemy was at Front Royal, and that Banks had moved to Winchester to protect his trains and would immediately return to Strasburg. A dispatch from Baltimore indicated that the First Maryland was largely from that city and added, "The friends and relatives of the men are stung to madness by the exultings of Rebel sympathizers." Dispatches dated Sunday continued the account of the violent reaction in Baltimore against Secessionists who congregated "at the corners, with radiant faces and words of rejoicing." Not a few of the Southern sympathizers had to be rescued by the police. All this news appeared on Monday in a paper that also carried Banks's first official report from Martinsburg, putting the number of the enemy correctly at 15,000 and saying that his own trains were in advance and would cross the river safely, that only two brigades had been engaged, and that "our loss was considerable, as was that of the enemy, but cannot now be stated." The whole story had modest headlines, and not even the first place on the page. There was nothing in the account to cause any alarm whatever, and the paper the next day gave the general's telegram to Stanton from Williamsport that his men were in fine spirits, ending, "Your dispatch read to the troops this morning amid the heartiest cheers." [73] Banks's report that he had lost only 50 out of 500 wagons should have done much to quiet fears about any disaster. Henderson's statements that "terror had taken possession of the nation" and that "in the cities of the North the panic was indescribable" seem made out of almost nothing—except perhaps a perversion of what took place in Baltimore.[74]

On the 25th Stanton sent a telegram to the governors of thirteen states that must have interfered greatly with Sunday habits: "Intelligence from various quarters leaves no doubt that the enemy in great force are advancing on Washington. You will please organize and forward immediately all the volunteer and militia force of your State." Part of the "intelligence" referred to was of course the report of the 24th from General Wool at Fort Monroe, so that the incident at Front Royal was by no means alone responsible for Stanton's disturbing the governors. A more alarming dispatch was sent to the governors of Pennsylvania, Massachusetts, and Rhode Island: "Send all the troops forward that you can immediately. Banks is completely routed. The enemy are in large force advancing upon Harper's Ferry." To

Governor Morgan of New York a special message went: "Send all the troops you can, and quickly. All the information from every source indicates a concentration of rebel power in this direction. Send the Seventh Regiment immediately." It looks as if the Secretary were really alarmed, though he may have touched things up in order to be sure the governors would not let war matters wait while they went to church and sat down calmly to good gubernatorial dinners in the state mansions. To expedite the movement of troops the railroads were taken over in accordance with a stand-by law that had been passed by Congress. Better news was passed on by Stanton as it came in from Banks in the course of the day; and on the 27th releasing of the militia began, and all the governors were instructed to accept nothing but three-year men in any regiments that were formed.[75] Calling out the militia and thirty-day volunteers was certainly an extreme measure, and it is not strange that the action has led to condemnation by those especially critical of Stanton.

The "incident" was used to resume the recruiting unwisely stopped two months before, and on May 30 Stanton telegraphed to seventeen governors, saying that 50,000 three-year men would be accepted. Ohio's new governor—David Tod—at once reported that he believed he could raise five new regiments within sixty days, and he queried, "Shall I attempt it?" Still on the 30th Stanton gave him the green light and added, "We want to finish this war at once." [76] The touch of boastfulness was stimulated by the news of the evacuation of Corinth by Beauregard that had just been telegraphed by General Halleck, and the happy Secretary broke it in his telegram to Governor Tod. Henderson's statement that 500,000 men offered themselves in one day "to save the Union" [77] is preposterous; as a soldier he knew that one should count only those who appeared before recruiting officers and signed oaths, or gave dependable proof of such intention. But there was real earnestness, and on May 31 Tod telegraphed that he already had about 1,500 men in camp and would have 5,000 by June 10—fifty days before his promised time. Following through, Stanton on June 5 issued an order that began, "A camp of instruction for 50,000 men—cavalry, artillery, and infantry, in due proportions— will be immediately formed near Annapolis." The training was entrusted to an officer of unrivaled competence, Major General Wool, who was brought to command at Baltimore; and Major General John A. Dix went thence to Fort Monroe. Such a camp would rival any single installation the United States had for either of the world wars, and Henderson leaves his reader believing that 50,000 men were kept "stationed permanently near the capital," though he well knew that this was not done. The next day Stanton directed that all the old recruiting offices be reopened.[78]

Though Freeman cuts down the story of the panic to a more just size, he takes an unwarranted jab at Stanton: "The Secretary had another attack of nerves on the 29th, lest Jackson advance on Washington." [79] The reference cited is Stanton's dispatch to McDowell asking if it were possible for the enemy to cross the Potomac below Harpers Ferry; this, he said, if in force would endanger Washington. He explained, "General Meigs suggests this latter contingency, and thinks the safety of the city requires an increase of its garrison." With his customary foresight and efficiency Stanton ordered transportation to be sent to Aquia Creek for bringing to the capital a part of King's division; but he left the decision to McDowell, who, having a good grasp of the situation, sent no men whatever and was very careful to explain to Shields that Stanton had made the suggestion "at the instance of General Meigs." [80] There was nothing whatever of "nerves" in the incident, only prudence and good administration of a type that we are now in a position to appreciate and admire.

Upon his operation in the period May 20 to June 10 much of Stonewall Jackson's fame is built; and no one who is proud of American soldiers would desire to lessen renown for courageous leadership as well deserved as his. But the reputation of one American general should certainly not be built on depreciation or distortion of the accomplishments of others. What Jackson achieved during those tense days, notable though it was, was not as great either in interest or in military instructiveness as the records of the Federals. Jackson was operating almost entirely upon his own responsibility, and there are not many written orders for the military student to ponder; but there are many pages of important Federal dispatches. Most of the time we know what the Federal commanders were thinking from what they themselves wrote; the story for the Confederates must be built largely out of secondary sources, which, accurate though they may be, lack the stirring quality of the messages between Washington and the field commanders and between the generals themselves. In this narrative the dispatches between the High Command and Frémont and Mc-

Dowell appear only in part; and it uses only a very few of the messages to and from Banks, which fill several pages of the Official Records. Entirely unused are those to and from Brigadier General Rufus Saxton at Harpers Ferry.

If Jackson is lauded for so neatly capturing 700 Federals at Front Royal with his column of 16,000, what should we say of the exploit of Colonel Carroll with his 150 troopers and four guns? Surely in the entire campaign there was no bolder action than his riding through the fords and into Port Republic. He did not know that Jackson himself was in the town, and if he did not capture the Confederate general it is also to be remembered that Jackson did not do the extensive damage to Banks he had hoped to do. A newsreel of Ashby's troopers riding in among the wagons of Banks's fleeing train while the drivers sought safety in flight would certainly give hilarious entertainment; but the sight of the great Stonewall Jackson coming hastily out of a house, mounting a horse, and galloping to the river bridge would not be exactly dull. Excellent as was the marching of Jackson's men back down the turnpike to escape the closing trap—especially that of General Winder's rear guard—it cannot stir the admiration as much as the road record of the Federals. Shields had more to contend with in mud between Front Royal and Port Republic, and Frémont more in the mountains between Moorefield and Strasburg, than Jackson had after he left Front Royal. But the really unbelievable marching exploit was that of Captain H. T. Collis and a small group who formed part of Banks's bodyguard. Cut off three times in his effort to reach Winchester, Collis turned westward with twenty-three exhausted men in wagons and fifty soldiers from various regiments and reached Hancock, Maryland, on the 26th at 2:00 P.M., reporting the next day to General Banks at Williamsport. On the 28th he wrote, in a detailed account of his adventures, "Incredible, General, as it may appear, my men marched 141 miles in forty-seven hours, as measured by Captain Abert." [81] Incredible it was, and the captain was worthy of the highest praise for skill and steadfast devotion to duty. To the general who inspired a subordinate with the desire to get back and stand before him in salute in the proud manner of a soldier, much credit too is due.

One must admire the two Federal columns that turned southward swiftly after their attempt at interception had failed, and did so in spite of the difficult country: the Shenandoah dividing into two intervening streams, both now flooded, while mountains suddenly interposed as if they had waited ages upon ages just for this occasion. Nor should we forget that McDowell threw his well led cavalry brigade and four guns to Frémont's pursuing column so as to make sure that there could be harassing contact with the enemy, while he strove to put Shields's toughened infantry ahead of the Confederates. Frémont too brought to the front of his column his pontoon train. Those were little points, but they are precisely the sort of incidents that give the Federal operation its great instructiveness. Then there is the final coming together of the two columns—except for a single intervening river—sixty miles below, after a week without contact.

In fighting as well as marching there is no question where the wreath belongs. It goes to the brigades of Tyler and Carroll—four infantry regiments from Ohio, two from Pennsylvania, one from West Virginia, two Ohio batteries, and one regular battery [82]—which for four hours maintained an unequal contest in such a manner that Confederate officers after the war could hardly believe their old antagonists when they told them that only half of Shields's division had been in the actions that day.[83] To some Union men it looked as if the fight had been unnecessary and to no purpose; and Shields himself blamed Tyler severely for accepting battle.[84] But it is hard to criticize a general who had been pushed forward on an intercepting mission and whose instinct was to stand his ground and fight, when he knew supporting troops were coming and when there was no danger that he would be cut off. Tyler's error—if error it was—was on the right side for a fighting man; and perhaps recollection of his experience on June 9 caused Jackson to hesitate on a fateful day later in the month.

There is instructiveness in the requisition that Shields sent forward on the first day of his return march, giving in detail what his needs were, and asking that they be put down where he could pick them up and have his division ready for the field once more. He said not a word about the necessity for rest; while with regard to McDowell's criticism that he had let his command get out of hand, he commented, "My greatest fault has been that I have not calculated upon the effect of sudden rain in this narrow valley." [85] Not always do generals make such prompt examination of their actions or write in the record so frank an intimation of possible mistakes.

The manner in which water and rail transportation were combined with marching in moving McDowell's troops was admirable. The spirit of a "blitz" was in the words "celerity and vigor" that Lincoln telegraphed to McDowell on the evening of May 24, and it haunted a dispatch he sent four days later: "I think the evidence now preponderates that Ewell and Jackson are still about Winchester. Assuming this, it is for you a question of legs. Put in all the speed you can." It was indeed an injunction that would arouse a high-minded officer, and presently McDowell telegraphed to Shields—who had then reached Rectortown—that the President was urging them to push after the enemy with all speed. Then, showing a preference for the vernacular of Lincoln over the learned French military terms he knew so well, McDowell said, "The question now seems to be one of legs— whether we can get to Jackson and Ewell before they can get away." [86] Already on the same day McDowell had shown how whole-heartedly he was working on the operation of which he had disapproved by writing to Shields, "We must not disappont the expectations of the President, if extraordinary exertions will enable us to fulfill them." The words reveal not only the character of the soldier in the field, but give a measure of the man in the White House.

The communication between Washington and the two columns was nothing less than remarkable. If the telegraph from Front Royal went out on June 1 with the result that an important message had to go back to Rectortown by mounted courier, it can be recalled that there have been comparable occurrences even with the highly perfected methods and instruments of the present day. Lincoln's scheme of command, with McDowell called back to Washington and Schriver operating a forward command post at Front Royal, was a happy one, and was at least as good as the Germans used in the opening phases of World War I. When their Supreme Headquarters—far to the rear at Coblenz—had a confused idea of the situation of the armies on the Marne, especially of the First and Second on the right flank, just east of Paris, a lieutenant colonel was dispatched to the front with authority to make decisions and issue orders even to generals commanding armies—an incredible procedure. So mixed up was the question of command that a court of inquiry could not decide beyond all possibility of doubt who ordered what or when.[87] Before Shields received his mandatory withdrawal order on June 9 a discretionary order had been sent, written by Schriver but carefully based upon instructions from McDowell; [88] but the final decision that Shields should return to Luray was made by Lincoln, not by an officer of low rank. To make certain that Frémont's order reached him, Schriver was instructed to send a copy direct through Strasburg and a duplicate to Shields for transmittal; more than that, a good "pilot" message was sent by McDowell to Schriver explaining what would soon come over the wire, and directing him to have commissioned officers ready to act as couriers on the long hard rides.[89] Who handled a difficult problem of command best—Moltke and his staff, or Lincoln, McDowell, and Schriver?

There is no question whatever that Lincoln made a blunder in the first order that went to Frémont. Whether he actually wrote it is uncertain, for it was not common for him to use the third person in his messages; but the signature was his, and so it was his order and he was responsible. The President should have told Frémont what had happened, directed him to march to Harrisonburg, told him to keep open communications with Washington through Franklin, but said not a word about relief to Banks—bad as was the predicament in which that general seemed to be. But criticism even of this blunder should not be too severe, for Lincoln definitely told Frémont to go to Harrisonburg. Furthermore he followed through well, carefully reading the messages that came from Frémont; thus he quickly detected the error that had been made and asked for an explanation. Very able professionals have sometimes failed to read with care important dispatches from their subordinates, even at critical times. Lincoln also made a mistake when he directed Frémont to halt at Moorefield on May 28, for there was little chance that Jackson would go to Romney, although he had made a famous march to that place early in the year. But no time was actually lost on account of the blunder, and great care was taken to get the order countermanded; thus the incident in the end gives another demonstration of good command.

Great distortions of the Federal operations began promptly after the war and have continued to the present day. In his well known work published in 1866 Robert L. Dabney, the theological professor who was a member of Jackson's staff, put into the record inaccuracies that have not yet been thoroughly expunged. In a summary of the May and June operations of Jackson, he said that McDowell's corps "was rendered inactive at Fredericksburg by the fear of his prowess." [90] Although the Official Records had not been published there was not an excuse for the statement. Too much enthusiasm also colors the contention of Freeman. He concludes a chapter that brings Stonewall up to the evening of May 29 with the stirring sentences: "McDowell was immobilized. That was Jackson's reward." [91] At that very moment three of McDowell's divisions were closing on Front Royal. The next morning Shields would seize the town from the Confederate garrison, and in the evening Jackson would start somewhat hastily down the turnpike to escape the "immobilized" McDowell.

There is much to support General Ballard's contention that Lincoln would not have stopped the march of McDowell to Richmond if the operations there had been in the hands of a Grant, a Sherman, or a Sheridan. But it is not necessary to excuse or apologize for Lincoln's action, because his effort to cut off and destroy Jackson was the first case of inspired warfare by the Federals in Virginia since Lew Wallace had made his sudden descent upon Romney and thereby jerked Joe Johnston out of Harpers Ferry. No one carried a heavier role in the great drama than James Shields. And this man who had once been highly offended over a political attack upon him that Lincoln had published in a paper wrote, while the marches, the rain, the uncertainty, the exertions, and the battle of Port Republic were fresh in his mind, "The plan for Jackson's destruction was perfect." [92] If Lincoln's keen strategic insight picked Harrisonburg as the proper place for Frémont, so it was his spirit and his drive that animated the divisions of McDowell: "It is for you a question of legs. Put in all the speed you can."

CHAPTER VIII

FLIGHT ACROSS THE SWAMPS

I shall do my best to save the army. Send more gunboats.
McClellan to Stanton

On June 6 McClellan learned that Johnston had been wounded and Smith had taken over his command; [1] but it is not clear when he discovered that Lee had at once taken over from Smith at the explicit order of President Davis. Lee was still under a cloud, because of his failure to regain West Virginia the previous fall. Davis, however, had retained faith in him, and his influence had been constant since the middle of March, when he had come to Richmond to be high military adviser to the President. The army of which Lee now assumed field command had recently received the designation Army of Northern Virginia; much larger than the old Confederate Army of the Potomac, it was not divided into corps as that army had been the previous summer, though without the authority of law. Lee's failure in West Virginia had affected the high opinion of him originally held in the North as well as in the South, and *Harper's Weekly* remarked on April 26: "Joseph Johnston is reputed a good soldier. Lee certainly is not." [2] The editor would shortly have the chance to reverse himself; but that would not be difficult for a man who had predicted an imminent advance by McClellan the preceding October.

Lincoln and Stanton of course knew that only half of McClellan's men had been engaged in the battle of Fair Oaks; and they were discerning enough to realize that a Confederate repulse could have been turned into a telling Union victory by a resolute general who would throw his full power into a contest. But they continued their efforts to give him more men, while still hoping for returns from the operation against Jackson. At 8:30 P.M. on the 5th Stanton telegraphed McClellan that five new regiments were going forward as fast as possible, the first to leave Baltimore the next day. They had orders to debark at Fort Monroe, and the Secretary said, "Please advise me if this be as you desire." [3] The next day McDowell, at Front Royal, was told to have McCall's division sent to McClellan at once by water from Fredericksburg. As usual there was efficiency. Meigs was sending transportation down from Washington and had directed Fort Monroe to forward shipping for the rest of the strong division of 10,000 men and five light batteries. While attending to such matters Stanton also found time to get off a brief but important dispatch that may have wounded the sensitive general on the Chickahominy: "Officers of your army, some of high rank, are sending details to their wives and friends, by telegraph, of the late disasters, in respect to the number killed and wounded." [4] There was no censorship of mail, but over the telegraph line from his position McClellan had easy and complete control.

Much more soothing was a telegram that came on the 7th announcing that either McCall's or King's division would be sent, depending on which could be moved first. Later in the day a message stated that four regiments had embarked the day before at Baltimore and one at Washington, while one more was to go on the 7th from each city. [5] Quite as if he doubted McClellan's ability to do simple sums, the Secretary gave him the total, seven regiments; and he added, "McCall is ready to move as soon as transportation arrives at Fredericksburg." However, the most notable sentence in the telegram was the concluding one: "Please state whether you will feel sufficiently strong for your final movement when McCall reaches you." It was indeed a direct question; and almost as unequivocal were the pertinent statements that the general made in a reply dispatched at 4:40:

I am glad to learn that you are pressing forward re-enforcements so vigorously. I shall be in perfect readiness to move forward and take Richmond the moment McCall reaches here and the ground will admit the passage of artillery. I have advanced my pickets about a mile to-day, driving off the rebel pickets and securing a very advantageous position. [6]

Though there was something of an escape clause, it looked like a pretty definite commitment. One would not be surprised to find some of

McClellan's defenders asserting that Stanton asked his categorical question just to trick the general.[7] When McCall arrived on June 12–13 McClellan had all of McDowell's original corps except King's division, and fully half of that force had been replaced by regiments from Washington and Baltimore. In addition to losing McDowell, McClellan had initially lost Blenker's division of Sumner's corps, which had been sent to General Frémont during the last days of March. But these troops were replaced by those of General Wool on June 1, when he and Dix exchanged positions at Fort Monroe and Baltimore, Dix being directed to report to McClellan, who received unequivocal command of the Department of Virginia.[8] Although McClellan had some of Wool's old regiments join him before Richmond, he left about 10,000 men at Fort Monroe, a place as secure as New York harbor after Wool had taken Norfolk on May 10 and all the naval installations and harbors in the vicinity the next day. It looked as if Wool still had something of the old touch, for he organized his operation one afternoon, carried it out the next morning, and, as one would expect, was personally at the head of the leading troops. Lincoln and Stanton were in Norfolk on the 11th when word came that the Confederates had blown up the *Merrimac* before departing, and the President issued an order of congratulations at once, stating he considered the destruction of the ironclad one of the greatest war successes to date.[9]

More should be said about McClellan's actual strength in June, compared with the end of March, because so much has been made of the loss of Blenker and the detention of McDowell.[10] In a statement vouched for by the adjutant general of the Army, as being based upon McClellan's own signed returns, the strengths of the Army of the Potomac on April 1 and June 20 are put in positions one above the other and compared. The strength "present and absent" on April 1—including the corps of McDowell and the division of Blenker—was 158,419, and the comparable figure for June 20 was 156,838.[11] In spite of the operation at Yorktown, battles at Williamsburg, Hanover, and Fair Oaks, McClellan's aggregate was only 1,581 below what it had been before the campaign started and before any withdrawals had been made. But the number of men reported as "absent" had grown from rather modest 13,128 to the sizable 29,511. When an examination is made only of strength "present," the case is as clear against excuses made by McClellan or offered in his behalf. No fewer than

40,000 men in the flesh had been sent to restore or to replace the 45,000 men who were actually present on March 31 in McDowell's corps and Blenker's division.[12] Altering words of the sturdy Joe Johnston, one could say: No one but McClellan would have complained so much or have sought to explain away his failure by ascribing it to the loss of one man in every twenty.

Lee had begun promptly to dig elaborate trenches, and the dirt thrown up tended to increase the suspicions and the misgivings with which he was regarded. The Southern soldiers did not take well at that stage of the war to pick and shovel, though they became apt and cheerful diggers later; and the people thought that trenches would not get the objectionable Yankees away from the neighborhood of their fine city. But Lee had no idea whatever of conducting a passive defense behind comfortable breastworks after the manner of Andrew Jackson at New Orleans. He intended to hold Richmond with a minimum number of men and take the remainder of his force into the field for aggressive purposes, for he, no less than the good people of the city, wanted to get rid of, or destroy, the Yankees, whom he sometimes referred to as "these people." As great an authority as Maurice calls Lee's plan a novel thing in war;[13] so it is not strange that neither his own men as they sweated with their shovels nor the perplexed citizens as they gossiped or read the papers understood their new general's plan or comprehended the full possibilities of ugly trenches.

In order to maneuver, Lee needed something more than a good solid fixed point to serve as pivot; he needed information about McClellan's right flank. So on June 12, he sent the really redoubtable and hard-riding Stuart with some 1,200 picked troopers on sturdy horses in search of the intelligence he needed. In accomplishing his mission, the bold cavalryman made the first of his celebrated raids and fought his father-in-law, Brigadier General Philip St. George Cooke. He led his troopers completely around McClellan's army, and early on June 15, weary from long hours in the saddle, and after an exhibition of fine courage and leadership, brought Lee amazing word indeed: the Federal commander's right flank was in the air, completely unprotected and easily accessible. The exploit was difficult for editors to explain to Northern readers, who naturally thought of Munson's Hill, the batteries on the Potomac, and the wooden guns reported to have been at Manassas.

Lee was receiving reenforcements, but nothing like the number that

McClellan believed from the reports of contrabands and Pinkerton's spies. How much of the misinformation resulted from the ignorance of those bringing or sending the reports, and how much from clever counterintelligence work, cannot be determined; but it all worked in the same direction. As early as May 30 McClellan reported that Beauregard was said to have arrived in Richmond with troops amid great excitement. Stanton promptly checked the rumor with General Halleck, who had been confronting Beauregard in far-off Mississippi, and on May 31 Halleck replied: "If Beauregard has been in Richmond, others have forged his signature, as I have received letters from him about the exchange of prisoners, and nearly every day for the last fortnight. . . . No troops have gone from here to Richmond, unless within the last two days." The efficient Secretary passed the word on to McClellan, as well as another dispatch from Halleck of June 2, after he had been in possession of Corinth for three days, stating, "No one has given any intimation that any troops have gone east." [14] Still Beauregard continued to haunt McClellan's mind, and on June 21 he telegraphed that the *Richmond Dispatch* had a Montgomery item of that date reading: "General Beauregard and staff are here on their way to Richmond. We hear that a large portion of the Army of the Mississippi will soon follow the general. A sufficient force will be left with the invincible Bragg to check any advance which the vandals under General Halleck may attempt to make into the interior." [15] Throughout the war, too much information of value to the enemy was published by papers in both the North and the South, and McClellan could not have been certain that there was not some truth in this dispatch even though it looked decidedly like an effort at deception. But he should have known that it would be some time before many of Beauregard's troops could reach Richmond, in view of the distance and the inefficiency of the railroads.

The next day letters were intercepted stating that Beauregard had been expected in Richmond a few days before, and on the 25th Porter wrote to McClellan that a contraband had come into his lines who had actually seen Beauregard and his troops arrive in Richmond. The army commander passed the message on to Stanton with the statement, "This only serves to corroborate previous information received from several sources today." [16] McClellan, who did not yet realize how badly his credulity had been imposed upon at Munson's Hill and Manassas, naturally did not break through the deception, which was strengthened by reports that Pinkerton's spies sent from Richmond. Two of the general's defenders do little service either to him or to Pinkerton when they say the operatives merely "confirmed McClellan's opinion," the general having settled upon 200,000 as the number of men the Confederates could and should have had in Richmond. The defenders do not point out where the men over and above the re-enforcements which were actually received could have been taken from, nor explain how 200,000 soldiers were to be fed near a city whose civilian population of 40,000 had at least doubled.[17]

Another apologist is even more inventive, for he asserts that "McClellan could rely only on the advice of his superiors and of the secret service over which he had no control at all." [18] The first part of the claim is not supported by a single figure for Lee's strength as given to McClellan by the administration; and if Lincoln and Stanton had deceived him in so important a matter the general who said they wanted him to fail would hardly have spared them when he wrote his memoirs. The charge that McClellan had no control over the secret service is completely disproved by the statements he made in his official report; there it was an instrument of his own creation, and Pinkerton was called the "trustworthy and efficient chief of the secret-service corps." [19] In his memoirs McClellan not only failed to mention Pinkerton but did not give Lee's actual strength—well known at the time he wrote—or state frankly in the text the strength he had believed Lee to have.[20] Evidently the entire thing was something the more mature man wished to forget, and his curt "No comment" by itself topples over many of the tall and grotesque excuses that recent writers have built up for him.

On June 12 McClellan acknowledged receipt of the word that McDowell's corps was being recalled from the Valley and would be sent to him. The weather changed for the better; and, with the ground rapidly drying, the general had the extra whisky ration stopped, while a stern order prescribed that without fail the men should all have hot coffee after reveille.[21] But there were clear indications that everything was not going to be easy and simple, even with soldiers who were perfectly sober and well braced by early coffee. On June 12, the very day that McClellan moved his headquarters to the house of Dr. Trent on the south side of the Chickahominy, where four of his corps had then been concentrated, he reported somewhat ominously, "The enemy are massing their troops near our front, throwing up earthworks on all the approaches to Richmond, and giving every indication of fight." That showed only too well that it was not going to be a case of just marching into Richmond with colors flying and bands playing tuneful selections, after the last puddle had been dried by the mellow June sun. Almost diffidently, Lincoln telegraphed on the 18th, "I could better dispose of things if I could know about what day you think you can attack Richmond, and would be glad to be informed, if you think you can inform me with safety." The next day the general replied: "After to-morrow we shall fight the rebel army as soon as Providence will permit. We shall await only a favorable condition of the earth and sky and the completing of some necessary preliminaries." [22]

They were brave words; but McClellan was worrying, and at 4:30 in the morning of the 22nd he telegraphed Stanton, "I am informed that General James has now completed two batteries of bronze rifled guns and one battery of steel rifled guns, all 3.80-inch caliber." The guns had been tried by officers in whom he had confidence, and he would be glad to have them, though he had been unable to get them from Secretary Cameron. Stanton promptly replied that he knew no James who was a manufacturer of guns; there was, however, a projectile maker of that name whose product McClellan himself had declined to recommend for purchase. "Where are the guns to which your telegram refers? There is no proposal for their sale on the files of this Department. Who has offered them to you?" the Secretary asked. In the evening McClellan came back with some rather indefinite information, ending: "General James informed me that he has the guns now ready, with projectiles. With these remarks I leave the matter in your hands." [23] The general who a few days before had been waiting only for the ground to dry was now grasping in desperation for some shadowy new weapon. Lincoln must have been reminded of McClellan's request from Yorktown for Parrott guns, which he had answered with the message about indefinite procrastination and the query whether anything was going to be done. History was repeating itself.

At midnight on the 24th, McClellan sent Stanton this important dispatch:

A very peculiar case of desertion has just occurred from the enemy. The party states that he left Jackson, Whiting, and Ewell (fifteen brigades)

Gordonsville on the 21st; that they were moving to Frederick's Hall, and that it was intended to attack my rear on the 28th. I would be glad to learn, at your earliest convenience, the most exact information you have as to the position and movements of Jackson, as well as the sources from which your information is derived, that I may the better compare it with what I have.[24]

This vies in excellence with the brief and soldierly message he had sent to Washington on May 24 when he was informed that McDowell was being detained. Under questioning, the deserter must have seemed much more convincing than the contrabands who had arrived from time to time with alarming reports; still a cautious attitude was maintained, and McClellan for once wished to check with higher authority instead of making immoderate conclusions that he expected his superiors not even to question.

Stanton's long reply must also be seen in full. We have viewed the Secretary doing careful operation work on Sunday May 25; caring for personnel when he inquired solicitously about McDowell; as a supply officer on June 22, trying to get fifty miles of telegraph wire salvaged. We have glimpsed him in late May giving the intelligence reports that became the basis of the charge that he went into panics easily. A more rounded picture of him as a G-2 is furnished by his telegram to McClellan on June 25:

We have no definite information as to the numbers or position of Jackson's force. General King yesterday reported a deserter's statement that Jackson's force was, nine days ago, 40,000 men. Some reports place 10,000 rebels under Jackson at Gordonsville; others, that his force is at Port Republic, Harrisonburg, and Luray. Frémont yesterday reported rumors that Western Virginia was threatened, and General Kelley that Ewell was advancing to New Creek, where Frémont has his depots. The last telegram from Frémont contradicts this rumor. The last telegram from Banks says the enemy's pickets are strong in advance at Luray. The people decline to give any information of his whereabouts. Within the last two days the evidence is strong that for some purpose the enemy is circulating rumors of Jackson's advance in various directions, with a view to concealing the real point of attack. Neither McDowell, who is at Manassas, nor Banks and Frémont, who are at Middletown, appear to have any accurate knowledge of the subject. A letter transmitted to the Department yesterday, purporting to be dated Gordonsville, on the 14th instant, stated that the actual attack was designed for Washington and Baltimore as soon as you attacked Richmond, but that the report was to be circulated that Jackson had gone to Richmond, in order to mislead. This letter looked very much like a blind, and induces me to suspect that Jackson's real movement now is toward Richmond. It came from Alexandria, and is certainly designed, like the numerous rumors put afloat, to mislead. I think, therefore, that while the warning of the deserter to you may also be a blind, it could not safely be disregarded. I will transmit to you any further information on this subject that may be received here.[25]

Stanton was recognized as one of the best trial lawyers of his day, and his telegram to McClellan suggests the reason for his success. One can doubt if many trained intelligence officers could have written as clearly and discerningly as he did, or more to the point. The letter also shows a touch of cordial sympathy for the man to whom it was addressed; it looks as if the Secretary were giving the general the very best he had.

Jackson, the master of deception, had overdone things; the contradictory reports he had spread about his moves had revealed that an important Confederate operation was being mounted. The master stroke—the Gordonsville letter—was correctly interpreted as a blind. Not the least alarm was revealed by Stanton over the safety of Washington, and from information in his own possession he thought that Jackson was Richmond-bound. Nor had the general been successful in keeping knowledge of his destination from the ranks of his command. Although the date the deserter gave for the projected attack on McClellan's rear was three days later than Stonewall had set in a conference with Lee on the 23rd,[26] he did not miss the date of the actual attack as badly as did the general. He put it only one day late.

Lincoln had done his bit in breaking through deception. A few days before, McClellan had reported that deserters stated that probably 10,000 men had gone from Richmond to reenforce Jackson; and confirmation soon came from General King at Fredericksburg, to whom a Frenchman gave the news that he had seen the troops en route. At first Lincoln was inclined to believe that perhaps a stubborn defense of Richmond was not intended, but on reflection he asked McClellan, "Have not all been sent to deceive?" [27]

So as Jackson on the 25th of June—hours behind the appointed time—moved his force of some 18,500 men toward Ashland, McClellan had not only the warning from the deserter, but much additional information from Washington and the clear injunction from his superior that the deserter's story "could not safely be disregarded."

Chapter XXV of *McClellan's Own Story* begins: "On the 26th, the day upon which I had decided as the time for our final advance, the enemy attacked our right in strong force." Actually, it was not until late that afternoon that a few enemy brigades attacked after a couple

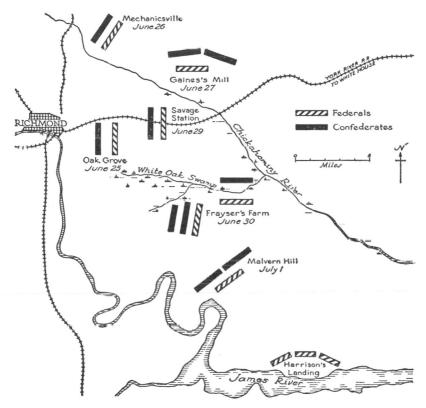

THE SEVEN DAYS' BATTLES, JUNE 25 TO JULY 1, 1862

of hours of brisk skirmishing; so McClellan had had most of the day to start a big "push" if he had really planned one. His statement is merely another falsehood, another boast as to what he had planned to do if the *weather,* or the *President,* or the *Secretary of War,* or the *enemy* had not prevented. For some days he had indeed been advancing his picket lines here and there, and on June 25 Palfrey entered in his diary: "Perfection of weather. Startling news that general advance of our

whole line has commenced." On that day there was indeed a successful action at Oak Grove, south of the Chickahominy, by the Third
Corps with some assistance from the Second and Fourth; and the
advance would probably have gone on if Lee had not decided to put
an end to it. But never for a moment had McClellan planned a real
attack to be pushed through with resolution in spite of intrenchments
and opposition—even before Lee had been reenforced by Jackson.
Everything he had done indicated a siege. The arrival of mortars on
June 22 confirmed an idea that Palfrey had long entertained, "that
we were now engaged in a siege, rather than as an advancing army." [28]
Lee, watching closely from the other side of the slowly advancing lines,
had formed the same conclusion, and on June 11 he wrote to Jackson
that McClellan was "apparently preparing to move by gradual approaches on Richmond." [29] McClellan's later claim, that he was about
to launch something decisive on the 26th, is in a way an admission that
the slow procedure in which he was actually engaged was neither
necessary nor well advised.

As late as five o'clock on June 25 McClellan was in the best of
spirits, telegraphing Stanton about the operation for the day: "The
affair is over, and we have gained our point fully and with but little
loss, notwithstanding strong opposition." [30] An hour later he was in
the depths of despondency and telegraphed about dying with his
troops.[31] The plunge into gloom was caused by additional intelligence
about the expected attack of Jackson upon his right flank and by the
arrival of another contraband or two announcing that Beauregard had
come again. He stated that he would probably be attacked the next
day by 200,000 men (which implied at least 250,000 Confederates at
Richmond). The dispatch of 6:15 P.M. is very unpleasant reading,
and naturally it disturbed Lincoln, whose reply was notable for its
tone of mild forbearance. Of the possibility of disaster, McClellan
said: "The responsibility cannot be thrown on my shoulders; it must
rest where it belongs." But even when overwhelmed with fears, his
vanity broke through. He did not say manfully that he would do the
best *he* could; he boasted, "I will do all that a general can do with
the splendid army I have the honor to command." [32]

McClellan cheered up a good deal when he visited the headquarters
of Porter, whose Fifth Corps, augmented to 35,000 men by the
attachment of McCall's division of McDowell's corps, alone remained
north of the Chickahominy. Porter also had late information that con-

firmed the approach of Jackson, but he was not the least dismayed. Signing off for the night, McClellan wired Stanton, "If I had another good division I could laugh at Jackson. . . . Nothing but overwhelming forces can defeat us." [33] Just one more good division! Then McClellan could not only repel, but laugh at the Confederate general who knew how to march hard and fight hard. As a matter of fact, McClellan had the equivalent of another division at Fort Monroe.

The night was quiet, also the next morning. McClellan, waiting, wired Stanton at noon: "The affair of yesterday was perfectly successful. We hold the new picket line undisturbed. All things very quiet on this bank of the Chickahominy. I would prefer more noise." Well, the general had plenty of cannon with which to make a very big noise indeed, as well as infantrymen to bring in a heavy roll of musketry; and he had had all morning to do it. This, it is to be remembered, was the very day when he said in the memoirs that the enemy beat him to the draw. Idly he was waiting, though two days before he had wired Burnside at New Bern, North Carolina, "I wish you to understand that every minute in this crisis is of great importance." [34]

In the afternoon of June 26 McClellan very creditably went to Porter's headquarters. At about three o'clock the covering detachments in front of Porter's main position along Beaver Dam Creek, just east of Mechanicsville, were driven in, and then his strong line was assaulted. At nine o'clock McClellan, still with Porter, wired Stanton: "The firing nearly ceased. . . . Victory of to-day complete and against great odds. I almost begin to think we are invincible." [35]

The victory was indeed complete, but all the advantage had been with Porter. His 35,000 well posted men, with splendid artillery support, had been attacked by A. P. Hill's division of 14,000 men, which had only a few guns in position. There had been plenty of ginger in the attack, for Hill had been McClellan's rival for the hand of Ellen Marcy. Whether it was explained by Hill's eagerness to get at McClellan, or by his inability to hold his men in check after their enthusiasm had been raised by driving in Porter's pickets, it is impossible to say. But the attack was quite out of line with Lee's wishes and brought about a serious situation. Hill had been expected to wait until the noise of Jackson's guns showed that Porter's flank was being turned by the Valley soldiers; but the general from the Shenandoah, famed for rapid movement, was not in position to attack at anything like the appointed hour. So the impatient Hill, with a score to settle, went in alone. His soldiers showed themselves the bravest of the brave in a hopeless situation, and many of them were killed by the volleys of Porter's infantry and the fire of his superior guns.

When darkness came and the noise of battle ceased, there was no doubt that Lee had lost the battle of Mechanicsville and McClellan had won it. But in a way McClellan failed completely. Here he had a chance to estimate the strength of the attacker from the length of his lines, the formation that was used, the number of units apparently employed, the number of guns he put in action, and from other signs. But he was no more successful than the detectives and the contrabands when it came to estimating enemy strength.

While at Porter's headquarters McClellan received some encouraging news from Washington and replied: "Dispatch as to reinforcements this moment read. I thank you for them. I am rejoiced that the troops in front of Washington are to be placed under one command. Keep at that and all will be well." [36] In a tactful way he was complimenting Lincoln on no longer trying to manage separately such forces as those of Frémont and Banks; and he probably thought that President and Secretary had learned a lesson from the unsuccessful effort to destroy Jackson. But on this same day he showed for a second time that he could not estimate an enemy force from combat actions—something he would have to learn if he were to be a successful general.

Then, after another quiet night, came June 27—a bad day for McClellan, a very bad day, one beyond all possibility of satisfactory explanation. All wagons and heavy equipment had been brought to the south bank of the Chickahominy, and Porter's troops were very skillfully brought back about three miles at daybreak to a strong new position. At ten o'clock McClellan reported to Stanton that the army was in a position to "take advantage of the first mistake made by the enemy." Here again the general spoke good words, appropriate to the situation; but, having uttered them, he forgot them. At noon he reported that the attack had been renewed against his right, and that he expected one against his left. But in a dispatch sent at one o'clock there was a great deterioration in tone. It closed with the gloomy words, "Goodby, and present my respects to the President." [37]

McClellan should have gone back to Porter's headquarters. There he could have learned more about war in a few hours than he had learned in the Crimea and in Europe. Against Porter's 35,000 men,

Lee—undaunted by failure the day before—was hurling 55,000, commanded by Jackson, Longstreet, A. P. Hill, and D. H. Hill. McClellan may have seen some good generals in Europe, but he saw none who wrote their names so high among the roll of good captains as Lee and Jackson. He may have seen some fine soldiers on his trip; Tennyson

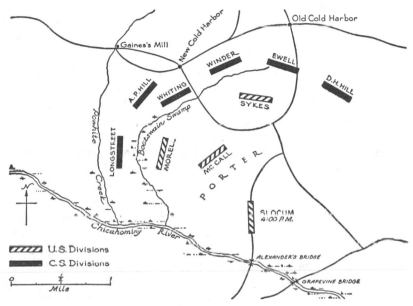

BATTLE OF GAINES'S MILL, JUNE 27, 1862

wrote imperishable lines about the bravery of the soldiers in the Crimea. But if McClellan had stood at the side of Porter in the late afternoon of June 27, he could have seen fierce attacks by Virginians and Carolinians broken by steady ranks of men from Northern states; then he could have seen Hood's Texans after staggering losses drive home an assault over bad terrain until the blue line was shattered and the victory won by Lee. But McClellan contented himself with sending greetings and thanks by wire, which Porter probably found it difficult to deliver to the soldiers. He also said: "I look upon today as decisive of the war. Try to drive the rascals and take some prisoners and guns. What more assistance do you require?" Somewhat incredible! But it is in the Official Records. On the day he described as "decisive of the war," McClellan did not visit the one corps of his army that was engaged.

When darkness came, the fighting stopped. Again, as at Bull Run, Sykes's regulars covered the Union withdrawal. Now they were a division—nearly 6,000 strong—and Sykes was a major general. They had stood firm in the battle, and in covering the withdrawal they were well aided by two fresh brigades from the other side of the river. The Union loss in this battle of Gaines's Mill was 6,837 in killed, wounded, and missing; and fourteen good rifled guns were left behind. The Confederate loss was probably 8,000 in killed and wounded. In some units the casualties almost exceeded belief. The First Texas lost 600 out of 800 and the Fourth Texas came out under the command of a captain —all the field officers were gone.[38] Lee had been with his troops all day, and he had had many puzzling problems to solve in locating the Federal positions and getting his divisions placed for a final coordinated attack after preliminary assaults had been broken with heavy loss. That night, Lee knew that he had won a significant victory, but he had only 25,000 men, under the command of Magruder, in front of Richmond; these men faced three times as many men in blue. In his official report Magruder stated: "From the time at which the enemy withdrew his forces to this side of the Chickahominy and destroyed the bridges to the moment of his evacuation—that is, from Friday night [June 27] until Sunday morning, I considered the situation of our army as extremely critical and perilous." [39] Lee, of course, was aware of this and had weighed the possibilities beforehand.[40] After saying that McClellan had the opportunity for an Austerlitz in case he attacked, Magruder wrote: "His failure to do so is the best evidence that our wise commander fully understood the character of his opponent."

In Federal headquarters—in the house of Dr. Trent—there took place that day the complete disintegration of the Commanding General of the Army of the Potomac. At 3:00 P.M. Marcy sent a message to Stanton designed to condition the Secretary for worse news; and at 8:00 McClellan sent the telegram:

Have had a terrible contest. Attacked by greatly superior numbers in all directions on this side; we still hold our own, though a very heavy fire is still kept up on the left bank of Chickahominy. The odds have been immense. We hold our own very nearly. I may be forced to give up my position during the night, but will not if it is possible to avoid it. Had I 20,000 fresh and good troops we would be sure of a splendid victory tomorrow. My men have fought magnificently.[41]

On the north of the river the odds were certainly heavy against McClellan—nearly two to one—because of Lee's magnificent concentration of force. But on the south bank, though he reported the enemy as greatly superior, the odds were three to one in his own favor. Next to the Chickahominy, looking toward Richmond, was the corps of General Franklin. After stating that he had been subjected to noisy but very ineffective artillery fire late in the morning and again after 6:30 P.M., and that there had been some enemy demonstrations in the afternoon, Franklin wrote in his report:

About sundown a severe infantry attack was made upon General Hancock, who with his brigade, held the picket line. The fight lasted about forty-five minutes, when the enemy retired, not having been able to gain an inch of ground.[42]

Next to Franklin came the veteran Sumner, then Heintzelman, and nothing happened on June 27 in their sectors for either to mention in his report. At the time that McClellan was longing for 20,000 fresh men, he actually had more than 60,000 that had not been engaged and were not to become engaged at that time.

Sometime during the evening—or perhaps well before—McClellan made the fateful decision to retreat to the James River, where a week before he had ordered supplies to be sent. At an unspecified hour before midnight he sent a dispatch to Flag Officer Goldsborough, saying that he had "met a severe repulse . . . having been attacked by superior numbers." He stated that he was "obliged to fall back between the Chickahominy and the James River." He wished the navy to send small gunboats up the former, and other craft up the latter, to guard his flank and to protect the supplies that had already been ordered to the James. Promptly the commodore—who may or may not have been surprised—replied that every request would be complied with.[43]

Soon after midnight McClellan wrote the famous dispatch to Stanton that ended:

I feel too earnestly to-night. I have seen too many dead and wounded comrades to feel otherwise than that the Government has not sustained this army. If you do not do so now, the game is lost.

If I save this army now, I tell you plainly that I owe no thanks to you or any other persons in Washington.

You have done your best to sacrifice this army.[44]

Strange as this was, it was in perfect harmony with other McClellan dispatches, and it was foretold in the Morris letter written a year before. Out of a confusion of unsoldierly, distraught utterances, one sentence alone stood out as worthy of the moment: "I shall draw back to this side of the Chickahominy, and think I can withdraw all our material." That would have been a soldier's decision and a soldier's words to his government. But it was lost in a mass of contradictory, hysterical lamentations unworthy of a man in uniform. The talk about the dead and wounded was just McClellan bombast; he had been in his headquarters all the day.

In almost unbelieving amazement the telegraph operator in Washington wrote the last sentences of the unnerved general's dispatch; then he summoned his chief, E. S. Sanford, military supervisor of telegraphs, whom Stanton had called from the presidency of the American Telegraph Company.[45] To Sanford the two final sentences seemed little short of treason, and being a man used to assuming responsibility, he boldly directed that they be dropped from the copy given to the Secretary. In what followed there was irony. William C. Prime, who wrote the very eulogistic biographical sketch in *McClellan's Own Story,* stated with regard to the grave charge that McClellan made against him, but which Stanton did not see: "The Secretary received the accusation in silence which was the confession of its truth." (We are not told who observed Stanton reading the message.) The sentences not being in the copy furnished by Stanton to the Committee on the Conduct of the War, the Secretary himself was accused of making the deletion—which was further evidence of his guilt! However, in 1907, David Bates made known what had taken place in the Washington telegraph office, though the inclusion of the complete dispatch in McClellan's report of August 4, 1863, may have revealed to Stanton that he—the chief censor of news—had himself been given a telegram significantly expunged by a subordinate.

The facts are simple. McClellan had 105,000 effective men, Lee had 85,000.[46] The Federal infantry was much better armed than the

Confederate, having many more rifles, fewer smoothbore muskets and no shotguns; the Union artillery was much the stronger—both in number and in quality of pieces. McClellan was on the defensive, and on the south bank of the Chickahominy his troops were behind good breastworks. To blame the government and say that McClellan needed more troops, when he had used only one-third of what he had and had 10,000 more men at Fort Monroe, is surely absurd. Nor can one excuse him because his intelligence agents deceived him. General Michie wrote: "Language is scarcely strong enough to condemn in appropriate terms the inefficient administration of the service of information whereby so gross a miscalculation should have been evolved, and especially since the two armies, with the exception of Jackson's corps, had been within close contact for more than a month." [47] Irrespective of what he may have been deceived into thinking on June 25, McClellan should have known the truth by 6:00 P.M. on the 27th.

For a resolute and able commander the road to Richmond was open; but the real indictment against McClellan is not that he did not have the courage that would allow him to make a vigorous and general counterstroke, but that he did not even act conservatively and maintain a position in front of Richmond, as he did after the battle of Fair Oaks, changing his base to the James River. [48] The change in base was already under way and was proceeding nicely, and as early as June 24 he had informed Heintzelman, "I have satisfactory communication from the gunboat fleet in James River." Stanton had told him on June 26 that reenforcements were coming, and the President had stated in a message of June 20 that more force would be sent as soon as the uncertainties about Jackson were cleared up. [49] McClellan knew that all forces in front of Washington were being put under the command of General Pope, and he had commended the move as one that promised well. On the 26th an order had been issued prescribing the cooperation of Pope's army with that of McClellan before Richmond as soon as the situation in the Valley made it possible. [50] By acting defensively and making local counterattacks, McClellan should have been able to use up Lee's offensive power and wear out the reserves that he had committed. With Pope's army approaching, the Confederate situation would have then been desperate.

Though his army was not defeated, McClellan was. So he decided to retreat.

A retreat from the Chickahominy to the James presented real difficulties, and military writers have very charitably said it was the best part of McClellan's campaign. The McClellan defenders have seized upon this mild praise, avidly and illogically magnifying the operation into a great achievement—even into a masterpiece of logistics that few generals could have carried out.[51] The great distortion has been aided by blending two separate and distinct operations—McClellan's change of base and his retreat—into one, and shifting part of the praise that rightly belongs to the former to the latter. The change of base was undoubtedly well carried out, but it was not difficult. It was not noticeably harder to load supplies onto ships at the White House on the Pamunkey River and move them around to the James, than it had been to load the ships originally at Washington or elsewhere and transport their cargoes to the White House. Much labor was involved, and the work had to be conducted as rapidly as possible; but no tactical questions were involved, and the enemy did not interfere. The operation was carried out under the direction of Lieutenant Colonel Rufus Ingalls, which was a guarantee of smoothness; American ship captains revealed their skill in getting the 400 vessels out of the narrow, tortuous Pamunkey without incident. Great efforts were made to comfort the disappointed Northern people with the thought that the entire operation was just a change in base; and even Freeman, careful as he is, and without illusions about McClellan—who, he says, was not far from panic for a week—more than compliments the retreat when he writes, "The Federal staff work during the change of base was well-nigh flawless." [52]

Although McClellan's staff had unquestionably improved a great deal after it had been in the field for more than two months, the retreat to the James is found to be incomprehensibly bad when it is carefully examined. He started the operation with little knowledge of available routes to the river, and—unbelievable though it may seem—he had no reconnaissances made. Through failure to use all the roads that existed, his retreat was greatly protracted, and as a result he fought two unnecessary battles, neither of which he desired, and in the first of which a part of his army might have been destroyed if Jackson had shown his customary drive and resolution. As a piece of logistics, therefore, the retreat was very poor—though the evidence remains to be given.

The map that accompanied McClellan's report shows a large

unexplored region almost directly between his position on the Chicka-hominy and Harrison's Landing on the James, to which he retired.[53] The region is bordered on the west by the Quaker (or Willis Church) Road which, according to his own statement in the report, was the only road he knew about. Speaking of his road information, not as of June 28, but *as of June 30,* McClellan said, "We then knew of but one road for the movement of the troops and our immense train." [54] The word "then" apparently indicates that subsequently—when it was too late—there was enlightenment on the all-important question of roads. As can be seen by referring to an excellent Confederate map dated 1864, the region that is blank on McClellan's map was crossed by two good roads, one past Smith's Store and one past Samaria Church, re-spectively three and five miles east of the Quaker Road.[55] These roads were actually used by the Army of the Potomac in 1864 when it rapidly crossed the Peninsula without the opportunity for reconnais-sance, and they were there awaiting use in 1862. McClellan is usually represented as a careful and methodical soldier who planned every-thing in advance. But here he failed to look ahead. For some weeks he had contemplated changing his base to the James River, and the proc-ess was under way when the retreat began. Even if there had been no retreat he would have needed to use all possible roads to the new base merely to supply his great army, because it took 150 wagons to haul one day's food for his soldiers and 300 wagons to haul one day's forage for his animals.[56] In his entire campaign of blunders none exceeded McClellan's failure to know of all the roads to the James River. The explanation probably was that in recent days he had been dwelling upon the political and military mistakes and deficiencies of Mr. Lincoln, and evolving a memorial on that attractive theme—when there was plenty of work to be done in his own back yard.

McClellan sought to move his entire army down the Quaker Road, where it was hazardously exposed to attack, and where it was attacked and was extricated with difficulty. Just how long the movement should have taken if there had been really first-class staff work is hard to say, because of various uncertainties about equipment, location of the troops, etc. The number of wagons involved has been greatly exag-gerated, sometimes about 100 per cent. McClellan's quartermaster put the number at 3,600 wagons and 700 ambulances; [57] but some-times it is stated that there were 5,000 wagons—with perhaps the implication that ambulances were included. But Lieutenant Colonel

Rufus Ingalls, who became chief quartermaster on July 11, gave Quartermaster General Meigs a much lower number on July 18. After stating that the number of wagons in the army had been greatly exaggerated, he wrote: "We have here now about 2,600 wagons for service with troops, engineer and supply trains; each regiment is allowed six." [58] If we accept the figures of Ingalls—who was a talented field quartermaster as well as an excellent arithmetician—120 miles would be a liberal estimate for the length of McClellan's army in a single column. The movement over one road could not possibly have been carried out in less than two days of constant uninterrupted movement. McClellan himself stated that the column was kept in motion with great difficulty; [59] and Ingalls reported that there was a mingling of all sorts of units, and that it was not the kind of march which is pleasing to the eye of a soldier.[60] Three days were used in place of two.

In the meeting at McClellan's headquarters about midnight June 27–28 General Keyes, commanding the Fourth Corps, was ordered to move his command—less one brigade left at the bridge over the Chickahominy on the Williamsburg road—with all artillery and baggage across White Oak Swamp before daylight, and to take position near the junction of the Long Bridge, Charles City, and Quaker roads.[61] This place, called Glendale, or Riddell's Shop, was a strategic point to be well guarded until the movement was completed. In spite of the shortness of the warning, Keyes evidently got under way promptly; but when he arrived at the bridge over White Oak Swamp, he found it had been partially destroyed by General Hooker. It was bad that it had been damaged; it was worse that the army commander and his staff did not know about its condition and got Keyes started in the dark, only to be delayed. It was not until two hours after daylight that Keyes was able to start crossing the repaired structure.

A second good bridge with corduroy approaches was thrown across White Oak Swamp at Brackett's Ford, about two miles above the regular bridge, and by evening of the 28th two crossings for wagons and guns and several fords for infantry and cavalry were available.[62] The engineer in charge of getting McClellan out of the clutches of Lee and his hard-hitting subordinates was General Barnard, the same officer who less than a year before had searched for roads by which McDowell could turn Beauregard's left flank at Bull Run. But though the work of bridging White Oak Swamp went on promptly and briskly nothing was done in the equally important search for more roads to the south of the obstacle. Late in the afternoon of the 28th both Barnard and McClellan instructed Lieutenant Colonel Barton S. Alexander to proceed to the James River with two other engineer officers in search of "an eligible position to which the army might retreat and establish a new base of operations." [63] But not until the next morning, Sunday, did Alexander pick up a cavalry escort and get under way. One entire day had been lost. Alexander was back by noon and reported: "I saw General McClellan, for whom I sketched the roads as far as I had seen them, and from whom I received orders to try and communicate with our fleet on James River." Evidently McClellan made no interrogation as to roads east of the Quaker Road.[64]

General Keyes showed himself far more inquisitive and enterprising in the discovery of roads than McClellan, for while waiting in his new position near Riddell's Shop on the 29th he sent out parties from the Eighth Illinois Cavalry and the Eighth Pennsylvania Cavalry on a road hunt; and the troopers turned up two new routes to the James, one of which was probably the road past Smith's Store, and the other a poorer road nearer to the Quaker Road.[65] Ordered to proceed that night, Keyes moved his trains over the good road—Eighth Illinois escorting—and led his combat troops—infantry, artillery, and remaining cavalry—through rain over the poor road, parts of which had not been used for years. Early the next morning he encamped on the banks of the James with all artillery and baggage in good order, but with no thanks due to the army commander or his staff. Then the roads that his good soldiership had provided fell idle. McClellan's staff was not only not directing the movement; it did not know what was being done.

On the afternoon of the 29th there was an engagement in the vicinity of Savage Station, about which the corps of Sumner (Second), Heintzelman (Third), and Franklin (Sixth) were located. McClellan had departed without giving adequate instructions or appointing a commander, and there was much confusion. Heintzelman saw a chance to cross White Oak Swamp on the bridge at Brackett's and did so in the late afternoon. If Jackson had repaired the "Grapevine Bridge" over the Chickahominy as early as Lee expected, and if he had crossed and joined forces with General Magruder, who was advancing down the Williamsburg Road, Sumner and Franklin would have been in difficulty. But the danger passed, and during the night the Second and

Sixth Corps crossed the swamp and destroyed the bridges. Porter's Fifth Corps, which had recuperated from the heavy battle of the 27th and had already crossed White Oak Swamp, was ordered on the evening of the 29th to proceed to the James. Because of inadequate guides—a black mark for someone—it got lost and spent the night covering six miles, reaching its destination at 9:00 A.M. on the 30th.[66]

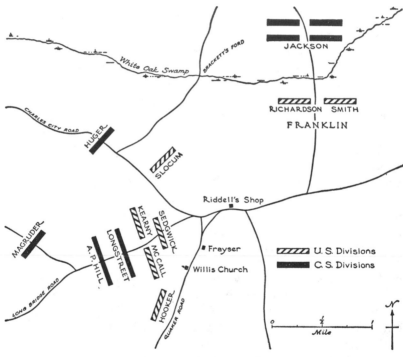

BATTLE OF FRAYSER'S FARM, JUNE 30, 1862

If the good road that Keyes had used for his wagons had been constantly used from the beginning, all trains and reserve artillery would have been out of the way by midnight of the 29th–30th, and the combat troops could have followed rapidly. But because of idle roads, trains were moving all day on the 30th down the exposed Quaker Road, and as a result the Second, Third, and Sixth Corps had to remain in position and fight the battle of Frayser's Farm, or Glendale, in the afternoon and evening.[67]

The battle of Frayser's Farm might well have seen the annihilation of a large portion of McClellan's army, and there would have been no escape for the remaining part. Though Lee had definitely raised the threat to Richmond, he wanted nothing less than the destruction of the invading force; and on the afternoon of the 30th all his army was closing around the three Federal corps caught in a trap near Frayser's farm because of McClellan's wretchedly handled retreat. At noon Jackson, with a force of 25,000 men, appeared on the north side of the destroyed White Oak bridge, facing a mixed command (Smith's division of Franklin's corps, and Richardson's of the Second) under Franklin on the south bank. Huger with a division of about 10,000 men was advancing down the Charles City Road, and later in the afternoon Longstreet and A. P. Hill came up the Long Bridge Road, followed by Magruder. In addition, a force of about 4,000 men under Holmes, who had originally been south of the James, was on a road to the south, not far from the Quaker Road. The full success of Lee's excellent but somewhat complex plan of concentration depended of course upon Jackson's getting over White Oak Swamp. He did not cross, and again pages have been written in explanation and condemnation—more even than about his failure to be in position to attack McClellan's right flank on the afternoon of June 26, or his failure to cross the Chickahominy on June 29. Contemplating the Union troops, Jackson must have recalled not only the battle of Gaines's Mill, where the inferior Federal force had been hard to dislodge, but also the smaller but significant action at Port Republic. To the extent that his state of mind on June 30 was due to memories of June 9, Tyler's accepting battle that day was paying rich dividends indeed. Certainly Jackson was no more aggressive than Frémont had been at Strasburg on June 1 or at Cross Keys on June 8. General Franklin wrote in his report:

> The enemy kept up the firing during the whole day and crossed some infantry below our position, but he made no serious attempt to cross during the day, and contented himself with the cannonading and the firing of his sharpshooters.

Longstreet attacked with skill and power, and A. P. Hill liquidated a little more of his personal account against his old rival. Again McClellan was absent from the battlefield, and again there was confusion about command. Franklin stated:

Night-fall having arrived, and the wagons having all disappeared, I took the responsibility of moving my command to the James River by a road to the left which had not been much used, and arrived at headquarters safely about daylight. I previously informed General Heintzelman of my determination.[68]

The road that Franklin used was probably the one Keyes had used the night before, which evidently had been used little if at all during the day of the 30th. In an article written after the war Franklin gave unstinted credit and generous praise for the discovery of the road "to the fertile brain of General Smith, who ordered the exploration." [69] Again no credit was due to McClellan or his staff for an act that contributed much to the success of the retreat, for it is very doubtful if Franklin and the two corps in action about Frayser's farm could have all extricated themselves by the Quaker Road. Though Sumner and Heintzelman got away successfully during the night they, like Franklin, took the responsibility of retiring without orders from McClellan.[70]

Having come unnecessarily into so dangerous a situation, the Army of the Potomac ended the day in good condition. Lee's disappointment was commensurably great; never again would he have so good an opportunity to destroy an adversary. Responsibility for the failure, however, must rest upon him as well as upon Jackson and other subordinates. Lee had held Longstreet and A. P. Hill inactive on the north side of the Chickahominy until morning of June 29, although dust clouds had indicated before noon of the 28th that McClellan was retreating. Of the 28th Freeman writes, "Thus ended a day that might have changed the whole course of the war if its ample hours of light could have been given to a march on the heels of the enemy." Might not some hours of the 28th have been used by Longstreet and Hill in marching to strike McClellan's flank at Frayser's farm several hours before they did—early in the morning of the 30th, perhaps? Lee's explanation in his report is far from satisfactory,[71] and Freeman's defense of him must be matched with that of Henderson's pleading and excusing Jackson's inaction on the bank of White Oak Swamp two days later.[72] Certainly no cleverness can be ascribed to McClellan for the minor uncertainty that strangely balked Lee—though this too is sometimes attempted.[73] After several days of heavy strain and one of great personal exertion, it is possible that Lee had a touch of battle fatigue on June 28. Certainly he did not show the quickness of decision that Lincoln revealed on May 24, when he decided to move Frémont to Harrisonburg and ordered McDowell to send two divisions to the Valley at top speed to cut off Jackson. Lee had just fought and won his first big battle, and it was not altogether strange that he failed to act as promptly or take the chances that he was willing to take later.

So, to hours of inaction of parts of Lee's army on June 28 and June 30, the Army of the Potomac may have owed its escape from Frayser's farm. By noon of July 1 it was in position on Malvern Hill, close to the James River, on terrain excellently featured for defense. After inspecting the disposition of his troops and batteries McClellan turned over the command to Porter and rode away to Harrison's Landing, where he had decided to put his base, and where supplies were already being landed. Lee, unwilling to give up the thought of destroying McClellan, decided to attack again, although a glance showed the strength of the position that the Federals had seized. His own troops were worn out by harder marches than the men in the heavy blue lines with the strong batteries on Malvern Hill; but their success had begun to create a little contempt for the invaders of Virginia, whom they had driven from the very threshold of the Confederate capital. The Union ranks on the other hand, though they had lost battles and had retreated, were far from disheartened—the men were made of the stuff that could take punishment and not lose morale or the will to fight.

Swamps and thick woods made deployment for attack very difficult, and coordination and control were bad. Partial assaults in the early afternoon were crushed largely by the fine Federal artillery. The final general attack did not come until late in the afternoon, and it too failed. Malvern Hill was a definite and costly defeat for Lee, who may unjustifiably have raised his opinion of his opposite number, not knowing that McClellan was sitting on the deck of a gunboat and that it was Fitz-John Porter who conducted the Union defense.

In spite of the victory, the Federal retreat was resumed that night and was continued the next day through heavy rain and over muddy roads to Harrison's Landing. (There is no object in raising the question whether another commander might not have followed up the repulse of the Confederates; another commander would not have had his army back at Malvern Hill.) Lee followed without delay, but the last battle had taught him discretion: he investigated but did not attack the new position.

The campaign was virtually at an end, a campaign full of interest for the military student because of the opportunities that McClellan missed, as well as because of the bold generalship of Lee. The Confederate commander failed to destroy his adversary, because of the difficulty of terrain, his own newness to army command, his faulty and imperfect control of troops, and the peculiarities of his subordinates. But there was another very important reason: the ability of Federal corps commanders to improvise in the absence of good orders from McClellan, fine leadership by subordinates, and the inherent fighting qualities of the Union troops, which matched the unexcelled bravery of the regiments that Lee hurled against them. Failure to accomplish all that he hoped for does not detract from Lee's achievement any more than failure to destroy Jackson detracts from the remarkable features of the offensive operation of the Federals that culminated at Port Republic. Lee had attacked a larger force commanded by a general who would go into a panic; Lincoln had sought to bring greatly superior forces against a general who would fight hard, was fleet of foot, and would not lose his head. Some very brilliant military work was done in the six weeks that ended July 1, 1862.

Casualties in the Seven Days' Battles were heavy. The Federal loss was 1,734 killed, 8,062 wounded, and 6,053 missing, giving a total of 15,849. About 2,500 sick and wounded were abandoned to the enemy at Savage Station, though an equal number of beef cattle was safely driven to the James. Rations, ammunition, and various stores, as well as tents and other camp equipage, were destroyed in enormous quantities. Lee's total casualties were approximately 20,000, mostly dead and wounded—a heavy toll indeed.[74]

The Confederates gained rich booty in spite of the great destruction the Federals had carried out. Lee reported as captured 52 excellent pieces of artillery and upwards of 31,000 small arms, as well as a great deal of other equipment and supplies. The great excess of weapons over casualties indicates that fully 15,000 of McClellan's soldiers found their rifles or muskets a nuisance under the changing fortunes of battle and abandoned them. An inaccurate statement by Lee in his report about the destruction of medical supplies for the sick and wounded that McClellan abandoned has been distorted to a charge of unjust brutality on the part of the latter.[75] That would have been totally out of character for the Federal commander, who had issued an order, "Subsistence must be left and medical stores for their use in liberal quantities." [76] The report of the Medical Director of the army reveals special care in carrying out the instructions,[77] and it is possible that Lee was wrongly informed, though some of the supplies may have been burned by mistake in a wholesale application of the torch.

In February, McClellan had written very derisively about the regiments which he had found "cowering on the banks of the Potomac" after the battle of Bull Run. Now after an abortive campaign of three months and a week of disaster at the hands of the newly formed Army of Northern Virginia—poorly equipped and smaller than his own army, but boldly commanded—he had the Army of the Potomac on the banks of the James, beleaguered by the enemy and protected by the navy's guns. When almost in despair on June 30, McClellan had wired the Secretary of War, "I shall do my best to save the army. Send more gunboats." [78] For a West Pointer who had graduated second in his class, Little Mac's fondness for gunboats was little short of heresy.

CHAPTER IX

PROFESSIONALS TAKE COMMAND

I expect to maintain this contest until successful, or till I die, or am conquered, or my term expires, or Congress or the country forsake me.   *Lincoln to Seward*

On Saturday June 28, the telegraph line along the railroad from McClellan's position to the White House was cut, and official information to Washington stopped abruptly. Fortunately McClellan's last dispatch to Stanton had been very calm and quite the sort of dispatch which a general should write; he stated that Jackson was driving in Union pickets north of the Chickahominy, and that telegraphic communication could probably not be maintained for more than an hour or two.[1] The dispatches that Lincoln and Stanton wrote in the hours and days that followed are among the most instructive that they sent during the period that they personally directed military operations. A month before, they had had to deal with the sudden attack upon Front Royal, Banks's retreat, and the threat upon Harpers Ferry. They had seen Frémont's misconceived march and torrential rains bring failure to their great counterstroke to destroy Jackson. Lincoln had been almost casual in referring to Frémont's blunder in his statement to McDowell; Stanton had not even intimated disappointment because the pincer had not closed in time at Strasburg. Nor was there any hint that the pursuit to Port Republic could have been more fruitful. While the Valley operations had given the civilians directing the war nothing worse than great disappointment, at Richmond they had to deal with a major reverse that had narrowly escaped being a catastrophe.

To General Dix, Lincoln at once sent the following dispatch, "Communication with McClellan by White House is cut off. Strain every nerve to open communication with him by James River, or any other way you can. Report to me." To Flag Officer Goldsborough went a longer telegram that is equally worthy of study; uncertain as to how well posted the sailor might be as to events on land, Lincoln described the situation and then concluded, "Also do what you can to communicate with him and support him there [McClellan, on the James]." At 3:30 P.M., on the same day a comforting message came back from the alert commodore informing the President that he was well up on current events, and concluding: "General Dix and myself will do everything in our power to communicate with General McClellan and to keep a communication with him open up the James River." [2]

Likewise on June 28 a dispatch went to General Burnside, who was operating against New Bern in North Carolina, "I think you had better go with any re-enforcements you can spare to General McClellan." Secretary Stanton followed this with two longer dispatches, the second of which reveals with what clear heads the President and he were working, and how careful they were not to interfere with McClellan:

> Since the dispatches of the President and myself to you of to-day we have seen a copy of one sent to you by General McClellan on the 25th, of which we were not aware.

> Our directions were not designed to interfere with any instructions given you by General McClellan, but only to authorize you to render him any aid in your power.

To General Halleck, at Corinth, Mississippi, Stanton sent a rather long dispatch—well written like all his dispatches—stating that the enemy had concentrated heavily at Richmond, and directing that Halleck prepare to send 25,000 infantry to McClellan at once by the quickest route.[3]

The grave mistake of stopping enlistments at the beginning of April had fortunately been offset by Lee's strategy in having Jackson threaten the line of the Potomac, so that the recruiting offices had already been ordered reopened. On the 28th the President received a message signed by eighteen governors, stating that the "people of the United States are desirous to aid promptly in furnishing all re-enforcements that you may deem needful to sustain our Government." Secretary of State Seward—himself a former governor—properly received the

task of negotiating with the state executives; and, to give him a firm
basis for his work, Lincoln wrote a memorandum beginning, "My
view of the present condition of the war is about as follows."

The note is an important document. Though McClellan's wildly
exaggerated reports had deceived the President somewhat about the
enemy concentration at Richmond, he still saw the situation clearly and
expressed himself characteristically. He was unwilling to endanger advantages already gained in the West by calling away too many troops,
lest the enemy "let us have Richmond and take Tennessee, Kentucky,
Missouri, etc." But no setback at Richmond was going to cause him
to relax his purpose:

I expect to maintain this contest until successful, or till I die, or am
conquered, or my term expires, or Congress or the country forsake me;
and I would publicly appeal to the country for this new force were it not
that I fear a general panic and stampede would follow, so hard is it to have
a thing understood as it really is.[4]

Thus armed, Seward went to New York to confer with some gov-
erners in person and with others by wire. He kept Lincoln and Stanton
posted, and they, in turn, kept him informed about the military developments in all parts of the country. In a dispatch at 7:00 P.M.,
June 30, Stanton assured his brother secretary: "You shall have all
the reliable news as fast as it comes. Dix is at work to establish a new
telegraph line between him and McClellan. Everything is moving
briskly and favorably. If the Governors will give us promptly 100,000
men the war will be over." [5] Simultaneously with the sending of this,
the governors' general program was received, and at 9:00 P.M.,
Stanton, the man of iron constitution, wired Seward: "Your pro-
gramme just received and I think it all right. The President has gone
to the country very tired. In [the] morning you shall have his answer.
I will send it [your message] to him immediately." [6]

The next day bad news was beginning to leak out, or to be suspected,
and Stanton wired Seward that some discreet persons were suggesting
300,000 more men, and that the President was inquiring as to the
practicality of 200,000. Seward replied that no one in New York was
thinking of fewer than 200,000, and that the governors were willing
to underwrite 500,000 men if they were needed; but it was left to the
President to fix the number. Later that day Lincoln telegraphed to the
governors that he accepted their offer of the 28th and had "decided to
call into the service an additional force of 300,000 men." [7] To get the

men quickly, $25 of the $100 bounty allowed by law was to be paid at the time of enlistment. With greenbacks in their pockets the new regiments would soon be singing lustily, "We are coming, Father Abraham, three hundred thousand more." And before long some of the fresh levies would be fighting with a stubborn valor that might shame some veteran units—one of the paradoxes of war. But it was much to be regretted that an effective method was not found to bring the thinning regiments already in service to full strength. Urgent recommendations of commanding officers were made known to the public, for an editorial in *Harper's Weekly* for August 16, entitled "In Earnest" closed with General Burnside's exhortation, "All is right; all is going right; only you must fill up the old regiments." McClellan wrote strong letters to the governors about the matter; but the efforts bore little fruit, for, although—with a success unparalleled in history— a second army numbering 421,465 men came into existence, only 49,990 men were obtained to fill the ranks of the veteran regiments.[8] Soon a draft of 300,000 militia for nine months was attempted.[9] Nowhere was the draft satisfactorily executed; but 87,000 volunteers for nine months, credited as draft, were accepted—a measure of doubtful value. But at least the words "draft" and "conscription" had been uttered, and people had the sound of them in their ears and the feel of them on their tongues.

The army to which the new levies would be added totaled 624,235 officers and men on June 30, with 501,663 reported as "present." [10] The number of absentees was far too great, and it was a matter soon taken in hand by the vigorous Stanton; but some of the worst evils were not corrected.[11] A soldier will naturally study the strength return detailed by departments, armies, and states to discover if there were an undue diversion at the expense of field armies.[12] If he recalls the way in which American forces had to be spread all over the world in World War II, he will probably refrain from much criticism.

Though absenteeism remained to be dealt with, another matter was being straightened out. On July 1 a report from two eminent and incorruptible citizens, Joseph Holt of Kentucky and Robert Dale Owen of Indiana, on War Department contracts was presented to Stanton.[13] Among other things they stated that Springfield rifle muskets should be made for $16 each, instead of $20, in a contract for as many as 25,000. If $4 per rifle seems a paltry sum to be concerned about in times of war, it should be remembered that at the period in question extravagance was merely in its infancy. But the honest commissioners also found fault with the public for its indiscriminate condemnation of all contractors.

The unjustified optimism that Lincoln and Stanton had on June 29, and part of June 30, was due largely to the arrival of C. C. Fulton of the *Baltimore American,* fresh from the Peninsula.[14] He had witnessed the withdrawal of Porter's force after the battle of Gaines's Mill, and stated it was according to plan and not under necessity. Ingalls also reported from Fort Monroe that he thought McClellan was fighting for Richmond.[15] This information was passed on to Seward, and Stanton went so far as to state that he thought McClellan had withdrawn from north of the Chickahominy in order to concentrate against Richmond; and he predicted at 6:00 P.M. June 29 "that General McClellan will probably be in Richmond within two days." Correspondents with the army also sensed the precarious position in which Lee had placed himself when he uncovered Richmond and moved the bulk of his army north of the Chickahominy; one of them wrote on June 28 that Jackson's attack on McClellan's right flank *"was strictly in accordance with Gen. McClellan's wishes and plans.* It withdrew them from and advanced him towards Richmond." [16] Stanton—whom McClellan accused of wishing him to fail—remained optimistic even after his prediction of the fall of Richmond tumbled upon him. On June 30 he wired General Wool at Baltimore: "McClellan has moved his whole force across the Chickahominy and rests on James River, being supported by our gunboats. The position is favorable, and looks more like taking Richmond than any time before." [17]

By July 1 the "change of base" was generally known and people had begun to dispute as to its significance. On July 4, as more news arrived or was released, there were such headlines as: "Our Army on the James River—The Enemy Still Press On—185,000 Rebels Against 95,000 Union Troops—The Rebels Repulsed Over and Over Again—The Bloodiest Fighting in Modern History—Stonewall Jackson Killed." [18] In general, exaggerated figures of enemy strength were accepted, and McClellan was reported as saying, "We fought a battle every day for the last week, and whipped them every day, though they had three to one." Naturally enough, the success of Farragut on the Mississippi River was given prominence; but it was inaccurately reported on July 7 that Vicksburg had fallen.[19] In a very judicial tone

Harper's Weekly sought to discuss on July 19 the delicate question "Who did it?" admitting candidly: "McClellan hoped to take Richmond and failed." Then it added, "The enemy hoped to annihilate him, and failed." On neither President nor general would the editor lay the blame: "We are all responsible. . . . Let us all be our own scapegoats." As to the Union force then under arms, "the general conviction of the country and of the Administration has been that there were men enough to do the work." More conservative than many writers in estimating enemy strength, he put Lee's force at between 120,000 and 140,000, but referred none the less to "overpowering odds." [20] Long extracts from Richmond papers appeared in Northern journals, and readers could see how exultation was mingled with disappointment in the "Rebel mind." On July 4 the *Richmond Examiner* [21] gave the invading army as 120,000 men: it was almost as accurate as if the writer had had McClellan's strength return before him. More correct estimates of the Confederate force began to compete with the exaggerated figures of McClellan. A Washington dispatch presently stated that Lee's army was not more than 91,000 strong at the beginning of the battles, according to "rolls in the Rebel War Department," and that "the muster roll shows the whole strength of the Rebellion from Richmond to Texas to be not more than 300,000 men" —about 100,000 below the number given by Livermore.[22]

Then the casualty lists began to appear, many columns of them, and the people of the Eastern states began to learn the real sadness of war, as they summoned their courage to read the papers. The people of the West had met the great ordeal two months before, when more men had fallen at Shiloh in two days than in McClellan's seven days of battle—1,754 killed, 8,408 wounded, as compared with 1,734 and 8,062, respectively. But the long lists of men evacuated from the Peninsula were not just of the wounded, for they contained a staggering number of men with "general debility," rheumatism, and typhoid fever. Men unused to swamps were paying for McClellan's weakness in geography and his yearning for a "brilliant campaign."

From Virginia to Texas there also were tears and heartaches, as mourning settled over the homes of the South and the people realized the great price at which a mere relaxation of the threat to Richmond had been secured. It was easy for a Convention to vote a state out of the Union, and it was not difficult to argue about the legality and constitutionality of it; *but the North would not let them go.* The

Southerners could make a new flag, and put eleven stars upon it; but
the North meant to keep those eleven stars upon the flag of the United
States. Defiantly, and perhaps a little humorously—if there can be
humor in a thing so grim—Northern regiments carried stars for the
Southern states into battle.

But the soldiers of Lee could mix a little humor with their mourning
for the men who had marched beside them, who had shared their
meager rations and their hunger, who had lain near them in many a
cheerless bivouac, and had stood shoulder to shoulder with them in
battle until they fell. As Richmond papers copied papers from the
North, the Confederates learned with some surprise that McClellan
had not really retreated after defeat but had only "changed his base"
in accordance with plans. From that time on, no one in their ranks
ever acted from discomfiture; he was only *changing his base*. An able
cavalryman recorded that if a dog were seen running ahead of another
dog as if wishing to get away, a shout would go up, "Look at him
changing his base!" Then too there were the almost unbelievable stories
of the fortunate men who had found some of the stores of the sutlers
with McClellan's army.[23] Confederates until then living on salt meat
and crackers feasted upon delicacies which some had not known existed
even in time of peace: iced lemonade, pickled oysters, eggs roasted in
blocks of salt, canned beef and ham, French rolls, cakes and confec-
tionery—all topped off with coffee and fine Havana cigars. Perhaps
after that some of the Southerners would march and fight not just for a
vague constitutional principle but for something more tangible and
immediately satisfying—the more than bountiful supplies and the
sutlers' stores that they knew were behind the Union lines.

Because of the decisions that the High Commands had to make, the
month that followed is of great interest to the military student. In the
North, Lincoln himself had to make them, at first; in the South, the
questions were largely for Lee, though Davis was certainly involved
at times. In spite of McClellan's retreat to the James and his complete
collapse as a field commander, Lincoln still held some very high cards,
and he intended to play them wisely. On June 30 he telegraphed Halleck not to send a man if it would endanger holding any important
place or compromise intended operations: "To take and hold the railroad at or east of Cleveland, in East Tennessee, I think fully as important as the taking and holding of Richmond." [24] On July 1 Halleck

reported, "All scouts, spies, deserters, and prisoners, without a single exception, report that no troops have been sent from here East." Probably Lincoln and Stanton had more confidence in his reports on such matters than in McClellan's; the thought of bringing troops from the West was dropped, though Stanton had promptly dispatched an Assistant Secretary of War to arrange transportation for the difficult move.[25]

On July 1 McClellan telegraphed, "I need 50,000 more men, and with them I will retrieve our fortunes." Patiently Lincoln replied next day: "Your dispatch of Tuesday morning induces me to hope your army is having some rest. In this hope allow me to reason with you a moment." He explained that he just did not have large numbers of available men to send, and concluded, "The Governors of eighteen States offer me a new levy of 300,000, which I accept." Unconvinced, McClellan on July 3 modestly raised his request to 100,000 and made the revealing admission that he did not think there were "more than 50,000 men with their colors." The same day the President wired: "I am satisfied that yourself, officers, and men have done the best you could. All accounts say better fighting was never done. Ten thousand thanks for it." These very gracious words appeared to bring some sense back to the hysterical general, and on July 4 he telegraphed, with his thanks for promised reenforcements: "I will do the best I can with such force as I have and such aid as you can give me. . . . Our whole army is now drawn up for review in its positions, bands playing, salutes being fired, and all things looking bright." The effect of the bands and the salutes lasted until the next day, and McClellan informed the adjutant general, "I have every reason to believe that our victory at Malvern Hill was a crushing one— one from which he [the enemy] will not readily recover." A few hours later, upon the statement of a single prisoner, all his confidence had evaporated. McClellan feared a heavy attack the following day and woke up corps commanders to read long orders.[26]

McClellan's lack of balance was growing worse instead of better; it was again revealed in the letter he handed to Lincoln when the latter came to Harrison's Landing on July 8, for a brief visit with the army and a talk with its commander. Perhaps no soldier ever presumed to write a document more out of order, and Margaret Leech is restrained rather than severe when she speaks of the "incomparable brass" it took to give it to the President. McClellan candidly stated that the contents of the letter had little to do with his army or its operation. The document was in fact purely a political one, and it dealt at length with questions that fell to the President and the Congress but not to the commander of an army.[27] None of the quiet sentences with which Michie so often blasts McClellan exceeds the devastating analysis he gives the July infraction:

With perfect confidence in his own military talents and political sagacity, he felt entirely competent to teach Mr. Lincoln something, whom, as President, he regarded as his official superior, but otherwise as his intellectual inferior. Seward, Chase, and many others less prominent, had committed the same error and learned to profit by it; but it was not the good fortune of McClellan, while in active service, to have this beam removed from his intellectual organs of vision.[28]

McClellan's offense was not in what he said, but in the fact that he should say anything. The actual document was not what appeared to be foreshadowed by a request he had made on June 20 for permission to indulge in some suggestions,[29] but it none the less shows that he had not been attending in a single-minded way to the very heavy duty before him. He had been thinking of the political principles on which the war should be conducted, when he ought to have been thinking of such things as the routes to his newly planned base on the James. He meddled in somebody else's business and neglected his own; and the neglect almost caused disaster. Never did Abraham Lincoln show more forbearance than when he merely thanked McClellan for the political composition and let the great transgression go unnoticed. Though the President had made no comment with regard to the sentiments expressed, McClellan did not hesitate to convey his beliefs even to the enemy. On July 11 he wrote to Hill Carter, owner of a great estate near Malvern Hill, in a letter expressing regret for the inconvenience and loss the Virginian had suffered because of the Union army: "I have not come here to wage war upon the defenseless, upon non-combatants, upon private property, nor upon the domestic institutions of the land. I and the army I command are fighting to secure the Union and maintain its Constitution and laws, and for no other purpose." There was nothing in this contrary to the objective of the war as Lincoln had previously expressed it, but, nevertheless, McClellan was taking sides on a very serious question which was emerging, and he was confidentially communicating his political views to the enemy.[30]

On July 11 Lincoln assigned Major General Halleck "to command the whole land forces of the United States as General in Chief," and directed him to report at Washington as soon as he could leave his headquarters at Corinth. There were no unnecessary flourishes in Halleck's reply, which was a through-and-through soldierly dispatch stating that he had ordered General Grant to report immediately to take over the Western command and would "start for Washington the moment I can have a personal interview with General Grant." [31] General Scott must have mentioned Halleck as his possible successor the previous fall, though he ended up with recommending McClellan. The suggestion was doubtless renewed and discussed at length when the President made a call upon the retired Lieutenant General at West Point late in June—an event which set correspondents and editors to conjecturing.[32]

Halleck had more to commend him than just Scott's approval: his *Elements of Military Art and Science,* first published in 1846, was in the field kit of many a new officer, and his *International Law,* published in 1861, was destined to run through several editions. He had not seen active campaigning of a hard kind. His Mexican War experience was confined mostly to California, and he had had a successful career there in both law and business since his resignation from the army in 1854. Back in the service promptly in 1861, he had been commissioned a major general in the regular army on August 19, which gave him rank next after McClellan and Frémont. Undoubtedly Halleck had helped straighten out administrative confusion in the West; and, though his move on Corinth had been slow, he had captured that important strategic point, and public and administrators alike naturally gave him credit as department commander for the sizable achievements of the Western armies.

The new General in Chief was completely free of political ambition, and found the Washington atmosphere of politics, intrigue, and gossip distasteful. Tightly buttoned up, with the unusual fringe of whiskers about a smoothly shaven mouth and chin, he would have been far happier among scholars than among Congressmen and their ladies.

Already Major General John Pope had been working hard for a few weeks in Washington to concentrate and recondition the troops of Frémont and Banks and other units that were to comprise his new Army of Virginia. Unfortunately, however, he had been talking too much. The press had given publicity to his achievements at Island No. 10 and elsewhere, and had built prestige he was shortly to compromise by boasts and indiscretions. Unwisely, in view of McClellan's inclination to classify a person quickly as a friend or an enemy, he had made some comments on that general's campaign. In spite of such talk, however, Pope wrote McClellan a long letter on July 4 that had in it a ring of frankness, capability, and sincerity. It ended:

You now know my position and resources. A movable force of 43,000 men (19,000 in good order), posted as I have detailed to you, are all I have, and I am made responsible for the security of this city.

I trust you will communicate your wishes to me, and give me the benefit of any views and suggestions which will enable me to aid you. I need not repeat that I stand prepared to do all in my power for that purpose.[33]

McClellan replied on July 7 with appropriate thanks, but also typical distortions and promises. He stated, that, although he should receive heavy reenforcements at once, the spirit of his army was such that he felt he would not be able "to restrain it from speedily resuming the offensive, unless reconnaissances should develop so overwhelming a force of the enemy in front as to render it out of the question. Even in that event we will endeavor to find some weak point in the enemy's lines which we will attack in order to break it." This "tall talk" was in line with his statement to Adjutant General Thomas on July 5 that he intended to ascertain the enemy's "position and prevent him from assuming a new line of operations." [34] He never had the slightest intention of making a serious reconnaissance, for he was still depending upon Pinkerton for his "intelligence"; nor had he thought of breaking any line or of preventing the enemy from doing anything he wanted to do. In fact, the day after McClellan made his boasts to Pope, Lee moved his army back to convenient and more healthy camping grounds near Richmond where he could refit and reorganize, leaving a brigade of cavalry to observe McClellan.[35] It was sufficient to detain him in position in spite of all his bold statements.

From his headquarters in Washington on July 14 Pope issued an address to the officers and soldiers of his army that marked the beginning of his trouble. He bragged, "I have come to you from the West, where we have always seen the backs of our enemies; from an army whose business it has been to seek the adversary and to beat him when he was found; whose policy has been attack and not defense." [36] Full of such bombast and boasting, it sat ill with the men Pope was to command; many of them had worn out much shoe leather fighting apparently to no purpose, and were sensitive to open comparisons between the East and the West, which Pope should have been most careful to avoid. Presently he was reported as having said that his headquarters would be in the saddle. When this boast reached the humor-loving Confederates, still laughing over the location of McClellan's "base," they made indelicate jokes about the general who had his headquarters where his hindquarters should be. The Southerners knew their own ability to march, endure hunger, and attack impetuously, and, trusting deeply in their own commanders, waited for the next contest somewhat scornful of Northern generals.

Four days later Pope ordered that as far as practicable his army should live on the country. The order did not justify pillaging, which he tried hard to suppress; supplies were to be purchased in all cases by the proper officers, and the order was in every way in strict conformity with military usage.[37] Nevertheless it showed that Pope was against a "soft war" such as McClellan had seemed to endorse in his letter to Hill Carter. The new order met approval in Pope's army, and a correspondent wrote: "Its very good sense compensates for the ill effect produced by the address to his army received here a few days since, which was generally disliked and laughed at." [38]

It would have been well if Pope had stopped writing orders after gettting himself out of one predicament. But on July 20 he issued an order which prescribed stern penalties for guerrillas, marauders, and "evil-disposed persons in rear of our armies." Though within the bounds of recognized warfare the measures and punishments that he prescribed seemed barbaric to people who believed they were fighting for their homes and their essential liberties. Still all might have been well; but Pope's busy pen kept on, and three days later came an order prescribing that an oath of allegiance be administered to all "disloyal male citizens" within the lines of the Union army. A person who refused to take the oath was to be expelled from the lines and, if later found within them, was to be considered as a spy; a person who took the oath and violated it was to be shot.[39] For this order there was no justification at all in the recognized rules of warfare, which did not consider as binding an oath of allegiance taken through force.

John Pope indeed was getting rough, "an ugly customer," as one correspondent put it,[40] and the radicals tended to acclaim him. Still he had not said one word about the war being for any other purpose than the restoration of the Union, and he had not referred to "the domestic institutions of the land" with approval or disapproval, or in a non-committal tone—as George McClellan had done. In fact, he had left his proposed order with the President before issuing it, and explained in a note what was back of it: "I find it impossible to make any movement, however insignificant the force, without having it immediately communicated to the enemy. Constant correspondence, verbally and by letter, between the enemy's forces and the so-called peaceful citizens in the rear of this army, is carried on, which can in no other way be interrupted." [41] Lincoln doubtless saw in the order nothing but a military object; but this did not change the fact that Pope had no right to consider reluctantly given oaths as binding—a fact that Halleck, careful student of international law and military usages, well understood.[42] The uproar and condemnation that the conservatives raised was out of all proportion to the new general's sin, for the order could not have been enforced, and could easily have been ignored by officers to whom it was especially repugnant.[43] Pope's subordinate commanders were very busy, and it was merely necessary for them to observe few "disloyal males" in order to render the general's unhappy order ineffective, and to compel him to deal with the troublesome problem without exacting oaths.

At last Halleck, for whom the President had been waiting both anxiously and impatiently,[44] arrived, and on July 23 the war passed again into the hands of a professionally trained General in Chief. Though no one would recommend that amateurs engage in the direction of a great war, the period when Lincoln was *de facto* Commander in Chief gives far more to commend than has been recognized. The new General in Chief, taking over direction at a difficult time, had to make one of the hardest decisions of the entire war: what should be done with the Army of the Potomac, confined by cavalry vedettes in a space too small for necessary sanitation and inadequate for maneuvering and training. There was no delay on Halleck's part. On the afternoon of the 24th he was off to visit the army and confer with its temperamental commander; on the 27th he gave Stanton a memorandum on the interview.[45] At first McClellan had suggested, instead of another move on Richmond, crossing the James and attacking Petersburg; but he had finally conceded the great difficulty of this operation. He believed that with 30,000 reenforcements he could

MAJOR GENERAL HENRY W. HALLECK

attack Richmond with "a good chance of success"; but he had to be told that the President could assure him of only 20,000 more men—and Halleck was not yet sufficiently familiar with the entire military situation to say whether the number could be increased. As to strengths, McClellan ran true to form. He stated he had only 90,000 effectives, although his strength return for July 20—certified correct by his own signature—gave him 101,691; he continued to estimate the enemy strength at 200,000, although he knew that both Jackson and Ewell had gone to the vicinity of Gordonsville because of the activity of Pope's force.[46]

After consulting with his officers McClellan believed that even with only 20,000 more men there was a "chance" of success against Richmond and expressed his willingness "to try it." His leading officers were about equally divided over the question of withdrawing from the Peninsula, or making another try at the Confederate capital.[47] The situation of the army was in many ways bad,[48] hemmed into a small area in an unhealthy region, with scant chance to mitigate the midsummer temperatures—which were more extreme than those to which most of the men were accustomed. The number of sick was high, 12,000,[49] and 39,000 men were still carried as absent; it was probable that half of the absentees had got away largely on account of McClellan's own negligence—as he had been forced to admit when the President asked for an explanation of the difference between the 170,000 men he understood had been sent to the Peninsula and the number on hand.[50] (Lincoln's passion for figures often was an annoyance to McClellan.)

In his memorandum General Halleck stated that he had had neither time nor opportunity to "investigate the facts upon which" McClellan had based the estimate of the enemy force at 200,000, and accordingly offered no opinion as to its correctness. The very next day, however, he received a remarkable memorandum about the enemy strength at Richmond from an unexpected source—the office of the quartermaster general.

Better quartermaster generals than M. C. Meigs do not often come along. He had a passion for thinking and doing sums; moreover, the enemy strength was a subject of real concern to him through its effect on the Union strength that had to be deployed, reflected in the number of horses, mules, wagons, and the amount of forage and clothing he would have to procure and get to the army (and also pay for). An orderly and logical mind was revealed in his letter that began: "From the Richmond and Wilmington published notices of the battles of the 26th and 27th of June north of the Chickahominy I have with some care made out the following organizations of the attacking forces." What followed was what would now be called the "enemy order in battle," and it showed that Meigs would have made as good an intelligence officer as he was a quartermaster. He identified the enemy divisions, brigades, and considerable of the artillery that had been in action, and he suggested that the sixty-odd infantry regiments that were apparently revealed "must be nearly one-half of the whole Richmond army." He supported this deduction by citing an article in the *Wilmington Journal* of July 8 by "an intelligent writer of Branch's division," which indicated 152 regiments in Lee's army. Allowing an average of 700 men—certainly very liberal—Meigs deduced "a total force of 105,000 men." The facts and reasoning that he set forth must have impressed Halleck, and they doubtless coincided with judgments of Lincoln and Stanton already given him.[51]

There was only one thing that a responsible administration could do: acknowledge the Peninsula Campaign to be a failure and not merely "a change of base," bring back the Army of the Potomac from its unhealthy camp, and start on a new line of action. If McClellan really believed that Lee had 200,000 men in and about Richmond, it was military stupidity to say that he had a good chance to take the city with 30,000 more men. If Lee had the great strength reported, a successful operation against Richmond would require a force of 200,000 to 250,000 men. McClellan was in no way qualified for such a gigantic field command, and even a Meigs would have been overwhelmed with the problem of its supply.[52] Large reenforcements were not available, and to hold the Army of the Potomac in an unhealthy area where the necessary training and maneuvers and relief from tedium were impractical was to insure its deterioration.

On the other hand, if McClellan did not believe his fantastic figures about Lee's strength, over and over again repeated, he was willfully deceiving his government; and truthfulness is the first essential of a field commander. A man deficient in intellectual integrity may plan a good campaign, but only a general who is honest with himself and honest with his government will ever lead a large body of troops successfully against skillful, hard-fighting opponents. Some such thought must have been in the mind of Marshal Foch when he remarked: "Intellect, criticism—Pah! A donkey who has more character is more useful." [53] Henderson touched the same note clearly in a sympathetic comment about the heavy and searching trials of the Northern people: "They had yet to learn that mere length of service is no test whatever of capacity for command, and that character fortified by knowledge is the only charm which attracts success." [54]

It has often been pointed out that McClellan's suggested move across the James against Petersburg was an anticipation of the operation that in the end succeeded under Grant's command. Here one should note another weighty remark of Henderson: "It is easy to conceive. It is less easy to execute." [55] McClellan, prone to be jubilant over a minor success and completely cast down by slight opposition or initial failure, was not the man to succeed with the very difficult operation he suggested to Halleck. Competent students of warfare who have studied the final Petersburg operation have seen that it required great steadiness and also the ability to appraise accurately the real meaning of events: qualities almost totally lacking in McClellan, as they are likely to be in a man not scrupulously honest with both himself and others. Some writers have pointed to McClellan's plans and suggestions as if they alone were sufficient; and, failing to understand what Henderson meant by capacity to command, they have confused it apparently with mere popularity with troops or with personal bravery.

The operation that lay ahead was both delicate and difficult, and it was to put a heavy test on Halleck, Pope, and McClellan. McClellan might be attacked by Lee after part of his force had been withdrawn; Pope, on the other hand, might be heavily assailed before the two Union commands could be joined. As soon as the movement was well started, the strategical initiative would pass to Lee, who was advantageously situated to take advantage of vulnerable Union armies. For a short interval he could be deceived and would be uncertain as to what the Northern program was; but, once it was revealed, the Confederate commander would not sit idly by with such an unusual opportunity to strike. There would be anxious days ahead for Lincoln as the race developed and each day brought its altered situation. Clear-thinking and fast-acting generals—and also steady ones—were needed.

Did Lincoln have them? Would the three generals work together? The President and the Secretary of War would give no orders; the generals were to be given full rein.

The move began, properly, with the quartermaster. On July 29 Meigs directed that all suitable steamers at Baltimore should be engaged to help evacuate the sick and wounded at Harrison's Landing, and the next evening McClellan was directed to send such men away as rapidly as possible.[56] On August 1 General Burnside, whose troops had been held at Newport News, was ordered to embark at once for Aquia Creek, on the Potomac, and proceed to Fredericksburg.[57] Movement of his force of 15,000 men presented something of a problem, because all its wagons, ambulances, artillery, and cavalry had been left in North Carolina; it, therefore, was not mobile and could not do heavy duty. On the evening of August 3 a dispatch communicated the final decision to McClellan, directing him to withdraw his army from the Peninsula and move it to Aquia Creek.[58] At noon the next day he protested in a long telegram stating, "It is here on the banks of the James, that the fate of the Union should be decided"; and he *entreated* that the order be rescinded. But the High Command was resolute, and the new General in Chief wired briefly that he had given the order with reluctance, but that it must be executed "with all possible promptness." [59] Although he must have known the views of the administration, he wrote a long and able letter of explanation manfully backing up the decision as if it had been entirely his own:

I must take things as I find them. I find the forces divided, and I wish to unite them. Only one feasible plan has been presented for doing this. If you or anyone else had presented a better plan I certainly should have adopted it. But all of your plans require re-enforcements, which it is impossible to give you. It is very easy to ask for re-enforcements, but it is not so easy to give them when you have no disposable troops at your command.[60]

That Halleck did not touch upon the delicate but all-important question as to what McClellan *really believed* to be Lee's strength is quite understandable. He stressed the great need for promptness in a telegram to McClellan on August 7: "I must beg of you, general, to hurry along this movement. Your reputation as well as mine may be involved in its rapid execution. I cannot regard Pope and Burnside as safe until you re-enforce them." [61]

Halleck was in a difficult position: he had to solve a hard military problem, without an adequate staff; and that problem was confounded by his relations with McClellan, an unfortunate type of officer ruined by premature stars, a vain, touchy, and suspicious subordinate who once had been his superior. At first their communications contained expressions of good will and the promise by McClellan of full coopera- tion, tiresomely repeated. But very soon Halleck began to speak openly in his dispatches of McClellan's delay. Doubtless this was unfair, for the General in Chief did not know all the difficulties that beset McClellan in sending away the sick and wounded and in making the other preparations for departure.[62] Nevertheless, McClellan need- lessly pretended not to understand the first directive sent him, and although he gave frequent assurance of his intention to execute orders received he made further attempts to persuade the General in Chief to change his mind—by renewing promises about taking Richmond.[63] The general who had written much more harshly to General Morris than any superior ever wrote to him, concluded a dispatch: "The present moment is probably not the proper one for me to refer to the unnecessarily harsh and unjust tone of your telegrams of late. It will however, make no difference to my official action." [64] It was indeed an unhappy moment for an army commander to indulge in pique, for on the day preceding, before any of McClellan's troops had started to move, the first blow had been struck at Pope, in a sharp and bloody battle at the base of Cedar—or Slaughter—Mountain.

John Pope had set to work in a thorough way organizing his com- mand and preparing it for operations. His headquarters, however, instead of being "in the saddle," had been in Washington, where the President had directed him to remain until Halleck should arrive and get things somewhat in hand. The First Corps of the new Army of Vir- ginia was to be composed of Frémont's command; but when Frémont, who had been Pope's superior in the West at one time, declined to serve under his former subordinate and asked to be relieved the admin- istration lost no time in granting the request.[65] The temperamental soldier, explorer, and politician remained inactive until 1864, when he resigned in order to become a Presidential candidate. His command was appropriately given to German-born Franz Sigel,[66] since the corps had a very German flavor, with divisions commanded by Briga- dier Generals Robert C. Schenck, Adolph von Steinwehr, and Carl Schurz. The troublesome old division of Blenker had been split up, each of the other three divisions receiving one of its brigades—which gives color to Barnard's statement that McClellan had more than once expressed his determination to rid himself of Blenker's division in some way,[67] in spite of his later complaint that Lincoln had sent it to Frémont.

Pope's Second Corps consisted of the troops of General Banks,

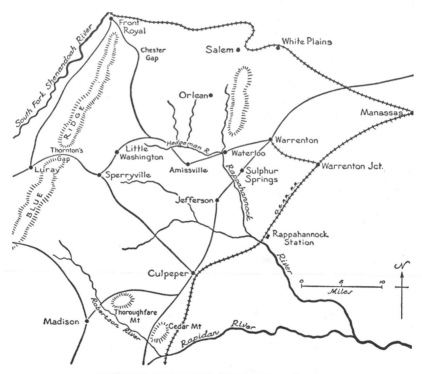

REGION OF POPE'S CONCENTRATION

comprising two divisions commanded by Brigade Generals Alpheus S. Williams and C. C. Augur, and a cavalry brigade under Brigadier General John P. Hatch. The Third Corps of the new army consisted, with some exceptions, of the three divisions of McDowell's force remaining after Morell's division had gone to McClellan. Shields's division, rather broken down,[68] was now split up, and part was sent elsewhere; so that McDowell had the divisions of Ricketts and King, separate brigades under Carroll and Brigadier General Abner Doubleday, and Bayard's cavalry brigade. In addition to the three corps constituting the real field force, the Army of Virginia included a Reserve Corps under Brigadier General Samuel D. Sturgis consisting of troops in and about Washington, and the detached command of Julius White at Winchester. Also included in Pope's army was the strong division of Brigadier General Jacob D. Cox in far-off West Virginia.

The administration had indeed gathered together quite a miscellany of forces for the command of a general who had some accomplishments to his credit. On July 31 Pope's returns showed a total of 77,779 officers and men as present for duty, of whom 56,098 were in the field force proper.[69] The new commander had shown in some correspondence with Brigadier General A. Sanders Piatt, White's predecessor in command at Winchester, that he really meant that there should be no retreating before mild shows of force; but he also showed himself very fair and considerate when he apologized generously for having been influenced by exaggerated rumor.[70]

Pope's plan was to operate down the Orange and Alexandria Railroad toward Gordonsville and beyond, and also to make a move from Fredericksburg toward Hanover Junction, at least as a distraction. In this way he would keep Washington covered, and at the same time he would threaten the Virginia Central Railroad, the vital link between Richmond and the Valley. Sigel and Banks had been moved as quickly as possible from the Shenandoah Valley, eastward through the Blue Ridge, and Ricketts's division had marched from Fredericksburg to join them. On July 17 Pope put his plans fully before McClellan:

There is no enemy in my front. My cavalry pickets extend 25 miles south of Fredericksburg, and Hatch, with 2,500 men, passes through Gordonsville to-day *en route* for Charlottesville. He will destroy the Virginia Central road and the road from Charlottesville to Lynchburg. If it be possible he will push cavalry in several directions to James River and destroy the canal. Culpeper is occupied by a considerable force, with Banks, Sigel, and one division of McDowell in supporting distance.[71]

Although Pope was correct in saying there was no enemy in his front on July 17, it is likely that he knew that Lee was being well informed of the gathering threat toward Gordonsville, and that he expected prompt reaction. Two days later Pope reported to McClellan that there were unconfirmed rumors that Jackson was moving on

Gordonsville. On July 20 McClellan informed Stanton that he had learned from returned prisoners and wounded that a force had moved toward Gordonsville; and in a dispatch to Lincoln he identified the force as Jackson's. On the same day Pope wired McClellan: "Ewell is at Gordonsville with about 6,000 men. Jackson reported to be at Louisa Court-House with 25,000." [72]

In spite of the grandiloquence in his unfortunate address to his army, Pope was a careful officer, and he intended to watch Jackson. On July 20 he directed Piatt at Winchester:

Spare no means through spies and others to inform yourself of the movements of the enemy's cavalry in the valley. It is reported to me that Jackson is on the road to Moorefield. Spend whatever money is necessary to keep yourself fully advised of what is going on within 50 miles south of you.[73]

Equally significant was his dispatch fifty minutes later to General Wool at Baltimore: "It is reported that Jackson is on his way toward Romney, with the purpose of making a descent into Maryland. It is possible, but I hardly think it probable." The fine old soldier instantly put all his troops westward along the Potomac on the alert and reported the fact to Pope; in spite of his seventy-eight years, this man who was every inch a general, was going into the field to assure himself that all was well. His dispatch closed with these significant sentences: "It is my intention to go as far as Cumberland to-morrow, visiting all the troops on this side. You ought, my dear general, to be with your troops. Jackson is an enterprising officer. Delays are dangerous." [74] Even the Peninsular Campaign might have succeeded if command of the Army of the Potomac when it reached Fort Monroe had been assigned to Wool. There would have been no overestimation of the enemy, and no supercaution. Instead, there would have been promptness, enterprise, and boldness.

Pope was not depending on money and spies alone to get information; he depended chiefly upon bold reconnaissance, and his accomplishments were little less than remarkable. Naturally rumor as well as fact flowed in. Thus Bayard reported on the 21st: "General Jackson is at Gordonsville, I think, with General Ewell and 30,000 men, says report. I know nothing." [75] No tired cavalryman could give a more teasing morsel than that to evaluate. But on the same day Banks sent in this definite word received from Colonel Henry Anisansel, First (West) Virginia Cavalry:

He left Friday, 18th, 3 p.m., and arrived within 4 miles of Louisa Court-House. Learned with a certainty that Jackson dined there Saturday, the 19th, at 2 p.m. Was received with great joy, and left for Gordonsville with 10,000 or 20,000 men and a large force of artillery by land, as he says, on the State road. Anisansel encountered a heavy body of cavalry near Louisa Court-House and withdrew to Culpeper. He reports hearing the cars running at Hanover Court-House and a great stirring up. No other news.[76]

The most thorough intelligence officer could have only one complaint here: the name of Stonewall's hostess and the dishes she served her famous guest had not been ascertained. But nothing was more significant or timely than the report of Banks that Jackson "was not bound for the valley, but more in this direction." [77]

Excellent information was also flowing to Pope about the entire Confederate force at Richmond, for McDowell reported from Warrenton that a Frenchman who lived at Richmond had just brought in word that there were only six Confederate divisions about the capital, "and that their force amounted to 90,000 at the outside." [78] The man was sent to Washington for further questioning; and the report, helping to show the hopelessness of McClellan, surely must have been in the hands of Halleck before he made his decision a few days later. Not only was McClellan a week later to more than double the enemy strength, but on July 20 he reported to Stanton: "In conversation the rebels boast of going to Baltimore, etc. Our information begins to be more full." [79] McClellan apparently evaluated the boasts quite as the enemy wished him to—as definite plans of action.

The instructions that Pope sent to Hatch through Banks were those of a forthright field general:

He must take nothing with him except what I specify and live upon the country. It does not matter what force of infantry the enemy has either at Gordonsville or elsewhere. Infantry cannot pursue cavalry. . . . Tell Hatch speed is the great thing by day and night. He ought not to think of stopping more than a couple of hours at any time. He can return by any other route he pleases. . . . Hatch must move at once and with the utmost rapidity.[80]

The expedition was a dismal failure; Hatch got no farther than Orange, because Jackson and Ewell were reported to be at Gordonsville.[81] Without delay Pope made him a foot soldier, and appointed Brigadier General John Buford—late major and assistant inspector general—to succeed him.[82] Few bolder or more enterprising soldiers ever rode at the head of a column of horse than this gallant Kentuckian. Buford was to be tireless in his search for information and always eager to fight: a fitting comrade for George Bayard. What these two excellent soldiers were to contribute won praise from Henderson:

> Very little that occurred within the Confederate lines escaped the vigilance of the enemy; and although Jackson's numbers were somewhat overestimated, Pope's cavalry, energetically led by two able young officers, Generals Buford and Bayard, did far better service than McClellan's detectives. Jackson had need of all his prudence.[83]

The great admirer of Stonewall also had a good word for Pope: "Nevertheless, with all his peculiar characteristics, Pope was no despicable foe." Indeed he was not, for all that Lee might think.[84]

Late in the afternoon of July 29 Pope and his staff arrived by rail in a shower of rain at Warrenton, and set up headquarters in a "female seminary" in the outskirts of the comfortable and attractive little village, untouched as yet by war.[85] The stay was brief, and the general moved the next day to a camp beyond Hedgeman River at Waterloo; the very observant Colonel Strother, who had now joined his staff, set him down as an accomplished horseman by his quiet pace. The next day Ricketts's splendid division of McDowell's corps was reviewed, and on succeeding days Banks's corps near Little Washington, and Sigel's corps near Sperryville—a mere crossroads hamlet—marched before their commanding general.

Pope lost no time; probably in his mind was the admonition from General Wool: "Jackson is an enterprising officer. Delays are dangerous." On August 3 he learned that cavalry from Crawford's advanced brigade of Banks's corps had had a tart little clash with the enemy in Orange—the outcome of which made Jackson try to get rid of a cavalry commander.[86] Two days later Pope reported to Halleck that Jackson was said to have 50,000 men; though he believed that this was an overestimation, he knew that A. P. Hill had recently joined Jackson with at least 10,000.[87] On the same day he set fully before the General in Chief the operation which was to start the next day.[88] He planned to take up a position along Robertson River, which would be strong and easily defensible; then by using his large force of cavalry he believed he could make Gordonsville untenable.

On the 6th things were developing south of Culpeper, where Crawford became somewhat anxious because his front was uncovered and there were several fords over the Rapidan within ten miles of his position. Bayard was working hard, but his pickets had been on duty for four days, and his horses were badly used up. To increase his troubles, the learned McDowell had bothered him with French words, and the young untraveled cavalryman wrote the general's chief of staff: "I have received your order to establish *estafettes* along the road. That means couriers, does it not? Excuse my ignorance, but I have no dictionary to see what it is." [89]

The next day, Friday the 8th, Pope had his headquarters at Culpeper, and he learned that Jackson had crossed the Rapidan with a force reported at 30,000.[90] Bayard was being forced back. Banks, whose corps had arrived, sent two regiments of cavalry, as well as Crawford's infantry brigade reenforced by two batteries, to Bayard.[91] Halleck telegraphed to Pope: "Do not advance, so as to expose yourself to any disaster, unless you can better your line of defense, until we can get more troops upon the Rappahannock." Pope was not alarmed and intended to hold at Culpeper. Orders went to Sigel to leave Sperryville that evening and to be at Culpeper by noon the next day.[92] General King, some of whose troops were just back from a very bold and somewhat destructive raid on the Virginia Central Railroad, was ordered to march as soon as possible to Culpeper with his entire division and Doubleday's brigade.[93] Pope could well feel that night that he had matters sufficiently in hand for the trial with Jackson that seemed to be developing. With the arrival of Sigel he would have about 32,000 men, and this number would be materially raised when the absent units of McDowell's corps joined.

Strother watched Crawford, commanding the Forty-sixth Pennsylvania, the Fifth Connecticut, the Tenth Maine, the Twenty-eighth New York, and ten guns of Roemer's and Knapp's batteries, move out to support Bayard; and he wrote in his journal, "It was the most inspiriting sight I ever beheld." [94] One may be sure that Bayard felt not only "inspirited" but grateful when Crawford came up and encamped one mile in advance of his "utterly exhausted troops." One night of rest would do much for himself and his men, but it would hardly rebuild broken-down horses. He promised, however, to be back at work in the morning, and informed McDowell's chief of staff, "The enemy are about 2 miles in advance of us." [95]

Saturday August 9 broke bright, and the thermometer mounted rapidly. But it was not excess of temperature that made the day unusual—for there had been a succession of very hot days; it was the fact that a Federal general was very bold in an attack. The general was none other than Banks. Jackson's soldiers, remembering some of the rations they had harvested from the Federal general's wagons, had

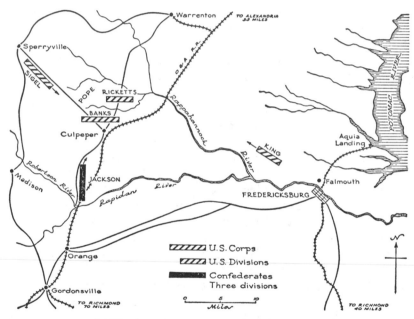

POPE AND JACKSON, AUGUST 8, 1862

named him "Commissary Banks"; but Stonewall himself asserted that the Northern people did not do Banks full justice.[96] Substantial indeed was Ballard's tribute, "Banks was always ready for a fight, and fought well." [97] Now, after being separated for two months, Banks and Jackson were to renew their associations in a new environment. Orders from Pope came to Banks through Colonel Louis H. Marshall, and inexcusably they were verbal. Desiring to have his instructions on paper, Banks had a staff officer write what Marshall dictated and then read it back to the colonel for verification. A little over two years later Banks asserted under oath that his records showed that this is what was written:

Culpeper, 9:45 A.M., August 9, 1862

From Colonel Lewis Marshall:

General Banks will move to the front immediately, assume command of all the forces in the front, deploy his skirmishers if the enemy approaches, and attack him immediately as soon as he approaches, and be re-enforced from here.[98]

General Lee had been much aggrieved by his own nephew Louis's serving under the "miscreant Pope," [99] but he probably would have felt better if he could have seen the masterpiece of ambiguity that his lamented kin uttered to Banks in the name of General Pope. What did it mean? Pope afterward stated that he wished Banks to take his entire corps (reduced to about 8,000 on account of detachments) out to the position occupied the afternoon before by Crawford, and to hold that position until the arrival of Sigel, making no attack except with skirmishers.[100] If that was his wish, he should have so directed in writing, taking no chance of a misunderstanding or a poor statement by Lee's nephew. Banks naturally had in mind Pope's declaration of July 14 with its strong condemnation of defensive action, and the maximlike sentence, "Success and glory are in the advance." Conditioned thus, Banks can be excused for seeing in the order only the words, "and attack him immediately as soon as he approaches." So "Commissary Banks" marched out prepared to fight—and fight he did.[101]

After Bayard's cavalry had been driven in, the enemy guns opened at about eleven o'clock from the slope of Cedar Mountain upon the position occupied by Crawford. About noon General Williams arrived accompanying Gordon's brigade (which with Crawford's brigade completed his division); about two o'clock Banks was up with Augur's division, accompanied by Brigadier General Benjamin S. Roberts, Pope's chief of cavalry, sent as a staff representative. Banks must have come to the conclusion that the enemy was making merely a "reconnaissance in force"—a view expressed by Pope's chief of staff in writing to Sigel the evening before [102]—or at least was not present in great strength. He decided to attack his former teacher, and not just with skirmishers (for one could not do much serious attacking with skirmishers), but with everything he had. Augur was to take the left of the Culpeper-Orange Road, and Williams the right, and they were directed to advance upon the enemy in their front.

As a matter of fact, Jackson had about 24,000 men and was trying to get them into position for an attack—but with much slowness.

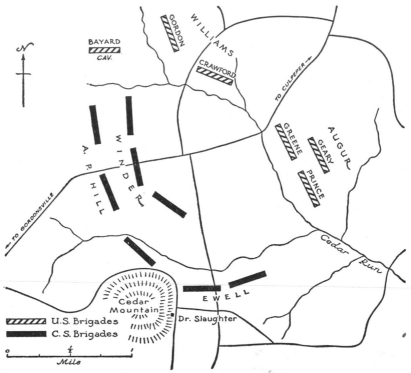

BATTLE OF CEDAR MOUNTAIN, AUGUST 9, 1862

Ewell's division was on the east side of the road toward Cedar Mountain, opposing Augur; Jackson's own old division, commanded first by Winder, then by Taliaferro (after Winder had been killed by artillery fire), was on the west of the road, opposing the division of Williams. Confederate reconnaissance had been inadequate, and about half past five Crawford's brigade, after working its way through some woods, burst with fury on Jackson's unsuspecting division. It was about 1,500 men against double the number; but Crawford broke the first Confederate line irretrievably (Henderson's word), and many Confederate regiments, including one from the famed Stonewall Brigade, were shattered and driven back in confusion. All of Jackson's battlefield skill and energy were required to restore the conflict, which he did largely through brigades from Hill's division, now close at hand. Crawford, unsupported, could not stand against the well directed counterattacks of fresh troops, and after suffering heavy loss he was forced back. When it was too late to do anything substantial for Crawford, Gordon, who had been in reserve, and who should have been held for Crawford to retire upon, was ordered to attack. This his brigade did bravely, but only to meet heavy loss from the now reorganized and superior enemy, and to be in turn compelled to retire. Augur too had attacked well on the east of the road, but without Williams's brilliant temporary success. He too was forced back as the great power of the enemy developed.

Darkness was coming as Banks fell back to about his original position, where Sigel's corps and Ricketts's division had been deployed at the direction of Pope, who assumed personal command of the field. A full moon illuminated the night, and Jackson tried to advance, but after shelling a woods with temporary demoralizing effect among men who had sought refuge there,[103] he received some well directed artillery fire himself and clear indications that it was a good time to desist. In the morning Pope had a good line of battle, with skirmishers out, but the enemy, well watched from Thoroughfare Mountain,[104] remained generally quiet, his aggressive mood apparently over for the moment. A courier was sent to General King, en route from Fredericksburg, informing him of the situation and stating: "It is all-important that you should be here as soon as possible." [105] Halleck, doing his part well, got everything necessary into a three-sentence message to Burnside: "The enemy has attacked General Pope at Culpeper. Are you ready to co-operate with him? Give me full information of your position and preparation." On the 11th there was general quiet; burial parties were busy under flags of truce, and the two commanders watched each other. Pope could hardly feel the affair was over, for his observers on Thoroughfare Mountain had reported "a large park of wagons 6 miles this side of Orange Court-House," which would indicate that Stonewall had contemplated something more than a week-end expedition. From some source inaccurate information reached him that large reenforcements had come to the enemy, including the division of Longstreet. At eleven o'clock, before turning in for the night, he wired Halleck, "I think it almost certain that we shall be attacked in the morning, and we shall make the best fight we can," a sentence quite in contrast with the hysterical message McClellan had sent to Lincoln at 6:15 P.M. on June 25. But the expected attack did not come, and at 7:30 A.M. on the 12th Pope reported to the General in Chief: "The enemy has retreated under cover of the night. His rear is now crossing the Rapidan toward Orange Court-House." [106]

Even the first accounts of the engagement that appeared in Northern papers were, in some cases at least, singularly accurate. Headlines in the *New York Tribune* for August 11 read: "The Rebels, 15,000 strong, attack Banks' advance. Large re-enforcement of the Rebels. Our troops hold their ground." An editorial began: "Gen. Pope and Stonewall Jackson have met at last, and a fierce battle has been fought, apparently without any decided advantage on either side, save that our advance held its ground, which considering the position, is equivalent to a victory." A Washington dispatch in the next day's paper read: "Accounts from Culpeper represent the enemy's estimated force at 20,000, and our own, exclusive of cavalry and artillery, as not exceeding 7,000." [107] Better reporting there could hardly be, and such statements would not have to be revised later to the detriment of the people's confidence and the public morale. A better official report could hardly have been written than Pope signed at 5:00 P.M., on August 13. Even if it had not already been removed by contact with him, and his good field behavior, any lingering resentment which his subordinates and his soldiers may have felt for Pope because of his unhappy address a month before, should have been removed by his honest, straightforward statements, and his just praise, free of extravagance. Fundamentally a good soldier, he closed his dispatch: "A full list of casualties will be transmitted as soon as possible, together with a detailed report, in which I shall endeavor to do justice to all." Halleck at once sent a telegram of warm commendation which Pope published to his army.[108]

There were many quirks to Stonewall Jackson. He had no taste whatever for lionizing at Richmond, and he was equally loath to have his Valley soldiers petted too much by the eager girls who would so willingly have given their hearts to Shenandoah heroes. Being very devout, he no doubt felt he should not overexpose his regiments of farm and village boys to the opportunities of a great city. So he was glad when he was ordered back on July 13 toward the Blue Ridge, where there was less distraction, and he could rediscipline his men with drill and catch up with the courts-martial of officers who had displeased him.[109]

But no peculiarity of Jackson was more pronounced than his close-mouthedness toward his subordinates with regard to his plans, and his volubility in giving thanks afterward for whatever he had done. Whether the ill will engendered by the first trait was sufficiently compensated for by the second habit must remain a matter of dispute. But when Lee on July 27 sent A. P. Hill to Jackson he wrote a rather famous note, in which he tactfully suggested that it might work for good if Jackson would confide somewhat in Hill. Acceptance of the very wholesome advice is not indicated by the unbelievably poor march that Jackson's column made on August 8.[110] Some observers, basing their opinions upon the results of the campaign and the quickness with which Jackson went back to Gordonsville, thought that Stonewall was laying it on pretty heavy in the thanks he gave for the battle of August 9.[111] Jackson set out with a tremendous train of wagons—no fewer than 1,200—quite as if he intended to go to Washington or farther and be away for months.[112] When all the wagons rumbled back within less than a week, it looked—on the surface at least—as if he had changed his plans or had encountered something more serious than a washed-out bridge or two. And many soldiers in his old division and in Ewell's division realized that their old friend Commissary Banks would have given them a sound beating if it had not been for the "light division" under A. P. Hill. Hill also knew it perfectly well—Hill, whose ranks had opened to let a routed Stonewall regiment through to safety, but who had received black looks and hard words from Jackson just the day before.[113]

Much has been made of the claim that for two days Jackson held the field of battle; but this is somewhat contradicted by a dispatch of the 11th from George Bayard: "Cedar Mountain is covered with rebel infantry, and *I am occupying the field of the late fight*,* and while they hold that hill I can go no farther." General Lee sent Jackson congratulations, and Southern papers renewed their praise; but within a few days captured Negro letter bearers from Richmond stated that

* Italics not in the original.

Jackson's wounded had arrived in the city on the 12th and that everyone "admitted that he had been badly whipped." Freeman entitles his chapter on the battle, "Jackson Fumbles at Cedar Mountain." [114]

On August 10, a day when the two armies faced each other grimly, each ready to repel attack, it rained hard—as it often seemed to do the day after a cruel battle. One of Jackson's officers—who saw many sad fields from Manassas to the war's end—recorded that the horrors of that day left a singularly lasting impression. In a barn where wounded were being sheltered, a Confederate and a Federal lay close together. For a while they eased their pain with banter and light talk. Then quiet fell, and presently the man who had lost a leg inquired calmly: "Why did you come down here anyway, fighting us?" In the suffering soldier there was none of the bitterness that there was in the adjutant general of Virginia when, on August 4, he called out men between thirty-five and forty-five years of age in the militia of forty counties "to rescue the soil of the State and our people from the pollution and tyranny of a detestable foe." Equally without emotion but with much pride, the man in blue, whose arm was gone, replied: "For the old flag." [115]

CHAPTER X

MANEUVER IN GRAND STYLE

Be patient as possible with the generals. Some of them will trouble you more than they will the enemy. *Watson to Haupt*

In a dispatch to General Halleck of 11:00 A.M. on August 11, Pope reported startling information: "Captured officers speak freely of General McClellan's move back from Malvern Hill the other day. They say that their skirmishers drove in our pickets in the afternoon, and next morning at daylight they found to their surprise that our forces were gone." [1] The morning referred to was August 7, the day when Jackson left Gordonsville; yet, incredible at is seems, his officers were well informed about the Richmond front. Pope, like the captured officers—and like General Lee, who had been carefully studying the behavior of General McClellan—immediately saw the significance of what had occurred. Malvern Hill was a feature McClellan had to hold if he intended another move on Richmond; and when he had seized it on August 5, after an abortive start to do so two days before,[2] Lee had moved considerable force down to meet him, and had gone himself to observe the situation.[3] If McClellan had merely held the hill, and had made some demonstrations from it, Lee would have been uncertain as to his intentions. But when the Federal general voluntarily abandoned the important position that gave good access to roads to Richmond he was putting his cards on the table—and he was putting them there face up.

Knowing what would happen, Pope told Halleck that more force would be sent against him unless McClellan kept them "busy and uneasy at Richmond." He stated that he could get along with the enemy then in his front, but requested Halleck to "make McClellan do something to prevent re-enforcements being sent here." A few hours later, still wanting to act against the enemy communications, he said: "The only hazard in such a policy is that supineness of the Army of the Potomac renders it easy for the enemy to re-enforce Jackson heavily. Of that, however, you must be the judge." Pope's aggressive mood continued, although the situation might rapidly deteriorate; and when he reported the next day that Jackson had retired he stated that he would follow as far as the Rapidan. Halleck sent the brief answer: "Beware of a snare. Feigned retreats are secesh tactics." [4]

"Please make McClellan do something." Poor Pope! It looked bad indeed for him if his safety depended on that. Lincoln surely needed all his sense of humor if he read Pope's request—as he probably did. Halleck, knowing the futility of further attempt to deceive Lee, concentrated on *hurrying* McClellan—which thought also must have brought a smile to the President's face. "I am doing everything in my power to hasten McClellan's movement," was the best promise that Halleck could send to the headquarters of the Army of Virginia at Cedar Mountain. In order to get help to Pope as quickly as possible, Burnside was directed to send from Fredericksburg as much of his force (which had now been provided with wagons, artillery, and a little cavalry) as could be spared, keeping only enough to hold the base.[5] There was no delay by Burnside; that same evening he had twelve regiments of infantry, four batteries, and two troops of cavalry on the way to Pope, under the command of General J. L. Reno.[6] Pope also was trying to reenforce himself to the utmost with troops under his own command; on the 11th he requested that White's brigade at Winchester be relieved by other troops, and he ordered Cox in West Virginia to bring 5,000 of his men by river and railroad.[7] On the 13th Halleck informed Burnside that a brigade of infantry and a regiment of cavalry should arrive that day at Aquia—the van of McClellan's army.[8] This small contingent had embarked at Harrison's Landing; the main army was to march to Fort Monroe, and so would be a number of days behind.

The race was on. Pope's army, situated a little hazardously on the Rapidan, was the grand prize. Good news at last came from the Peninsula: McClellan's army was really on the march.[9] Porter's corps had taken the road to Williamsburg on the evening of the 14th, eighteen hours after McClellan had wired Halleck: "Richmond prisoners state that large force, with guns, left Richmond northward on Sunday [the 10th]." [10] At Williamsburg on the evening of the 16th Porter learned from intercepted letters and from Negroes that a heavy movement of troops from Richmond against Pope had begun on the 13th, and that it was known in Richmond on the 10th that McClellan was about to leave.[11] Porter passed the word to both McClellan and Halleck, hastened his march, and sent word to have transports ready.

Lee had the start of a day. He had a much shorter distance to go; he had a railroad instead of steamboats to use; he had only to entrain and detrain men, instead of embark and debark them. Pope, though not alarmed, was aware of the hazard in his position—a fact generally overlooked or denied.[12] On the 16th he reported that there was danger that forces coming from Richmond would unite with those of Jackson and turn his left, adding, "So soon as McClellan's move is understood I have little doubt this will be done." Halleck, replying, told Pope it would be far better if he were in rear of the Rappahannock, and he ordered: "If threatened too strongly, fall behind the Rappahannock. Every possible exertion is being made to increase our forces on that line." Pope was of good cheer; he made no threats as to who would be responsible if he met disaster; he only asked for a more efficient quartermaster to replace one who was "too old and too easy," and who was not getting sufficient forage. The next morning he requested 1,500 horses as soon as they could be sent, to remount his broken-down cavalry. Immediately Halleck approved both requests; but good quartermasters are not easy to find, and the most efficient quartermaster general in the world never could keep many horses ahead in his remount depots—Meigs at once raised the question of the abuse of animals and other extravagances.[13]

Fredericksburg was a strategic point in the Federal operations. It was only fifty-five miles from Richmond, with which it was connected both by direct road and by railroad, and only twelve miles by the reconstructed railroad from the port at Aquia Creek on the Potomac. From the old historic town, closely associated with the early days of George Washington, raids could be launched to break the Virginia Central Railroad, and a serious movement could be directed toward

Richmond itself, which would have endangered any Confederate force about Gordonsville. Thus Lee, while he was studying the difficult problem of what the Federals meant to do, had to give much thought to the forces at Fredericksburg and had to keep them watched by cavalry and by other observers. Halleck, on his part, needed a reliable and steady officer in command at the important point. Although Pope in a gracious manner opened the way for a solution of the problem of command in case Burnside joined him, Halleck sent only the troops, keeping Burnside himself at Fredericksburg.[14]

For a few days, however, Halleck sent Burnside away from his important station on a diplomatic mission for which he was particularly well fitted, as a close and trusted friend of McClellan's. On the 14th the General in Chief ordered him to Washington, and then dispatched him on a good-will mission and as an expediter to McClellan. Good results seemed to come quickly, for on the morning of the 17th McClellan wired from Barrett's Ferry, where one of his columns was crossing the Chickahominy on a pontoon bridge: "I have seen Burnside. Now that we are committed to the movement, you may be sure that it will be carried out without the delay of a moment. Not an hour has been lost thus far. Count on my full co-operation." [15] A rather peculiar message certainly, with various interpretations possible, especially in view of the many assurances previously given. Late in the day he wrote, in a note that was delivered to Halleck by Burnside: "I am glad to say that Burnside has satisfied me that you are still my friend; in return I think he can satisfy you that I have loyally carried out your instructions, although my own judgment was not in accordance with yours." [16] This was a strange declaration for a man wearing the two stars of a major general. McClellan, like Frémont, seemed to think that the first sentence of Army Regulations was not intended for him; and he was heedless of the injunction that an officer should not only obey strictly but "execute with alacrity and good faith the lawful orders" of his superiors.[17]

More important than reams of telegraphic promises from McClellan was the soldierly dispatch that Halleck received from Burnside, giving an excellent summary of the situation, and closing: "All reports agree that the enemy is pushing all their troops to re-enforce Jackson. All right. Will leave for your headquarters this afternoon." [18] Burnside found everything quiet at Fredericksburg when he got back, and his mission had accomplished something, for McClellan pushed things vigorously and with unwonted energy, for a few days at least; but presently a special messenger brought a "confidential" note to "Dear Burn," ending "Ever your friend." He was again unhappy, because of rumors or news he had received from "confidential sources" in Washington, and asked, "Please keep me posted as to all you know." [19]

Although his horses were breaking down, Pope kept his troopers at work. On the 16th Colonel T. F. Brodhead's First Michigan Cavalry, of John Buford's division, was sent out in the direction of Louisa.[20] On their return on the morning of the 18th, they came near picking up something far more valuable than any piece of information. General Jeb Stuart and some of his staff had spent the night on the airy porch of a house near the village of Verdierville, and were preparing to leave when Brodhead's troopers came along on their way to Raccoon Ford over the Rapidan.[21] Though the great cavalryman, famous for embarrassing others by his unexpected appearance, made good his escape into a woods, he had to leave his cloak and the hat with the famous plume. Off the Michiganders rode with these fine trophies, after chasing and firing their revolvers at the scattering Confederates. But there was much more valuable booty. Major N. R. Fitzhugh, Stuart's adjutant, had already been picked up carrying a letter with the signature of R. E. Lee.[22] It was an item for which any collector would have paid a fair price, regardless of the contents. But this was more than a pleasant chatty note of good wishes; it set forth the Confederate plan to overwhelm Pope before he could be reenforced by McClellan's army. Pope had been expecting this, but he had not known the details; and it was nice to have it all official over the signature of Lee. Because of the success of the Federals, Brigadier General Robert Toombs, eloquent secessionist, whose brigade was supposed to cover Raccoon Ford was that day put in arrest.[23]

At 1:30 P.M. on the 18th Pope reported to Halleck that the enemy, heavily reenforced, was advancing on Raccoon Ford from Gordonsville, Louisa, and Hanover Junction with the intention of turning his left. His trains were already in motion for the Rappahannock; his troops would soon take up the march in three columns, and he hoped to be entirely over the river by noon the next day. Halleck, who earlier in the day had sent new warnings of the reenforcements going to Jackson, approved the retirement, and directed Pope to stand firm on the line of the Rappahannock, saying, "Fight hard, and aid will soon come." [24]

The Confederates had also had the advantage of a fine observation station, for from Clark's Mountain, just south of the Rapidan, Pope's army could be well watched. There, Lee and Longstreet witnessed on the 18th the beginning of the withdrawal of a fine prize: "Miscreant Pope" and Nephew Louis. Lee would have liked to attack on the 18th, but it was quite out of the question: infantry, cavalry, artillery, and commissary, were all unready.[25] His organization and his army were not such that he could start numerous units from Richmond on the 13th and open up a good offensive against Culpeper on the 18th. Henderson's assertion that the design to attack on the 18th "was thwarted by one of those petty accidents which play so large a part in war" is not in accord with the facts, being as much in error as his assertion that "a sudden attack against his left was the last contingency that [Pope] anticipated." [26] Even the next day, Lee did not move forward, and it was not until 4:00 P.M. on the 20th that his troops began to cross the Rapidan.[27]

Pope certainly tarried as long as was prudent—there can be no question about that. But generals have often almost overstayed their time in exposed positions and then escaped. Pope's error was in believing that his army was a fine machine that could quickly and smoothly execute a march. He was retiring by three columns,[28] which showed that basically he had matters well planned for prompt action, and his march order stipulated: "Very heavy rear guards of reliable troops, well supplied with artillery and commanded by discreet and prudent officers, will follow the march of the columns at a distance of at least 3 miles in the rear." [29] But there was confusion and slowness in his columns. Strother noted this in his journal and added: "But the General rode here and there, infusing some of his Western energy into the caravan, and every thing began to move in accordance." [30] It was well that Pope could do this, but he should not have had to do it.

As Pope was moving out of the clutches of Lee, Halleck enjoined General Dix at Fort Monroe: "Not a moment should be lost. Employ everything that can be procured for transports." Porter's corps was already at Newport News and Hampton Roads, and word came from McClellan that the rear guard of his army had crossed the Chickahominy at 10:00 A.M., and that his long pontoon bridge had been dismantled and was being towed to Fort Monroe.[31] It still was anybody's race; but the chances were that Pope might have to fight alone before any sizable reenforcements came.

Although the short march had not been of the sort that pleases a

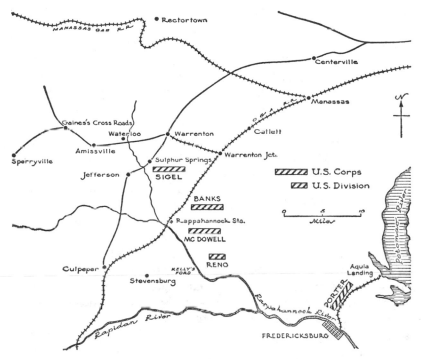

POPE'S SITUATION AT EVENING OF AUGUST 20, 1862

soldier—leading units arriving at initial points exactly on the appointed minute, vehicles moving smoothly at correct distances, infantry marching easily, well closed up—still General Pope's army was over the Rappahannock on the afternoon of the 20th "without leaving any article whatever." McDowell with 18,000 effectives and Banks with 8,000 were in the vicinity of Rappahannock Station; Reno with 8,000 was some five miles below at Kelly's Ford; Sigel with 12,000 was about the same distance above Sulphur Springs. Pope reported at once that the Rappahannock did not furnish a very strong defensive line, for it dwindled rapidly in size above its junction with the Rapidan, to break again above the railroad crossing, and then repeatedly until it disappeared in small tributaries that rose east of the Blue Ridge. Pope in fact stated clearly that he thought the "true position," if the enemy should "advance with his whole force," was considerably in rear of the Rappahannock, until the Federal strength was built up sufficiently to allow an advance.[32] Pope, however, was a soldier who did not think that war was a sort of cooperative matter; unlike McClellan he knew the first sentence of Army Regulations, and fully intended to carry it out. He had been told by Halleck to stand firm on the line of the Rappahannock, and that was all there was to it. Every dispatch that he wrote and every action that he took showed that he intended to carry out the full spirit of the General in Chief's order.

Pope's aggressive turn was in no way dimmed by his retirement and the knowledge that most of the Army of Northern Virginia with Lee in command was opposed to him. On the morning of the 21st he directed Reno to send Buford (temporarily attached to Reno's detachment of the Ninth Corps), with two or three regiments of cavalry, four of infantry and a battery, on a strong reconnaissance toward Stevensburg,[33] a village only five miles east of recently abandoned Culpeper. As was usual with Buford, a lively skirmish was developed, and he reported that he had been in contact with Longstreet,[34] the first positive identification of that general's presence on the right bank of the river. A Federal cavalry regiment dispersed an enemy infantry regiment, took seventy cattle the Confederates had been counting on eating, and seven horses. Halleck directed Pope: "Dispute every inch of ground, and fight like the devil till we can re-enforce you. Forty-eight hours more and we can make you strong enough." [35] To this Pope replied: "There need be no apprehension, as I think no impression can be made on me for some days." Information received later in the evening changed the prospects, and Pope wired that his right might be attacked the next morning, but: "We are all ready, and shall make the best fight we can." [36] Again John Pope showed up as a good soldier. He would do the best he could with what he had, and if he were defeated he would leave it to history to decide whether it was his fault or the fault of higher headquarters in giving him an impossible mission. He would not place the blame ahead of time as McClellan had done on June 25.

Pope immediately gave orders to Reno at Kelly's Ford about supporting him in case the enemy attacked, and informed Reno that McCall's old division of 8,000 men, now under the command of Brigadier General John F. Reynolds (just exchanged after six weeks of captivity), which was leading the advance of Porter's corps from Fredericksburg, should reach Kelly's Ford the next morning; and he gave instructions for its use.[37] Most of the Fifth Corps had in fact already debarked at Aquia Creek; but the knapsacks of the men were on schooners still at Fort Monroe, and there was little ammunition with the troops.[38] At 10:40 that night McClellan telegraphed to Porter: "Tell your men and those of Heintzelman when they arrive that I will leave here to-morrow and will be with them when they are engaged. . . . Whatever occurs, hold out until I arrive." It was a somewhat amusing message for McClellan to send, in view of his absence from the battlefields of the Peninsula. Nevertheless the general had been pressing the departure of his troops, for he had written to Porter the day before: "Please push off your troops without one moment's delay. The necessity is very pressing—a matter of life and death—See me before you sail." [39] One would not have wanted more —except the knapsacks and plenty of ammunition. Later, strange events were to take place, in view of which it would be interesting to know about the final meeting of McClellan and Porter. Did it take place, and if so, what was the information communicated, or what final instructions were given by McClellan to his favorite subordinate?

While Reynolds's good division of "Pennsylvania Reserves" was marching to Pope from near-by Fredericksburg, the troops of General Cox—an excellent "political general"—had begun to entrain in far-off Parkersburg. With just pride he wired, "On marching from Flat Top to the steamboats we made 90 miles in three and a half days." [40] It was a fine record indeed for a mixed command—cavalry, infantry, artillery, trains—even though small, on hilly roads. Probably it was history's first instance of a movement by forced marches, steamboats, and railroad, and it remains a model for smooth planning and smart execution. The War Department, the Baltimore and Ohio Railroad, the steamboat company, and Cox worked together efficiently, while the Ohio regiments of the Kanawha Division—men and animals alike— made a road record that is inspiring to contemplate. The move took place at a time when guerrillas were threatening to attack the railroad, but prompt and effective action by General B. F. Kelley with a force from Cumberland gave the necessary security. The fleet of trains passed safely, and the first of the Western units were due in Washington on the 23rd.[41]

Troops and supplies were to come to Pope both from Fredericksburg and from Alexandria. The two bases were an embarrassment as well as a convenience, for it was difficult for Pope to tell at first which line of communications he must keep open, as Lee seemed to threaten first one of his flanks and then the other. If Lee turned the left flank Pope's connection with Fredericksburg would go out, and that base would be threatened; if Lee on the other hand turned the right, the important railroad to Alexandria would be endangered. On the 22nd the enemy showed definite signs of moving up the Rappahannock; but renewed activity below the railroad at Kelly's Ford made it necessary for Pope to give attention to that locality as a possible danger point.[42] Because of the draft of the vessels and the inadequacy of docks at Aquia, it was decided on the same day to send Heintzelman's corps to Alexandria, instead of having it debark at Aquia.[43] On the following day Halleck directed that the corps of Franklin should likewise go on to Alexandria; and eventually that of Sumner proceeded to the same place. Thus Pope's uncertainty as to which was his more important line of communications began to disappear; but doubt as to Lee's exact strength remained a disturbing factor. On the evening of the 22nd he reported to the General in Chief in regard to the enemy force, "Its numbers you can estimate as well as myself." [44]

In spite of the uncertainty as to how many men Lee had, Pope reported to Halleck that he favored crossing the river with his force at Rappahannock Station and striking the enemy's flank and rear. He was perfectly well aware of the great risk involved in the operation, but it seemed to be the only way in which he could hold Lee south of the Rappahannock. Although Pope's dispatch was not sent until 9:15, the General in Chief's approval was back at 11:00 P.M.[45] If Halleck approved an offensive against a superior enemy, it would look indeed as if he were determined that Lee must be held beyond the Rappahannock,[46] and as if he thought he could get substantial reenforcements to Pope without delay.

All plans were changed by two events which took place while the telegrams were passing to and fro: a heavy rain, and a heavy raid by Jeb Stuart on Catlett, where Pope's trains were located. On the morning of the 23rd the Rappahannock was up six feet, and Pope's very best dress-up coat was gone from his tent at Catlett. The rise of the river made Pope change his plans, but the loss of the coat did not apparently disturb him much,[47] the weather being what it was—though presently the fine garment with the handsome shoulder straps of a major general was on public display in Richmond, where it served to

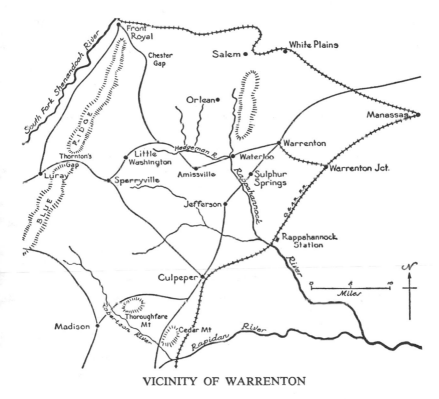

VICINITY OF WARRENTON

offset the chagrin for the loss of Jeb's plume. The raiders also picked up many of Pope's papers and a talkative quartermaster; but these could hardly have given them as valuable information as is sometimes claimed.[48] Pope saw the chance to destroy the enemy troops that had crossed the river in the vicinity of Waterloo bridge, who now would be marooned by impassable fords and washed-out bridges. (Even the coat might be retrieved.) An order went to Sigel at 7:15 to move vigorously against such forces;[49] he was supported by Reno and

Banks, who already had been started from Kelly's Ford toward Rappahannock station.[50] McDowell's corps was ordered to Warrenton,[51] and the bridgehead force which Pope had always kept across the river at the railroad crossing was withdrawn—though not without difficulty. At 8:30 the General in Chief was informed of the quick change in plans of his enterprising field commander,[52] who himself moved headquarters to Warrenton in a justifiably optimistic frame of mind. There seemed to be the chance to fall on a sizable fragment of the enemy with overwhelming force—which is something a soldier enjoys doing, and is highly honorable, because the enemy can surrender if he does not want to be annihilated. The new move would have none of the hazard of the one Pope had planned the night before; fortune seemed to have taken a part, and in addition, Reynolds's division was at hand, and some of Birney's division of Heintzelman's corps was arriving by cars from Alexandria.[53] Pope's chances had indeed risen with the river.

Late in the afternoon Sigel gained contact with the enemy not far from Sulphur Springs, and a brief action took place in which the Confederates were driven across a small tributary of the Rappahannock with the impressive name Great Run; then night stopped operations. Pope knew that the Rappahannock would fall rapidly, and he was up early the next morning. At five o'clock he wrote to Sigel, "Our work must be finished here to-day; we have no time to spare." [54] Already it was too late, for the enemy was safely back across the river shortly after daylight; the force was not as great as Pope had thought—and hoped—for it consisted solely of the brigades of Lawton and Early, of Ewell's division. The Confederates felt that their escape had been a narrow one, and in his report Early wrote: "My command was thus rescued from almost certain capture, as it has since appeared from General Pope's report that he had brought up his whole force to attack what he supposed to be General Jackson's whole force." [55]

On account of lack of orders from Halleck, uncertainty confronted Pope after his hope to destroy part of the enemy had ended in "frustration." He had been told to hold the Rappahannock line securely; this he had done, for Lee's entire army was again on the far side of the stream—and some of the units very happy to be there. But what was Pope's new mission to be, now that units of McClellan's army had begun to arrive, and the period of danger to himself seemed to be rapidly passing? Pope did not like to sit quietly on the defensive, and he was not long either in making decisions or in doing things; but above all else he was a conscientious soldier, and he wanted his actions to conform strictly to the plans of his superior. Because he was quite in the dark as to the purposes of the High Command, Pope submitted to Halleck that very day a proposed order for the posting of his army.[56] It would change its orientation, facing it more toward the west to conform to his adversary's shifted position; the lower fords, however, were not to be left unguarded, and communication would be kept with parts of Porter's corps still en route from Fredericksburg; army headquarters would be at Warrenton Junction. The army would be somewhat dispersed, but the situation prevented greater concentration.

The fact that Lee had not crossed the Rappahannock in force raised again the question of his intentions. It might have been that the rain had interrupted his plans, or it might have been that his crossing had been made to mask a move toward the Shenandoah Valley. Both Pope and Halleck had kept the possibility of such a move in mind ever since Jackson had moved to Gordonsville.[57] During the 24th word had come from General White at Winchester that the train from Harpers Ferry the day before had been attacked and burned. The president of the Baltimore and Ohio—J. W. Garrett—also reported the incident, and stated: "Reports are current and believed that a column of the enemy is marching up [down] the valley, leaving Winchester to the left. Indications are that heavy movements are in progress in that vicinity." [58] Since White had almost no cavalry, he was practically blind, except as to events close at hand. Obviously Pope would have to find out whether Lee was moving toward the very touchy Shenandoah whose flanking mountains gave protection to forces operating in it, for forces there could easily break the important Baltimore and Ohio, and cross into Maryland above Washington. At 9:00 P.M. he wired Halleck that he was sending out spies and scouts to investigate the situation, anticipating the alert General in Chief's order to do just this.[59]

It had been a long hard day for Pope; he had begun writing messages as soon as it was light and probably did not stop until midnight or after. His own movements had put him out of touch with Halleck, for there was no telegraph to Warrenton from the Junction, and the Junction operator had had difficulty getting important messages to him.[60] Although the day that had begun with hope of success against the enemy had ended with disappointment, Pope had shifted quickly and skillfully to new lines of thought and had worked hard to keep his part in the rapidly changing operations well under control. With Halleck's prompt approval of his suggested order there also came the statement that directions might be issued for Pope "to recross the Rappahannock and resume the offensive in a few days." [61] To this Pope replied that he would be ready to recross the river at a moment's notice; but he added very significantly: "Please let me know, if it can be done, what is to be my own command, and if I am to act independently against the enemy. I certainly understood that as soon as the whole of our forces were concentrated you designed to take command in person, and that when everything was ready we were to move forward in concert." [62]

Pope, when he made his plain hint about taking the field, of course did not know of the disturbing situation in another theater of war for which Halleck was as much responsible as he was for Virginia. The Confederates had seized an opportunity after the failure of McClellan's campaign, while the Federal High Command was burdened with difficult moves in Virginia, to strike elsewhere and to cause confusion. On the 16th word came to Halleck from Major General D. C. Buell at Huntsville, Alabama, that a Confederate force of 12,000 to 15,000 under Kirby Smith was advancing into Kentucky, with the evident intention of threatening Union communications, and regaining much of Tennessee. Presently the much larger army under General Braxton Bragg joined in the threat; and by the 25th Halleck was having a hard time to prevent the removal of Buell, whose slow movements greatly displeased both the Secretary of War and the President.[63] Under such circumstances it was probably quite out of the question for the General in Chief to take the field,[64] however desirable it would have been in the Virginia situation. Sound command considerations indicated that the Army of Virginia and the Army of the Potomac should be directed —for a period at least—as a little army group. Except for a corps or so given to Pope as an emergency reenforcement, the Potomac army should have been conveniently assembled—perhaps at Manassas, where the branch railroad to the west gave highly necessary trackage, with McClellan in command of it alone.

More was involved, however, than sound command principles. Not only McClellan but some of his subordinates were touchy and vain; and others who were not so afflicted had been understandably affronted by Pope's ill advised address to his army. At a time when all officers should have been able to concentrate on defeating the enemy, animosities and dislikes were present. Probably to appease McClellan, Halleck on August 7 had written in answer to a "private letter": "As I told you when at your camp, it is my intention that you shall command all the troops in Virginia as soon as we can get them together; and with the army thus concentrated I am certain that you can take Richmond." Burnside must have confirmed that assurance in his good-will mission ten days later, for McClellan's melancholy note of the 20th to "Dear Burn" stated that "confidential sources" indicated that Halleck either would not or could not carry out his intention.[65] For McClellan to take over the active field command of the operation that Pope was conducting would have been unwise. But a brief assumption by the General in Chief of field command of the two armies would not have repudiated any commitment to McClellan. Pope had already expressed the desire to return to the West,[66] so that a final adjustment affecting him would not have been difficult. Just what Halleck might have done if Bragg and Smith had not erupted into Kentucky cannot be said, but their offensive, with its threat to Louisville and Cincinnati, certainly had an effect on the command problem in Virginia.

Close at hand there was an officer who would have been an excellent temporary commander for the group of two armies: that was John Wool, whose headquarters were now in Baltimore. He held an important position with peculiar responsibilities; but General Dix was already familiar with it and could have been recalled from Fort Monroe; and his position in turn could easily have been taken over by Keyes, whose corps of the Army of the Potomac remained there temporarily instead of going on at once to the Potomac. Wool, now a major general in the regular army, stood in seniority just below Halleck. He knew McClellan thoroughly and had effectively squelched him at the first sign of presumptuousness, without apparently being classified as an enemy. He also had ventured in a friendly manner to give Pope a very good piece of advice, though perhaps misapprehending the reasons that had detained him in Washington; but the younger man must have kept the admonition in mind: "Jackson is an enterprising officer. Delays are dangerous." Halleck, who was well aware of Wool's fine qualities, had wired on August 19 to Harrisburg, where his duties had taken him: "From information received here it is feared that an attempt may be made in Maryland to destroy railroad bridges, so as to interrupt the transportation of troops. It is hoped that you will give the matter your usually prompt attention." The reply was immediate and gratifying: "I have received your dispatch of to-day. I had previously attended to the subject alluded to; will, however, repeat my orders." [67] General Wool's age of course did not permit continued and hard field service; but this would not have been necessary in the operation in front of Washington. In seizing Norfolk on May 10 he had quickly taken the saddle, at the head of troops; and in October he was to endure three days strenuous enough to exhaust younger officers on his staff.[68] All things considered, John Wool would have been almost a perfect temporary commander for the little army group; and authority for placing a junior over a senior of the same grade had already been given to the President by Congress—authority Lincoln had used when he put Pope over Frémont, thereby freeing himself of the latter. Under Wool's efficient, steady, but bold direction, the junction of the Army of the Potomac and the Army of Virginia could have been safely carried out; and Halleck could have dismissed most of the problem from his mind and given greater attention to the threatening developments in the West, as well as to the organizing of new troops.

Halleck was at fault in not giving an order that would fix without ambiguity the command status of the first corps of the Army of the Potomac that was to arrive from the Peninsula. McClellan did not want any elements of his army to come under the orders of Pope; he wished to give them a supporting or a cooperating sort of mission. Quite likely the final interview that McClellan wished to have with Porter was to impress upon the latter that he should support and cooperate with Pope but should also seek to maintain an independent command. Halleck's instructions for Porter after his arrival at Aquia were communciated through Burnside, and merely spoke of the importance of moving up the Rappahannock with the greatest speed.[69] But the General in Chief made his meaning clear enough to McClellan in a dispatch sent the same day—the 22nd: "Porter's corps is moving up the river to re-enforce Reno at Kelly's Ford." [70] Reno was definitely under Pope's orders, not just vaguely cooperating with him, and the meaning of "reenforce" is hardly open to debate. Porter, however, continued to pretend to be an independent commander, protecting Pope's rear by guarding the Rappahannock. In a carefully written directive to General Morell, one of his division commanders, he spoke of Reynolds as "supporting" Reno at Kelly's Ford. Then presently he directed Morell: "If you are called upon to go to Rappahannock Station move up to the support of the army there."[71] More shrewdly chosen language would hardly be possible; and Porter, in his subsequent trial, took pains to use phrases like "co-operating with and supporting General Pope against the enemy" in such a way as to cause a pointed question from the court.[72]

McClellan arrived at Aquia on the 24th and soon became fearful that Porter was getting away from his command, for he sent the message: "Have you had anything new from Washington since I saw you which causes you to say you shall push on to Rappahannock Station? Please inform me at once." A query which he addressed to Halleck at the same time received the prompt reply: "Porter and Reno should hold the line of the Rappahannock below Pope, subject for the present to his orders. I hope by to-morrow to be able to give some definite directions. You know my main object, and will act accordingly." For the time being at least McClellan was to keep his hands off Porter; and the last sentence suggests that Halleck was weary of his quibbling. In order to have no doubt about Porter's status, the General in Chief presently telegraphed Burnside that Porter should push forward and reenforce Pope in the direction of Sulphur Springs, where Pope had fought the day before. Before receiving the instructions that terminated all doubt as to his relation with Pope, Porter significantly closed a dispatch to Morell and Sykes—a division commander—with the words, "All goes right," which might have several meanings. After Porter's mission was well disposed of, Halleck wired McClellan: "You can either remain at Aquia or come to Alexandria, as you may deem best, so as to direct the landing of your troops."[73] The cool indifference of the General in Chief was rather confounding, and the man who had been called a young Napoleon appeared to be offered the choice of two ways of doing almost nothing. He already knew that Heintzelman's corps had been sent to Pope,[74] and he could expect the same thing to happen to Franklin. But at the time Sumner was still under orders to debark at Aquia, and McClellan elected to remain there. However, he preceded that corps to Alexandria, without the prospect of being more than a debarking officer. The journey with his large staff could not have seemed to him like a triumphal return to the capital of the nation. The whispered warnings of his Washington agents doubtless appeared only too true: Halleck was not his "friend." But presently McClellan's estate was to rise again.

Halleck had sought to counter the enemy movements in Kentucky by throwing a tight veil of secrecy over the Virginia operations. On August 19 he directed Pope to remove all newspaper reporters from his army, to stop all telegrams except those from himself, and to "suspend the transmission of any mail matter other than that of official communication." The General in Chief seemed to be contending with his army commander in being tough and harsh; but instead of making war a grim business for the Southerners he was taking stern measures with his own men and the "home folk." How much needed his order was, Halleck saw the next day when he read about it in the New York papers before he released it. To Pope went the wire, "I think your staff is decidedly leaky," together with the admonition to seek out the offenders and get rid of them. As Pope believed he already had his own household in good order, he had the chance to carry out a little more disciplining of corps commanders and their staffs.[75]

Since Halleck's assumption of command, neither Lincoln nor Stanton had issued an order; all the messages in the Official Records are to or from the General in Chief. But President and Secretary alike kept well posted; copies of outgoing messages went to them,[76] and early every morning the President went to the War Office to read incoming dispatches so that he could keep informed without intrusion on the General in Chief. But though instructions to generals no longer appear, there is an occasional brief inquiry. The man who under the Constitution was Commander in Chief could not put one bit of his ultimate responsibility on the shoulders of any other person, and he wanted to know what was taking place each day, each hour. Lincoln knew full well the importance of the battle at Cedar Mountain; he thought the engagement might break out again on the 11th after quiet on the 10th, and he wanted King's fine division to be there. To Burnside there went a telegram of just one sentence: "Has King's division, in part or in whole, joined Pope yet?" [77] Not a single word of instructions, but the President, who had a penchant for figures, wanted all his information to be exact. With still greater anxiety Lincoln must have kept pace with the leading corps of McClellan's army as they crossed the Chickahominy, marched along the dusty roads to Williamsburg, and thence to the ports to embark and sail for Aquia Creek. On the morning of the 21st, when his early call at the War Department disclosed nothing about the arrivals at Aquia that he had hoped for, there again went to Burnside a dispatch of just one sentence, "What news about arrival of troops?" It was a tonic for generals to know that the President was at the side of a telegraph operator at seven o'clock in the morning, and within an hour Burnside had a detailed and encouraging reply back in Washington.[78]

Harmless news was not kept away from the public by an unintelligent censorship, and there was writing about the war that was all that one could wish. On August 25, when the danger period appeared to have passed, the *New York Tribune* revealed and commended Pope's retirement, and realizing that the enemy had intended his destruction, the editor praised the rigid censorship which had blacked out his moves. With a touch of relief he stated:

The city has been full of ill-defined rumors of battle and disaster, and the people have been in most painful anxiety all the week. But now there seems to be no reasonable fear of disaster. That a great portion of Gen. McClellan's army has been added to the force under Pope, McDowell, Banks, Sigel, and Burnside, is very certain; and it is equally certain that such a combination of strength will cause Jackson and Lee to think twice before they hazard an attack. Their golden moment has passed, thanks to the bravery of Banks and his men at Cedar Mountain, and the wide-awake caution of Gen. Pope.

So it would seem, and doubtless Lee and Jackson did think twice before they hazarded an attack. But hazard it they did.

On the morning of historic August 25, 1862, Pope's observation stations, well placed on hills in the vicinity of Waterloo, were alert. Hardly had dawn given way to more certain light when columns of the enemy were seen. At 8:45 Colonel John S. Clark of Banks's staff reported: "The column of rebel infantry and artillery still passing; are evidently on the road between Jefferson and Amissville, and going toward the latter place. Cavalry and wagon train passing. A large camp, with wagons parked, in neighborhood of Jefferson. An officer reports the column to have been moving for an hour and a half." A wide-awake man who knew his business made that report, for every word had meaning. Clark kept watching, and in forty-five minutes he again reported: there had passed four six-gun batteries (not twenty-four guns or six four-gun batteries), a few ambulances, six wagons (not a number of vehicles), and six or eight regiments of *well closed* infantry, and the column was moving *rapidly* (not just some infantry). The enemy also had established a signal station near his line of march. Colonel Clark kept watching, and having written a good message, then a better one, he reached perfection at 10:30: "Column been moving since daylight, composed principally of infantry and artillery. Comparatively few wagons or ambulances. Column appears well closed up and colors flying." He stated that within an hour and a half thirty-five wagons, five batteries, one regiment of cavalry and thirteen of infantry had gone past. He had seen every bit of it himself with signal corps telescopes, and visibility had been excellent. The eyes of officers other than Clark were also watching carefully. At 8:45 Lieutenant P. A. Taylor reported to General McDowell from Watery Mount: "Long lines of enemy's infantry are moving toward Sulphur Springs from a town southwest of Sulphur Springs. These [their?] trains are concentrated at town, extending westward." [79]

The important observations of Colonel Clark were forwarded to Pope at Warrenton at 11:45 A.M., and shortly after midday Pope reported to Halleck that a column plainly seen by his lookouts, and estimated by them at 20,000, was on the march to Amissville and Luray or Front Royal.[80] He had already alerted McDowell's corps to follow as soon as it was certain that the enemy was bound for the Valley; he hoped to know the truth within a few hours. Uncertainties, however, did not resolve themselves as rapidly as the optimistic general hoped, for during the day the enemy was very active in the vicinity of Sulphur Springs, where he crossed the river with infantry, artillery, and cavalry, and showed an aggressive or even a vindictive spirit.[81] This complicated the picture considerably, and the only certainty when Pope summarized the situation for Halleck at 9:00 P.M. was that the enemy column had passed Gaines's Cross-Roads (five miles northeast of Little Washington), and when last seen, near sunset, was moving northeast, in the direction of Salem. He believed that the column was merely covering the flank of the main body, which he thought was moving toward Front Royal and Thornton's Gap; and he intended to push a strong force across the river at Waterloo Bridge and Sulphur Springs early the next morning to discover whether the main body of the enemy had actually departed. In that case he would push forward on their rear. He was certain there was no longer any force opposite Rappahannock Station.[82]

Bayard and Buford were working hard, and the horses of the fine cavalrymen were breaking under heavy use. At midnight Buford, though probably very tired, wrote to McDowell, to whose corps he was now attached: "I have sent one regiment in the direction of Miller's ford [unidentifiable], another to Waterloo Bridge, and have scouts toward Salem. If the enemy advances I can do very little. My command is almost disorganized." [83] Scouts toward Salem! One could rely on John Buford to know where to send patrols, but it broke the heart of the good soldier not to have something left to fight with. For glamour, neither Bayard nor Buford could compare with Jeb Stuart—even when wearing his second-best plume; but in substantial ways they were showing themselves his equal—perhaps now and then his superior.

Pope reported to Halleck that the only really reliable force that he had was McDowell's corps; Banks's corps amounted to no more than 5,000, and they had not completely recovered from Cedar Mountain; Sigel's corps, potentially good, could not be depended upon because of its commander. Plainly he wrote: "Sigel's corps, although composed of the best fighting material we have, will never do much service under that officer." While sending in such an adverse report Pope did not fail to inform Sigel of his displeasure, writing: "I am not satisfied either with your reports or your operations of to-day, and I expect to hear to-morrow early something much more satisfactory concerning the enemy." Tired of trifling, he told Sigel bluntly, "You will force the passage of the river at Waterloo Bridge to-morrow morning at daylight and see what is in front of you." [84]

Although Reynolds's division of Porter's corps was firmly attached to McDowell's corps, and Kearny's division of Heintzelman's corps had arrived from Alexandria, other troops of the Potomac army, as well as Cox and Sturgis of Pope's own command, were overdue. For this fact the general was in part to blame, for he had been a hoarder, as generals often are; he had kept railroad cars and engines at his end of the railroad. This brings to the front a very important element of the drama and the capable man who had it in charge—Herman Haupt. After graduating from West Point in 1835 at the age of eighteen, Haupt had resigned from the army, and had quickly become known as a railroad engineer, builder, and operator. In April, 1862, Stanton called him into the service, and he reconstructed the railroad from Aquia Creek to Fredericksburg, building among other things a high bridge over the Potomac Creek—out of "cornstalks and bean-poles," according to Lincoln. After that he put the Manassas Gap line back in order, and presently returned to private affairs in connection with the building of the great Hoosac tunnel. After a few weeks of operation under the quartermaster department, the Orange and Alexandria Railroad was in considerable confusion, and on August 14 Pope requested his recall. Haupt reported to Cedar Mountain without delay, and on the 18th Pope placed him in control of the railroad.[85]

Railroads were a new instrument in warfare, and there was no experience as to the best way to handle one which, like the Alexandria line, lay in enemy territory and could not therefore be operated by its normal owners. The powers and duties given to Haupt were wisely formulated; but he was placed under Pope, when he should have been directly under War Department control, or under Army Headquarters. On August 20 Pope directed him to keep nearly all of the rolling stock of the road on the sidings at Catlett or Warrenton Junction so that in case of necessity he could carry off the superabundant baggage and supplies of the army at short notice.[86] This arrangement soon hampered higher headquarters in getting reenforcements to Pope. On August 22 Assistant Secretary P. H. Watson broke into the picture and informed the general: "You can use the cars for either warehouses or for transportation, but not for both." Two hours later Major John J. Key, assistant to Haupt, notified Halleck that Pope had 200 cars, enough to transport 10,000 men.[87] Troops of Heintzelman and Cox were being detained by want of cars and engines idling near the Rappahannock.

The next morning communications were interrupted by Stuart's raid on Catlett, and there was uncertainty about bridges. No fewer than six trains were lost somewhere on the line, and confusion was general.[88] In addition, Pope had hurried into the field to try to destroy the enemy forces that had been cut off by the rising river; thus he did not receive Haupt's urgent requests to have the western end of the line put in charge of an officer who would see that the cars and trains were promptly emptied and returned. There were also troubles a plenty for Haupt at Alexandria. General Sturgis, apparently eager to join his commander in the field, seized the railroad some distance west of Alexandria and declared he would take over its operation. Everything was stopped for a number of hours and many troops were delayed. Haupt finally found the offending general, who was in a deteriorated condition and who informed him bluntly, "I don't care for John Pope a pinch of owl dung." [89] Trouble was also to come from the thirstier of McClellan's officers. After weeks and months on the dreary and inhospitable Peninsula many of them were famished and eagerly sought relief in the well appointed bars of the city. When Haupt had cars ready to load Joseph Hooker's division, the handsome general, already famous for the white horse he rode in battle, was absent. Haupt sent two telegrams to Watson, entreating help from that efficient "trouble-shooter," and received a reply stating that a search would be made of the Willard Hotel the only place that the absent general was apparently known to frequent. It was after midnight, but Watson, who probably was sleeping and eating as little as Haupt, was still able to put a little of his characteristic touch into his message to the perplexed railroader. He admonished Haupt—who may have been wishing he was back digging at the Hoosac tunnel: "Be patient as possible with the generals. Some of them will trouble you more than they will the enemy." [90]

Tuesday August 26, which ended with a great surprise for General Pope, began with a great disappointment, occasioned by General Sigel's falling back upon Warrenton from Waterloo. Pope's change of orders the day before was partly responsible. Early in the morning he had issued the order that he had submitted to Halleck on the 24th; but before it was executed the long column of the enemy had been seen going northward. This called for a modification of the previous order after the movements it directed had begun. To stop them and to slip into new movements was difficult. Even a modern trained staff, in close touch with lower units by radio and telephone, might tie things up badly. Success in such an operation also depends much upon the intelligence and the temper of lower commanders. It is not possible to tell with precision everything that happened in Pope's army on the afternoon and night of August 25, but it seems clear that McDowell grasped the new situation quickly and changed his movements, but that Sigel did not.[91] McDowell not only made the needed alterations; he also discovered early in the morning of the 26th what Sigel had done and what he had not done, and he inquired of Pope at 5:30 A.M. whether instructions to himself would consequently have to be again changed.

But Pope—at Warrenton Junction—had been sleeping no more than dependable Irwin McDowell at Warrenton, and sent him this important dispatch at 5:00 A.M.:

> Please ascertain in some way whether the enemy be really in force at Waterloo Bridge. Sigel insists that he is, while Banks, who was there late yesterday afternoon, asserts positively that there was no enemy during the day there. You will easily see how important it is for us to know positively what has become of the enemy's force which was in front and where the column has gone which took yesterday the road toward Salem. Please use every means possible to ascertain this at once. Reno will cross at Rappahannock Station and push forward a reconnaissance to Culpeper. Nothing is expected from Sigel. I wish you would send me a regiment of cavalry; I have not a mounted man here; send one of Buford's or Bayard's.[92]

Perhaps during the uncertain night Pope had had the half-hour or so of sleep that can mean much to a commander and that may change a battle. At least there had been a noticeable alteration in his views, for at 9:30 the previous evening he had wired to McDowell by the telegraph line that had been constructed between Warrenton and the Junction: "I believe that the whole force of the enemy has marched for the Shenandoah Valley by way of Luray and Front Royal." [93] An hour later he sent a similar dispatch to White at Winchester, with instructions to keep a sharp lookout, and to keep his men in camp and his supplies up.[94] With the coming of day Pope was no longer certain of the destination of the well closed column of infantry and artillery which Clark and others had seen. He needed eyes; he wanted a regiment of cavalry; and he wanted one of Bayard's or Buford's, for he thought that it would have some of the bold and earnest spirit of those fine brigadiers.

The request for cavalry shows how foolish it was for Pope to have no "army cavalry"—but only "corps cavalry"; but it may be noted that the very next day Lee would be suffering badly from wrong use of his mounted arm and would have to grope blindly at a critical moment.[95] Presently Pope learned that Buford had said his brigade was disorganized, and that Bayard had reported that he had not a regiment that could make a charge or sustain one. Nevertheless one of Buford's weary regiments was ordered to Pope, while McDowell told that tireless officer to get information by "scouts, spies, and reconnaissances" about the direction the enemy column had taken, and had directed, "Use money freely to pay for it." [96]

The cavalry horses had broken down not only because of heavy use, but also because of lack of forage. In the rather desolate country, barns were empty of corn, oats, and hay, and operations were too continuous to allow adequate grazing. The railroad was overburdened, but animals would fare better after August 25 when Haupt set up the priorities: "Subsistence for men, forage, ammunition, hospital stores, veteran troops, raw troops." [97] Perhaps there was not enough oats on the market; perhaps some quartermaster had blundered; perhaps there was a bottleneck above Washington; whatever the cause, Pope started the critical day of August 26 under handicaps.

From McDowell at 3:30 P.M. a good report about his operations toward Waterloo contained this statement:

What is the enemy's purpose is not easy to discover. Some have thought he means to march around our right through Rectortown to Washington. Others think that he intends going down the Shenandoah, either through Thornton's or Chester Gap. Either of these operations seems to me too hazardous for him to undertake with us in his rear and flank. Others, that it was his object to throw his trains around into the valley, to draw his supplies from that direction and have his front looking to the east rather than to the north.[98]

This was an excellent presentation of "courses open to the enemy" that a commander must weigh in making his "estimate of the situation." McDowell was neither the first nor the last to dismiss as "too hazardous" precisely the course that a bold enemy followed; but the record is not often so clear and interesting.

Soon after McDowell's dispatch Colonel Clark reported, "Trains and troops still passing over the same route." He related that an enemy deserter had just come in and had stated that Longstreet's corps, embracing such-and-such divisions, was in the woods back of Waterloo, and that Jackson's corps was somewhere above Longstreet. The deserter appeared truthful, and Clark credited his story.[99] (It was in fact accurate.)

What other information came in cannot be told with certainty, but in a dispatch to Banks which unfortunately does not show the hour McDowell stated that Negroes and scouts reported that the enemy force which had reached White Plains at noon on the 25th had marched in the direction of Thoroughfare Gap. He added, "General Pope wishes all the troops in hand ready to march, with three days' rations (cooked), at a moment's notice." [100]

Pope and his trusted lieutenant were alert on August 26, 1862. General White at Winchester, who had been warned the night before, had also been seeking information and had reported to both Pope and Halleck, and the General in Chief at 11:45 had told Pope that discovery of the enemy's position had become the order of the day.[101] Both Halleck and Pope have been criticized for believing that Lee meant to strike at the Shenandoah. So they did believe at first, as was natural; and Lee had directed a feint toward the Valley, expressly for the purpose of confusing the Federals, on the same day that he ordered the march of the column observed on the 25th.[102]

Pope made his estimate and decisions, and set them out in a letter to Porter at 7:00 P.M.—about as fine a letter as a general could put on paper. After giving instructions he set forth the disposition of all his forces, and the enemy position. This he gave as generally facing east, in accordance with the last of McDowell's estimates, adding that the enemy had a "strong column still farther to his left towards Manassas Gap Railroad, in the direction of Salem. . . . I do not see how a general engagement can be postponed more than a day or two." And he directed Porter: "Make your men cook three days' rations and keep at least two days' cooked rations constantly on hand. Hurry up Morell as rapidly as possible, as also the troops coming up in his rear."

John Pope was getting ready for battle; and John Pope would fight.

At 11:00 P.M. Porter sent an answer which left nothing to be desired in his apparent attitude as a subordinate but included one little bit of bad news. He had been drawing supplies from Fredericksburg, and now would like to receive from Pope grain for 800 animals for three days, and he had only forty rounds of ammunition per man.[103] It looked as if the railroad would have more work to do; but before Pope could pass on the cheering news to his perplexed quartermaster something had happened that changed everything.

At 8:00 P.M. the telegraph operator at Manassas reported that a body of Confederate cavalry had rushed into that place, firing into a train.[104] That was all that got through before the wires were cut; but it was quite enough. Within a few minutes Pope had the message in the hands of General Heintzelman, whose corps was at Warrenton Junction, with orders to send a regiment immediately by train to Manassas to find out what was up, repair the wires, and protect the railroad. The regiment was sent, and about daylight the commanding

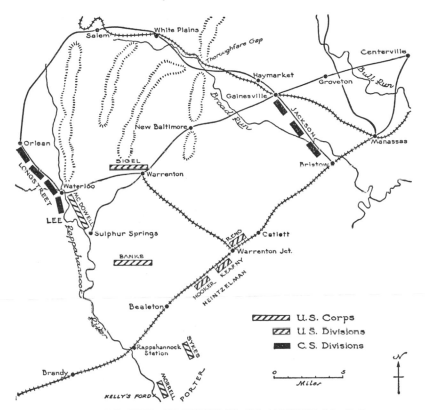

POPE AND LEE AT EVENING OF AUGUST 26, 1862

officer—a captain—reported by wire that he had proceeded almost to Bristow, and had found "a train of cars burning and telegraph wires broken, and enemy in very heavy force." [105] The only response from Warrenton Junction that clicked out was an ambiguous "Wait a little," and not a clear "Understood." The little force of 300 men was hardly enough to cope with the infantry, cavalry, and artillery that the enemy threw against it, and so the commanding officer entrained his men and returned to Warrenton Junction, where he gave a full report.

Even before the regiment had reached Bristow, Pope knew the truth, that it was not just a raid like that on Catlett four nights before, in spite of Henderson's most unjust statement to the contrary.[106] Before midnight he was conjecturing that Lee's entire army, or the larger part of it, had gone in that direction.[107] At 10:00 McDowell reported confirmatory reports from Sigel's scouts, but was elated rather than depressed by the prospects: "If the enemy are playing their game on us and we can keep down the panic which their appearance is likely to create in Washington, it seems to me the advantage of position must all be on our side." Then, after he had raised a question about food, ammunition, and forage, the general who had complained so much about the Federal waste of rations stated: "We have wasted a good deal of artillery ammunition." [108]

The headquarters of Pope and McDowell would have been interesting places to visit on that historic night. The generals were both cool men who understood warfare, and they had some very good staff officers. It would have been instructive to observe such soldiers suddenly called upon to deal with the difficult problem which night had brought at the end of a busy and confusing day. Faithfully they worked, in spite of exhaustion, writing and reading messages, and studying maps by candle and lantern light, talking quietly about roads, distances, ammunition, rations, oats, guns, wagons, ambulances, regiments, brigades, divisions, and corps in the atmosphere of composure, suspense, anxiety, laughter, and profanity that makes a military headquarters unique. Over it all there brooded the awful sense that they dare not fail, even though there were great uncertainties in their knowledge. So the heavy hours of a stuffy night dragged on, and some who had been fortunate enough to get a little sleep shook themselves into consciousness and returned refreshed for tasks that might begin anew with the arrival of an unexpected horseman.

Outside Pope's headquarters were two tired, faithful troops of the First Ohio Cavalry. They were the men who took the messages and watched over the headquarters of the army. From time to time as the night wore on, a trooper would arrive, give the reins of his tired horse to waiting hands, go within the circle of the flickering candles and the smoky lanterns, stand momentarily at attention, salute, and report the safe delivery of a message; then he would vanish into the dark and drop exhausted into sleep that no longer could be denied—after he had removed his saddle and had patted and talked to his horse a little in the easy manner of a cavalryman. Doubtless the commanding general sometimes seemed a little abrupt to the weary boys from Ohio farms. But Pope knew full well what they were doing, and no event could crowd from his mind a consciousness of that. His report stated, "As orderlies, messengers, and guards they passed many sleepless nights and weary days," and pinned a medal on the breast of each with the observation that they "performed the most arduous service probably of any troops in the campaign." [109]

What had taken place was the prototype of an airborne operation of World War II. Between Pope and Washington was Stonewall Jackson with some 23,000 infantry and artillery and Stuart's cavalry. Not by gliders and parachutes had they arrived there, but by their legs and feet, after one of the famous marches of history. "Close up, men, close up," was the constant urging of Jackson to the column that Colonel Clark's discriminating eye the day before had reported as "well-closed infantry." All of Jackson's men were worn out, and not a few were nearly dead from exhaustion; but it was night, and for several hours they would be safe, and most of them could rest: all except the inevitable few who must fight sleep and stay awake on outpost duty. (After seizing Bristow, Stuart and two regiments of infantry were sent to Manassas, but had arrived before midnight.) Jackson was squarely on Pope's line of communication and in possession of a great advanced supply depot.[110] But as Irwin McDowell had stated quickly: there was also the opportunity that a soldier dreams of—destroying a large part of an enemy force which had been hazardously divided. In the entire situation there was only one really unfortunate element: at the same hour that Jackson reached Bristow, McClellan arrived at Alexandria from Aquia Creek.

Lee has been soundly criticized by military writers because of the great hazard he took when he divided his force in the face of an enemy who was becoming his superior and put one part of it in a most exposed position. Not a few writers have derived cheap amusement by stating that the move revealed his contempt for Pope. But such a claim is a reflection upon Lee, and not on Pope. At no place in Virginia had the Confederates received a more significant rebuff as that administered to Jackson by Banks and Pope at Cedar Mountain; and although Lee had hoped to capitalize on Pope's remaining too long in that vicinity he was too much of a general to lack admiration for the boldness that Pope had shown. He might have had contempt for Pope personally and might have disliked him because of the orders he had issued; but a general whose place in history is built upon boldness carried almost to a fault would correctly evaluate the trait in an opponent. Then for four days Pope had definitely outgeneraled him on the Rappahannock, and had done so with an inferior force. This Lee knew full well, as did every one of his lieutenants. With regard to Lee's thrusting vainly first at one flank of Pope and then just as vainly at the other, Freeman writes: "The operation was becoming tedious. Wherever Lee moved, there was Pope, apparently confident and fully the master of the situation." [111] After the war, Lee replied to his critics correctly: that, being the weaker—with everything to gain and little to lose—he had to resort to moves that were overbold. All soldiers know that operations have often succeeded merely because they were foolhardy and completely unexpected. But not many generals have the moral courage necessary to try them, for the price of failure is usually complete and overwhelming disaster. Lee's maneuver was more hazardous than the moves that McDowell ruled out as too dangerous for Lee to entertain, and its very boldness helped bring it success.

Only a general with superb courage could have sent Jackson on his perilous mission, and fewer still could have done it and then remained serene and calm.[112] Everything depended upon the man at the head of the marching column—upon Stonewall Jackson—and in him Lee had one of the few subordinates to whom such a daring enterprise could have been committed. Lee had perfect confidence in Jackson, and was always duly thankful for having such a rare lieutenant; but he did not know when Jackson marched away in the early dawn of August 25 that Providence would also intervene in his favor by having McClellan get control of the Alexandria end of the railroad while Jackson was sitting on it at Manassas. No blow by Jackson could be quite as paralyzing as an order by McClellan.

Word that something was amiss at Manassas reached Washington promptly; before 9:00 Halleck had a copy of a dispatch Haupt had received from the operator at Manassas, which announced that the engine *Secretary* had been fired on at Bristow, had handsomely scattered a pile of ties placed on the track to wreck her, and, though riddled with bullets, had safely pulled her train to Manassas, for which the conductor thought the enemy was heading.[113]

At 9:30 P.M. Haupt's instrument clicked out a message from Halleck that General Smith, General Slocum, or General Sturgis, or any other general officer that could be found, should take all the men Haupt could transport to Bristow or Manassas.[114] Armed with that authority, Haupt about midnight found General Hancock, senior officer present of Franklin's Sixth Corps, who ordered Brigadier General G. W. Taylor to execute the mission of protecting the bridge at Bull Run. To this force the Eleventh and Twelfth Ohio infantry, under Colonel Scammon of Cox's command, were added. In reporting his actions to Halleck, Haupt had to break the bad news that brave little *Secretary,* after her heroic escape through a rain of bullets, had ingloriously dashed into the rear of a train two miles east of Bull Run bridge and had piled things up badly. Haupt suggested to the General in Chief that what had happened at Manassas—bad though it might be—was really a matter for the history books, and that attention should be concentrated on saving the bridge at Bull Run, the destruction of which would be a serious matter. He said he was dispatching a wrecking and construction train to clear up the muss that *Secretary* had unhappily caused, that he hoped that the 3,000 or 4,000 men he was sending could save the bridge.[115]

But the bridge was not saved. Instead of obeying his orders carefully, and putting his brigade in a strong defensive position to cover the bridge, Taylor crossed it, proceeded toward Manassas, and without any artillery support attempted to attack a strong Confederate division that had artillery support. Soon his four New Jersey regiments were in retreat, and the retreat became something of a rout. Blankets, shelter tents, and haversacks containing three days' rations were left on the far side of the stream. General Taylor was mortally wounded, and the command fell on Colonel Scammon, who had arrived later, and who reported that the behavior of Taylor's troops was most discreditable. With the exception of two officers and ten men, whose names Scammon secured and reported, Taylor's regiments would not join in the defense of the bridge.[116]

Such was the first contribution that McClellan's troops made in the battles before Washington. Scammon held on as best he could, and reported in the afternoon to General Cox that he had taken a position about three miles from the bridge and would do his best. The Eleventh Ohio had driven the enemy "handsomely," and if he had more men and some guns the affair might still be made a success. Presently, however, encirclement threatened him; he withdrew his force and marched back to Alexandria that night.[117] One of Taylor's regimental commanders said in his report that Hancock's orders had been "to hold the bridge over Bull Run at all hazards." [118] If Taylor had handled his force properly the mission might have been fulfilled. The enemy could have brought an overpowering force against him; but it was a day of jollification and feasting at Manassas, with matters tending to be lax, and it is not certain that the enemy would have done so.

Hoping that the expedition that he had dispatched would be successful, and believing that the Confederates would not remain long upon the railroad, Haupt at 11:00 A.M. suggested to Halleck that, as soon as cars were back, he should make a subsistence train of rations and grain, protect it with 1,500 or 2,000 more men, and try to force it through; for he feared that Pope's men might be hungry, and his animals starving. Halleck, who had only an hour before received notification of McClellan's arrival at Alexandria, replied: "If you can see General McClellan, consult him. If not, go ahead as you propose."

Haupt was soon off on an errand whose success he later regretted. He procured a rowboat and, after some search, located McClellan in a transport below Alexandria; the general returned with him. News had arrived about Taylor's unfortunate little battle, and when Haupt submitted his plan for the subsistence train immediately after this McClellan stated that it "would be attended with risk."

Haupt suggested that risk was quite usual in military operations, and added that he did not consider the hazard involved in his proposal to be excessive, for the trains could be withdrawn if the enemy were found in firm possession of the railroad. Of the interview he wrote as follows:

> My representations and arguments availed nothing; the General would not give his consent, or assume any responsibility, and would give no orders, instructions, or suggestions of any kind!!
> After a time the General had a sudden attack of indisposition, became very pale, and asked if I had any brandy.
> I replied that I did not use it, but would send for some.
> On its arrival he drank a portion, which revived him.[119]

Though there may be some questions whether Haupt added any embellishments with the passing of time, the incontrovertible facts about the meeting, together with his high character, make it necessary to accept his story as essentially reliable. He had no reason to disparage McClellan in order to make his own record look better, because his contributions to the war were beyond dispute, though they may not have been known to the general public. Furthermore the statements that he made about McClellan that really mattered were quite in character for the latter. The first unit of McClellan's army to be engaged with the enemy had been defeated. Though Taylor's culpable departure from orders and the bad behavior of his regiments was still to be told, the first report about losses was badly exaggerated. It had been sent by Haupt's Manassas agent, who had escaped to Fairfax Station, and the report McClellan had seen closed with the statement that the sender did not know how reliable it was.[120] But McClellan's first maxim of war seems to have been that bad news should never be distrusted, and he did not wait for fuller information before making decisions. At 1:15 he telegraphed to Halleck: "Should not Burnside take steps at once to evacuate Falmouth and Aquia, at the same time covering the retreat of any of Pope's troops who may fall back in that direction? I do not see that we have force enough in hand to form a connection with Pope, whose position we do not know. Are we safe in the direction of the valley?" Twenty minutes later he sent a message with more defeatist thoughts: "I think our policy now is to make these works perfectly safe and mobilize a couple of corps as soon as possible, but not to advance them until they can have their artillery and cavalry. I have sent for Colonel Tyler to place his artillerymen in the works. Is Fort Marcy securely held?"[121] (Fort Marcy was near the west end of the Chain Bridge, three miles above Washington.)

McClellan was again thinking of retreats and of defeats; he would wait once more until everything was ready before moving forward—even though it might then be too late. The contrast between McClellan and Haupt stood forth immediately and sharply, and it was significant. Both had stood high at West Point; both had become engineers after quitting the army. Though Haupt had never held responsible military command, he had made other kinds of decisions where the stakes were high. It was he, for example, who had said the Hoosac tunnel could be built and at such-and-such a cost. While McClellan, without inquiry as to the enemy strength, was stating to the General in Chief that he did not think that he had force at hand to make a connection with Pope, Haupt was wiring his agent at Burke (ten miles east of Bull Run) that there had been 20,000 enemy at and around Manassas the night before (an amazingly accurate figure), and that, the railroad being out for a time, the army *must cut its way through*.[122] The digger of tunnels was of a courageous bent and used words apt for the occasion.

At an hour not given—though it would be interesting to know whether it was before or after the receipt of McClellan's melancholy messages—Halleck informed him of his own occupation with the problem of new levies and with matters in the West, and directed: "You will therefore, as ranking general in the field, direct as you deem best; but at present orders for Pope's army should go through me."[123] An order went promptly to Burnside from McClellan to prepare for the evacuation of Falmouth and Aquia; but it drew at once an effective protest addressed to Halleck.[124] A few weeks later the General in Chief told Pope that McClellan had not been given control over the Army of Virginia, though he had wished to have it.[125] Perhaps Halleck thought that the proviso he had inserted kept Pope's command subject to himself alone; and in a way that was true. But in spite of the saving clause that flowed from Halleck's pen, Fortune played loosely and dangerously with the Union during those hot hours of Wednesday August 27, 1862.

Haupt, who had encountered both timid opposition and knavery in connection with the Hoosac tunnel, did not surrender easily his wish to get succor to Pope, and his native determination was no doubt strengthened by a one-sentence message from the President he had received that day: "Is the railroad bridge over Bull Run destroyed?" Although at 7:15 P.M. he wired pessimistically to Colonel D. H. Rucker, one of Meigs's indefatigable quartermasters, "Everything that we now have awaits the orders of General McClellan," he shortly took matters somewhat into his own able hands. At 9:50 P.M. he sent McClellan a message which asked no advice or permission, but told the general what the railroader was *going to do*!

I propose to start at 4 o'clock precisely, a wrecking and construction train bound for Bull Run; also a forage train and a subsistence train. It is perhaps proper that 200 good skirmishers should be sent with the trains, who should be at the depot at Alexandria before 4 A.M. to-morrow morning. General Pope will be notified by courier to-night to have his wagons at Sangster's Station by daylight to-morrow. If the troops are not here by 4 A.M., we propose to go ahead without them.[126]

Sangster was three miles east of Bull Run, and Haupt had no way of knowing whether Pope could get wagons to that place at the time set—it looked impossible. But the provisions could be there and be waiting, and Haupt knew that the reserve supplies at Manassas were in flames. No answer came from McClellan to the invitation extended; but, undaunted, the builder of bridges and digger of tunnels again went out lantern in hand at midnight, four miles to a camp where he knew there was a soldier. He wrote: "I found General Hancock in bed in his tent. He arose immediately and cheerfully agreed to give me the force I required, promising that they should be on hand at 4 A.M. punctually. They were there on time and performed good service in the operations of the next day." When Haupt sent McClellan a report of the accomplishment of the expedition, the general wrote back, "I am very glad you have sent out the reconnaissance," belittling what had been done and covering his error by misnaming the expedition.[127] Though August 27 was a day heavy with fate for the United States, when Haupt, Halleck, and Pope were giving all their efforts to their duty, McClellan still had time to listen to gossip and indulge in personal pique. He took no notice of Haupt's note but sent to Halleck an impertinent, if not insubordinate message, stating that he had heard the General in Chief had made an unfair and a slighting remark about him, and implying that if it were true—which he hoped was not the case—cooperation between them would deteriorate. However exasperated he must have felt, Halleck took time to answer mildly and considerately.[128]

Just as Haupt and his staff worked tirelessly with the railway problem, so Meigs and his efficient helpers labored unremittingly with heavy quartermaster problems. Steamers and schooners had been piled up at Fort Monroe and Yorktown until some of them stood idle, though there may have been a shortage at first of ships suitable for animals.[129] A heavy gale on the 24th had interfered badly with the forwarding of cavalry and teams, but the movement in general had been smooth and well handled.[130] Over the one railroad that served Washington from the north, trainloads of supplies and equipment had been moving for the two armies that were to be united; loaded cars were forwarded to the yards in Alexandria on the rails that had been laid over Long Bridge. On August 23 the 1,500 horses that Pope had asked for, together with 230 mules and 75 new ambulances, were on hand, and efforts were being made to get them to the general.[131] On the evening of the 27th a War Department quartermaster informed his opposite number in Alexandria that there were 78 cars of grain on Maryland Avenue in Washington, and that Haupt had reported the cars already brought over were more than could be unloaded.[132] In the manner of a good desk soldier he inquired, "Can you not double your force and unload the cars?" It all looked reasonable, for the railroad was crying for its cars so that yet more forage and more of everything could be brought from the rich Northern states that had begun to develop a war potential never equaled before by any nation. Reasonable though it looked, the Alexandria quartermaster did not like the message; and the next morning he wasted no words on Washington: "All the cars that have arrived here from Maryland avenue have been unloaded promptly. We want more cars instead of more force." [133] Doubtless there was a comment about Haupt's little slip that did not get into the record.

Amid the trains of supplies and equipment for the great army to be based on Washington—150,000 men, and probably 25,000 animals— there were also troop trains. Not just trains of men who had seen some action and much marching, such as Cox's Kanawha division, whose trains had sped over the Baltimore and Ohio with top priorities, but trains of new troops. When they arrived in Washington they came under the care of Brigadier General Silas Casey,[134] and great pains were taken that they should be well received, with a bit of thoughtful welcome. When the telegraph announced an approaching train, a meal was prepared, and the men were soon marched away from the cars, to be seated at tables where they were served well prepared and wholesome food.[135] They would have plenty of chance later to learn about campaign fare, and to march and fight with empty stomachs—the Army of the Potomac still had virtually as much to learn of such things as it had to learn about offensive battle.

In the Twenty-third Ohio Infantry that Cox brought from West Virginia, there were two future Presidents of the United States. After a welcome that impressed them well, Lieutenant Colonel Rutherford B. Hayes—the commanding officer—and Commissary Sergeant William B. McKinley first saw the impressive Capitol with its unfinished dome, rising steadily in spite of war, and the arrested monument to the great First President.[136]

CHAPTER XI

THREE GENERALS AND THREE DAYS

"You are getting the value of your ammunition. Yes, sir," he said, "you are giving them just what they need."
General Kearny to Captain McGilvery

At 8:45 A.M. of the 27th McDowell wired Pope: "Can you spare time to come to the instrument and have a conversation with me?" [1] The two generals then engaged in shop talk, and their questions and answers form one of the most interesting pages of the entire Official Records. One of the questions Pope asked was: "What became of that regiment of cavalry I directed you to send me yesterday?" McDowell had the answer ready. Not having been able to check with Buford, he had already directed Bayard to send a regiment. And he added: "This may result in your having two regiments." Both Buford and Bayard were hard to locate during those eventful days, and when and where any horsemen reported to Pope—if ever—is not discoverable. The questions the generals explored covered a wide military range: intelligence of the enemy, location of their own troops, their movements, supplies, and trains. The record they wrote shows how badly they were in need of the modern well trained general staff officers to take over the different lines of work and pursue every important item carefully and ceaselessly.

The entire campaign had suddenly reversed itself. First, the Federal Supreme Command had undertaken the difficult and delicate task of uniting the Army of Virginia and the Army of the Potomac, and Lee had striven to destroy Pope before it could be done. Lee had failed.

Then he in his turn had made a much bolder move which had thrown part of his army into a hazardous position. Both Pope and McDowell knew that the remainder of Lee's army would move rapidly to the support of the endangered part, for Clark had reported the day before that troops were following the road on which the enemy column had been seen on the 25th, and McDowell in the telegraphic conversation informed his superior, "Reynolds reports from Sulphur Springs that the indications are that the enemy has left that place." Now Pope would in his turn have the chance to attempt to do what Lee had failed to do—destroy a portion of the enemy.

A decision had practically been made several hours before the two generals talked with each other over the telegraph, as shown by a dispatch that Pope's chief of staff wrote to Porter as the first touches of day were appearing in the east. After acknowledging receipt of the latter's message of 11:00 P.M., Colonel Ruggles explained clearly what had happened: the enemy cavalry had interrupted railway communications near Manassas, and a heavy force seemed to be advancing along the Manassas Gap Railroad. A move would probably be made to attack this force the next day in the neighborhood of Gainesville. The colonel said he would attempt to keep the commander of the Fifth Corps informed, and ended, "You should get here as early in the day to-morrow as possible, in order to render assistance should it be needed." [2]

At 10:00 A.M. Pope himself sent to Halleck by way of Fredericksburg an excellent description of the situation and of the movement he had started:

The enemy has massed his whole force at White Plains, with his trains behind him. A strong column penetrated by way of Manassas Railway last night to Manassas, drove off a regiment of cavalry and one of infantry, and I fear destroyed several bridges. My position at Warrenton is no longer tenable. I am now moving my whole force to occupy the line from Gainesville to railroad crossing of Cedar Creek [near Catlett], on Alexandria and Central [Orange and Alexandria] Railroad. Neither Heintzelman nor Porter has any transportation and but little ammunition; cannot move off the railroad. . . . Under all the circumstances I have thought it best to interpose in front of Manassas Junction, where your orders will reach me. Neither Sturgis' nor Cox's commands have come up. Heintzelman's has no artillery. I am pushing a strong column to Manassas Junction to open the road. I do not know yet what damage has been done. You had best send a considerable force to Manassas Junction at once and forage and provisions, also construction corps, that I may repair the bridge and get the railroad trains to the rear. I . . . will endeavor to communicate with you from Manassas to-night.[3]

Although two corps of the Army of the Potomac had been sent to him with little ammunition—one with no transportation and no artillery, and the other with little transportation—John Pope blamed no one. In his subsequent report he did assert that he understood that Manassas was being guarded under the authority of higher headquarters.[4] The accuracy of his understanding is not strongly supported, though the information is incomplete.[5] It is true, however, that the great accumulation of supplies was not primarily for him but for the combined armies when the expected offensive should begin. Wherever the responsibility to protect Manassas may have rested, Pope on the morning of August 27, like Haupt, regarded what had happened as history; and in good cheer he marched his divisions without delay toward the enemy.

Pope's order moved McDowell with his own corps and that of Sigel from Warrenton along the turnpike to Gainesville; Reno with his detachment and Kearny's division of Heintzelman's corps from Catlett to Greenwich; Porter to Warrenton Junction. General Banks was placed in command of the combined trains of the army, and full instructions were given in regard to this important responsibility, made difficult by the reversal in direction of the army. Hooker's division was sent down the railroad toward Manassas, a mission that obviously would quickly lead to a collision.[6]

Pope estimated his effective force as: Sigel, 9,000; Banks, 5,000; McDowell, including Reynolds's division, 15,500; Heintzleman and Porter, 18,000; Reno, 7,000.[7] The figures totaled 54,500, which the general thought might be over the correct number. Heintzelman's and Porter's commands were by far the freshest, for Pope's own men had been marching and skirmishing almost constantly since August 18. On paper Pope's cavalry had the impressive strength of 4,000 sabers; but so badly had the horses broken down that the general stated he had fewer than 500 troopers who could do the service that should be expected of cavalry.

More knowledge of the enemy was the great need as the columns moved on their objectives for the 27th. At 2:20 P.M. Pope reported to McDowell that aides of General Banks had observed a hostile column moving from Sperryville in the direction of Salem on the previous day. He said, "It is this movement of the enemy that I desire very much to know about, if it can be ascertained by observation." Halleck had early sent Pope a dispatch through Burnside and over the wire up the Rappahannock saying that the enemy seemed to be concentrating near Manassas, with the order not to allow himself to be separated from Alexandria and the promise that some force would be sent from Washington to meet him, in spite of a shortage of transportation. Burnside was doing everything he could to clear the picture for the General in Chief, and telegraphed at 12:40 that there had been no considerable body of the enemy in the vicinity of the fords the day before, and that all his information tended to show that the mass of the enemy was moving toward Pope's right flank; he did not believe that there was any large force between Fredericksburg and Hanover.[8]

By midafternoon Hooker, advancing down the railroad with two batteries and two extra infantry regiments that had been sent to him, came into contact with Ewell's division, which was protecting Jackson's command, about four miles southwest of Bristow.[9] A sharp action took place, and Ewell was forced back to Broad Run. Pope, who arrived on the scene about sunset, afterward spoke warmly of the gallant conduct of Hooker, conspicuous but heedless on his white horse. Hooker bivouacked that night along Broad Run, with only about five rounds of ammunition left per man.

Pope's movement on the 27th has generally been praised as the correct one for him to make. Writes Henderson: "This move, which was complete before nightfall, could hardly have been improved upon. The whole Federal army was now established on the direct line of communication between Jackson and Lee and although Jackson might still escape, the Confederates had as yet gained no advantage beyond the destruction of Pope's supplies." [10]

But there was one officer who, taking a hasty look at Pope's excellent order, behaved contemptuously. When Porter arrived at Warrenton Junction in the afternoon he found a copy of the order waiting for him; and at 4:00 P.M. he wrote a long letter to Burnside that has in places an unsoldierly tone:

I send you the last order from General Pope, which indicates the future as well as the present. Wagons are rolling along rapidly to the rear, as if a mighty power was propelling them. I see no cause for alarm, though

I think this order may cause it. . . . We are working now to get behind Bull Run, and I presume will be there in a few days, if strategy don't use us up. The strategy is magnificent, and tactics in the inverse proportion. . . . I do not doubt the enemy have large amounts of supplies provided for them, and I believe they have a contempt for this Army of Virginia. I wish myself away from it, with all our old Army of the Potomac, and so do our companions. . . . Most of this is private, but if you can get me away please do so. Make what use of this you choose, so it does good.[11]

It would not have been a pretty letter for any officer to write. It was particularly unbecoming for a general who had taken part in the great seven days' retreat to the James River from a strong position in front of Richmond—a retreat so precipitate that great quantities of supplies and equipment were destroyed while 2,500 wounded and sick were abandoned to the enemy. Pope's wagons were indeed "rolling along," but not to the rear as Porter stated; they were moving toward the enemy, toward the new front. As to the enemy's regard for the Army of Virginia, Porter himself had reported ten days before that intercepted persons stated that Richmond gossip was that at Cedar Mountain Jackson had been defeated by Banks and Pope. And he should have seen that for four days Pope with the smaller force had maneuvered so skillfully that Lee had been unable to cross the Rappahannock successfully, though he had tried first one place and then another.

The letter indicated that Porter's heart was not fully in the work to which competent authority had assigned him. A crucial battle was hour by hour coming closer—Pope had told him that—and Fitz-John Porter wanted to be away from it. He wished to be back with McClellan; perhaps because the latter was in the habit of turning over the management of battles to him, while Pope would stay in the fight and direct his own battle. The letter entered both Porter's court-martial for disobedience of orders and the subsequent rehearing of the case. Whether the letter "did good" as he hoped it would, is hard to determine, and the answer might depend upon what one thinks about Fitz-John Porter. In spite of this letter revealing some animus, he sent a very good directive to Morell about bringing his division up promptly; but in a way, instead of mitigating the letter to Burnside, it makes it seem worse. He had closed that letter with the statement, "Our provisions are very short." To the directive his adjutant sent to Morell, Porter himself added in a postscript: "Do all you can to get up provisions, and put as much bread in haversacks as possible—three days. We go right to the railroad, and with your cattle will manage to get all that is wanted." That sounded like a good soldier, and the ending was still better: "Hurry up Griffin. Don't wait for him. Hope you are improving." [12] The hour of writing is not shown; but, whether or not it was before or after the Burnside epistle, the latter left doubt as to what Porter would do when the pinch came.

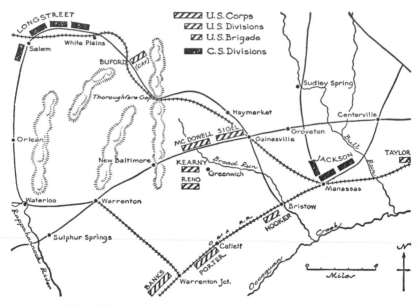

POPE AND LEE AT EVENING OF AUGUST 27, 1862

That night Pope was at Bristow; and he was in very good spirits, as well he might be. His columns had executed their march missions, and he was closing his 50,000 men on the enemy, which he knew to be Jackson with about 25,000 men—consisting of his own old division, and those of A. P. Hill and Ewell. Pope also was certain that Stuart was present with all his cavalry, including the former command of Ashby, now led by General Beverly Robertson.[13] Though his total force was double that of Jackson, Pope was for the moment in a very precarious position, for he had in hand near the enemy only Hooker's 4,000 men with almost empty cartridge boxes.

While Pope watched the sky glowing with flames of burning warehouses and railroad cars at Manassas, he made the first bad decision of his campaign. He thought it probable that Jackson would mass his whole force and attack the right of the Federal line as it then faced northeast. Undoubtedly that was Pope's weak spot, and Jackson might have done him great damage; but such an operation would have isolated Stonewall from the rest of the Confederate army. In accordance with his view, Pope at 6:30 P.M. sent an order to Porter to march the next morning at one o'clock for Bristow, and he furnished an officer as guide. At nine o'clock an order went to Kearny to march "at the very earliest blush of dawn" to Bristow and to McDowell to march rapidly at daylight on Manassas with his own and Sigel's corps.[14] Approaching battle certainly did not make John Pope nervous; it made him a bit poetical. But the Kentuckian could not remain a poet long; he quickly lapsed into practical thoughts and instructed Kearny to do unpoetical things such as to obtain receipts for messages, and to furnish an escort for officers carrying dispatches. He himself sent the high-spirited Kearny a guide, knowing that strange country roads are hard to find "at the very earliest blush of dawn." To the trusted McDowell he wrote: "If you will march promptly and rapidly at the earliest dawn of day upon Manassas Junction we shall bag the whole crowd." The sentence will make anyone smile, but not because it is ambiguous or shows a frightened general. Pope can also be pardoned for touching up the end of his letter to McDowell just a little: "Be expeditious, and the day is our own."

After he had indulged himself in these flashes of poetry, mixed with hardheaded orders and admonitions, Pope sat with his staff by the embers of a fire, and smoked and watched the glowing sky above Manassas, where Jackson with 25,000 excellent soldiers was supposed to be.[15] But already Jackson's rested, washed, and somewhat rehabilitated columns were on the march to a place of hiding—a confused march that rivaled his bad performance on August 8.[16] There was some excuse this time, for it had been a day of great jollification, when even his iron hand could not suppress plundering and indulgence.[17] He tried hard to see that the stores of liquor on the sutler's shelves were absorbed by the thirsty ground and not by his still more thirsty soldiers, and in this he had quite a measure of success. But officers and men who were perfectly sober had stomachs too well stuffed with substantial food and uncommon delicacies to make a good march record. And the men were burdened without as well as within. No wagons for rations, only wagons for ammunition had accompanied Jackson on the 25th—though some beef cattle had been driven in the rear of the column; and his men loaded themselves to the limit with the stores of Manassas as they trudged away, leaving the rest in flames.

John Pope outlasted the others at the camp fire. He—the commanding general—could not shake off the sense of responsibility as he watched the flames grow low, and one by one his staff officers went to sleep with such comfort as could be found in the bivouac. His orders had gone out. But had he forgotten something? And it was Pope's voice that roused the sleepers at "earliest dawn," telling them to eat their breakfast and make ready. The poetic vein had passed, but Pope again used vivid language, though no longer calculated to evoke a smile. Strother wrote: "Anxious and moody the General sat smoking his cigar, listening for the opening sounds of battle, and occasionally ripping into delinquents of all grades." It was a great relief not to hear musketry from Hooker's weak outpost lines, but it was a disappointment not to see the expected columns of Porter and Kearny arrive. Porter's failure to comply with the order sent him was the basis for one of the charges against him, though by itself it probably would have been ignored, because Jackson did not make the attack that Pope had feared. Sigel as usual was late, in part because he had retained 200 wagons with his command, instead of concentrating them as ordered with the other trains under Banks.[18] In one important particular McDowell departed from the order sent to him, for he sent Ricketts's division and Buford's and Bayard's cavalry toward Thoroughfare Gap to stop up that important avenue of approach for reenforcing enemy troops.[19] The day before, Buford had had contact with an enemy column between Salem and White Plains, west of the Gap. The tireless cavalryman did not know how great a prize came near falling into his hands; but his troopers narrowly missed capturing General Lee, who was incautiously riding near the head of Longstreet's column without cavalry protection.[20]

But Pope did not spend all his time ripping into delinquents, so as to keep things moving briskly and tone up the atmosphere of headquarters; as he awaited the overdue troops he busied himself with important logistical considerations. Orders went to Banks about bring-

MAJOR GENERAL JOHN POPE

ing both the railroad and the wagon trains forward to the new position of the army.[21] The railroad bridge over Kettle Run two miles west of Bristow had been burned, and until it could be repaired only the wagons could go farther. Priority was given to ammunition, and Pope ordered that a box or two of that essential commodity be thrown into every wagon that passed the railroad cars halted at the destroyed bridge.[22] The enemy who had denounced Pope's orders as barbaric would have been surprised to read a note that went to his medical director: "Major-General Pope directs that you take measures to hunt up the wounded of the enemy, and to provide for them the same as for our own soldiers." [23]

About noon Pope rode on to Manassas. Waste and destruction were everywhere. Strother wrote:

While here I amused myself strolling about observing the debris of the recent rebel carnival. On the railroad track and sidings stood the hot and smoking remains of what had recently been trains of cars laden with ordnance and commissary stores intended for our army. As far as the eye could reach the plain was covered with boxes, barrels, cans, cooking-utensils, saddles, sabres, muskets, and military equipments generally; hard-bread and corn-pones, meat, salt, and fresh beans; blankets, clothes, shoes, and hats, from brand-new articles, just from the original packages, to the scarcely recognizable exuviae of the rebels, who had made use of the opportunity to refresh their toilets.

From the Federal skulkers, stragglers, and sutlers Pope gathered such information as he could as to when and whither Jackson had departed, and at 4:15—after an earlier note of 2:00 P.M.—he wrote to McDowell: "The enemy is reported in force on the other side of Bull Run, on the Orange and Alexandria Railroad, as also near Centreville. I have ordered Sigel to march on Centreville immediately, as also Kearny and Reno. I will advance Hooker as reserve. Please march immediately with your command directly upon Centreville from where you are." [24] The day was well advanced, and every lost hour brought Lee's succoring column nearer to Jackson.

By early afternoon Jackson had posted his command generally west of Sudley Springs, there to await the arrival of Lee, with escape possible through Aldie Gap in case the Federals should prevent the rest of the Confederate army from coming through Thoroughfare. Blackford, Stuart's engineer officer, wrote:

The position was a wonderfully strong one along the line of an old railroad where there were successive cuts and fills of from eight to fifteen feet, making most formidable breastworks for infantry both in the cuts and behind the banks, while the elevated ground in rear gave position for artillery to fire over their head.

The left flank was covered by Bull Run and the right rested on the crest of a ridge which could be crowned with batteries to enfilade the whole front. The high ground was wooded, and in these woods Jackson massed his corps, hiding them completely, while Stuart surrounded them by a curtain of cavalry to keep off [Pope's] scouting parties who were in search of Jackson's dreaded men.[25]

The appraisal of the defensive value of the position should be reliable, and in speaking of Jackson's men as being "dreaded," Blackford was merely indulging in an old soldier's privilege. But Blackford's clear insinuation that Pope could have easily found Jackson if he had been a commander of talent and enterprise, does not come from thorough and objective study of the situation and problem that confronted the Federal general. With advancing years Stuart's enterprising engineer officer remembered vividly the long rows of stacked arms, so close together that one could hardly ride between them, as well as the card playing and other merriment of the Confederates, as they rested and feasted on that historic day; but he forgot that Pope was operating in enemy territory where the inhabitants did not hasten to him with helpful information about the enemy, and where even a professed Unionist had to be regarded with some suspicion until he proved his case. Freeman's statement that Jackson might never have been able to reap the advantage of his excellent position if his adversaries had been alert, may likewise not be based upon careful consideration.[26] Pope's wrong decision the night before as to what Jackson would do caused some countermarching of McDowell's troops; but he himself believed that if the order he had given Porter to march at 1:00 A.M. had been executed he would have engaged some of Jackson's force before it left Manassas.[27] Be that as it may, it is clear that Pope was alert enough; the most that can be said is to charge that he was not shrewd enough to divine what Jackson would do, and thus anticipate his move by ordering McDowell and Sigel to a position to intercept him.

The hiding place of Jackson was found in the early evening, when King's division of McDowell's corps proceeded, under its new orders, down the turnpike towards Centerville. Jackson was under no compulsion to attack it, for he had not been directed to engage Pope and hold on to him; but the opportunity offered by the Federal column marching across his front was more than he could resist. No writer has described what took place so well as Henderson:

The reports of the engagement at Groveton are singularly meagre. Preceded and followed by events of still greater moment, it never attracted the attention it deserved. On the side of the Union 2800 men were en-

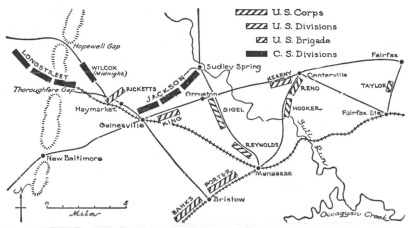

POPE AND LEE AT EVENING OF AUGUST 28, 1862

gaged, on the side of the Southerners 4500, and for more than an hour and a half the lines of infantry were engaged at the very closest quarters. The rifled guns of the Federals undoubtedly gave them a marked advantage. But the men who faced each other that August evening fought with a gallantry that has seldom been surpassed. The Federals, surprised and unsupported, bore away the honours. The Western brigade, commanded by General Gibbon, displayed a coolness and a steadfastness worthy of the soldiers of Albuera. Out of 2000 men the four Wisconsin and Indiana regiments lost 750 men, and were still unconquered. The three regiments which supported them, although it was their first battle, lost nearly half their number, and the casualties must have reached a total of 1100.[28]

This battle where "men fell like leaves in autumn," was a costly engagement for Jackson. The rifles of Gibbon's unshakable farmers and villagers reduced the famed Stonewall Brigade to about 400 men. Southern loss of officers was very heavy; Taliafero, an excellent division commander, was badly wounded, and Ewell lay long on the field with a shattered leg. After that evening the Badgers and the Hoosiers called themselves the Iron Brigade; and no one disputed their right to the title or hinted that they were immodest—least of all their opposite numbers in the Stonewall Brigade.

Jackson had now sampled two of Pope's corps, and had been roughly handled, though in both cases he had had much the superior force. Apparently Pope's tactless order to his troops had not made them fight any the worse; and it took a general of great courage and ample confidence in his subordinates and his soldiers to remain in position that night, with the knowledge that Pope could now concentrate his corps for attack. With Taliafero and Ewell gone it would not be an easy matter to hold out until Lee arrived with the rest of the army. Perhaps Stonewall remembered how difficult it had been to drive the two Federal brigades from a good position at Port Republic and believed his men should rival their superb fighting.

From near Centerville Pope wrote to Halleck at 10:00 P.M. a dispatch wrongly headed "Manassas Junction," which did not reach the General in Chief until 6:45 the next evening. Giving an excellent summary of operations to date, he told of Hooker's success the day before, and said, "Late this afternoon, a severe fight took place, which was terminated by darkness. The enemy was driven back at all points, and thus the affair rests." He asked to have a construction corps sent to rebuild the bridges over Bull Run and Kettle Run, and provisions and forage as far as the railroad could bring them. He had a thousand prisoners, many arms, and one captured piece of artillery, and did not see how Jackson could escape without heavy loss. Most important for the sequel were his statements with regard to Thoroughfare Gap. Referring to the 27th, he said:

McDowell was ordered to interpose between the forces of the enemy which had passed down to Manassas through Gainesville and his main body moving down from White Plains through Thoroughfare Gap. This was completely accomplished, Longstreet, who had passed through the Gap, being driven back to the west side.[29]

Pope misunderstood badly what had taken place at the Gap, and his operation the next day was accordingly predicated upon an erroneous hypothesis. Where responsibility for the blunder lay cannot be determined now with certainty; perhaps inaccurate reports reached him that are not in the records. Few commanding generals have had to face a more elusive situation than that which confronted Pope on August 27 and 28; and no general perhaps was ever more in need of good general staff officers than Pope was on those days. One cannot take from him all responsibility for his error, but anyone who has ever done any staff work in the field and realizes the great burden a commanding general carries in a long continuing operation will feel a great deal of understanding and sympathy for John Pope.

Longstreet had not been driven back through the Gap, to be somewhat stunned by failure—as Pope seemed to believe. On the contrary, Lee had arrived only that evening at the Gap and had just deployed in order to force the weakly held passage. Pope's misconception of the situation helped lead to his undoing.

The 28th was a day of critical decisions in Washington, where so much depended upon taking advantage of the unusual opportunity to deal a fatal blow to the Confederates. At an early hour Pope's order of the previous evening to Porter should have been in the hands of Halleck, for Burnside had forwarded it by wire at 5:00 A.M.,[30] after receiving it from his advanced telegraph station up the Rappahannock. The order gave information about Hooker's fight of the 27th and the movements ordered for the 28th. Other information forwarded during the day by Burnside revealed that there were only weak enemy forces south of the Rappahannock;[31] so Pope was in no danger of being assailed in the rear as he moved on Jackson. Information had also been received from Colonel Miles at Harpers Ferry and from General White at Winchester; the enemy activity they reported looked like that of guerrillas, who had also been in evidence between Alexandria and Manassas.[32] From such information as he had received, the General in Chief could have made quite a good situation map.

McClellan wrote on the 28th some of the strangest dispatches of his career, though they were not quite so hysterical as some he had sent from the Peninsula. In a message received by Halleck at 1:00 P.M., he stated that it had been learned from an officer passing through with dispatches from Pope that the latter had put the enemy force at Manassas at 20,000. Such a figure would hardly suit McClellan, and with characteristic disdain he wrote, "I expect to learn some reliable information from the front." A much longer communication that arrived at 2:45 began as follows: "From a full conversation with

Colonel Scammon I am satisfied that the enemy is in large force between us and Pope. One of his surgeons, who was taken and released, saw Jackson, A. P. Hill, and three other generals. At about 5 P.M. yesterday there was heavy cannonading in direction of Manassas. It is my opinion that any movement made from here must be in force, with cavalry and artillery, or we shall be beaten in detail." [33]

Scammon in his official report, written the same day, stated that about six enemy regiments with six guns had been engaged in the Bull Run bridge affair the day before, and mentioned also a strong cavalry force of 1,000 to 5,000.[34] From such figures, together with the report of the surgeon who saw what Jackson wanted him to see, and a little artillery fire—which should have been encouraging, since it proved that Pope was attacking—McClellan made up his mind, after calmly rejecting Pope's good estimate.

A soldier who had been captured and had then escaped came in while McClellan was writing—as opportunely as the contrabands had dropped in when McClellan was in front of Richmond. This man reported that the enemy was 30,000 strong at Manassas, and was being constantly reenforced. That settled it. McClellan at once recommended to Halleck that Pope be ordered to retreat and "change his base" by falling back between the Occoquan and the Potomac. The frightened general in Alexandria wrote: "I do not think it now worth while to attempt to preserve the railway. The great object is to collect the whole army in Washington, ready to defend the works and act upon the flank of any force crossing the Upper Potomac."

But McClellan had not finished. At 10:00 P.M.—perhaps after some more of the "reliable information" had arrived—he sent a dispatch in which he put the enemy force at 120,000 and stated that it was Lee's intention to march on Washington and Baltimore.[35] Consideration of supply alone made his figure utterly fantastic, and it is to be hoped that the overburdened General in Chief was in bed and sound asleep before the final nonsense clattered out of the telegraph instrument at 12:20 A.M.

Though Halleck could not get orders easily to Pope, the latter had seized the initiative himself and the General in Chief was quite well informed about the Army of Virginia. Of the Army of the Potomac, Franklin's corps of 16,000 men had reached Alexandria on

August 24,[36] and the bulk of Sumner's corps (14,000 infantry and some artillery) arrived on the morning of the 28th.[37] In addition, much of Cox's good, though small, division had fallen to the command of McClellan on account of its inability to join Pope at an earlier date. McClellan's dispatch at ten o'clock that night indicated clearly that the troops of both Sumner and Cox were in condition to move forward, for he said to Halleck in what seems almost like mockery, "If you wish any of them to move toward Manassas please inform me." Heavy arrivals of artillery, cavalry, and wagons were expected at Alexandria on the 28th.

One again has the chance to compare McClellan's pronouncements with his actions. On July 30—when the use of his army was still undecided—he had wired Halleck: "We are losing much valuable time, and that at a time when energy and decision are sadly needed." [38] He had stated that the place to defend Washington was not close to it, but on the Peninsula, and he had spoken of watching for mistakes by the enemy in order to take advantage of them.[39] While at Fort Monroe on the 22nd he had bravely directed Sumner, "Your corps should be in condition to fight immediately upon landing, as you ever are." [40]

The general who had made these statements advised on August 28 that the defenses of Washington be manned and preparations be made for a close-in fight about the city, and recommended in addition that Pope be ordered to retreat in a roundabout manner—although reports on his operations of the 28th were not yet in. What took place on the 27th and 28th of August was merely a repetition of what had taken place on the 27th and 28th of June. The scene was different, the situation different, but the man was the same.

There is no chance to put any responsibility upon Secretary Stanton, because more than a month had passed without a communication from Stanton to Halleck about operations in Virginia—so far, at least, as the records reveal. However, on the 28th the Secretary broke silence with a note to the General in Chief which, with characteristic precision of thought, asked three questions. The first two referred to McClellan's withdrawal from the Peninsula, and the third inquired about any order for the movement of Franklin's corps to reenforce Pope which had recently been issued, "and whether it was obeyed as promptly as the national safety required." The note may have been responsible for the directive that Halleck sent to McClellan at 7:40 P.M.:

There must be no further delay in moving Franklin's corps toward Manassas. They must go to-morrow morning ready or not ready. If we delay too long to get ready there will be no necessity to go at all, for Pope will either be defeated or be victorious without our aid. If there is a want of wagons, the men must carry provisions with them until the wagons can come to their relief.[41]

In that message there was a touch of the spirit of Joffre's great order of September 4, 1914, a touch of the boldness that would have brought victory on the banks of Bull Run as surely as it did a half-century later along the Marne.

Through orders issued in the final hours of the 28th Pope sought to move his troops into position to attack Jackson as soon as it was light the next morning. His plan was to have McDowell's corps and Sigel's corps—a total of 25,000 men—attack from the south and west, so as to prevent Jackson from escaping through Thoroughfare Gap; at the same time Heintzelman's corps, Porter's corps, and Reno's detachment would attack Stonewall with another 25,000 from the east.[42] But about daylight a change in plans became necessary because McDowell's corps, with the exception of Reynolds's division, was not where Pope had believed it to be. King's division of the corps had fallen back to Manassas after the Groveton action, perhaps because of the supply situation, or perhaps because King had had to give up command after fighting illness for some days. On the other hand Pope learned that Ricketts's division had been sent to Thoroughfare Gap, which according to Pope's idea of the situation was a useless precaution. In reality, however, Ricketts was no longer at the Gap, for in the evening Lee had sent three brigades under Wilcox through Hopewell Gap to the north, and Hood's division over the trails to the south, while Jones kept up pressure on the gap itself.[43] Finding that his position was fast becoming untenable, Ricketts fell back on Manassas via Centerville and Bristow. McDowell quite as well as Pope had lost contact with both King and Ricketts; and he did not locate them until the next morning.

Pope's new plan was to shift Porter from the eastern attacking force to the western group, which was not difficult because Porter had spent the night near Bristow and was only starting his march toward Centerville in accordance with the earlier order. The new order was sent probably about 5:00 A.M., and an hour and a half later Pope sent a joint order to McDowell and Porter, directing both generals to move on Gainesville, and discussing the situation at some length. The question of supply had begun to disturb him, and he stated that he wanted his whole command to halt as soon as McDowell and Porter should gain contact with Heintzelman, Sigel, and Reno, and added, "It may be necessary to fall behind Bull Run at Centreville to-night. I presume it will be so, on account of our supplies." The order said not a word about attacking, but contained the very general sentences: "If any considerable advantages are to be gained by departing from this order it will not be strictly carried out. One thing must be had in view, that the troops must occupy a position from which they can reach Bull Run to-night or by morning." [44]

It was hardly a good order to send to Porter, though McDowell was an officer who could and would probably interpret it and work with it satisfactorily. That Pope believed he had ample time to dispose of Jackson was shown by the sentence, "The indications are that the whole force of the enemy is moving in this direction at a pace that will bring them here by to-morrow night or the next day." Tomorrow night or the next day! At the moment Pope wrote that sentence Lee's leading troops were safely through the Gap and only five miles from Gainesville.

Porter's corps was leading in the march on Gainesville from Manassas. Presently the column halted, and while McDowell was on the way forward he was overtaken, or met, by a courier with an important message:

Headquarters Cavalry Brigade
[August 29, 1862]—9:30 A.M.

General Ricketts:

Seventeen regiments, one battery, and 500 cavalry passed through Gainesville three-quarters of an hour ago on the Centreville road. I think this division should join our forces, now engaged, at once.

JNO. BUFORD, Brigadier General

Please forward this.[45]

The incomparable Buford! After sending a message earlier in the morning that the enemy was coming from the Gap in force, he had counted the colors and could give the number of regiments observed so far. He had done all he could as eyes for the army, and now he wanted to fight. Temporarily attached to Ricketts, he suggested to that general that they get into the battle that had begun. Their commands had marched and skirmished the day before; they were tired from the long night march back from the Gap, and no orders had reached them. But such things made no difference to John Buford. A battle was on: one needed no orders.

The regiments that Buford had reported were the advance elements of Lee's column hastening to the aid of Jackson, and his message was one of the most important of the campaign. It should have gone on to Pope by the freshest horse that was available. But according to Pope's testimony the following January at Porter's trial it was not sent.[46] No slip is more likely to occur than for a commander to fail to pass on to higher headquarters information that comes to his attention, engrossed as he is with making decisions for his own command. On that account it is necessary that there be on all staffs intelligence officers who are in constant communication with one another "up and down," who have no responsibility of command but responsibility solely for securing, comparing, coordinating, and disseminating information. If McDowell had that day had a good intelligence officer, Buford's important dispatch would probably have quickly found its way to army headquarters. Whether it would have changed the dispositions that Pope made for the rest of the 29th is one of the points in this interesting campaign that can never be settled. From a hill near Centerville some of Pope's staff that morning saw dust clouds from the direction of Thoroughfare Gap and surmised their meaning.[47] Though a dust cloud might be puffed aside by sanguine John Pope as not conclusive, a precise note from clear-thinking John Buford held before his eyes by a good intelligence officer should have brought conviction. Buford's postscript was significant—as his postscripts always were. He was the perfect cavalryman. Through Stuart's covering screen he had fought his way close enough to the infantry column to count the colors amid the clouds of dust, and he wanted that precious information to go all the way to the top. McDowell might well have taken the hint from the three momentous words, "Please forward this"; and it is strange that he did not, for throughout the campaign he had foreseen many needs, and had been much more than a corps commander ready to obey orders. No task had been too heavy for him, no danger too great. Even now, as the senior commander addressed in the joint order, he had a responsibility for Porter's corps as well as his own.

Seeing in Buford's note need for decisions on his own part, McDowell apparently put it into his pocket and trotted on past the halted corps of Porter to the head of the column, where he found its commander observing from a slight eminence the dust clouds rising above the trees, raised by the feet of the infantry regiments that Buford had reported—or dust that Stuart's men had stirred up by dragging a road.[48] From the northeast there came the angry noise of artillery fire. After discussing the situation somewhat, McDowell remarked to Porter, "You put your force in here, and I will take mine up the Sudley Springs road, on the left of the troops engaged at that point with the enemy." With the divisions of Ricketts and King—still enthusiastic in spite of the marching and fighting of the day and night before—McDowell joined that of Reynolds, which he had previously directed to support Sigel, and which took part in some of the later action of the day.

The battle that McDowell had joined had been begun soon after daylight by Sigel in an attack a mile or two east of Groveton; it grew from the fire of skirmishers to an engagement of all his artillery and infantry. About 10:30 the enemy counterattacked with superior numbers, but Sigel's outnumbered men were opportunely joined by Kearny's and Hooker's divisions of Heintzelman's corps and also by Reno. The attacks of Pope's divisions and corps may not have been well coordinated, but they were repeated, and many of them were bitterly pressed up to the strong enemy position along the railroad grade and through difficult woods and undergrowth. A. P. Hill held the left of the Confederate position, and against him the attacks were particularly severe; few officers and few troops could have sustained them. Most of the Confederate reserves had to be put in, and Gregg's South Carolinians were driven to the last tenable position, where they held under the words of Gregg: "Let us die here, my men, let us die here!" [49] In some previous battles the Confederates had seen the coming of darkness with regret, as it helped save an enemy on whose destruction they were bent. But not so on this day. Douglas wrote that it seemed the sun would never set, and he added that no one knew how slowly time could pass "unless he has been under the fire of a desperate battle, holding on, as it were by his teeth, hour after hour, minute after minute, waiting for a turning or praying that the great red sun, blazing and motionless overhead, would go down." [50]

Kearny and Hooker, who had chafed under the restraint and inaction of the Peninsula, at last had a chance to reveal their appetites for offensive fighting, and they vied with each other in the attacks which they pushed resolutely against a stubborn foe. Three days later Kearny was to die in battle, but not until he had written his report of the 29th, in which he said: "My regiments all did well, and the remiss in camp seemed brightest in the field." A battery commander, whose guns were temporarily detached from Banks and attached to Heintzelman, and who had made a forty-mile march the day before, put into his battery diary a remark that showed how closely Kearny watched the field of battle. Wrote Captain Freeman McGilvery, Sixth Maine Battery: "During the fight General Kearny came to me and said, 'You are getting the value of your ammunition. Yes, sir,' he said, 'you are giving them just what they need.' " [51] Never would that battery commander forget the general with the empty sleeve.

From early afternoon Pope had expected the arrival of McDowell and Porter upon his left. Though his final order had not given them any attack objectives, they would become aware of the battle, and the words about departing from instructions would be ample. After he had learned of McDowell's approach he sent at 4:30 P.M. a definite order to Porter:

> Your line of march brings you in on the enemy's right flank. I desire you to push forward into action at once on the enemy's flank, and, if possible, on his rear, keeping your right in communication with General Reynolds. The enemy is massed in the woods in front of us, but can be shelled out as soon as you engage their flank. Keep heavy reserves and use your batteries, keeping well closed to your right all the time. In case you are obliged to fall back, do so to your right and rear, so as to keep you in close communication with the right wing.[52]

It was primarily on account of his failure to obey this order that Porter was court-martialed. In reality the order was based on an altogether erroneous view of the situation, and it could not have been obeyed. The exact hours at which events took place on that day are still somewhat in dispute; but certainly before Pope wrote his order Lee had arrived with all of Longstreet's troops, and had put them in position, with the left toward Jackson's right, the line running almost north and south across the Warrenton-Centerville turnpike, extending well to the south of it to the vicinity of the railroad from Manassas.

Although Porter knew he was in contact with the enemy, he was not aware of the latter's great strength in his front. To General Pope's 4:30 order—which was delivered about 5:00 according to the positive testimony of Captain Douglass Pope,[53] who carried it—a written reply was made, which unfortunately does not appear in the records. It seems unlikely that the reply said anything convincing about the enemy strength, because Porter, at his trial, did not ask Captain Pope if he had delivered the message, nor question General Pope as to

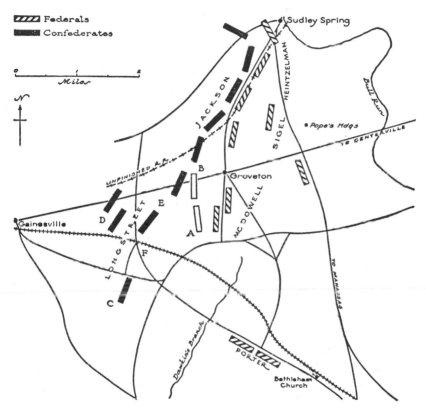

SECOND BATTLE OF BULL RUN, 4:30 P.M., AUGUST 29, 1862

Pope ordered Porter to attack the enemy right, which he believed to be at AB, while in reality it was at CD. The court that later cashiered Porter thought he had fallen back from F.

whether he had received it. And if the reply had been of special significance, Porter should have had a retained copy, which could have been put into the trial record. Though completely indifferent to the answer he had made to General Pope,[54] Porter made great efforts to discredit Captain Pope's testimony as to the time the message was delivered—

a matter of no consequence whatever if Porter knew that the enemy strength was so great that an attack upon him was out of the question. As a matter of fact, Porter promptly ordered General Morell to attack with *two regiments*, supported by two more.[55] A sentence in the diary of Porter's corps shows that his reconnaissance had been insufficient to determine the enemy situation with any precision. The statement—apparently not presented at the trial—reads: "On the afternoon of the same day [the 29th] had a slight skirmish with the enemy." [56] Captain Pope gave other revealing testimony as to how matters were regarded at Porter's headquarters. He affirmed that a lieutenant, whom he took to be an aide to General Porter, instructed him within the general's hearing to inform General Pope that a scout had come in, reporting that the enemy was retreating through Thoroughfare Gap. The statement was not challenged in any way by General Porter. Perhaps strangest of all was the testimony of General Sykes at the trial.[57] His division of regulars had not been deployed, but was—in part, at least—in column along the road. Sykes himself had been near Porter when the 4:30 order was received and "continued with him from that time all night." But Porter did not mention to Sykes the fact that he had received a positive order to attack—an action that passes understanding. Twelve hours earlier Porter had not been so reticent about what Pope was doing. In a letter written at 6:00 A.M. to Burnside, enclosing an order he had just received from Pope, he had been lavish enough with sneers as to the operations of the day before, and he said, "I hope Mac is at work, and we will soon get out of this." [58]

"Mac" indeed was "at work"—badgering Halleck, who, in the absence of his chief of staff,[59] had only one regular officer on duty, and that at a time when the situation was growing more critical in Kentucky as well as along Bull Run. In spite of the peremptory order of the General in Chief for Franklin to march to the aid of Pope, ready or not ready, McClellan had him stop at Annandale, five miles from his starting point. Then he began quibbling, and at noon he asked Halleck if he really wanted Franklin to go any farther. By that time word must have come in that Pope and part of his army had been at Centerville the night before, so that communication was assured and all danger to the capital was removed. Nevertheless, McClellan also started to bring pressure on Halleck to detain Sumner,[60] who had camped the night before on the Centerville turnpike with instructions to be ready to resume the march the next morning.[61] In this effort he was successful, and the harassed General in Chief, who stated that he had no time for details, capitulated at three o'clock, and directed McClellan, "dispose of all troops as you deem best." [62] That evening and night, after convincing news had been received that matters were going in Pope's favor, Sumner's corps was marched back and took position to guard the aqueduct bridge at Georgetown,[63] a move that shows clearly McClellan's military incapacity—or his lingering hope that Pope would be defeated.

At 2:45 P.M., in reply to a request from the President for news from Manassas, McClellan sent the famous dispatch in which he stated that either all forces should be concentrated to open communications with Pope, or Pope should be left "to get out of his scrape," while all efforts were directed toward making the capital secure.[64] McClellan knew that communications were already open, and his phrase about letting Pope "get out of his scrape," and his open and brash bid to bypass the General in Chief,[65] should have aroused a holy wrath on the part of the President. Only a mild rebuke was sent by the too patient Lincoln:

> Yours of to-day just received. I think your first alternative, to wit, "to concentrate all our available forces to open communication with Pope," is the right one, but I wish not to control. That I now leave to General Halleck, aided by your counsels.[66]

Halleck had received a copy of McClellan's dispatch, and it afforded him the last chance he had to put the command problem in a really satisfactory form. He should have ordered McClellan to proceed to Centerville with both Franklin's and Sumner's corps, and at the same time summoned Wool from Baltimore for the purpose of going into the field and taking over command of the two armies. In that way he would have been freed from McClellan's ceaseless heckling (which the scholarly soldier did not know how to counter); all available strength would have been put against the enemy; and the corps of the Army of the Potomac could have been united under their own commander for more harmonious action. (Heintzelman's corps, however, should have been left with Pope.) But full power should of course have been given to Wool to remove McClellan as commander of the Army of the Potomac and substitute one of the corps commanders if he found him quibbling, or showing the slightest tendency to disobey an order, or revealing indecision that unfitted him for field responsibility. A broad order from the President would have been needed; but it should not have been difficult to obtain after McClellan's dispatch had revealed his attitude toward Pope.

Halleck contented himself with issuing at 7:50 P.M. another order for Franklin to march. His dispatch expressed sharp disapproval of the fact that Franklin had been stopped at Annandale, in disobedience of his orders; but it also showed that the General in Chief was tired and somewhat confused after what must have been a very busy day.[67]

CHAPTER XII

SECOND BULL RUN

> My dear General: You have done nobly. Don't yield another
> inch if you can avoid it. All reserves are being sent forward.
>
> *Halleck to Pope*

Pope was up early the next morning—August 30—and with an
apparently rested mind he wrote a letter to Halleck at five o'clock
from near Groveton, a letter so important as to be given in full:

We fought a terrific battle here yesterday with the combined forces of
the enemy, which lasted with continuous fury from daylight until dark, by
which time the enemy was driven from the field, which we now occupy.
Our troops are too much exhausted yet to push matters, but I shall do so
in the course of the morning, as soon as Fitz John Porter's corps comes
up from Manassas. The enemy is still in our front, but badly used up. We
have lost not less than 8,000 men killed and wounded, but from the
appearance of the field the enemy lost at least two to one. He stood strictly
on the defensive, and every assault was made by ourselves. ·Our troops
behaved splendidly. The battle was fought on the identical battle-field of
Bull Run, which greatly increased the enthusiasm of our men. The news
just reaches me from the front that the enemy is retreating toward the
mountains. I go forward at once to see. We have made great captures, but
I am not able yet to form an idea yet of their extent.

I think you had best send Franklin's, Cox's and Sturgis' regiments to
Centreville, as also forage and subsistence.

I received a note this morning from General Franklin, written by order
of General McClellan, saying that wagons and cars would be loaded and
sent to Fairfax Station as soon as I would send a cavalry escort to Alex-

andria to bring them out. Such a request, when Alexandria is full of troops and we fighting the enemy, needs no comment.

Will you have these supplies sent without the least delay to Centreville? [1]

It would be hard to imagine a much better letter; it breathes the steadiness of a good commanding general. If there was some exaggeration, it can be remembered that this was Pope's first major engagement. The extravagant statements about enemy losses had been taken from reports by Kearny and Hooker, who had led assaulting troops.[2] The phrase "combined forces" is significant and presents a riddle. Apparently it indicates that, although he had very erroneous ideas the day before as to when Longstreet would arrive, he had learned during the night that Longstreet's troops had been present during much of the preceding day. This view harmonizes well with a statement in a letter of September 3 to Halleck, but it cannot be fully reconciled with Pope's final report written the following January.[3] However that may be, there was only one conclusion that Halleck could draw from the first sentence of Pope's five o'clock dispatch: all of Lee's army had been present and in the action of the day before, and Pope had done well against it.

A very careful reader of the messages that were coming in was Edwin Stanton; and though he was giving no instructions about field operations there was work for him to do with a great battle raging not far from Washington. He wired the competent T. A. Scott at Philadelphia, giving the news that Pope had fought all the day before with the combined forces of the Confederates, who had acted entirely upon the defensive and had been "driven at all points." That was pleasant word, and, though reflecting Pope's optimism, it was not too far out of accord with the facts. But the War Secretary had to think of grim things—of the men who had fallen; so, after stating that a large number of prisoners had been taken, he got to the real point of the dispatch: "The loss in killed and wounded is great on both sides. Volunteer surgeons are needed. Send all you can to report to the Surgeon-General, and see that they are furnished with transportation." To Stanton there came from the surgeon general, William A. Hammond, a note suggesting that the 3,000 convalescent soldiers in hospitals in and about Washington be at once evacuated to Philadelphia, New York, and Portsmouth Grove. The note went immediately on to General Meigs with the indorsement, "You will please carry into effect the foregoing recommendation of the Surgeon-General and report to this Department." A postscript said that Hammond had suggested that all the hacks and carriages in town be seized if necessary in order to hasten the move of the convalescents to the railroad station; ships also would be used to speed the evacuation.[4] Washington was preparing itself—perhaps a day or so late—for the terrible aftermath of a great battle.

The different official reports mention little if any gunfire during the morning of the 30th, but Strother wrote in his diary, "There is nevertheless sharp practice going on in the front both with small-arms and artillery."[5] Miles away in Alexandria, McClellan heard the noise of the cannon and grew alarmed. At 9:15 he wired Halleck that there was heavy artillery fire and he believed it to be "this side of Fairfax," adding, as if in the last hope of retaining Sumner, "It seems that the garrisons in the works on north side of Potomac are altogether too small." This looked as if he expected the Confederates to soon be across the Potomac; and, as though to emphasize the idea of a last-stand battle, he chose as the countersign for the day the word "Malvern." Pope's dispatch, however, was more convincing to Halleck; and, again assuming the role of a real General in Chief, he directed McClellan: "Franklin's and all of Sumner's corps should be pushed forward with all possible dispatch. They must use their legs and make forced marches. Time now is everything." At 2:00 P.M. he telegraphed Pope: "Yours of 5 A.M. is received. All matters have been attended to. Thirty thousand men are marching to your aid. Franklin should be with you now and Sumner to-morrow morning. All will be right soon, even if you should be forced to fall back. Let your army know that heavy re-enforcements are coming." As a fitting and grateful encouragement for the fighting general who was still on the top of a hard campaign, the General in Chief wrote above his signature, "Yours, truly."[6]

Throughout the morning contradictory reports came to Pope, but by noon reconnaissances by McDowell and Heintzelman on the right seemed to give assurance that the enemy was retreating.[7] He wished to forgo none of the possible fruits of his marching and fighting, and issued orders for pursuit. Presently, however, Reynolds reported from personal knowledge that the enemy was not falling back, but was massing his troops heavily south of the turnpike apparently to turn the Federal left.[8] In the meantime Porter's corps—less two brigades which had mysteriously wandered off to Centerville—debouched from

a wood to attack the center and left of Jackson's position of the day
before, only to come under the enfilading fire of many guns that Longstreet had in position.[9] Within a few moments the entire aspect of
the battle changed.

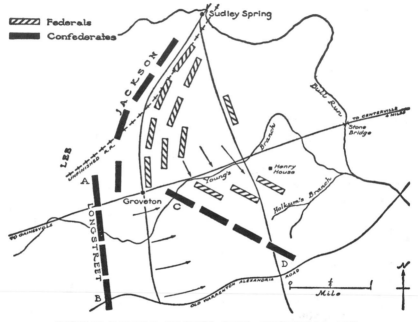

SECOND BATTLE OF BULL RUN, AUGUST 30, 1862

Pope's left was enveloped by the heavy counterattack of Longstreet, who
had been in a concealed position AB, and who advanced to CD.

The Confederate commander, who was about to launch one of the
great counterstrokes of military history, was no longer the novice of
the Peninsula confused by the difficulties of high command, and handi-
capped by past defeats and the distrust of his people. Nor was Jackson
any longer the man who strangely had failed on three occasions before
Richmond; away from the swamps of the Chickahominy he was again
the resolute, dependable soldier of the Valley. Longstreet in his turn
had grown until he could handle a corps as readily as a lesser man
could handle a battalion. In addition, the strategical initiative that Lee
had seized on the 25th enabled him to take into the combat many
fresh men, for most of Longstreet's troops had not been in the battle

of the day before. On the other hand, McClellan's "work" and Halleck's failure to be uncompromising had kept from the field 30,000 fresh and excellent Union soldiers. The orders of Halleck and Meigs, and hard and faithful work on the part of many, had brought the troops to Alexandria in plenty of time; but they did not draw a trigger in the battle. History perhaps has no more mournful episode.

The rested troops of Longstreet had chafed with some impatience. Freeman writes: "He had noticed, as he had ridden up, that the battery commanders, with instincts surer in this case than his own, had been anticipating an order to advance and had their horses harnessed and the men standing to the guns." [10] At the word of command the Confederate line, in which was concentrated heavy power, swept forward, overlapping the Federal left, and driving back the divisions that were marched from the right in haste to strengthen the point of danger. The fighting was stern and resolute, and it became especially bitter in the vicinity of the Henry House Hill, already famous for the battle of the year before. Though they again were excellent, Sykes's regulars did not stand out this day in contrast with other troops, as they had a year before. When it became apparent that he must retire, Pope handled the difficult task well, having completely recovered from the momentary excitement he had revealed when the heavy counterattack first became apparent.[11] About seven o'clock McDowell was given a covering mission; at eight a written order went to Heintzelman to retire to Centerville by Sudley Springs.[12] Strother states that after it was dark Sigel heard the verbal order: "General Sigel will fall back on Centerville with his command, seeing that the movement is executed smoothly and with deliberation." Then to the members of his staff who were present, the commanding general said: "If we could be of any further service I would remain, but as every thing is now arranged we will ride back to Centreville." Without more words the party rode away, and Strother recorded, "The turnpike was crowded with the retiring army, moving in silence and in perfect order." [13] McDowell, who a year before had witnessed a confused retreat from the same field, wrote in his report that the retirement was well conducted; likewise did Sigel, whose troops came last and blew up the stone bridge. Sykes stated that he reached Centerville "at midnight intact and in excellent order." [14]

At 9:45 P.M. Pope sent a good dispatch to Halleck, telling of the fortunes of the day and of the orderly retirement of the troops upon Centerville: "The battle was most furious for hours without cessation, and the losses on both sides very heavy. The enemy is badly crippled, and we shall do well enough. Do not be uneasy. We will hold our own here." [15] Fifteen minutes later Lee wrote to Jefferson Davis a dispatch in which he gave his customary reverential thanks to "Almighty God." [16] How much he was indebted to the "work" of McClellan, the Confederate general did not know.

Franklin had reached Centerville at six o'clock, in time to form a straggler line,[17] and Sumner arrived the following day. Before the Committee on the Conduct of the War, Sumner testified:

> If I had been ordered to advance right on from Alexandria, I should have been in that second Bull Run battle with my whole force. As it was, I lost some forty-eight hours, by remaining in camp for a time near Alexandria and then marching up to the Aqueduct Bridge.[18]

Had Franklin and Sumner been on the field with their corps, in addition to the 40,000 men that Pope probably had in battle, the 30th of August would have had a different ending. Halleck saw the possibilities clearly, and at 6:10 P.M. he had wired McClellan: "News from Pope favorable. If re-enforcements reach him in time we shall have a glorious victory, which will enable us to push Burnside in another direction." [19] The General in Chief's mind was apparently running toward a full exploitation of the hoped-for results at Manassas.

Rain was falling at dawn of Sunday August 31. The hungry, tired men set themselves to cooking and eating. Mixed-up units were straightened out, camp sites were arranged, outposts were strengthened, and patrols sent out. For the first time in his campaign there was a touch of uncertainty in the dispatch that Pope sent to Halleck at 10:45 A.M.:

> Our troops are all here in position, though much used-up and worn out. I think it would perhaps have been greatly better if Sumner and Franklin had been here three or four days ago; but you may rely on our giving them as desperate a fight as I can force our men to stand up to.
>
> I should like to know whether you feel secure about Washington should this army be destroyed. I shall fight it as long as a man will stand up to the work. You must judge what is to be done, having in view the safety of the capital.
>
> The enemy is already pushing a cavalry reconnaissance in our front at Cub Run—whether in advance of an attack to-day I do not know. I send you this that you may know our position and my purpose.[20]

Administrative matters were promptly taken in hand. The retirement on Centerville had left Banks badly exposed at Bristow, where he had both railroad trains and wagon trains. He had not been forgotten in the confusion of battle, and at 6:30 the evening before instructions went to him to destroy warehouses and railroad equipment, which could not be extricated on account of the destroyed bridge over Bull Run, and to retire on Centerville. Although flames and explosions revealed to the Confederates what was going on, Banks got away with his wagons, and by taking a back road arrived safely at Blackburn Ford and rejoined the army at Centerville.[21] On the 30th he had put through 100 wagons with ammunition, and the extrication of the rest of his train, after he had been left almost in the enemy's rear, was something of a feat. Haupt also had been working successfully, in spite of what he thought was insufficient assistance from McClellan, and was pouring supplies into Sangster and Fairfax Station, including 500 tons of ammunition, with provision for eleven different types of small arms.[22]

Halleck, who had been wishing for a decisive victory as recently as evening of the 30th, responded sympathetically to the news of Pope's reverse, and wired at 11:00 A.M.:

My dear General:
You have done nobly. Don't yield another inch if you can avoid it. All reserves are being sent forward. Couch's division goes to-day. Part of it went to Sangster's Station last night with Franklin and Sumner, who must be now with you. Can't you renew the attack? I don't write more particularly for fear dispatch will not reach you. I am doing all in my power for you and your noble army. God bless you and it. Send me news more often if possible.[23]

This note revived Pope's spirits and checked the tendency toward discouragement that had crept into his note of the morning. He promptly wired the General in Chief his warm appreciation, with the wish to have the commendation put into form to share with the army. Stating that "the whole secession army engaged us yesterday," he again divined Lee's next maneuver: "The plan of the enemy will undoubtedly be to turn my flank. If he does so he will have his hands full. My troops are in good heart." Once more he asked for cavalry horses, having failed to receive a single one.[24]

On the evening of the 31st the situation was still good so far as Pope was concerned; but the General in Chief had had a trying day.

Besides the bad news from Bull Run, word had arrived that a Union force had been defeated on August 30 at Richmond, Kentucky, so that the road was open to Lexington and possibly to Louisville and Cincinnati. On top of all this he was harassed by McClellan, who had wired at 10:30 P.M. of the 30th:

I cannot express to you the pain and mortification I have experienced to-day in listening to the distant sound of the firing of my men. As I can be of no further use here, I respectfully ask that, if there is a probability of the conflict being renewed to-morrow, I may be permitted to go to the scene of battle with my staff, merely to be with my own men, if nothing more; they will fight none the worse for my being with them. If it is not deemed best to intrust me with the command even of my own army, I simply ask to be permitted to share their fate on the field of battle. Please reply to this to-night.[25]

The appeal was pure hypocrisy, and it shows how little intellectual honesty McClellan possessed. Except for the short action at Mechanicsville he had apparently never yet been on a field of battle with his men; and he certainly knew it. Sumner had fought the battle of Williamsburg while he was back at Yorktown doing things a staff officer should have done. Sumner and Keyes had fought the battle of Fair Oaks while he was indisposed at his headquarters. Porter had commanded at Gaines's Mills while he remained in the house of Dr. Trent, in a panic preparing for his unnecessary retreat. Sumner and Heintzelman had conducted the affair at Savage Station, almost without orders, while he was again doing what a staff officer should have done. Sumner, Heintzelman, and Franklin fought the battle of Frayser's Farm, cooperating as best they could under vague instructions, while he was again away. Finally Porter had commanded at Malvern Hill while he sat—part of the time at least—on a gunboat in the James. The record was well known. On August 9 an editorial in *Harper's Weekly* defended McClellan, under the interesting title "McClellan Under Fire." Though it was a column long, there was no mention of any of the recent battles of the Peninsula, but only of battles in the Mexican War. Readers must have thought that the editor had raised rather than answered questions; and Halleck's aide, who received McClellan's message on the night of the 30th must have been amused at the touching appeal. At least the aide had the thoughtfulness when he read the message to the hard-worked General in Chief to omit the request for an immediate reply, and did not call attention to it until the next morning, when Halleck stated that he would have to take the request up with the President, since Pope was in command of the department.[26]

At 3:30 A.M. of the 31st McClellan wired Halleck: "My aide just in. He reports our army as badly beaten. Our losses very heavy. Troops arriving at Centreville. Have probably lost several batteries. Some of the corps entirely broken up into stragglers." The entire thing was of course irregular and somewhat underhanded. The only place from which a report should have been secured was Pope's headquarters, and there is no likelihood that Major Hammerstein, the officer in question, went there. It is a very serious thing to report to a General in Chief that one of his armies has been badly beaten, and it is not at all certain that Hammerstein made the unqualified report that McClellan attributed to him. That there had been much exaggeration on the part of the latter, if not a willful and malicious distortion, is shown by the fact that at 9:50 A.M. McClellan's assistant adjutant general wired Burnside in reply to a request for information, "Pope fought all day yesterday, but retired in evening to Centreville. He did not gain a victory I fear. We have little definite information." [27] Failure to gain a victory is quite another matter from being badly beaten.

The poison in McClellan's early morning dispatch, like his alarm over the artillery firing of the day before, evidently did not have any effect upon Halleck, for his message to Pope at 11:00 A.M. was one of encouragement and firmness, and even spoke of renewing the offensive against the enemy. Sometime during the day a wire from Major General H. G. Wright, commanding the Department of the Ohio, with headquarters at Cincinnati, was received. It contained the information that Major General William Nelson's defeat the day before at Richmond, Kentucky, had been very decisive: his forces were hopelessly broken and routed. Confirmation of the disaster came from Brigadier General J. T. Boyle at Louisville, who also wired the President: "News grows worse from Lexington. Many of our troops captured. Rebels on the Lexington side of Kentucky River. Lexington will be in their possession to-morrow morning. We must have help of drilled troops unless you intend to turn us over to the devil and his imps." [28]

Great alarm naturally was felt in both Cincinnati and Louisville, and fear spread also into other parts of the North which for months had been feeling secure. The problem that had suddenly descended upon Halleck as a result of Nelson's defeat would have been enough for one day, without the distorted accounts of events near at hand that McClellan, now acting thoroughly in character, was to give him. At 7:50 P.M. McClellan wired that he understood that there were some 20,000 stragglers between Alexandria and Centerville, and he slyly closed his dispatch, "The armament of Fort Buffalo is very incomplete." [29] The General in Chief should have been shielded from all such communications after he had made his decision in the morning with regard to Pope; but apparently he was not. It was, of course, his own fault that he was not sufficiently supported to be able to work calmly and quietly at this critical time, for he had been in Washington long enough to build up a proper headquarters. At 10:07 he capitulated again, as he had two days before, and closed a dispatch to McClellan, "I beg of you to assist me in this crisis with your ability and experience. I am utterly tired out." [30]

Here was McClellan's cue, and at 10:25 he answered: "I am ready to afford you any assistance in my power, but you will readily perceive how difficult an undefined position, such as I now hold, must be. At what hour in the morning can I see you alone, either at your own house or the office." [31] An hour later the General in Chief's aide replied that Halleck had gone to bed, which was the proper place for him to be. But in bed Halleck was not allowed to remain. At 11:30 McClellan sent a dispatch of considerable length which contained these sentences:

I apprehend that the enemy will or have by this time occupied Fairfax Court-House and cut off Pope entirely unless he falls back to-night via Sangster's and Fairfax Station. I think these orders should be sent at once. I have no confidence in the dispositions made as I gather them. To speak frankly—and the occasion requires it—there appears to be a total absence of brains, and I fear the total destruction of the army. . . . The occasion is grave and demands grave measures. The question is the salvation of the country. I learn that our loss yesterday amounted to 15,000. . . . It is my deliberate opinion that the interests of the nation demand that Pope should fall back to-night if possible, and not one moment is to be lost. . . . Please answer at once. I feel confident that you can rely upon the information I give you. I shall be up all night, and ready to obey any orders you give me.[32]

It was unbecoming a general who, through failure to make a reconnaissance, had tried to have a great army retreat by one road when others were available to speak of lack of brains in anything or anyone.

But McClellan's great offense was much worse than that. The only "information" in his dispatch (in sentences not reproduced above) had been obtained from a cavalry sergeant, who had been no nearer to the front than Fairfax; and its most important item was the completely false report that Pope's entire left had been driven in—a report which had very obligingly been given to the sergeant by a Confederate major. Doubtless McClellan exaggerated the report of the sergeant, as he had distorted the origin of the artillery fire the day before and had magnified the report of his aide and had stretched the number of stragglers and the number of casualties. Without any hesitation he stated, "It is clear from the sergeant's account that we were badly beaten yesterday, and that Pope's right is entirely exposed." He was trying to alarm the General in Chief and was doing so by false information in which he said reliance could be placed.

Fortunately for the record of the day, the tired Halleck resisted the falsehoods of the frightened and scheming McClellan. He replied at 1:30 A.M. of the 1st:

My news from Pope was up to 4 p.m. and he was then all right. I must wait for more definite information before I can order a retreat, as the falling back on the line of works must necessarily be directed in case of a serious disaster. Give me all additional news that is reliable. I shall be up all night and ready to act as circumstances may require. I am fully aware of the gravity of the crisis and have been for weeks.

The dispatch was not all that McClellan probably had wished, but the last sentence looked hopeful, and he graciously telegraphed at once:

We will be on the alert here. It will not be necessary for you to remain up all night so far as news from here is concerned, for anything new of the slightest importance will be communicated to you instantly.[33]

It was an error for McClellan to let Halleck go back to bed after once arousing him; it allowed the General in Chief to pick up some sleep, after which he felt better and wired Pope:

Yours of last evening was received at 4 a.m. I want to issue a complimentary order, but as you are daily fighting it could hardly be distributed. I will do so very soon.

Look out well for your right, and don't let the enemy turn it and get between you and the forts. We are strengthening the line of defense as rapidly as possible. Horses will be sent to you to-day. Send dispatches to me as often as possible. I hope for an arrival of cavalry to-day.[34]

Again Halleck ended, "Yours, truly"—a little touch that was not going into his dispatches to McClellan. The request for more dispatches, and the postscript, "Acknowledge hour of receipt of this," indicated that Halleck was wanting more news direct from Pope than he had been getting.

On the morning of September 1, Halleck was clearly expecting Pope to go on with his battle. Any note of uncertainty which he may have detected in Pope's dispatch of 10:45 A.M. of the preceding day had been removed by the field commander's later message.

Sometime during the morning McClellan received a long letter which Porter had written the evening before, and which fortunately found its way into the records. The document goes far toward removing any thought a person might have that Fitz-John Porter was unfairly treated when he was cashiered, even though the actual charges against him were doubtfully sustained. He had been in action only on the afternoon of the 30th, and his troops had marched less and fought less than any other division that Pope had. Still he wrote: "The men are without heart, but will fight if cornered." Part of the reluctance to fight, he said, came from the knowledge that they would be left on the field if wounded—a strange criticism from the man who had left so many dead and wounded when he retreated from Gaines's Mill. He stated that Pope had told a meeting of corps commanders the army was going to stay and fight, and that the decision had given general disappointment, adding, "However, we obey, and do what Halleck thinks is best." Perhaps the sentences most likely to affect McClellan were these: "I do not wish to see the army back if it can be helped; but I fear it may be kept here at the will of the enemy, to cripple it so that when it does get back it will be so crippled that it cannot defend the forts against the powerful enemy who will hold it here while they cross into Maryland. . . . I expect to hear hourly of our rear being cut and our supplies and trains (scarcely guarded) at Fairfax Station being destroyed, as we are required to stay here and fight." The letter concluded, "The bearer will tell you much." [35]

There is a twofold mystery about the Porter letter. The original, written in pencil on both sides of two small sheets of paper, is among the McClellan Papers, and how the compilers of the Official Records came by a copy of it is not clear.[36] A little of the right-hand copy of the second sheet is burned away, quite as if the writer, who had not signed the document, but whose identity was all too obvious from references to Morell and Sykes, had had an attack of fear—or conscience. But it was only for a moment; and after the flame had been put out, the destroyed words were carefully crowded into the corner of both sides of the damaged sheet. It would look as if Porter realized for a moment that he was not being loyal to Pope, to whose army his corps had been officially attached. That other letters were written by Porter to McClellan is proved by an entry in Strother's diary. Strother had known Porter as chief of staff for Patterson, but had not seen him for a year when he delivered the 3:30 A.M. order of August 29 directing him to move on Gainesville. Strother found the commander of the Fifth Corps asleep in his tent upon arriving at 5:20, and recorded that Porter, while dressing, quizzed him a good deal about the general situation. He was invited to stay for breakfast, and recorded that Porter at the table was engaged in writing, stopping to inquire how to spell "chaos," with the explanation that simple words sometimes bothered him. "Completing his dispatch he folded it, and asked if any of us had letters we wished to send to Washington. I gladly embraced the opportunity to hand in a letter to my wife, written in pencil and kept ready. The general then remarked that he had daily communication with Washington, and they made frequent and anxious inquiries after General Pope there, having nothing from him lately." [87] All of this fits in well with the fact that McClellan wrote twice on the 28th to Halleck about instituting means of getting information from the front.[38] News from the front should have been sought only from Pope, and one wonders if Halleck was not suspicious of what was going on. Pope's reference a few weeks later to "Porter's intercepted dispatches" in a letter to the General in Chief is significant and leaves one wishing for the complete story of what took place.[39]

Lee on his part sent a dispatch to the Confederate War Department. The humility that was in his dispatch to Davis on the night of the 30th was gone, and there was free use of the personal pronoun: "The enemy attacked my left, under Jackson, on Thursday [August 28], and was repulsed. He attacked my right, under Longstreet, on Friday, and was repulsed; and on Saturday I attacked him with my combined armies, and utterly routed the combined armies of Pope and McClellan on the plains of Manassas." [40] A professional writer of communiqués could not have done better; but the message hardly squared with the facts. Speedily it was put on the wires by Adjutant General Cooper in dispatches to the Western generals as welcome news that might lead to other Southern victories.

Pope—the lover of dawn—was at work early, and at three o'clock he directed Sumner: "It is essential that your right be carefully watched. I desire you at daylight to push a reconnaissance of not less than one brigade, supported, if necessary, by a second, toward the north of your position, to the Little River turnpike and beyond." At 5:45 he wrote again to Sumner: "The reconnaissance is only designed to ascertain whether there is any considerable movement of the enemy's infantry toward our right and rear. . . . I do not wish any engagement brought on at present on that ground, but when the information required shall have been obtained by the brigade withdraw it." [41]

None of the dispatches that Pope had sent to the General in Chief had intimated any distrust of his subordinates, although as early as the 28th Brigadier General B. S. Roberts, his inspector general—formerly his chief of cavalry—and Lieutenant Colonel T. C. H. Smith, an aide, had told Pope that Porter would fail him. [42] Even if Pope had dismissed the fact that Porter took no part in the fighting on the afternoon of the 29th, the prophecy of Roberts and Smith seemed fulfilled by Porter's retreat that night to Manassas without orders. [43] In his early dispatch to Halleck on the 30th Pope said nothing about Porter's retreat, but observed merely that he was expecting the latter to come up from Manassas. Whether or not there was proper determination in Porter's attack in the afternoon is difficult to say; in his final report Pope stated that there was not, and Strother recorded that Lee's engineer officer confirmed the view. [44] Be that as it may, it was certain that Griffin's brigade of the corps wandered away to Centerville and kept out of action, [45] although Piatt's brigade of Sturgis's corps, which had followed Griffin to Centerville, was led back to the battle when the error was discovered by its commander. Doubts began to multiply in Pope's mind, and they finally came to include Franklin, who was another of McClellan's favorites.

At 8:50 A.M. of the 1st Pope sent a long dispatch to Halleck, in which he spoke frankly of the situation:

All was quiet yesterday and so far this morning. My men are resting; they need it much. Forage for our horses is being brought up. . . . I shall attack again to-morrow if I can; the next day certainly. I think it my duty to call your attention to the unsoldierly and dangerous conduct of many brigades and some division commanders of the forces sent here from the Peninsula. . . . You should know these things, as you alone can stop it. Its source is beyond my reach, though its effects are very perceptible and very dangerous. . . . My advice to you—I give it with freedom, as I know you will not misunderstand it—is that, in view of any satisfactory results, you draw back this army to the intrenchments in front of Washington, and set to work in that secure place to reorganize and rearrange it. You may avoid great disaster by doing so. . . . When there is no heart in their leaders and every disposition to hang back, much cannot be expected from the men.[46]

Without mentioning names, he briefly described the conduct of Porter and Griffin.

Pope, however, continued to prepare for battle. At noon he ordered McDowell:

You will march rapidly back to Fairfax Court-House with your whole division [corps], assume command of the two brigades now there, and immediately occupy Germantown with your whole force, so as to cover the turnpike from this place to Alexandria. Jackson is reported advancing on Fairfax with 20,000 men. Move rapidly.[47]

The precision with which Jackson's force was given was remarkable; Jackson himself could not have given his strength with more accuracy. In a personal conference with Sumner, Pope arranged for that commander to attack the flank of the enemy the next morning with 25,000 men.[48] The situation, however, developed more rapidly, and late in the afternoon of September 1, during a heavy storm, a very sharp action was fought at Chantilly—four miles northeast of Centerville—in which Kearny and Major General I. I. Stevens, an able division commander in Reno's detachment from the Ninth Corps, were killed. Few officers have had a finer tribute than Winfield Scott paid to Philip Kearny: "the bravest man I ever knew, and a perfect soldier."

It is not recorded when Pope's dispatch of 8:50 A.M. reached Halleck, nor is there any record of the interview that McClellan had that morning with the General in Chief. But Halleck must have been loath to close the campaign, for no order was sent to Pope until September 2, after the latter in a telegram sent from Fairfax at

7:30 A.M. had repeated the recommendation of the preceding morning. Pope reported that the enemy had been repulsed the preceding evening by McDowell and Hooker, and his own will to fight was again revealed; but there was a definite note of futility in his dispatch. He stated, "The straggling is awful in the regiments from the Peninsula." One might think unjust the implication that straggling was worse in McClellan's regiments than in his own, if it were not that he urged Halleck to "come out and see the troops." [49] Heintzelman's subsequent report also supported Pope's complaint about McClellan's troops, for he stated that he had "a large amount of straggling," not only after the battles but also at Alexandria upon arrival from the Peninsula.[50]

Pope's statement in his dispatch that 57,000 men were present for duty on the morning of the 1st is proof that he was watching things carefully. If the figure, based on the reports of corps commanders, was correct, he had things well in hand, for he had had casualties amounting in all to 15,000. He expected the enemy to continue his turning operation, and he stated, "Every movement shows that he means to make trouble in Maryland." It was the first dispatch in which he spoke of a "greatly superior force." As a matter of fact Lee did not have as many men as the 57,000 that Pope acknowledged the morning before; but the morale of his army was good, and he could depend upon his subordinates.

After the receipt of Pope's dispatch from Fairfax there were only two courses open to Halleck: to go out and look at the situation, or to accept Pope's recommendation. Much could be said in favor of the first course, for Pope still had the will to fight and the mere presence of the General in Chief should have been sufficient to bolster some of the less resolute generals, and perhaps stamp out the tendency toward disaffection or insubordination. But Halleck claimed he could not leave Washington, and accepted Pope's recommendation after its second offering. The grave decision having been made, the General in Chief about noon sent to the army commander the direction, "You will bring your forces as best you can within or near the line of fortification." [51]

A written order for the retreat was issued at Fairfax, and it was an excellent document. Tactical matters were well thought out, and administrative questions received equal consideration. Banks was to evacuate stores at Fairfax Station, and take care of the movement of the consolidated trains—of which not a wagon was lost. Corps commanders were to send capable officers to Alexandria, to take over their trains when they should be released. The order closed: "The commanders of these various corps will send forward, several hours in advance, staff officers to notify General McClellan of their approach to the points which they are to occupy."

Soon a report was made to Halleck that the retreat was under way and was proceeding nicely:

The whole army is retiring in good order, without confusion or the slightest loss of property. The enemy has made no advance this morning, owing no doubt to his severe loss last evening. . . . Our whole wagon train is far in advance of us toward [Alexandria]. Our whole force is less than 60,000 men. Everything is being safely moved back to the intrenchments. When the stragglers can be assembled our force will be largely increased. I shall leave here with the last, and encamp to-night near Ball's Cross-Roads.

From his announced destination Pope reported again to the General in Chief at 7:10 P.M. in a dispatch that closed: "I await your orders. The enemy still continue to beat around to the north. I do not myself believe that any attack here is contemplated. The troops are very weary, but otherwise in good condition." [52]

Washington had been full of excitement born of a mixture of rumor and information, and something like a panic spread when it was learned that Pope's columns were marching back to the fortifications, for this was an unmistakable recognition of defeat. In June the people had been optimistic about the taking of Richmond, only to have all their hopes dashed by McClellan's retreat to Harrison's Landing, disguised though it was by the description "change of base." Now Pope's campaign had collapsed after its auspicious start at Cedar Mountain and the encouraging reports about the fighting on August 28 and 29. It was not strange that the people believed the capital itself to be in danger, for they could not read the excellent order that had been written at Fairfax; nor would they have comprehended it if they had read it. The document was as steady and as calm as if it had been written in a staff school and had been leisurely corrected so as to have something with the perfection of a model. Every sentence in it proved that in spite of many stragglers the basic organizations were all formed and in good control. The rear guard was composed of Sumner's corps—men who had not been in battle, under a general that nothing would shake. Back of everything were Buford and Bayard—dangerous even in defeat and with tired horsemen. But such things the "man in the street" did not know.

After wisely seeking volunteer doctors in Philadelphia on the 30th, Stanton ill advisedly the same day asked for volunteer surgeons and male nurses to go to Centerville to help care for the wounded. Whether or not this was contrary to the judgment and recommendations of the surgeon general does not seem to have been recorded; but Haupt protested at once to Watson, for he knew full well that the plan would only cause confusion.[53] He was working hard to bring back the wounded and using his transportation to the limit; it only disrupted his work to send trains to Washington to pick up the medical volunteers. The persons who filled the cars that he hauled to Alexandria and to Fairfax had not been properly "screened"; not all were competent or even had an honest desire to help; there were the inevitable curious and many who were drunk. When the farcical procedure was stopped the next day, Haupt had to get the hungry and wretched "nurses" out of the way and back to the city.

In addition to the important dispatches that were written on September 1 by the generals, the long entry which John Hay made in his diary also has real significance, because it gives us some of Lincoln's thoughts and views that we would not otherwise have. Hay recorded the high opinion the President had of Colonel Haupt, mentioning how much Lincoln liked the railroader's precise and satisfying messages, "which contrasted so strongly with the weak, whiney, vague, and incorrect dispatches" of McClellan. Secretary Chase had commented that Haupt had a major general's head upon his shoulders, and though Hay's words were mild when he summed up between McClellan and Haupt, they cut deep: "If heads or shoulder-straps could be exchanged, it would be a good thing, in either case, here. A good railroader would be spoiled but the General gained would compensate." [54] Halleck too would have derived much pleasure and also great reward for fatiguing hours of heavy responsibility from the unhesitating judgment that Lincoln passed after seeing him cope with his duties for six weeks. Realizing how important it is for a General in Chief to be fair and impartial, and perhaps giving a thought to proper documentation for the history that he and Nicolay had early made up their minds to write,[55] Hay had asked Lincoln if Halleck had any prejudices. A very

direct question it was; but it was met without evasion, and history is
the richer and more certain for the answer: "No! Halleck is wholly
for the service. He does not care who succeeds or who fails so the
service is benefited."

On the evening of the 30th the young secretary was with his chief
at Stanton's house for dinner. In spite of the fact that the smiles of the
handsome Madam Secretary were rare and seemed to pain her, there
was good cheer, for the three men had just come from the telegraph
office, where the latest bulletins from Bull Run were encouraging.
Lincoln and his young aid returned to the White House in good cheer
and "went to bed expecting glad tidings at sunrise." It was the older
man who was astir first the next day—another Sunday—and after
reading the message that Pope had sent at 9:45 the evening before,
he went to the room of his secretary—who made a point to record that
he was dressing—and remarked, "Well, John, we are whipped again, I
am afraid." Concern for the future soon took hold of Lincoln, for
he had seen Porter's letters to Burnside, which the latter had forwarded to Halleck on account of their strange content,[56] and he also
read the long dispatch that Pope sent the General in Chief on September 1. That afternoon Lincoln sent for McClellan and frankly told
him that he did not trust what Porter might do.[57] No accurate record
of the meeting exists, but in view of the letter which had come to him
directly from Porter in the morning, one wonders if the general pretended to be surprised when the President stated that he was alarmed
about his possible behavior. Certainly it is not to be believed that
McClellan sought to allay Lincoln's fear by drawing from his pocket
the letter which stated that Porter's men would fight "if cornered,"
and which had the intriguing ending, "The bearer will tell you much."
At the President's request McClellan sent a telegram to Porter; the
message did not tell Porter abruptly to obey orders like a soldier, but
asked him and McClellan's "other friends" to give to Pope the same
support that they had always given him. Porter's reply was the to-be-
expected assurance of cooperation and a reference to his casualties.[58]
(Porter's corps had 301 men killed, of whom 76 were in the Fifth New
York.[59] A twenty-fifth of his command had sustained a fourth of
his killed.)

When he learned of the retreat, Lincoln gave no orders about the
use of troops, but directed that all clerks and employees in public
buildings be formed into companies, and be given arms and ammuni-

tion.[60] It was a last-resort measure, not of much value, but the man on whom ultimate and final responsibility rests must think of such steps. On his part, Stanton ordered that the contents of the arsenal should be shipped to New York. On learning of this, McClellan wrote to Halleck that he believed the Secretary was being hasty, and he said very bravely, "I do not despair of saving the capital." The general did another thing which showed restraint. At 1:15 P.M. of the 2nd he ordered that the houses in Arlington should be vacated and be prepared at once for burning. But there was to be no precipitate earth scorching; the order said, "The houses will not be burned until the enemy comes near." [61]

McClellan's courage had increased a little from what it had been three days before when he had written his wife: "I do not regard Washington as safe against the rebels. If I can quietly slip over there I will send your silver off." As the years passed he became in his own mind a very great hero, and the pages he wrote in his memoirs contain in the present connection, as in others, historical distortions, if indeed they were not deliberate and vindictive falsehoods. He stated that neither Lincoln nor Halleck thought the city could be saved.[62] Both men were dead and so could not protest; and it made no difference to Little Mac that his slanders were contradicted by his own official report or by his private letters. His thoughts about the security of Washington in the last days of August did not escape Hay, who recorded in his diary September 1 that Lincoln had spoken of "McC's dreadful cowardice in the matter of the Chain Bridge." He had actually given an order for its demolition—an order countermanded, presumably, by Lincoln himself.

In addition to his reflections on the President and the General in Chief, McClellan gave a derogatory account of his meeting with Pope and McDowell outside the fortifications which one can suspect to be largely fiction—and malicious fiction at that. "He and McDowell," McClellan wrote, "both asked my permission to go on to Washington, to which I assented, remarking at the same time that *I* was going to that artillery-firing. They then took leave and started for Washington." [63] In his report, written only a year after the event, McClellan spoke of meeting Pope and McDowell, but made no aspersions. It would have been quite in character for him to say that he was going to the artillery firing, for it was at a distance; but it was quite out of character for either Pope or McDowell to go to Washington under the circumstances. Furthermore, Pope had reported to Halleck in the morning that he would go to Ball's Cross Roads in the evening; and to Ball's Cross Roads Pope went, where he reported to the General in Chief, and asked for orders. On his part, McDowell stated in his report that his "corps fell back to Hall's and Upton's hills, in front of Washington." He emphasized the fact that in spite of the marching, fasting, and fighting of his men, "they preserved their discipline." And he added that it was "an abuse of words to say they were either demoralized or disorganized." [64] A written order covering the retirement, issued at Fairfax in the morning,[65] as well as McDowell's unimpeachable character, stands behind his statements, made only two months after the event. And the general was too conscientious a soldier not to remain with his men.

On the morning of the 3rd, Pope reported to Halleck's adjutant general that everyone in the Army of Virginia blamed McClellan for having held back Franklin, Sumner, and Cox, and that the troops that had finally reached him had brought only forty rounds of ammunition per man. (In his own army Pope had a standing order requiring his men to go into action with 100 rounds.[66]) "Beg the general," Pope said, "if nothing else can be done, to command himself. It is easy to do so from Washington, as the telegraph lines are all through these works." [67]

While men were waiting with their matches ready to fire the evacuated homes in Alexandria, Pope wanted to fight again and resume the offensive. At 1:30 P.M. he sent his chief of staff to Halleck with a dispatch that read:

We ought not to lose a moment in pushing forward the fresh troops to confront the enemy. In three days we should be able to renew the offensive in the direction of Little River pike, beyond Fairfax Court-House. We must strike again with fresh men while the enemy is weakened and broken down. I am ready to advance again to the front with the fresh troops now here. Those I brought in can remain for two days. Somebody ought to have the supreme command here. Let us not sit down quietly, but push forward again. . . . The enemy is in the direction of Leesburg, with his left resting on Dranesville road, far as he can be traced by his pickets. I have just received advices from that direction. Lee himself is on the Leesburg turnpike.[68]

Pope was asking for nothing strictly personal—only that there be aggressive action, and that the confused command question be straightened out. Very important too was the wish to take immediate advantage of the enemy's exhaustion. Colonel Ruggles brought back the answer: "Reorganization of an army for the field will be immediately made. Till then General McClellan, as senior and as commanding the defenses of Washington, must exercise general authority." The preparation of a force to take the field had been directed that day in an order written by Lincoln's own hand.[69]

Pope persisted, recommending the next day that his army be reconstituted, to consist of the First Corps, under Banks, with his old command reenforced by ten of the new regiments; the Second Corps, under McDowell, to consist of his old corps and ten new regiments; the Third Corps, under Reno, to consist of his old command reenforced by the troops of Hunter and six new regiments; the Fourth Corps, under Hooker, to consist of Cox's command and the American regiments that had been with Sigel, and six new regiments. Pope wished to have Buford and Bayard, and he said that he had an abundance of artillery. The army which he proposed would give him an effective force of 40,000 to 60,000 men, who, he stated, "are anxious to serve with me."[70] It would indeed have been a force imbued with the thought of fighting. He added that the organization of the command could be perfected in a day or two at such a place as Upton's Hill.

The proposal was not accepted, and the utter confusion in command which had taken place was shown by a dispatch that Pope sent on September 5 at 12:05 P.M. to General Marcy, McClellan's chief of staff:

Your order to have my command ready to march with three days' rations received.

Please inform me what is my command and where it is. General McClellan has ordered my troops to take post at various places, and I have never been notified in a single instance of their positions. He has communicated directly with them, and I know, and can know, nothing of their whereabouts.[71]

This was a strange commentary on a general whose *forte* is supposed to have been organization and administration, and who a few days before had spoken contemptuously of "absence of brains." In a way Fate was kind, and Pope was relieved of his embarrassment by a one-sentence order which presently came to him from Halleck: "The Armies of the Potomac and Virginia being consolidated, you will report for orders to the Secretary of War." [72]

At four o'clock on this important day McClellan had time to write his wife as follows:

It makes my heart bleed to see the poor, shattered remnants of my noble Army of the Potomac, poor fellows! and to see how they love me even now. I hear them calling out to me as I ride among them, "George, don't leave us again!" "They shan't take you away from us again," etc., etc. I can hardly restrain myself when I see how fearfully they are reduced in numbers, and realize how many of them lie unburied on the field of battle, where their lives were uselessly sacrificed. It is the most terrible trial I ever experienced. Truly, God is trying me in the fire. [73]

Heaven protect a nation with a commanding general who could write like that just a few weeks after he himself had left many dead and wounded at Gaines's Mill, Frayser's Farm, and Malvern Hill, and who had abandoned 2,500 sick and wounded in his hospitals, and had reported that only half of his army was with the colors.

CHAPTER XIII

PRELUDE TO ANTIETAM

> I have all the plans of the rebels, and will catch them in their
> own trap if my men are equal to the emergency. . . . Will
> send you trophies. *McClellan to Lincoln*

It never occurred to Abraham Lincoln that God was trying George
McClellan in the fire. In fact, the President's views about recent events
were very different from those expressed in the general's note to his
wife at four o'clock on September 5. On that same day John Hay, able
and devoted secretary, wrote in his diary that he had spoken to his
chief about "the general feeling against McClellan as evinced by the
President's mail," and that Lincoln had responded: "Unquestionably
he has acted badly toward Pope! He wanted him to fail." [1] That was a
harsh judgment, but it certainly was not as unreasonable as the accusation that McClellan made in later years that Lincoln and Stanton had
wanted his Peninsular campaign to fail.[2] Lincoln's charge may have
been hasty; McClellan's assertion on the other hand was very deliberate
and rather childish. But the question of the motives behind McClellan's
acts during the last days of August need not be raised, for his Peninsular campaign is itself a character reference for him—though a
strange one. His actions at Alexandria while Pope was fighting about
Manassas harmonized with his actions the last week in June while in
front of Richmond. After he had wrecked his own campaign it was
not strange that he could wreck Pope's.

It had become necessary to choose between two generals, both of
whom had failed in a campaign. If only the actual field and command
records were to be considered, the choice would not have been difficult
to make. After his year of bitter experience and discerning observa-

tion of his generals, Lincoln had certainly learned something about generalship, and knew well the truth of General Fuller's striking sentence: "In order to understand this word we must at once strike from our minds the popular illusion that generalship can be measured by victory or defeat; for there is something more subtle than this in the drama of war, namely, the art of those who wage it." [3] In every important particular Pope had shown himself superior to McClellan. In the first place, he obeyed orders, without quibbling or seeking to evade; he obeyed in the full spirit enjoined by the first sentence of Army Regulations. When Halleck had instructed him to hold on the line of the Rappahannock, he held that line for a week, although he did not think it was the best place. After he had retired on Centerville he received the injunction, "Don't yield another inch if you can avoid it." Though by this time he had doubts about some of the commanders in the corps from the Army of the Potomac, it was his purpose to stay and fight. It was not until—after recommending what he thought was necessary in view of the disaffection in his army—he had received an *order* to retire to Alexandria that he broke off fighting. In marked contrast, McClellan's retreat to the James River from his position in front of Richmond *without orders* could well have been the subject of a court of inquiry, although uncertainty as to Lee's strength would probably have saved the operation from the condemnation it deserved.

Pope had also demonstrated that he had fortitude, which Fuller states must be a general's first quality.[4] Throughout his campaign he had been aggressive and bold—again in contrast to McClellan. If he was inclined to be too sanguine, his errors were in the right direction, because it is easier for a bold man to learn caution, than for a very timid one to become aggressive. Lee learned much from Malvern Hill, and Pope would certainly have profited from his unwise attack of August 30—which was not made precipitately or without reflection.[5] On that day he was in his first big battle, pitted against able generals who had already learned important lessons from previous errors. But unlike them, and many other Union generals, Pope was never to have the chance to show that he had learned from a mistake— a fate singularly harsh when it is recalled that his retirement upon Centerville was in itself not a serious matter, and was well conducted.

In the important matter of orders Pope rated much above McClellan. After April 2 McClellan never issued what could be called a field order for his entire army—so far as his final report shows. A good march order for his whole command to move on April 4 had initiated his Peninsular campaign; [6] but after the enemy had once fired at him McClellan never risked a general order; instead he resorted to piecemeal directions. After an order has been issued to an entire command, the commander of the army loses control; and he must have the courage of his convictions while the order is being executed. McClellan was simply too timid to issue such orders. He had an excellent opportunity to issue a written order for the retreat to the James. There was ample time, and the occasion demanded it. Although his defenders assert he issued splendid orders on the night of June 27, they do not quote convincingly from any order. The movement was apparently conducted largely on verbal orders; corps commanders did not always know what others were doing, and coordination had to be improvised; often commanders were uncertain of their own orders.

It was quite otherwise with Pope. He made the bad mistake of not sending a clear written order to Banks on the morning of August 9; but after that he did well and often excellently. He was forced to retire in haste on August 18; nevertheless there was a written order for his entire army—everyone knew what everyone else was to do. A good order for all the corps was issued on August 24; and there was even a written order for the final retirement on Alexandria. When a developing situation made it necessary to issue orders for different corps, Pope usually took pains to give their commanders full information about other parts of the army.

Both the President and the General in Chief were satisfied with what Pope had done. After having attended a cabinet meeting, Halleck wrote to Pope about his failure to issue the order of commendation he had spoken of and said: "Do not infer from this that any blame attaches to you. On the contrary, we think you did your best with the material you had. I have not heard anyone censure you in the least." [7] The failure to get Franklin's and Sumner's corps to Pope in time was obvious, visible to everyone in the capital and soon known throughout the country; and something of popular sentiment toward McClellan is revealed by John Hay's reference to Lincoln's mail. Persons of judgment also had the opportunity to read accounts of the fighting of August 30 in which the correspondents had stressed the fact that the retirement on Centerville was well conducted, with major parts of units well in hand.[8] Only the ill informed or those without military understanding then or now call Second Bull Run a debacle.[9]

But the command of the single army made by the absorption of the Army of Virginia into the Army of the Potomac went to McClellan, and Pope was virtually reduced to inactive service by being given command of the Northwest Department with headquarters at St. Paul. From that far-off place he requested that his campaign be made the subject of an official investigation, or that the President and the General in Chief make public some of the comments made to him in private, or that he be given an assignment that looked less like complete condemnation of his two months in the East.[10] However reasonable it appears, Pope's request was not granted; and the thought is almost irresistible that he was shabbily dealt with, while the country practically lost the services of a soldier who had many of the qualities of a good general. Toward McClellan he felt very bitter; and if divination is a quality of a general he had that, too, for on September 30 he wrote to Halleck: "McClellan will inevitably be set aside. I know of nothing conceivable that can prevent it before many months go by." [11] The thought probably eased the wound he felt in apparent repudiation and banishment; and in weeks instead of months Pope's prediction was to be fulfilled.

The cabinet was practically unanimously opposed to McClellan's return to command, and Stanton was the author of a vigorous letter to Lincoln on the subject, which, however, was never presented.[12] The Secretary's belief that McClellan was totally unfit for field command had been steadily growing, and fortunately a private and confidential letter to a cherished friend and former teacher preserves a long and frank statement of his views as of May 18. The letter sheds light on many things—for instance, the reason for the much criticized War Order No. 1 of Lincoln. It traces the change of Stanton's sentiments toward McClellan from the time he entered the cabinet "the sincere and devoted friend of General McClellan." In a forthright manner he faced the charges already being made against him by the McClellan followers, which had prompted an anxious letter from the disturbed clergyman, who had helped him when he "was a poor boy at school." In part Stanton wrote:

Now, one word as to political motives. What motive can I have to thwart General McClellan? I am not now, never have been, and never will be a candidate for any office. . . . If I wanted to be a politician or a candidate for any office, would I stand between the Treasury and the robbers that are howling around me? Would I provoke and stand against the whole newspaper gang in this country, of every party, who, to *sell news,* would imperil a battle? I was never taken for a fool, but there could be no greater madness than for a man to encounter what I do for anything else than motives that overleap time and look forward to eternity. I believe that God Almighty founded this Government, and for my acts in the effort to maintain it I expect to stand before Him in judgment.[13]

The War Secretary's unfavorable opinion of McClellan was strengthened by Halleck's answer to his inquiry of August 28 about McClellan's execution of orders. The General in Chief went at length into the delay in the movement of Franklin's corps and forwarded copies of all pertinent orders and letters.[14] Thus Stanton had the strongest sort of basis for opposing the reappointment of McClellan to the army command.

Though President Lincoln probably did not differ significantly, if at all, with Stanton and other members of the cabinet on past events, he had the responsibility for positive and immediate action. There was work to be done, and apparently he thought that the first point was the restoration of morale to the Army of the Potomac, and he believed that McClellan could do that one thing better than anyone else.

The situation in the army at that time makes unpleasant reading. Halleck wrote to Pope: "The differences and ill-feeling among the generals are very embarrassing to the administration, and unless checked will ruin the country. It must cease. It is discreditable to all parties. We must all act together or we shall accomplish nothing, but be utterly disgraced." [15] Palfrey, who was in the army, recorded and condemned the bickering and factionalism that were present.[16] On the affection for McClellan, Strother wrote in his diary: "This is worth something; but the enthusiasm of the American volunteer for any individual leader, either in war or politics, is an unreliable and evanescent sentiment." [17] But the fault lay not only with the volunteers; some regular officers were most pronounced in their partisanship, and it was much to their discredit as professional soldiers that they did not give the country an example of soldierly behavior. "I have only just now found out what military jealousy is," stated the unhappy President to his secretary.[18]

In late June, Lincoln had written some remarkable words about how hard it was to have a thing understood as it really was; in early September he must have deeply regretted the basis on which he felt compelled to act when he allowed Pope to go and restored McClellan. Frankly he admitted to his cabinet that little could be hoped for from McClellan in determined aggressive action, because he had the "slows" and never would be really ready.[19] Like Pope, Lincoln must have known that McClellan's reinstatement could not be for long. But for the moment he felt that he had to use him.

No time could be lost. Pope had predicted that Lee would move toward the Potomac rather than upon Washington; and on the 3rd he had reported that the Confederate army was in the direction of Leesburg, with Lee himself on the road thither. Though he had time for a chatty note to his wife in midafternoon of a crucial day, McClellan threw himself energetically into the work ahead. Lincoln described him to Hay as "working like a beaver," and added that the "snubbing" he had received the previous week had been wholesome.[20] Much had to be done in straightening out and readjusting the army; but it was not the feat claimed by some writers, who have exaggerated the way in which a word from McClellan brought order out of chaos.[21] In the first place, only three divisions of the Army of the Potomac had been heavily engaged at Bull Run—those of Hooker, Kearny, and Ricketts. The corps of Franklin and Sumner had had little more than practice marches under tactical conditions, and Brigadier General Alfred Pleasonton's cavalry, which had finally arrived at Alexandria from the Peninsula, had not been used at all. In the second place, few things are easier than to straighten out confused military organizations. After a soldier has picked up some sleep he will find his own unit if it is at all possible. No one can understand the attachment of a soldier for his "outfit" unless he has witnessed it; if a soldier cannot be at home, he wants his own company and his own regiment. At best, a bivouac is a cheerless place; but a soldier's contentment increases when he is among his comrades, men with whom he has slept, marched, hungered and thirsted, and perhaps fought—men for whom he feels an affection only less strong than for his family.

The actual reorganization that took place was not extensive. McDowell had asked to be relieved of command of his corps because of grave but sensational charges made against him, of which he was soon cleared by a court.[22] The corps was given to Hooker, and Burnside took over the command of his old troops, which had been led so well at Bull Run by Reno. Heintzelman, Sumner, Banks, and Porter con-

tinued as corps commanders. In all, there were on September 6 seven
corps, and the independent division of Major General Darius N.
Couch. Losses were made good by the distribution to the different
corps of thirty-five new regiments—Eastern troops except for three
regiments from Michigan.[23] It was a strong field army, backed up by a
considerable force—old and new troops alike—assigned to the defenses of Washington. With regard to getting things ready for the field,
one could safely say it was the quartermasters who had had the heavy
work; and Ingalls must have had many knotty problems to straighten
out. Although he was probably not the master he later became, he must
already have been good.

In all likelihood a great deal of unreliable enemy information came
in at first; but knowledge of the Confederate crossing of the Potomac
could not have been long delayed. Just when it occurred is not clear.
In his official report, a year later, Lee wrote indefinitely that "the army
was put in motion . . . and between September 4 and 7 crossed the
Potomac at the fords near Leesburg, and encamped in the vicinity of
Fredericktown." [24] What appears to have been the first accurate report
came—as one might expect—from General Wool at Baltimore. At
1:15 P.M. on the 6th he telegraphed to Halleck a report of a Baltimore
and Ohio train supervisor who had explored toward the Monocacy
River by engine and on foot. Talking with a foreman the supervisor
learned "The enemy were advancing to Frederick in large force, by
the Georgetown road, and . . . 5,000 had then passed, and still more
were following," as far as the foreman could see. Of the invaders the
supervisor said: "They are very quiet and orderly. Many barefoot and
clothes much worn out. This information is correct." [25]

By the next day Pleasonton had part at least of his cavalry out
toward the enemy, and at 7:00 A.M. he began to send an impressive
series of dispatches to army headquarters. In one at 10:15 A.M. he
did badly in saying, "All reports agree that Baltimore is their destination." He did not make it clear whether he was referring to rumors
picked up from the countryside, or to actual reports of patrols that
had observed the direction of the enemy columns. An hour later he
did better, and passed on some good information obtained from an
Englishman who had come through Leesburg, and had crossed the
Potomac with Longstreet's corps. He stated further that he had been
told that Jackson had moved on ahead of Longstreet.[26] Like the railroaders, the Englishman reported that the "rebel soldiers" were

badly cared for, many being without shoes. He was turned over to the
Provost Marshal General, who was a good person to take care of him,
and who probably interrogated him further.

At 6:40 P.M. on the 7th Pleasonton reported more facts as well as
rumors, and said positively: "The rebel train finished crossing the
river at Conrad's Ferry this morning, and passed in the direction of
Frederick. This is probably the end of all that are coming over." [27]
Both the fact and the conjecture it caused were important. About the
same time another event of importance took place, reported the next
morning by a *New York Tribune* correspondent: "At an early hour
last evening Gen. McClellan and staff, with the 2nd United States
Cavalry as bodyguard, rode through Georgetown toward the front to
take command of the army in the field." [28] Perhaps it was reflection
over the imposing cavalcade that caused a Massachusetts sonnet writer
to break out with a creation that began, "Once more we hail thee,
Chief!" and ended stirringly:

> Press on, young Chieftain, foremost in the van!
> The Hour of need has come—be thou the Man! [29]

McClellan pressed on that evening to Rockville, a village twelve
miles north by west of Washington, where he set up his headquarters
and remained for several days. The next afternoon at five o'clock
Lincoln broke into the new campaign for the first time with a brief
telegram, "How does it look now?" McClellan replied promptly and
at some length, though there was not much of importance in what he
said. At eight o'clock he sent a long telegram to Halleck, reporting the
results of reconnaissances: "Our information is still entirely too indefinite to justify definite action. I am ready to push in any direction,
and hope very soon to have the supplies and transportation so regu-
lated that we can safely move farther from Washington, and clear
Maryland of the rebels." [30] It would appear that the destruction of
Lee's army was not part of his program.

A few moments later McClellan sent a dispatch to Wool—and a
copy to Halleck—which plainly showed that he had no intention of
aggressive action at all, in spite of the bold-sounding sentence with
which he had just closed his message to Washington. The statement
to Wool, "Our information regarding the enemy's movement is very
vague and conflicting," must have brought a sigh from the vigorous
old soldier in Baltimore, who knew that uncertainty and conflicting

reports are the rule in warfare. The dispatch ended with the announcement, "I shall also push out reconnaissances in various other directions." [31] This was the proper thing to do, but McClellan should have known that unless his reconnaissances were bold enough to penetrate Stuart's cavalry screen, they would bring back some new conflicting reports. An hour later he ended his dispatch writing for the day with a message to the General in Chief that began, "After full consideration, I have determined to advance the whole force tomorrow." [32] The movement which the "young Chieftain" outlined could hardly be described as "pressing on." The procedure of the Peninsula was in fact being again put into effect—slow, cautious moves without a bold march order for the whole army. Instead of forcing Lee to change his program by himself calling the tune and marching rapidly upon him, McClellan was waiting for his adversary to reveal his plans. He well knew the condition of Lee's army—ragged, feet bare, stomachs full of green corn. Not only did new reports coming in show this, but the fact had been clearly revealed after Bull Run. On September 8 the *New York Tribune* headed a story: "A glimpse behind the rebel lines—The strength of the rebel army exaggerated—Its true condition." The dispatch, sent from Washington on the 6th, was based on the stories of Union soldiers who had been captured and released, and on the admissions of Confederate prisoners. All this information was available to McClellan, but apparently he brushed it aside, while the newspaper correspondent drew the devastatingly accurate conclusion, "This is the plain unvarnished truth; we have been whipped by an inferior force of inferior men, better handled than our own." [33] It was this same enemy force that now confronted McClellan. This he knew, but he knew also that the Confederate army had the same higher commanders who had defeated him on the Peninsula and—with aid from himself—had just worsted Pope. There was the rub. But McClellan could scarcely admit it, his natural self-esteem having probably been stimulated by such published statements as, "It is generally admitted that there is no soldier in the South whose military capacity is equal to McClellan's." [34] Perhaps the North needed to have its confidence bolstered a little; but what about the effect of such nonsense on McClellan?

Naturally enough the reports of Lee's strength that came in from Frederick were contradictory. For the first time the Federals had the advantage of a population for the most part sympathetic; but, while many persons might be eager to report about the Confederates, few knew how to estimate military forces. In addition, the Confederates were busy spreading false reports as to their numbers and their purposes. Nevertheless, Wool reported to Stanton on the night of September 8, "The person I sent out last evening brought me back word that the rebel army was generally estimated from 30,000 to 50,000." This was far more significant than the estimate of 75,000 men given Wool by a resident of Westminster, which he also forwarded. The next morning McClellan informed Halleck: "Pleasonton's report of last night that there were 100,000 rebels on this side of the river was derived from the notorious Captain White; it is not fully reliable. We shall know better to-day." This, from McClellan, could mean only one thing. At 10:00 P.M. he was in something of a panic, and his chief of staff wired Burnside, who was at Brookville, twenty miles north of Washington: "General Pleasonton telegraphs that Jackson's headquarters are to-day at New Market, and J. E. B. Stuart's at Urbanna. This indicates that enemy intends moving on Baltimore." [35] New Market is eight miles east of Frederick and Urbana seven miles south, and there was nothing in Pleasonton's report to indicate a recent movement of headquarters. McClellan's confident deduction, and the fright which succeeding sentences of the dispatch reveal, are very significant. Lee was a bold general, and took many great chances—especially with McClellan. But he was not a madman; and only a madman would have moved on Baltimore with the entire Army of the Potomac on its flank.

McClellan was the same man: the man of Yorktown, of June 27, and of the last days of August. Stanton understood him perfectly, and very properly was having no correspondence with him nor with Halleck, but was devoting his great energy and capacity to the proper affairs of the War Department. Nor was Lincoln giving directions; but from time to time the worried President repeated to McClellan the brief question, "How does it look now?" On the 12th, the dispatch bore the hour 4:00 A.M. [36]

Early on the 11th McClellan must have received reports that Lee had evacuated Frederick and had moved westward. At 1:50 P.M. Colonel Miles, commanding at Harpers Ferry, wired Halleck: "Report here that Jackson and Lee encamped at Boonsboro last night with 40,000 to 60,000 men, and that the enemy is leaving Frederick."

About the same hour McClellan wired Governor Curtin of Pennsylvania: "I ought to-day to know definitely whether the enemy are still massed near Frederick; whether they have any force east of the Monocacy; whether they have moved on Hagerstown in large force. I now think that nearly all their available force is on this side of the Potomac." At eight o'clock a reply was in from the governor:

We have advices that enemy broke up whole encampment at Frederick yesterday morning, 3 o'clock, and marched in direction of Hagerstown, with three hundred pieces artillery, large bodies of infantry and cavalry, Stonewall Jackson leading. Jackson is now at Hagerstown. Man who gives information said rebel army marching 5 a.m. to 9 p.m. yesterday out of their camps at Frederick. Men all believed they were going to Pennsylvania. We shall need a large portion of your column in this valley to save us from utter destruction.[37]

In a telegram to the President the governor gave some details: "Jackson's troops are represented to be in a very bad condition, a large portion of them without shoes or hats, and with ragged clothing. Cavalry are in better condition—well equipped and armed, except that they have no carbines." [38]

Washington correspondents were prompt in reporting the evacuation of Frederick, and they did not tend toward extravagantly large figures for the enemy force, though definite figures were not attempted. On the 11th a dispatch put the force between 10,000 and 80,000, and added that the Confederates had only 500 wagons, which were filled with green corn as subsistence for men and animals. The next day a correspondent narrowed the limits to 15,000 to 60,000 men, and added that the man who had brought the figures from Frederick was inclined to give a lower estimate than the Federal generals.[39]

At 6:00 P.M. on the 11th Halleck's headquarters received a long dispatch from McClellan evidently written before the news of the evacuation of Frederick had been received—or at least confirmed:

All the evidence that has been accumulated from various sources since we left Washington goes to prove most conclusively that almost the entire rebel army in Virginia, amounting to not less than 120,000 men, is in vicinity of Frederick City. . . . Everything seems to indicate that they intend to hazard all upon the issue of the coming battle. They are probably aware that their forces are numerically superior to ours by at least 25 per cent.[40]

After dwelling upon the critical nature of the battle which lay ahead, McClellan asked that his field army be reenforced by some of the troops which had been retained about Washington as a precautionary measure until it had become certain that the "rebel" irruption into Maryland was not a mere diversion.

One simple fact in the dispatch from Governor Curtin which had arrived at eight o'clock should have proved to McClellan the absurdity of his estimation of the enemy, for the message gave him the time length of the Confederate column—which is next best to consolidated morning reports. McClellan certainly remembered how long it had taken him to get his army of about 105,000 from the Chickahominy to the James, as well as the time required to march away from Harrison's Landing. Lee was moving under more normal march conditions without pressure upon him, and if he had cleared Frederick with all his trains in something like sixteen hours, it was certain that he did not have half the gigantic figure which McClellan had set down. Halleck himself had received precisely the same important information in a telegram Wool had dispatched at noon, the intelligence having come from a resident of Baltimore—vouched for by General Edward Shriver—who had been in Frederick on the 10th and had witnessed the evacuation.[41]

Although the General in Chief—as well as the President—must have felt heavy discouragement at McClellan's final "oriental" figures —Palfrey's description—there was no disposition to withhold troops from him. Immediately Lincoln sent back word that Porter with 21,000 men was being ordered forward, and that he hoped others could soon follow. At nine o'clock Halleck sent the more definite information that Porter was marching the next morning. Shortly before midnight McClellan acknowledged the information and stated he would also like to have the remainder of Keyes's corps as soon as possible.[42] But his dispatch contained no suggestion that recent intelligence forced him to revise his estimate of the enemy strength, and that he was glad to announce that Lee had probably had no more than 50,000 men. The next day McClellan closed a dispatch, "If the rebels are really marching into Pennsylvania, I shall soon be up with them. My apprehension is that they may make for Williamsport, and get across the river before I can catch them." [43] Here was an intimation that McClellan knew that Lee's army was after all very weak; but it would have been out of character for him to make a frank admission and deal candidly with his superiors.

Some units of the Army of the Potomac occupied Frederick on the 12th, but the army commander himself did not arrive until the following day. As he was now forty miles from Washington, he had been "pressing on" at an average of about six miles a day. Though the soldiers of his army enjoyed cheering lustily for him, they revealed the real character of their regard by marching poorly; and straggling was so general in the first short marches that on September 9 McClellan found it necessary to issue a circular upon the question. This document stated that the army "cannot be successful if its soldiers are one-half skulking to the rear"—words which leave no doubt as to the extensiveness of the evil. McClellan "entreated" his general officers to stop "the military vice of straggling," which ought to be terminated "in a single week," instead of directing his corps commanders to have the evil stopped at once. On the same day a long general order on the subject directed some procedures that should have been in effect for months, and others that were questionable and would not have been necessary if proper discipline had been exacted earlier. Grimly it was ordered: "Marauders will be at once brought to trial by division commanders, and the sentence of death will be executed, if awarded by the court, with promptness and as publicly as possible. Any officer of any regiment or corps whatever is authorized to order forward or arrest any straggler of any regiment in the army. Resistance to such exercise of authority will be at the risk of death." [44] Though McClellan was "cracking down," he was protecting the population of generally friendly Maryland with orders less stringent than Pope had issued to guard the inhabitants of hostile Virginia. Pope had ordered, "Parties caught plundering the country will be treated as common robbers and shot upon the spot, whenever and wherever found by the patrols from any army corps or any detachment sent out for that purpose," with no waiting on courts-martial.[45] McClellan's order as well as Pope's was illegal; but Pope's was more likely to be carried out than the apparently less drastic one of McClellan.[46]

The town of Frederick, so lately held by the enemy, gave the Union army and its general a hearty welcome and made the day one of rejoicing and festivity. Flags were everywhere; people lined the streets and cheered; and the young "National commander," showered with flowers and burdened with garlands, could hardly make his way through the streets.[47] If it had not been seen before, the proclamation which General Lee had issued on the 8th must have been read promptly and with much interest. It was a worthy and high-minded document by means of which the Confederate commander had hoped to win the people and bring supplies to his army and recruits to his regiments. But the attempt was a failure, though some of Lee's soldiers were fed by Southern sympathizers, had buttons sewed on their clothes, patches inserted and rips sewed up. The proclamation stated: "Our army has come among you, and is prepared to assist you with the power of its arms in regaining the rights of which you have been despoiled." [48] There was no denying the fact that the Southern regiments had splendid battle records, but the army was neither large enough nor well enough clothed and accoutered to look convincing. Lee's own great renown, and that of Jackson, Longstreet, Stuart, and some of their subordinates, were not sufficient to win the favor of a people who were unconscious of being oppressed or despoiled of many rights. The girls might call Jackson's soldiers "dirty darlings"; but not many of the men wished to join ragged and barefoot regiments. Many interesting incidents of the "Rebel occupation" must have been told—especially stories about Jackson. Soon after he had reached the north bank of the Potomac, the Valley Hero had been presented with a fine horse. Stonewall, forgetting that he was not mounted on reliable Little Sorrel, imprudently put his spurs into the animal, and the horse reared over backward and fell on its rider. His back was hurt so badly that he had to take to an ambulance—a conveyance which Lee also had been using since an injury to both wrists caused by his horse on August 31. But by Sunday the pain in Old Jack's back had sufficiently subsided for him to sleep through a sermon in the "Reformed Church" in Frederick, where the minister was so unreformed as to take advantage of the general's condition and utter a fervent prayer for Abraham Lincoln.[49]

But McClellan was to obtain information in Frederick far more valuable than the assurance that a prayer for the Union cause had been pronounced under the very nose of Stonewall Jackson; and he was to be presented with a sheet of paper worth far more than the flattering notes that may have been attached to the great bouquets of flowers which were presented to him. On ground where the division of General D. H. Hill had camped, Private B. W. Mitchell of the 27th Indiana found a package of three cigars—something which no well trained soldier would pass by. The Hoosier soon discovered that he had a find far more valuable than mere cigars, for the paper wrapped about them was a copy of Special Order No. 191, Headquarters Army of Northern Virginia.[50] This was the very important order that Lee had issued on the 9th, setting his army in motion early the next day, and governing its operation for about a week. Mitchell showed the order to a sergeant and the two men went to the colonel of the regiment, who in turn carried it to division headquarters, where the authenticating signature of Colonel R. H. Chilton, an adjutant on Lee's staff, was recognized by an officer who had served with Chilton. That the priceless paper was in McClellan's hands late in the morning is revealed beyond question by the telegram that he sent to the President at noon:

I have the whole rebel force in front of me, but am confident, and no time shall be lost. I have a difficult task to perform, but with God's blessing will accomplish it. I think Lee has made a gross mistake, and that he will be severely punished for it. The army is in motion as rapidly as possible. I hope for a great success if the plans of the rebels remain unchanged. We have possession of Catoctin. I have all the plans of the rebels, and will catch them in their own trap if my men are equal to the emergency. I now feel that I can count on them as of old. All forces of Pennsylvania should be placed to co-operate at Chambersburg. My respects to Mrs. Lincoln. Received most enthusiastically by the ladies. Will send you trophies. All well, and with God's blessing will accomplish it.[51]

Over twelve hours were to pass before McClellan's message reached Washington at 2:35 A.M. on the 14th; and it would be interesting to know just what Lincoln thought as he laid down the telegram that almost quivered with excitement. Did he suspect that his general was once more not being entirely frank with him? McClellan said he had all the plans of the enemy and would catch them in their own trap; but he did not say that he had much more than plans. Why did he not tell the President that a copy of Lee's order had fortuitously come into his possession, and that he was certain that it was perfectly genuine? Though the touch of mystery in the dispatch may well have annoyed Lincoln, we may be sure that he had no doubt that the men of the Army of the Potomac, as well as most of the subordinate commanders, would be fully "equal to the emergency," but that he did doubt whether McClellan himself would measure up to the great opportunity he vaguely described. It was one of the critical moments of the war for Lincoln, and it is interesting to conjecture whether there was anything that he could have done. He needed a real general at Frederick—that was the sum total of what he required for perhaps a decisive victory. He certainly could not have replaced McClellan by any other general, after having so recently restored him to command; and it would have been perfectly futile to send Halleck to Frederick in an effort to instill energy, promptness, and some real boldness into the commander of the army. Halleck, in fact, was giving much attention to the situation in Kentucky, for Bragg's invasion had been progressing ominously for the North, and there was intense excitement and alarm in both Louisville and Cincinnati. Buell was marching north from Nashville with a force perfectly able to handle the Bragg threat, but Lincoln had been vexed with his delays and may not have had a great deal of confidence in what he would do. But if Halleck had been really adequate, it would probably have been advisable to let affairs in Kentucky develop in accordance with instructions already issued, while the General in Chief joined McClellan's army. For there, forty miles northeast of Washington, a great and positive opportunity lay.

However much uncertainty surrounds Lincoln's thoughts and actions on the critical morning of September 14, it is safe to assume that he did not hurry to Mrs. Lincoln to present his general's regards, or send a messenger to Mrs. McClellan with the thrilling news that her husband had been well received by the ladies of Frederick. Nor did he probably give much thought to the promised trophies or directions to prepare for their reception.

Few generals in history have had a greater piece of fortune than that which had befallen George McClellan. The order which Lee had issued, and which the Federal commander had in his possession, was for an operation bolder than any that Lee had before executed. Once more the Confederate general had divided his forces, and the operation he had begun was certain to keep them divided for a number of days. And McClellan knew the whole program in detail. Well might he feel a touch of excitement at the possibility open to him; but it is hard to see why he could reasonably have been wanting more "blessings," unless that were an indirect way of expressing a doubt about himself. It is to be hoped that some capable smokers derived more good out of the three cigars than McClellan was to get out of the order in which they were wrapped.

The reason for Lee's division of his forces lay in a situation which is full of interest but cannot be explained without a turning back in time. On September 2, when events were taking a doubtful turn at Centerville and there was uncertainty as to what might happen in the Shenandoah, Halleck had directed General White, commanding at Winchester, to send his heavy guns to Harpers Ferry at once by rail, and march there with his brigades and field guns. The order seemed timely, for simultaneously White received the report—a false one— that an enemy column of 20,000 was descending upon him; and his precipitate abandonment of Winchester necessitated the destruction of many rations and stores.[52] At Harpers Ferry, White came under the command of General Wool, in whose department it was. On the 4th Wool ordered him to leave his troops with the forces of Colonel Dixon S. Miles, the local commander, go to Martinsburg, and take command of troops in that vicinity, defending the town and the railroad. The dispatch closed, "The most sleepless energy is expected"—which, coming from John Wool, meant exactly what it said. Two days later White protested his removal from his old troops, and received a somewhat equivocating answer from Halleck's chief of staff; but at Martinsburg the unhappy general remained.[53]

After Lee had crossed the Potomac the question of what to do with the Harpers Ferry force, so often bothersome, was up again. On September 10 or 11 McClellan asked to have the troops under Miles, which he understood to be about 9,000 men, ordered to join him. Halleck declined, saying the movement was impracticable and added "His only chance is to defend his works till you can open communication with him." [54] Certainly the only way in which Miles could have been safely withdrawn would have been by a circuitous route toward the west, crossing the river at Williamsport. In his long dispatch of the evening of the 11th, McClellan again urged that Miles be ordered to join him; only now he put the force in question at 25,000—which was double its actual strength. But Halleck firmly kept Miles where he was. (Persons forgetful of the important railroad bridge over the Potomac at Harpers Ferry have criticized this action severely as a violation of the principle of the concentration of force.) Furthermore, the presence of Miles at Harpers Ferry and of White at Martinsburg caused Lee to divide his already small army and give McClellan the remarkable opportunity utterly to destroy a good portion of his command.

When it became evident that the people about Frederick were un-friendly and were unwilling "to open their stores," Lee decided to move westward to a location where he would be protected by the mountains. He chose Boonsboro and Hagerstown as suitable places of observation, hoping that events would make it possible for him to move into Pennsylvania and threaten Harrisburg.[55] But he did not want to leave Federal garrisons upon his line of communications through the Shenandoah Valley. Consequently he decided to send about half his force straight toward Hagerstown and the other part on an expedition to capture the Union troops in Martinsburg and Harpers Ferry, this half to move to Hagerstown after its mission had been performed.

The plan looked well enough on paper, but it was boldness itself. Harpers Ferry might fall less quickly than Lee calculated, spoiling his plans and leaving his divided forces dangerously exposed. One recalls the value to the French in 1914 of Maubeuge, which like Liége and Namur, did not fall as quickly as the Germans had expected. The invaders were thereby deprived of a railroad which was important for their supply, and the corps they had left to capture the fortress was absent from the battle of the Marne. Thus Maubeuge played an impor-tant part in the great victory that France won in September, 1914. Surely Halleck's refusal to move Miles out of Harpers Ferry was right, even if it was without the least thought that it would lead to one of the great opportunities in military history; and neither this fact nor the fact that the opportunity was bungled detracts from the credit due to the General in Chief.

Lee's army amounted to about 50,000 men [56]—less than half the colossal figure that McClellan had stated so confidently on Septem-ber 11. After the recent battle near Bull Run, he had received from Richmond the divisions of D. H. Hill, Lafayette McLaws, and John G. Walker. Totaling about 9,000 men, they did much toward making good the casualties suffered in late August. But the army was not in good condition in many ways; many men were sick from the green corn on which they had been subsisting, and others without shoes were footsore. In addition, some of the soldiers were reluctant to invade the North: they would fight hard to defend the South but wished no part in an offensive war. They were willing to let the Yankees alone in exchange for the corresponding favor: with the Union army out of Virginia, they would have been prepared to let well enough alone. All these causes combined to produce excessive straggling as Lee marched toward the Potomac. Because stragglers would be liable to capture and would not look well once he was across the river, he had them gathered together at the Potomac and marched toward Winchester, with the idea that they would rejoin his army later; and this body of men got into Federal intelligence reports from time to time in ways that were hard to identify and interpret. Thus it happened that there were only about 50,000 "Rebels" about Frederick, and not 120,000; but they were very good "Rebels" indeed. "None but heroes are left," one Southerner wrote.[57]

In accordance with the famous "lost and found" order,[58] Jackson led the advance out of Frederick on the Hagerstown road, leaving his bivouacs—as one would expect—at an early hour. Under him were his three old and well tried divisions, now badly depleted by marching and fighting, and with new commanders: John R. Jones had the old "Stonewall Division," A. R. Lawton had that of Ewell, and L. O'B. Branch had the "Light Division" of A. P. Hill. Hill was a casualty, not to a Union bullet or shell, but to Jackson's stern idea of discipline, having again aroused displeasure on the march to the Potomac from Chantilly.[59] With nothing to worry about, he was marching at the rear of the column, pondering probably the fortunes of war and the peculiarities of his hard-fighting superior, perhaps thinking as well of the Maryland fried chicken and biscuits which he might have been able to get during his sojourn near Frederick if he had not been in arrest. So, with Hill still in arrest, Jackson set out to execute Lee's instructions to proceed from Middletown to Sharpsburg, cross the Potomac at a suitable place, capture the Union forces at Martinsburg, and intercept those that might attempt to escape from Harpers Ferry.

McLaws with his own division and that of R. H. Anderson was to turn south from Middletown toward Harpers Ferry "and by Friday morning [the 12th] possess himself of the Maryland Heights and endeavor to capture the enemy at Harper's Ferry and vicinity." Walker's division was to cross the Potomac below the old ferry town, seize Loudoun Heights, help cut off the Union forces, and assist Jackson and McLaws in their capture. Longstreet was to march straight to Boonsboro, where he would halt with the supply and baggage trains of the army. D. H. Hill—brother-in-law of Jackson—was to follow Longstreet and the trains, as rear guard. Stuart, after giving Jackson, Longstreet, and McLaws appropriate mounted detachments, would "cover the route of the army, bringing up all stragglers that may have been left behind." In conclusion—this was a particularly important paragraph—"The commands of Generals Jackson, McLaws, and Walker, after accomplishing the objects for which they have been detached, will join the main body of the army at Boonsborough and Hagerstown."

Such were the provisions of the famous order which McClellan read near noon of the 13th; and well might he have gasped at what Lee had ordered. Jackson had a long march to make, and the operation at Harpers Ferry was complicated and required good coordination, rendered especially difficult by the rugged terrain. McLaws on Maryland Heights was in a badly exposed position, inviting destruction or capture. Lee with Longstreet and D. H. Hill and the cumbersome trains of the entire army was isolated at Boonsboro, with a river between himself and a large part of the army. Reports which were already in McClellan's hands indicated that the order was *bona fide,* and not an artful deception. It was evidently in process of execution; but as the pressure on Harpers Ferry was just beginning, a number of days would be required before Lee's army could be brought together. Therein lay the great chance.

Carelessness on the part of D. H. Hill and inadequate procedure at Lee's headquarters had been responsible for the loss of the important Confederate order.[60] But the Federal commander made a compensating blunder by allowing strangers to be near his headquarters, or at least close to him when important matters were being considered. A man with Southern sympathy saw McClellan read the lost order and heard him exclaim jubilantly, "Now I know what to do." [61] By evening the Marylander had found and told Jeb Stuart, and soon a horseman was riding westward through the night, with the result that Lee, who had gone on to Hagerstown with Longstreet's troops, learned at ten o'clock that McClellan knew his program. He did not think it necessary to change his plans in any essential way, but the information he had received was to explain to him why McClellan moved the next day with a little more energy and hurry than was his custom.

On the 8th McClellan had closed a dispatch to Halleck, "As soon as I find out where to strike, I will be after them without an hour's delay." [62] But it was not until evening of the 13th that he issued an important order, and none of his troops were directed to march until daylight. General Ballard comments: "Sixteen hours delay! Jackson would have got his men on the move within one hour." [63]

Though the delay in issuing orders gave ample time for a good order for the entire command, none was written; individual instructions to different corps were again to be employed. At 6:20 P.M. a long message went to Franklin, whose corps was bivouacked at Buckeystown. After explaining the dispositions and plans of the enemy, McClellan directed Franklin to move at daybreak on Rohrersville— a move which would take him over South Mountain by Crampton's Gap. Franklin was told, "Having gained the pass, your duty will be first to cut off, destroy, or capture McLaws' command and relieve Colonel Miles." As a military order the message was too verbose, and it concluded: "My general idea is to cut the enemy in two and beat him in detail. I believe I have sufficiently explained my intentions. I ask of you, at this important moment, all your intellect and the utmost activity that a general can exercise." [64] To beat Lee in detail was an excellent thought and ambition; but it was not necessary for McClellan to cut him in two for the purpose; Lee had already obligingly cut himself not into two pieces, but into four.

If activity was wanted, why was Franklin not started at once? Palfrey was positive in his judgment: "The weather on the 13th was extremely fine, and the roads in good condition. There was no reason why Franklin's corps should not have moved that night, instead of at daybreak the next morning." [65]

During the evening orders were also issued for movements beginning at daylight of the 14th to concentrate most of the rest of the army at Middletown, where Burnside's corps—now under Reno—less one of its three divisions, was already camped.* But no orders were issued for movement toward Turner's Gap in the South Mountain, on the road to Boonsboro and Hagerstown. It was through this pass that McClellan would have to force his way in order to strike the enemy main body—if what remained of Lee's army after the large detachments deserved that impressive name. Evidently McClellan wished for daylight before he attempted the operation; but concentration nearer the place of expected battle could well have taken place during the night, so that the work of forcing the pass could begin early. It

* Burnside was in command of the "right wing" of the army, consisting of his own and Hooker's corps.

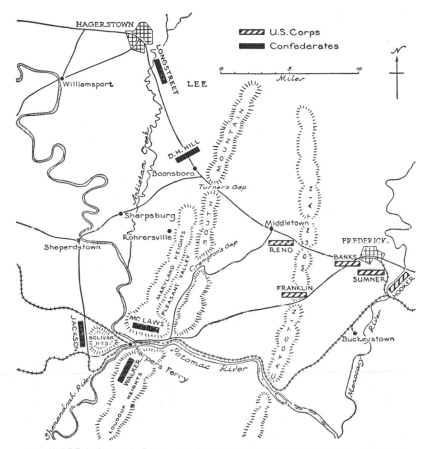

McCLELLAN AND LEE AT EVENING OF SEPTEMBER 13, 1862

was just one of those little matters which test a commander and reveal whether he is a good or an indifferent general.

At 11:00 P.M. McClellan wrote a long dispatch to Halleck (received the next day at 1:00 P.M.), in which he left out the touch of mystery which was in the one sent to Lincoln at noon, but inserted a distortion in its place. The message began:

An order from General R. E. Lee, addressed to General D. H. Hill, which has accidentally come into my hands this evening—the authenticity of which is unquestionable—discloses some of the plans of the enemy [he had told Lincoln "all the plans of the rebels"] and shows most conclusively that the main rebel army is now before us, including Longstreet's, Jackson's, the two Hills', McLaws', Walker's, R. H. Anderson's, and Hood's commands.

It is surprising that McClellan did not realize that the hour on his message to the President would reveal his effort to deceive the General in Chief as to when he had come into possession of the enemy order. After describing the Confederate operation against Harpers Ferry he said: "It may, therefore, in my judgment, be regarded as certain that this rebel army, which I have good reasons for believing amounts to 120,000 men or more, and know to be commanded by Lee in person, intended to attempt penetrating Pennsylvania. The officers told their friends here that they were going to Harrisburg and Philadelphia." After referring to a dispatch that Halleck had sent at 10:00 P.M., McClellan concluded, "I feel confident that there is now no rebel force immediately threatening Washington or Baltimore, and they outnumber me when united." [66]

It was indeed true that Confederate officers had stated that they were bound for Philadelphia, and Lee himself revealed that such stories had been deliberately planted. Jackson too was up to his old tricks; in leaving Frederick he had officers inquire ostentatiously for a map of Chambersburg,[67] just as if he would soon be in the Keystone state; but this stratagem apparently was not reported to McClellan. Midnight had brought a notable deterioration in the tone of the Union commander's telegram. At midday he had been aware of his great opportunity and had spoken of making Lee pay heavily for his mistake; twelve hours later he was magnifying the hazards that confronted him. He reminded Halleck that he faced Lee in person; he again accepted a fantastic figure for the Confederate strength, and spoke of a united enemy though he knew how badly divided Lee's army was.

It is inconceivable that accurate estimates of Lee's strength were not given to McClellan at Frederick. The telegram of Colonel Miles on the 11th spoke of only 40,000 to 60,000 men; and although it did not state definitely that the estimate was for Lee's entire army, the figures it gave are suggestive of what McClellan could have learned from other sources. Fairly precise information concerning the time lengths of Confederate columns, the time intervals between brigades and divisions, how well they were closed, etc., could without question have been obtained. A brief survey by experienced officers of the camping areas of some of the major units of Lee's army would have also given valuable data. One must believe that McClellan had staff officers sufficiently energetic and competent to do these things, and some of them must have found it boring to have flowers thrown at them and have been ready for serious business after getting a good meal and looking over historic Frederick. Palfrey, in fact, wrote that officers in the Second Corps did not share the views of the army commander about the Confederate strength, and cited as proof the statement "We outnumber the enemy," from a letter that he wrote at Frederick on the 13th. That good officer went even further and deliberately challenged McClellan's honesty by asserting: ". . . but it must be said without reservation that it is impossible to believe that McClellan believed that on the Peninsula or in Maryland the Confederates had the forces he attributed to them." [68] Whether McClellan knew that Lee's force was very small and was consciously dissembling may be open to question. But there can be no question as to how a competent commander would have estimated the opposing force; nor is there any question that McClellan knew that Lee's army would be divided for several days, whatever he believed its total strength to be.

Colonel Strother noted in his diary the important fact that General Marcy talked with him about the position at Harpers Ferry and whether Miles could hold out.[69] That place was very clearly the key to the entire situation, and if it did not fall to Lee's forces quickly, his plans would be ruined. Strother, a native of the locality, described in detail to the chief of staff the peculiar topography of the region. He expressed the belief that Miles could defend Maryland Heights against any force that could be brought against it—though a problem of food and water was involved; and the heights completely dominated the town. General Marcy replied that all would be well if Miles could hold out for only forty-eight hours; but he feared a premature surrender. According to McClellan's own report, no message or instruction was sent to Miles on September 13. McLaws already had possession of the all-important Maryland Heights by afternoon of that day, so that the oversight made no great difference. Still it was a bad omission, for it was more important for McClellan to attempt to get word to Miles than to report to the President about the graciousness of the Frederick ladies or to send his respects to Mrs. Lincoln.

It remains only to note how McClellan treated September 13 in his memoirs. He wrote, "On the 13th an order fell into my hands issued by Gen. Lee, which fully disclosed his plans, and I immediately gave orders for a rapid and vigorous forward movement." [70] Although he did not state the hour at which the order was found, it is notable that he did not say it was found in the evening. As he published the order in full in his book, it would have been futile to deny there the extensiveness of the information that had come to him. But did McClellan in his later years actually believe that he "immediately gave orders for a rapid and vigorous forward movement"? The facts in the case were well known at the time; but the claim he made has probably imposed upon those who have depended upon his statements as a trustworthy account of his campaigns and his troubles with the administration.

On the 14th [71] at about 9:00 A.M., just after McClellan had finished his Sunday breakfast,[72] an officer from Miles's command reported with the information that Maryland Heights had been evacuated the afternoon before, and gave the additional information that the Harpers Ferry garrison had subsistence for only forty-eight hours. If he could not be relieved within that time, Miles would be compelled to surrender. After he had refreshed the courier with a good meal, McClellan sent him back with a written message for General Franklin, according to a sworn statement of the officer, but with a verbal message to Miles—if he could get through—according to McClellan's report.[73] In the afternoon a message was written for Colonel Miles, asking him to reoccupy Maryland Heights with his entire force if that were possible. Three riders bore copies of the dispatch by different routes, but the fate of none of the messengers seems to be recorded.[74]

Franklin evidently had his breakfast earlier than McClellan, even though it was Sunday, and perhaps about noon his advance was stopped near the base of South Mountain by an enemy force which was deployed behind a stone wall. In his later formal report Franklin did not mention the hour, or approximate hour, at which anything took place; but it was accepted by the army commander.[75] Slocum's division was deployed; and *perhaps* about 3:00 P.M. it made a good vigorous assault, which must have been well handled in spite of difficult terrain, for without a serious setback the charging ranks went all the way to the crest and secured possession of Crampton's Gap.[76] The position was held by inadequate forces under Brigadier General Howell Cobb, who had been sent back by McLaws to protect his rear.[77] The night before and part of the morning the important gap had been completely unprotected; and if Franklin had been ordered only to the foot of the mountain on the evening of the 13th he could have marched through without any opposition and placed his strong corps squarely in the rear of McLaws. Instead he moved with great caution after having handsomely carried the pass, and as night settled McLaws sent back troops and established a defensive line across Pleasant Valley. This was the region between South Mountain on the east and Elk Horn Ridge on the west, the ridge being merely the northward continuation of Maryland Heights. On the Federal inclination to "call it a day" Freeman writes: "Thanks to their willingness to let night overtake them ere they overtook the Confederates, McLaws's hastily drawn line was not assailed." [78]

Turner's Gap, on the famous old "National Road" five miles north of Crampton's, presented a much harder problem than Franklin had to meet. Under Lee's order, both Longstreet and D. H. Hill were supposed to be at Boonsboro, just a few miles beyond the gap. But in reality, Longstreet, with Lee accompanying him, had moved on thirteen miles to Hagerstown, because a Federal force was reported to be approaching the town, and because it was believed that supplies would be found there. Lee had given the important task of protecting the rear of his army to D. H. Hill, and a noticeable point in his order was the absence of any instructions whatever. Had Jackson received the assignment, instructions might not have been needed; but Hill, though a hard fighting officer, was a very different commander from his brother-in-law. Lee had been much displeased a month before by the fact that Hill—in command at Richmond—had allowed McClellan to march away from Harrison's Landing without being impeded or annoyed in any way, and it is strange that he gave him only uncertain verbal orders. In fact, if McClellan had shown proper enterprise on the night of the 13th he could have taken the important gap without much of a price. But his negligence did much to offset the shortcomings of D. H. Hill.

About the battle at South Mountain there is much uncertainty, largely because of the difficult terrain and the inconspicuous roads and trails, small clearings, little valleys, and other features that test troop leading. As his spearhead McClellan did not use one of the corps of the old army of which he was so proud; instead he used Burnside's corps, now under Reno, who had been initiated into offensive fighting by John Pope—the general now in unhappy banishment at St. Paul. Reno took for his leading division the Kanawha Division Cox had brought from West Virginia, where the Buckeye regiments had learned something about bad roads and rugged, wooded mountains. Cox in his turn threw a heavy load on the brigade of Colonel Scammon—the man who might have done something at Bull Run bridge if he had been in command on that eventful August 27. Scammon gave the really crucial task to a man who was to become President of the United States. No other than Rutherford B. Hayes, at the head of the Twenty-third Ohio, appears to have been the first to make a lodgment atop the coveted mountain.[79] The regiment was to have more killed than any other regiment in the battle,[80] but it hung tenaciously to the position. Working on the problem of getting food up to the fighting men was Sergeant William McKinley. Hayes himself did some fine troop leading and was where the fire was hot. Scammon wrote in his report: "The regiment moved up promptly and effectively. Early in the encounter, Lieutenant Colonel Hayes, commanding the regiment, who had gallantly and skillfully brought his men into action and charged the enemy in his front, was severely wounded and carried to the rear. He remained on the field a considerable time after receiving the wound, and left it only when compelled to retire."

The corps of Reno by itself was not sufficient for the task of forcing the gap. Longstreet's command had been marched back over the thirteen dusty, thirsty miles from Hagerstown, and, tired though the men were, they were put in to help Hill.[81] In addition to Reno's Ninth Corps, the First Corps of Joe Hooker—who also had had his experience in offensive fighting under banished John Pope—was heavily used. Night had come before the two corps of Burnside's "right wing" had firm hold on the mountain top; but they had it. The way was open to the west—twelve hours later than it well might have been.

One of McClellan's defenders has written, "McClellan never was a 'killer,' and his men knew it and loved him for it." Perhaps. But General Michie, a soldier and distinguished scholar in the very practical and exacting subject of mechanics, and who understood warfare, wrote: "The Union losses on the 14th were eighteen hundred and thirteen at Turner's and five hundred and thirty-three at Crampton's Gap, the greater portion of which may justly be regarded as the penalty exacted by the procrastination of the commanding general of the Union army." Among the trees and in the clearings on the forbidding slopes of the mountain there were 324 dead in the Union blue. Among them was one with two-starred shoulder straps: brave, aggressive, hard-fighting Reno. Strother told some touching stories of the Confederate dead that he saw the next day, in their dirty, ragged clothing.[82]

Naturally McClellan was much pleased when he learned the next morning that the Confederates had withdrawn from Turner's Gap and had disappeared toward the west. The battle had not been an easy one—an attack up a mountain never is. But numbers had been much on McClellan's side, though almost a year later he wrote in his report that the enemy had held the mountain with 30,000 men—a claim which Palfrey states "is one of those extraordinary, inconceivable, aggravating things that stirs everything that is acrid in the nature of those who follow his career." [83]

The messages which McClellan sent to Washington on the 15th showed his tendency to accept optimistic accounts of the magnitude of the defeat he had administered to the enemy. In his dispatch to Halleck at 8:00 A.M. he quoted Hooker as saying that there was "perfectly reliable" information not only that the enemy was "making for Shepherdstown in a perfect panic," but that Lee had stated publicly "that he must admit they had been shockingly whipped." A telegram two hours later contained the sentence, "It is stated that Lee gives his loss as 15,000."

In his hour of success the thoughts of the victorious commander turned to Winfield Scott; and he wired to the retired general at West Point an account of the signal victory and the valiant behavior of old and new regiments alike, ending: "R. E. Lee in command. The rebels routed, and retreating in disorder this morning. We are pursuing closely and taking many prisoners." [84] Scott, still with a fondness for gold-braided language, replied: "Bravo, my dear general! Twice more and it's done." [85] Lincoln telegraphed: "Your dispatch of to-day received. God bless you and all with you. Destroy the rebel army if possible." [86] Like Scott, the President thought of what remained to be done, and he did not even inquire about the promised trophies.

NOTES

NOTES TO CHAPTER I

1. *War of the Rebellion, Official Records of the Union and Confederate Armies*, Series I, Vol. XXXVI, Pt. II (Serial No. 68), p. 332. Abbreviated as *O.R., 68*, 332. For further explanation see Bibliography.

2. *Ibid.*, p. 377.

3. *Ibid.*

4. *Ibid.*, p. 390. "Chapman'" is here corrected to "Chapman's."

5. Schaff, *Wilderness*, p. 55.

6. *O.R., 68*, 390–391.

7. *Ibid.*, p. 390 n.

8. *Ibid.*, p. 390.

9. Dana, *Recollections*, p. 73.

10. *O.R., 68*, 374.

11. *Ibid.*, p. 375.

12. *Ibid.*

13. *Ibid.*, p. 378.

14. *Ibid., 67*, 276–279.

15. *Ibid.*, p. 277. The number of mules given by Ingalls was decreased by 20 to give his probably correct total.

16. *Ibid., 68*, 354–355.

17. Porter, *Grant*, pp. 43–44.

18. *O.R., 68*, 370.

19. *Ibid.*, p. 372.

20. *Ibid.*

21. *Ibid.*, p. 380.

22. *Ibid.*

23. *Ibid.*

24. *Ibid.*, p. 372.

25. *Ibid.*, p. 371.

26. *Ibid.*, p. 948.

27. Porter, *op. cit.*, p. 47.

NOTES TO CHAPTER II

1. *O.R.*, *1*, 2.
2. *Ibid.*, p. 3.
3. *Ibid.*
4. *Ibid.*, p. 90.
5. Hendrick, *Lincoln's War Cabinet*, pp. 251–252.
6. *O.R.*, *1*, 115–118.
7. *Ibid.*, p. 118.
8. *Ibid.*, pp. 120–125.
9. *Ibid.*, p. 119 n.
10. Greeley, *American Conflict*, I, 411.
11. *O.R.*, *1*, 137.
12. *Ibid.*, pp. 125–128.
13. *Ibid.*, p. 105.
14. *Ibid.*, p. 112.
15. *Ibid.*, p. 114.
16. *Ibid.*, p. 119.
17. *Ibid.*
18. *Ibid.*, p. 114.
19. *Ibid.*, p. 128.
20. *Ibid.*, pp. 130–131. The letter quotes the telegram. There is no way to tell whether the latter was in code; but even if coded it would not necessarily have been safe, for there were clerks who were in the conspiracy, as well as Adj. Gen. Samuel Cooper. There must have been a peculiar arrangement as to keys for offices, for Thomas said: "After leaving you, I obtained the key of the outer door of the office, but could nowhere find the key of your door or of mine, so failed to get the chart." He added, however, that the captain of the steamer knew the entrance to Charleston harbor. At a later date, in a telegram to his headquarters in New York, Gen. Scott said, "Afraid of the wires" (*ibid.*, p. 177).
21. *Ibid.*, p. 132.
22. *Ibid.*, p. 133.
23. Report of Charles R. Woods, 1st Lieut., 9th Infantry, commanding the relief expedition, *ibid.*, pp. 9–10. Woods said nothing about expected fire from Sumter, but merely: "The American flag was flying at Fort Sumter, but we saw no flag at Fort Moultrie, and there were no guns fired from either of these fortifications." A reporter for the *New York Evening Post*, quoted later in the text, is authority for the statement that fire from Sumter was expected.
24. The scene at Fort Sumter is described at some length by Crawford, *Fort Sumter*, pp. 185–186.
25. *O.R.*, *1*, 134. Whether or not the *Star of the West* was fired upon by Moultrie would seem to be a simple question of fact, but the record is very contradictory. Lieut. Woods's official statement that it was not, is corroborated

by the very dramatic story of the reporter on board, who said the vessel turned away from the harbor before it came within range of the heavy guns of Moultrie. Anderson referred to batteries, but did not give their location. In a letter of Jan. 9, Foster wrote, "The firing upon the *Star of the West* this morning by the batteries on Morris Island opened the war" (*ibid.*, p. 136). James Chester in his article "Inside Sumter in '61" (*B. and L.*, I, 50–73), and Abner Doubleday in "From Moultrie to Sumter" (*ibid.*, pp. 40–49), stated the ship was fired on by guns at Moultrie; but their versions do not agree, and they differ from Crawford, who writes of very inaccurate firing at a long range (*op. cit.*, p. 184). Crawford gives the report of Col. R. S. Ripley commanding Moultrie as authority. The only report by Ripley in *O.R.*, Serial 1, is that with regard to the bombardment of Fort Sumter (*ibid.*, pp. 39–41). The firing must have been at very long range and very inaccurate if Lieut. Woods and other observers were not aware of it.

26. *O.R.*, *1*, 135–136.

27. *Ibid.*, p. 253. Greeley described Wigfall as "a Carolinian by birth, a Nullifier by training, and a duelist by vocation" (*The American Conflict*, I, 448).

28. *Harper's Weekly*, V, 52, 54 (Jan. 26, 1861)—the words quoted from the *New York Evening Post*.

29. *Ibid.*, p. 55.

30. Clippings forwarded by Anderson to the War Department, *O.R.*, *1*, 155.

31. *Ibid.*, p. 140.

32. Adams, *Education of Henry Adams*, p. 172.

33. *O.R.*, *1*, 166–168.

34. *Ibid.*, p. 143.

35. *Ibid.*, p. 139.

36. *Ibid.*, p. 138.

37. *Ibid.*, p. 212.

38. On Mar. 23, Anderson reported some "pretty good" practice firing by the Confederates, and added: "I have no ammunition to spare, and therefore do not show them our proficiency in artillery practice" (*ibid*).

39. *Ibid.*, pp. 181–182.

40. *Ibid.*, p. 254.

41. *Ibid.*, pp. 254–257.

42. *Ibid.*, pp. 258–259.

43. *Ibid.*

44. *Ibid.*, p. 261.

45. *Ibid.*

46. *Ibid.*, pp. 263–264.

47. *Ibid.*, p. 197.

48. *Ibid.*, p. 200.

49. *Ibid.*, p. 273. (For a discussion of the manner and extent to which Secretary of State William H. Seward contributed to the belief that Sumter would be abandoned, see Hendrick, *op. cit.*, pp. 166–168.)

50. *O.R.*, *1*, 274.

51. *Ibid.*, p. 275.

52. *Ibid.*, p. 277.

53. The much debated author of the baffling fragment *The Diary of a Public Man* wrote Mar. 11, "Mr. Lincoln has assured Mr. Douglas positively, he tells me, that he means the fort shall be evacuated as soon as possible, and that all his Cabinet whom he consulted are of the same mind excepting Mr. Blair, which is precisely what I expected" (p. 92). What Lincoln may have said to Stephen A. Douglas, what Douglas understood him to have said, and what he later reported him as saying, may of course have been quite different things. (See, Anderson, *"Public Man"*—published after above was written—, p. 174.) Consult Hendrick for a seemingly positive statement by Lincoln on the abandonment of Sumter reported by Francis P. Blair, Sr., to Samuel W. Crawford. As Crawford wrote twenty-five years after the incident, his story has not been unquestioningly accepted by historians. Hendrick's own analysis is judicious, and he concludes that, although Lincoln may have had periods of doubt, not even the words addressed to Blair—if accurately reported—"represented a mature presidential program" (*op. cit.*, pp. 164, 165).

54. *O.R.*, *1*, p. 208.

55. *Ibid.*, pp. 200–201. Scott stated, "An abandonment of the fort in a few weeks, sooner or later, would appear, therefore, to be a sure necessity, and if so, the sooner the more graceful on the part of the Government." He suggested the abandonment of Fort Pickens in Pensacola harbor in addition to Fort Sumter as a means of winning support in the eight slaveholding states that had not seceded. Nicolay and Hay quote Scott's memorandum at some length and imply that it was written by Scott and received by Lincoln on Mar. 28, and state that, greatly disturbed over it, he laid it before the cabinet after a formal dinner that night (*Lincoln*, III, 394–395). The editors of the *Official Records* stated that memoranda, of which Scott's was one, were "probably submitted to the Cabinet March 15, 1861" (*O.R.*, *1*, 196 n.).

The question is perplexing. On Mar. 15 Lincoln sent to all his cabinet members the following inquiry: "Assuming it to be possible to now provision Fort Sumter, under all circumstances is it wise to attempt it?" (Nicolay and Hay, *op. cit.*, p. 385). Cameron's rather long reply was not dated, but bore the signed endorsement, "There was a signed copy of the within placed in the hands of President Lincoln," dated Mar. 17 (*O.R.*, *1*, 198). Filed with Lincoln's question and Cameron's answer were eight enclosures, "A to H," among which were "General Scott's memoranda for the Secretary of War." At the head of the memoranda appears the statement, "Memoranda read before the President and Cabinet, General Scott and Commodore Stringham, and Mr. Fox, late of the Navy, Washington, March 15, 1861, by Bvt. Brig. Gen. Joseph G. Totten, Chief of Engineers" (*ibid.*).

Nicolay and Hay state that Cameron's reply was dated Mar. 16, as well as those of Smith and Bates (*op. cit.*, pp. 387–388). Thus the statement that Scott's memorandum was read to the cabinet on Mar. 15 may be open to question. Unfortunately Nicolay and Hay ignore the assertion in the records as well as the note of the editors. There would seem to be no doubt that the memorandum was written well before Mar. 28, and came as a result of the formal request that Lincoln made on Mar. 15. It is also to be observed that Lincoln asked a question as to *policy*, and this may have been the reason why

Scott went beyond the mere practicality of provisioning Sumter. Nicolay and Hay say that Montgomery Blair "charged Scott was transcending his professional duties and 'playing politics'" (*op. cit.*, p. 395).

56. Sandburg, *Lincoln,* I, 190.

57. *O.R.*, *1*, 211.

58. *Ibid.*, p. 294.

59. The cause of the misunderstanding was explained in Anderson's letter of Apr. 1: "I told Mr. Fox that if I placed the command on short allowance I could make the provisions last until after the 10th of this month; but as I have received no instructions from the Department that it was desirable I should do so, it has not been done" (*ibid.*, p. 23). As soon as he learned of the intended relief expedition, Anderson put the garrison on half-rations.

60. Lincoln Papers, XXXVIII, 8388–8403. Nicolay and Hay (*op. cit.*, III, 391–392) give about half a page to a quotation from Hurlbut.

61. Nicolay and Hay, *op. cit.*, p. 391.

62. Lamon, *Recollections of Lincoln,* p. 74.

63. *O.R.*, *1*, 222.

64. *Ibid.*, p. 241.

65. Nicolay and Hay, *op. cit.*, p. 395.

66. Hendrick, *Lincoln's War Cabinet,* pp. 24, 130–132.

67. Lincoln Papers, XXXVIII, 8470–8472.

68. *Ibid.*, p. 8476.

69. *Ibid.*, p. 8457.

70. *Ibid.*, pp. 8458–8459.

71. *Ibid.*, p. 8483. The replies of the cabinet members carry in Lincoln's writing the notation, "In Cabinet." They are given in full in Nicolay and Hay, *op. cit.*, 430–432.

72. Hendrick (*op. cit.*, p. 224) says that Cameron in accordance with his political nature "refrained from attending the session and made no response to Lincoln's request for his written opinion—in itself an act of insubordination." There may have been a valid reason for Cameron's absence; and, because Lincoln had not intended to ask written opinions (Nicolay and Hay, *op. cit.*, p. 429), it seems more than likely that no subsequent request was made on him. Cameron had not hesitated to express his view two weeks before.

73. *O.R.*, *1*, 196–198.

74. *Loc. cit.*

75. *O.R.*, *1*, 226.

76. The first note in the records from Lincoln was that of Mar. 15 to the Secretary of War, asking for his opinion as to whether it was possible to provision Sumter (*ibid.*, p. 196). The signature was added by the editors.

77. Nicolay and Hay, *op. cit.*, IV, 27.

78. *O.R.*, *1*, 235.

79. *Ibid.*, p. 294.

80. *Ibid.*, pp. 235–236.

81. *Ibid.*

82. *Ibid.*, p. 291.

83. *Ibid.* As a matter of fact, to guard against accidents, duplicate instructions had been given to Talbot (*ibid.*, p. 245). A facsimile of the remarkable document is in Crawford, *op. cit.*, p. 396.

84. *O.R., 1*, 252.

85. *Ibid.*, p. 289.

86. *Ibid.*, p. 285.

87. *Ibid.*, pp. 291, 286.

88. *Ibid.*, p. 248.

89. *Ibid.*, p. 292.

90. *Ibid.*, p. 249.

91. *Ibid.*, p. 294.

92. *Ibid.*, p. 297.

93. *Ibid.*, p. 299, 302, 303.

94. *Ibid.*, pp. 284, 297, 302.

95. *Ibid.*, p. 13.

96. *Ibid.*, pp. 301, 14.

97. *Ibid.*, pp. 284, 285.

98. Although his mail had been stopped, Anderson still wrote daily letters—submitted with his final report—and they show the last measures taken by a competent officer: what he was doing to strengthen defense; the arrangements to get the relieving expedition into the fort; and the care with which he was observing hostile preparations to bring heavy fire upon the landing place. His last letter—Apr. 11—ended thus: "The officers and men, thank God, are in pretty good health; and, although feeling aware of the danger of their position, have greater anxiety about the fate of those whom they expect to come to their succor than they entertain for themselves" (*ibid.*, p. 251). It is the same devout thankfulness that filled the first sentence that Anderson wrote from Sumter; and all soldiers will see his character as an officer revealed in his admiration for his steadfast officers and men.

99. Chester, *op. cit.*, p. 63.

100. *O.R., 1*, 16–25. Incidents of the contest are drawn from this report unless otherwise noted.

101. For complaint by Whiting see *ibid.*, p. 306.

102. *Ibid.*, p. 41.

103. Whiting to Beauregard, *ibid.*, pp. 313–334.

104. *Ibid.*, p. 41. Lieut. Col. R. S. Ripley, a former U.S. officer, commanding at Fort Moultrie, also spoke of the precision of Moultrie's gunfire. His detailed report of ammunition expenditure proved him a careful and thorough officer.

105. *Ibid.*, p. 64.

106. *Ibid.*, pp. 14–15, 107.

107. *Ibid.*, p. 12. Crawford (*op. cit.*, p. 449) stated that on account of his physical and mental condition Maj. Anderson requested Capt. Fox to write the brief report which was telegraphed to Washington upon the *Baltic's* arrival in New York.

108. *O.R., 1*, 11.

109. In a telegram on Apr. 13 Beauregard stated: "Six vessels outside in

signals with Sumter" (*ibid.*, p. 308). Neither Foster's journal nor Fox's report mentions signal communication between Sumter and the warships. Furthermore, early on the 13th, Harstene reported from Moultrie and Whiting from Morris Island to Beauregard about the ships and the possibility of relief. Harstene identified the ships, and both these professional officers would have been quick to observe signals; but neither spoke of any. Chester (*op. cit.*, p. 68) stated that the fort flag was lowered three times on the 12th when the ships first appeared, as a sign of recognition, but he mentioned no other communication.

110. *O.R., I,* 150.

111. Cooper's wife was a Virginian and a member of the distinguished Mason family—and on Mar. 7 the following telegram (*ibid., 127,* 132) was sent by J. M. Mason to President Davis: "My friend and connection has resigned from the Army, resignation accepted; will be with you in five or six days. Have written by private hand."

On Oct. 21, 1860, Capt. G. W. Hazzard, of the regular army, had prepared Lincoln for the defection of Col. Cooper and other officers of rank. In a long letter from Cincinnati he described the situation with regard to forts and arsenals and also the higher personnel. "Every Military Bureau is presided over by a Virginian or the husband of a Virginia wife," he wrote; and he went into detail and named names (Mearns, *Lincoln Papers,* I, 298).

112. Nicolay and Hay, *op. cit.,* IV, 36; Hendrick, *op. cit.,* pp. 179–183; Crawford, *op. cit.,* pp. 405–410.

113. Hendrick, *op. cit.,* p. 198.

114. Fox, *Confidential Correspondence,* II, 43–44; Nicolay and Hay, *op. cit.,* IV, 56.

115. Fox, *op. cit.,* II, 18. Included also is a note of instruction for the pilot.

116. Morley, *Recollections,* I, 18.

117. Charles W. Ramsdell, "Lincoln and Fort Sumter," *Jour. of Southern Hist.,* III, 259–288 (Aug., 1937), after referring to Lamon's visit states, "Lincoln now had the information directly from Charleston that *any sort of relief* would result in an attack upon the Fort" (p. 274, italics supplied). He also appears to go a little too far in criticizing Nicolay and Hay. After giving the last sentence of Lincoln's letter of May 1 to Fox, he states (p. 286), "Lincoln's two secretaries, John G. Nicolay and John Hay, in their long but not impartial account of the Sumter affair come so close to divulging the essence of the stratagem that one cannot but suspect that they knew it." In support of his statement Ramsdell quotes three sentences from the authors cited, but he does not observe that though they omitted some sentences of Lincoln's letter to Fox, *they did give the important last sentence* (*op. cit.,* IV, 56). That sentence constitutes the most significant *fact* in the whole question and quite outweighs reports that So-and-so heard Lincoln make such-and-such a statement with reference to the firing on Sumter. There is no question that Lincoln wrote the sentence, or that Nicolay and Hay publicized it; but there can be much disagreement as to the exact interpretation, especially when one remembers the great pressure upon Lincoln at the time he wrote to Fox.

118. *O.R., I,* 25.

NOTES TO CHAPTER III

1. Nicolay and Hay, *Lincoln*, IV, chap. iv, provides the details in the introductory paragraphs.

2. *O.R., 122,* 67–69, for the proclamation, letters, quotas, places of rendezvous, and replies from the governors.

3. *Ibid.,* p. 69; Phisterer, *Statistical Record,* p. 3.

4. *O.R., 122,* 95–96.

5. *Ibid.,* p. 160.

6. *Harper's Weekly,* V, 274 (May 4, 1861).

7. Nicolay and Hay, *op. cit.,* p. 65.

8. *O.R., 122,* 40.

9. Andrew to Scott, *ibid.,* pp. 36–37.

10. *Harper's Weekly,* V, 307 (May 18, 1861), quoting a letter to the *N.Y. Times.*

11. *O.R., 122,* 90.

12. Craig to Holt, *ibid.,* pp. 42–43.

13. Freeman, *Lee,* I, 444 (photograph), 464–468; Cameron to Thomson, *O.R., 2,* 603–604; Kennedy to the President, Mearns, *Lincoln Papers,* II, 587–589.

It is to be noted that the Confederate Army Regulations repeated exactly the provision of the U.S. Army with regard to resignations: "No officer will be considered out of service on the tender of his resignation, until it shall have been duly accepted by the proper authority."

14. *O.R., 122,* 146.

15. Kirkwood to Cameron, Andrew to Cameron, *ibid.,* pp. 162, 164.

16. *Ibid.,* p. 161.

17. *Harper's Weekly,* V, 356 (June 8, 1861).

18. Lee to Johnson, Feb. 25, 1868, in Capt. R. E. Lee, *Recollections and Letters,* pp. 27–28. Lee stated that he understood his conversation with F. P. Blair, Sr., was "at the instance of President Lincoln," and that he declined the offer made. Nicolay (*Outbreak of Rebellion,* p. 109) calls the offer "informal and unofficial." Nicolay and Hay (*op. cit.,* pp. 98–99) state definitely that Lincoln requested Blair "to ascertain Lee's feelings and intentions"; and they note the contradictions in reports as to Lee's reply to Blair.

19. *O.R., 2,* 652.

20. *Ibid.,* p. 881.

21. On June 3 Lee wrote to Johnston, "As regards Harper's Ferry, its abandonment would be depressing to the cause of the South" (*ibid.,* p. 901). On June 7 he spoke of having referred the question to Davis and said: "He places great value upon our retention of the command of the Shenandoah Valley and the position at Harper's Ferry. The evacuation of the latter would interrupt our communication with Maryland, and injure our cause in that state" (*ibid.,* p. 910).

22. Patterson to Townsend, *ibid.,* pp. 660–661, 668–669; Patterson to

Cameron, p. 672; Townsend to Patterson, pp. 680–681; McDowell to Townsend, pp. 664–665. When the text speaks of a dispatch to Scott, the message was frequently addressed to his adjutant, Col. Townsend.

23. *Ibid.,* pp. 670–671.

24. *Ibid.,* p. 687. Many reports that Harpers Ferry was being abandoned had been received the day before, but they were not believed because they were not confirmed by spies (Porter to Townsend, *ibid.,* p. 684).

25. Patterson to Townsend and to McClellan, *ibid.,* pp. 686, 689.

26. *Ibid.,* pp. 688–689, 680–681.

27. Morton to Cameron, *ibid., 122,* 244.

28. Wallace's report, *ibid., 2,* 123–124. *Harper's Weekly,* V, 423 (July 6, 1861), contains a full account of the expedition, from a correspondent.

29. Johnston's report, *O.R., 2,* 471.

30. Cooper to Johnston, *ibid.,* pp. 923–925. On June 20, Johnston reported to Cooper from Winchester on the Federal forces, "All the information I could obtain from their vicinity in Maryland, and from friends in Baltimore, was to the effect that 18,000 men would advance from Chambersburg to co-operate with an army from Ohio" (*ibid., 108,* 143). Johnston was well deceived as to Patterson's purpose.

31. *Ibid., 2,* 691, 694–695, 696. There were three ways to get the troops to Washington: march all 80 miles; march to Frederick, 30 miles, then rail to Washington, via Baltimore, 70 miles; rail from Hagerstown via Harrisburg and Baltimore, 165 miles. All three methods were used to expedite the movement.

32. Burnside's report, *ibid.,* pp. 715–716. The Rhode Island troops were in Washington at 6:00 A.M., June 19. Some of the troops were across the Potomac at Williamsport on the morning of the 17th when the unexpected order to return to Washington—which they had left only on June 10—was received.

33. *O.R., 2,* 695. *Harper's Weekly,* V, 424–425 (July 6, 1861), contains an impressive two-page illustration of the review.

34. Davis wrote to Beauregard on June 13: "But I have not anticipated the necessity of your retreat, and have struggled rather to increase your force and look hopefully forward to see you enabled to assume the offensive" (*O.R., 2,* 922–923).

35. *Ibid.,* p. 700.

36. *Ibid.,* pp. 104–105.

37. *Ibid.,* pp. 108, 111–112.

38. *Ibid.,* p. 178.

39. *Ibid.,* pp. 719–721, 722–723. The summary, based upon information furnished by an intelligent observer, dealt with the enemy strength, organizations, positions, movements, armament, equipment, supplies, transport, etc.

40. Nicolay and Hay, *op. cit.,* p. 323. Chap. vii is devoted to "Scott's Anaconda" plan.

41. *O.R., 2,* 710–711.

42. *Ibid.,* pp. 702–703.

43. *Ibid.,* p. 168.

44. The service of volunteers counted from the date of muster into the service

of the United States, and therefore varied with different units (Scott to Patterson, *ibid.*).

45. *Ibid.*, pp. 314–315; R. M. Johnston, *Bull Run*, p. 99.

46. For service records of the regular officers, see Johnston, *op. cit.*, pp. 91–95.

47. *Harper's Weekly*, V, 435 (July 13, 1861). The article explicitly says "in and about Washington," and adds that the regiments opposite Leesburg (Stone's force) were not included. A check against the roster of McDowell's regiments and the list of those at Baltimore (*O.R.*, 2, 67) shows that the 64 regiments did not include any of the latter, with a few possible exceptions.

48. *Ibid.*, pp. 303–305.

49. McDowell's report, *ibid.*, p. 324.

50. *Ibid.*, p. 236.

51. *Ibid.*, p. 305.

52. *Ibid.*, p. 308.

53. *Ibid.*, p. 156. Patterson had withdrawn his command to the north bank of the Potomac on June 17, after all his artillery had been taken from him. He recrossed promptly after receiving a battery or two. For strength given, see *ibid.*, p. 187; Simpson gave 10,000 as the approximate figure (*ibid.*, p. 179).

54. *Ibid.*, pp. 179–90, 182.

55. Johnston's report, *ibid.*, p. 472; Jackson's report, *ibid.*, pp. 185–188. Johnston recommended Jackson and Stuart for promotion.

56. *Ibid.*, pp. 157, 158–159.

57. *Ibid.*, pp. 163–165.

58. Scott to Patterson, *ibid.*, pp. 165, 166.

59. The U.S. *Field Service Regulations* (1944) state, "Simple and direct plans promptly and thoroughly executed are usually decisive" (Sec. 113).

60. Patterson to Scott, *O.R.*, 2, 159.

61. Between 1866 and 1868 D. H. Strother, a native of Martinsburg and a writer and artist of considerable prominence, published a series of articles in the form of a diary entitled "Personal Recollections of the War." The second paper, *Harper's Magazine*, XXXIII, 137–160 (July, 1866), covered Patterson's campaign. Strother joined Patterson's staff on July 9, and was placed in the topographical section. When Johnston evacuated Harpers Ferry June 15, Strother was in Charles Town, and he had recorded the Confederate strength as 14 regiments of infantry, 23 pieces of artillery, 600 cavalry, and 240 wagons. On his inability to convince Patterson's staff that they were exaggerating the size of Johnston's force, Strother wrote: "I must confess I was somewhat irritated at the cavalier manner in which my estimates were received by these men of war. They seemed to be entirely satisfied with information received from other quarters, and I was equally well satisfied that this information had been furnished them by persons in the employ of the enemy" (p. 152). Distinguishing real Union sympathizers from mere pretenders was not simple, but the appointment of Strother to the staff indicates that his loyalty was not questioned.

62. *Ibid.*, p. 155. The evidence was based upon the reports of two deserters from Johnston, whose accuracy and reliability Strother checked with his own knowledge of Winchester.

63. *O.R.*, 2, 701–702, 166–167.

64. *Ibid.*, p. 167.

65. Cameron to Curtin, *ibid.*, p. 166.

66. *Ibid.*, pp. 167–168.

67. *Ibid.*, p. 168.

68. *Ibid.*, p. 159.

69. *Ibid.*, p. 164.

70. *Ibid.*, p. 168.

71. *Ibid.*

72. On July 17 Beauregard was authorized to stop and retain a North Carolina regiment which was on the way to Johnston (Cooper to Beauregard, *ibid.*, p. 980).

73. Patterson to Townsend, *ibid.*, pp. 169–170. On July 20 Strother (*op. cit.*, p. 157) wrote: "All the while our force, composed of three months' volunteers, was rapidly melting away. The time of nearly all of them had expired. One or two regiments turned back at Martinsburg before the march began. Three regiments left at Bunker's Hill, marching homeward while the guns were sounding at the front. To-day other regiments were departing. General Patterson had several regiments whose terms were expired paraded near headquarters. He came out and addressed them, urging them to remain until the campaign was ended. Colonel Wallace's Zouaves volunteered to remain ten days longer. Some other organizations followed their example. The general feeling among the troops, however, was to go home on the day their engagement terminated, without regard to circumstances." Patterson said nothing in his dispatches about regiments leaving at Martinsburg or from Bunker Hill. The orders issued July 19–23 at Charles Town and Harpers Ferry covering the discharge of eight regiments may be found in *O.R., 107,* 424–426.

74. *O.R., 2,* 172.

75. On July 18 Strother wrote: "After dark this evening I was informed that Joe Johnston was crossing at Berry's Ferry, moving towards Manassas." The next day he recorded: "Clear and warm. This morning before breakfast I received positive information that Johnston's whole army had crossed the Shenandoah at Berry's Ferry. A loyal citizen, who was an eye-witness of the fact, had ridden during the night to bring the news." Strother told Capt. Simpson, topographical engineer, who believed the report; but the news was discredited at headquarters, perhaps because Strother would not divulge the identity of his informant.

76. Beymer, *On Hazardous Service,* p. 182. According to this account Mrs. Greenhow said she had "received a copy of the order to McDowell." There is no such order in the records, and McDowell seems to have been under orders to move when practical. For statement about Mrs. Greenhow's code, see Jordan to Benjamin, *O.R., 5,* 928–929.

77. *O.R., 2,* 469–470; R. M. Johnston, *Bull Run,* pp. 103–111. For the quoted telegram see *O.R., 2,* 439–440.

78. Cooper to Holmes, *O.R., 2,* 980.

79. Indorsement by Davis on Beauregard's report, *ibid.*, p. 504.

80. *Ibid.*, p. 980.

81. *Ibid.*, p. 470; R. M. Johnston, *op. cit.*, pp. 107–109.

82. In acknowledging receipt of instructions to move to Beauregard's aid, if practicable, Johnston said: "General Patterson, who had been at Bunker Hill since Monday, seems to have moved yesterday to Charlestown, twenty-three miles east of Winchester" (*O.R.*, 2, 982). In his report he said: "On the 17th he [Patterson] moved to his left to Smithfield. This created the impression that he intended to attack us on the south, or was merely holding us in check while General Beauregard should be attacked at Manassas by General Scott" (*ibid.*, p. 473). Apparently Johnston now realized that Patterson was not to cooperate with a force coming from the west.

83. Johnston's report, *ibid.;* J. E. Johnston, *Narrative*, pp. 34–36. Stuart withdrew his cavalry screen at dark and followed Johnston's main body. At 9:00 A.M. he had furnished information that there was no evidence of a Federal advance from Smithfield, which confirmed Johnston's belief that his march would not be interfered with. Proper instructions from Scott to Patterson on the night of the 17th might have resulted in holding Johnston. Strother recorded that a reconnaissance was made on the 18th toward Berryville, but he did not give the hour, or its strength. Johnston set out with the idea of marching all the way to Manassas; but the performance of his troops was disappointing, and he sent a staff officer to Piedmont to arrange for rail transportation from there. Inefficiency of rail operation delayed his last units.

84. McDowell to Townsend, *O.R.*, 2, 307.

85. Report of Maj. John G. Barnard, *ibid.*, p. 330. Barnard was McDowell's chief engineer, and his report is drawn on extensively for the reconnaissance, the plan of the battle, and the movement.

86. McDowell's report, *ibid.*, p. 324.

87. *Ibid.*, p. 308.

88. Reports of Capt. Henry F. Clarke, Lieut. George Bell, Lieut. James Curtis, and Lieut. John P. Hawkins, pp. 336–344. Clarke was chief commissary officer for McDowell. A train of 56 wagons with 64,700 rations and 90 beef cattle, under Hawkins, intended for the Second and Fifth divisions, reached Fairfax at seven o'clock, July 18, after marching all night. Since it was feared that the trains under Bell and Curtis for the Third and First divisions, respectively, would be badly delayed, Clarke was directed (by whom, he did not say) to distribute the rations in Hawkins's train to all four divisions. Bell's train of 54 wagons with 60,000 rations and 70 beef cattle actually reached Fairfax at 4:45 P.M. on July 18 and Centerville at 8:00 A.M., July 19. Curtis's train of 64 wagons and 65 beef cattle reached the rear of the army at Centerville just after dark on July 18. McDowell apparently sought to justify a two-day delay in issuing rations by a half-day delay in part of his trains.

89. James B. Fry, "McDowell's Advance on Bull Run," *B. and L.*, I, 183.

90. *O.R.*, 2, 317. It was the second time that McDowell had deferred to others on an important matter. He had wanted to make the reconnaissance of the 19th in force, and drive in enemy patrols to obtain the desired information (*ibid.*, p. 308).

91. Both Johnston and Beauregard referred to Evans as a colonel, but Evans signed his report (written before those of the generals) as a brigadier general (*ibid.*, pp. 558–560).

LINCOLN FINDS A GENERAL

92. Burnside's report, *ibid.*, p. 396.

93. Johnston's report, *ibid.*, pp. 470–478. Beauregard submitted a long, florid, and somewhat bombastic report (*ibid.*, pp. 484–504).

94. Griffin's report, *ibid.*, p. 394. Griffin, without specifying Barry, said that "an officer on the field" had pronounced the regiment to be Union. He also said that "every cannoneer was cut down." Ricketts was wounded.

95. Jackson's report, *ibid.*, p. 482.

96. *Ibid.*, p. 316.

97. Scott to McDowell, *ibid.*, p. 748.

98. At an undesignated hour, but probably at about 8:00 P.M., Capt. B. S. Alexander, Engineer Corps, who was on the staff of the First Division, sent to an unidentified person the message: "General McDowell's army in full retreat through Centerville. The day is lost. Save Washington and the remnants of this army. All available troops ought to be thrown forward in one body. General McDowell is doing all he can to cover the retreat. Colonel Miles is forming for that purpose. He was in reserve at Centreville. The routed troops will not reform" (*ibid.*, p. 747). Though there was some good information in the dispatch, no telegrams should have gone except those authorized by McDowell or responsible members of his staff.

99. Richardson's report and correction, *ibid.*, pp. 372–376.

100. Special Orders, No. 39, *ibid.*, p. 745.

101. *Ibid.*, p. 327.

102. *Ibid.*, p. 570.

103. *Ibid.*, p. 328.

104. *Ibid.*, p. 477.

105. *Ibid.*, p. 324.

106. Livermore puts the Federal "effectives" at 28,452, the Confederates at 32,232 (*Numbers and Losses*, p. 77). *B. and L.* (I, 194–195) gives 18,572 as the number of Federals "engaged," and 18,053 as the figure for the Confederates. The figures for killed and wounded in the text are those of Livermore.

107. The figures were obtained by using the killed and wounded numbers in the text, with 18,500 as the number of Federals and 18,000 the number of Confederates engaged. Using his figures for effectives—men available for combat—Livermore gives for the Union army: hit in 1,000, 52; hit by 1,000, 70. For the Confederates: hit in 1,000, 61; hit by 1,000, 46.

108. *O.R.*, 2, 390–391.

109. *Ibid.*, p. 326.

110. Patterson to Townsend, *ibid.*, p. 172.

111. McDowell's report, *ibid.*, p. 324.

112. *Ibid.*, pp. 690, 701–702. Whether Patterson had had an engineer report on the extent of damage to the bridge and the time needed for repair cannot be said.

113. Col. Stone joined Patterson by marching from opposite Leesburg, through Hagerstown and Williamsport to Martinsburg. If Patterson had moved to Harpers Ferry, Stone would have had hardly any march, and some of his transport would perhaps have been available for McDowell.

114. *Ibid.*, p. 171.

115. *Ibid.,* p. 746.

116. *Ibid.,* p. 671.

117. Patterson wrote to the Secretary of War on Nov. 1, 1861, requesting an investigation of the charges against him; but the request was denied on Nov. 30, on the grounds that he was no longer in the service and Gen. Scott was in Europe. In 1865 his *Narrative of the Campaign in the Valley of the Shenandoah in 1861* reported an interview in which the Secretary of War had said to him "that a court would throw the blame on General Scott, and this he would never consent to" (p. 17), and quoted a letter from Col. George H. Thomas on Aug. 25, 1861, to an unnamed colonel with the postscript, "I think, however, that time will set the General [Patterson] all right, as I see the papers are much more favorable to him than at first." The unfavorable opinion of Patterson had persisted, and Greeley had denounced him bitterly in 1864 (*American Conflict,* I, 536–538), citing at length Gen. Sandford's testimony before the Committee on the Conduct of the War. The records show that much that Sandford said about events at Bunker Hill was incorrect. Livermore's long investigation of "Patterson's Shenandoah Campaign" (*Papers, Mil. Hist. Soc. Mass.,* 1895 ed., I, 2–58) was very unfavorable and put emphasis on what Scott *intended* him to do and not on a careful consideration of *all* the orders. It failed to point out the disingenuousness of Scott's telegram of July 18, which, read by itself, gives a false impression. Livermore did not refer to Strother's account of the campaign. Lincoln remarked to Buell in a letter of Jan. 13, 1862, that he thought "less harshly of Patterson than some others seemed to" (*O.R., 7,* 928).

118. *Military Genius of Lincoln,* p. 59. Some of the greatest "nonsense" centers around the claim that Washington could have been easily captured if the Confederates had only been a little more enterprising and not content with a good day's work. Jackson is reported as lamenting—as he nursed a slight wound—that he did not have 10,000 fresh men to follow the retreating Federals in sort of a "My Kingdom for a horse" fashion. Stonewall was in no position to know the number of men in McDowell's force who had not been engaged, or the number of fresh regiments in the Washington defenses west of the Potomac, or again the number of other regiments in the Federal capital that did not belong to McDowell's command. There would also have been the question of supplying a force on an offensive operation in contrast to a purely defensive battle. Neither Johnston nor Beauregard had adequate transport or a good supply service.

Even among soldiers in Richmond erroneous ideas persisted. Thus Josiah Gorgas, the very able Pennsylvania-born ordnance officer who "went over" to the South, wrote in his diary almost a year after the battle—on June 12, 1862 —that 25,000 Confederates had completely routed 45,000 to 50,000 Federals. Ruefully he added, "Unfortunately the victory was not followed up, or Washington would have fallen into our hands without further contest" (Gorgas, *Civil War Diary,* p. 2). When a trained soldier could entertain such illusions and write such amazing nonsense, it is not strange that the Southern public should have taken false hopes through magnifying what their forces had done and what more they could have done. The criticism of Joe Johnston that is clearly implied in Gorgas's statement was not very becoming in an officer unfamiliar with field command.

119. Whitman, *Prose Works,* pp. 24–25.

NOTES TO CHAPTER IV

1. *O.R.,* 2, 746, 747, 749.
2. *Ibid.,* pp. 752–753.
3. Mearns, *Lincoln Papers,* II, 598–601. The letter is given with the indorsement in *O.R., 107,* 338–339; Scott's reply, *ibid.,* pp. 369–370.
4. *Ibid.,* 2, 656.
5. Report of Morris, *ibid.,* p. 67.
6. *Ibid.,* pp. 194, 196–197.
7. *Ibid.,* pp. 208–209.
8. *Ibid.,* pp. 198–199.
9. *Ibid.,* pp. 209–210.
10. McClellan to Townsend, *ibid.,* pp. 198–202.
11. Report of Rosecrans, *ibid.,* 214–215.
12. McClellan to Townsend, *ibid.,* p. 206.
13. Beatty, *Memoirs,* p. 27.
14. McClellan to Townsend, *loc. cit.*
15. *O.R.,* 2, 202, 203.
16. *Ibid.,* p. 204.
17. *Ibid.*
18. *Ibid.,* p. 207. Reports of Morris and Capt. H. W. Benham, *ibid.,* pp. 218–223.
19. *Ibid.,* pp. 288–290, 743, 744. Cox discussed the operations later in *B. and L.,* I, 139–140, under the title "McClellan in West Virginia."
20. *O.R.,* 2, 288.
21. *Ibid.,* p. 284.
22. Some kind of affront to Rosecrans is indicated by his letter to McClellan on June 29 (*ibid.,* pp. 212–213). Morris—builder and president of railroads—went out of service in the end of July, somewhat discredited. He later declined reappointment as well as a subsequent offer of a major generalship (*D.A.B.*). For some strange addresses that McClellan used in writing to Confederate commanders, see *O.R., 2,* 252, 267.
23. McClellan, *Own Story,* p. 53; Townsend to McClellan, Scott to McClellan, *O.R., 107,* 382, 386–387.
24. McClellan's report, *ibid.,* 5, 42.
25. *O.R.,* 2, 754–755. Scott wrote to Gen. Mansfield, who was in command at Washington: "The enemy is still pressing McDowell, and you need every man in the forts to save the city. Now is the time for effectual service." It is notable that on July 17 Townsend had informed McDowell, "In case of emergency, a reserve is held ready for you in Washington" (*ibid.,* p. 742).
26. Scott to P. B. Snyder, *ibid.,* pp. 756–757. Snyder had inquired at an

unspecified hour on July 22, "Shall I allow anything to go forward this morning?" Scott made an indorsement stating that messages might go if their substance conformed to the dispatch that Gen. Scott had sent to McClellan. Then he gave his appraisal of the situation, intended evidently as a guide in censorship. On the 22nd Cameron wired (*ibid.*, p. 756) in reply to an inquiry from New York: "Our works on the south bank of the Potomac are impregnable, being well manned with re-enforcements. The capital is safe. . . . There is no danger of the capital nor of the Republic."

27. *Ibid.*, pp. 755–756.

28. *Ibid.*, *122*, 301–310. Bassett uses figures drawn from the report (*Short History of the U.S.*, p. 517); Rhodes makes a specific reference to it (*History of the U.S.*, III, 360). Channing makes no mention of the call of May 3, but only of those of April and July (*History of the U.S.*, VI). Actually there was no call in July (see n. 31, *infra*). J. K. Hosmer (*The Appeal to Arms*, p. 33) mentions the call of May 3 but without comment as to the number of men it produced.

Randall does not discuss the question of how many men were raised by the call of May 3 and how many were in service at the time of the meeting of Congress; very critical of the "unmilitary democracy struggling to improvise a war machine for an emergency," he refers to the "blundering incompetence of politicians" and states, "The haphazard method of raising the emergency force took no heed of the importance of using the regular army as a nucleus" (*The Civil War and Reconstruction*, pp. 263, 266). There was nothing haphazard in what was done, and the regular army was used approximately as it was used in both world wars, when existing regular divisions were completed and others formed. In *Lincoln the President* (Vol. 1, p. 374, Vol. II, p. 290) he is not so harsh, but he again leaves the impression that no three-year volunteers beyond the 40 regiments were raised until after the passage of the acts of July 22 and 25.

Shannon's treatment of the question of raising volunteers is considered in Appendix VII.

29. *O.R.*, *122*, 303–304. Many of the regiments were apparently still in state camps, had not "come forward," as the saying was, and so did not show on the army strength return for June 30 (*ibid.*, p. 301). Rhodes noted the discrepancy between Cameron's figures for July 1 and the provost marshal general's (*op. cit.*, p. 360). In view of the work involved it is not strange that there was delay in getting organizations on Federal strength returns; but just what Cameron meant by "active service" is not clear.

30. For the acts see *O.R.*, *122*, 380–383. There has been misunderstanding as to whether the second act (signed July 25) provided 500,000 men in addition to the 500,000 provided by the first act (signed July 22), or merely changed certain details about enlistment. Quartermaster General Meigs wrote to Cameron Oct. 30, 1861, that 500,000 volunteers had been authorized (*ibid.*, pp. 608–609). Phisterer makes the somewhat ambiguous statement, "Under the call of May 3 and the acts approved July 22 and 25, 1861, 500,000 men were required" (*Statistical Record*, p. 4). Nicolay and Hay (*Lincoln*, VII, 2) state clearly that the two acts gave the President authority for 1,000,000 volunteers, and their

view is confirmed by the reading of the acts as well as by statements in the *Congressional Globe.*

31. *O.R., 122,* 383–384, n. The quotas for all states and the number of men furnished are given. It is sometimes said that Lincoln's answer to Bull Run was a call for 500,000 additional troops. This is not accurate. Congress answered with additional authorization; but the President made no new call, and, as noted in the text, all 700,680 men are credited to the call of May 3.

32. Shannon makes strong criticism. See Appendix VII.

33. Lincoln's message, *O.R., 122,* 316. It is significant that Gen. Maurice quotes this sentence and finds a parallel in Kitchener's perplexity in 1914 (*Statesmen and Soldiers,* pp. 63–64).

34. *Harper's Weekly,* V, 542 (Aug. 24, 1861).

35. Delafield, *Art of War,* p. 110.

36. *O.R., 122,* 694–697, 375–376. The November report gave a general description of what Myer had done.

37. *Ibid.,* pp. 455–456. The amount of cavalry and artillery is impressive. Myers (*op. cit.,* pp. 209–210) states, "Furthermore, two important arms of the service, cavalry and artillery, had been almost entirely neglected until McClellan took command"—a charge quite out of harmony with the facts. According to the Field Artillery Regulations of 1861 the number of guns per 1,000 men varied from one to four, and three was the number recommended for the "American Service." On the other hand, McClellan wrote to the Secretary of War Oct. 1, 1861, asking for 400 guns for 180,000 men, which was only 2.2 guns per thousand men. Thus he lowered rather than raised the estimates of artillerymen.

38. General Order 54 (War Department), Aug. 16, 1861, pp. 11, 13–14. Minors were not accepted for enlistment without the consent of parents or guardians (G.O. 66, Aug. 28), but minority was not a basis for discharge (G.O. 74, Sept. 17). The height requirement was reduced to five feet, three inches (G.O. 59, Aug. 17).

39. *O.R., 122,* 349.

40. *Ibid.,* p. 380.

41. Delafield, *op. cit.,* p. 8. The discussion of the breech-loader is amplified in Appendix III, where authorities for the statements in the text will also be found.

42. For discussion of Shannon's comments see Appendix VII.

43. *O.R., 12,* 767.

44. Using strength of 460,000 for Aug. 3 (*ibid., 122,* 455–456, omitting the 25,000 regulars listed as "raising"), and 17,113 for Apr. 5 (Nicolay and Hay, *op. cit.,* IV, 65).

45. The strength of the army on Apr. 1, 1917, was 190,000; on Aug. 1, it was 551,000 (War Department, *Report for 1918,* I, 11).

46. *G.O.* 54, Aug. 10, 1861, p. 5.

NOTES TO CHAPTER V

1. Johnston to Davis, Davis to Johnston, *O.R., 5,* 790, 798; various messages, *ibid.,* pp. 872–873.

2. *Ibid.*, *5*, 785; *127, 555, 572.* Before hostilities broke out there had been efforts to procure not only arms but powder in the North. On Apr. 9, Walker telegraphed to Tucker, Cooper & Co., No. 70, South Street, New York, "Increase weekly supply of 'rope' [gunpowder] to the utmost" (*ibid., 127,* 213). The bracketed explanation is by the *O.R.* editors.

3. Order to Huse, *ibid.*, p. 220. Huse reported May 21 (*ibid.*, pp. 344–345) that Northern agents had bought up a lot of "rubbish" at very high prices, but had not secured many good arms. He added, "The agent sent by the United States Government to purchase arms is the best man for that duty that could have been selected." On July 22 he wrote from Paris (*ibid.*, p. 566) that since he had been in Europe his limited funds had embarrassed him in competition with agents from the U.S., Italy, Spain, Russia, and Peru, all well financed: "The U.S. agents and the agents of the individual Northern States appear to have been unlimited, both as regards price and quantity, and they paid cash in every instance. Under the circumstances I am certain that you cannot fail to appreciate the difficulties under which I have had to execute my orders. I should state, moreover, that the U.S. ministers to England, France, and Belgium have been very active in their endeavors to discover what the agents of the Confederacy are effecting. They have agents employed for no other purpose, and it is of the highest importance that these agents should be kept in ignorance of all the acts of any agent of the Confederacy." Huse persevered, however, and on Aug. 11 he reported that he had bought about 10,000 good Enfield rifles, and that other contracts would be coming in (*ibid.*, pp. 583 ff.). Hendrick (*Lincoln's War Cabinet,* p. 223) denounces Cameron for slowness in making foreign purchases: "When Cameron finally woke up and began scouring the European field, prices, because of these Southern purchases, had reached a high figure, and in many cases arms could not be acquired at any price, for the agents of Jefferson Davis had cornered the supply." No authority is given, and the statement is beyond reconciliation with the reports of Huse.

4. *O.R.*, *5*, 829 830, 834.

5. Johnston to Davis, *ibid.*, p. 777.

6. *Ibid.*, pp. 121–122.

7. *Harper's Weekly,* V, 643 (Oct. 12, 1861), stated: "Munson's and Upton's Hills and Fall's Church have been abandoned, and are now occupied by the Union troops. The position of the rebels at these points appears to have been not very formidable. There were no signs found of guns having been mounted."

8. Beauregard to Johnston, *O.R.*, *5*, 990.

9. *Ibid.*, *2*, 908, for statement to Lee; *ibid.*, *5*, 847–848, Johnston to Whiting, for reference to the "redoubtable McC."

10. Explanatory note, *O.R.*, Atlas, I, Plate VI–1.

11. McClellan, *Own Story*, pp. 172, 84, 173.

12. *Ibid.*, p. 84.

13. *O.R.*, *14*, 3, 4. Eckenrode and Conrad defend McClellan's break with Scott by asserting that Washington was really threatened and Beauregard was "at that very time" considering an invasion of Maryland. The records prove the contrary. On Aug. 24 Johnston asked Davis for more guns and cavalry,

with clear implication of defensive needs and intentions; and on Aug. 11 Beauregard wrote to Johnston about posting his forces so as "to prevent a *coup de main* from McClellan" (*O.R., 5,* 777, 778–779). Although Beauregard stated that he thought a bold move would capture the Union forces at Annandale—provided all the artillery was in good shape—there was no serious intention to undertake an offensive. A few weeks later there was some wishful thinking about a movement into Maryland; but it did not get to the planning stage.

14. McClellan, *op. cit.,* pp. 106–107.

15. Leech, *Reveille in Washington,* p. 118. More can well be quoted: "A touchy vanity lay at the base of McClellan's arrogance. He liked only subordinates and uncritical admirers, and could find comfort in the approval of his horse, writing that 'he, at least, had full confidence in his master.'"

16. Myers, *General McClellan,* p. 211. McClellan also requested that no officer whom he recommended for promotion to a general officer be taken from him without his permission, "and that no one, whatever his rank may be, shall give any orders respecting my command without my being first consulted." A requisite of successful war making is that the High Command have the power to assign an officer to the position where he can render the best service; and every commanding officer from captain to general must expect to lose some of his best officers from time to time. McClellan wanted to be made an exception to this essential rule. The last request sounds more reasonable. But no commander should be bound never to interfere with a subordinate; McClellan himself often gave orders to division commanders over the heads of corps commanders. His letter was the result of an injudicious letter of Sept. 7 from Cameron which mentioned the imminence of a great battle and asked advice (McClellan, *op. cit.,* p. 105).

17. McClellan's report, *O.R., 5,* 9–11.

18. *N.Y. Tribune,* Oct. 23, 1861. Complete censorship was evidently not established until Feb. 25, 1862. For Stanton's order taking over the telegraph lines, see *O.R., 122,* 899. News had to be cleared through commanding officers. Newspapers publishing information that had not been properly passed would be "excluded thereafter from receiving information by telegraph or from transmitting their papers by railroad." No direct punishment seems to have been provided for publishing uncensored news.

19. *Harper's Weekly,* V, 531 (Aug. 24, 1861).

20. *N.Y. Tribune,* Sept. 20 and Aug. 17, 1861.

21. Quoted in *N.Y. Tribune,* Sept. 27, 1861.

22. *O.R., 122,* 39, 902–905. The number of rifles in the hands of the militia of North Carolina, Alabama, and Tennessee looks very high. The large number of muskets (57,000) in Virginia agrees in general with a statement by Davis, describing them as flintlocks (*Rise and Fall,* I, 971).

23. *O.R., 122,* 247, and elsewhere. See also the references to Huse, early in this chapter.

24. The figure given is an upper limit. Davis (*loc. cit.*) stated that in the arsenals, the states, and organizations there were 150,000 rifles and percussion muskets for the use of the Confederates.

25. McClellan to Townsend, *O.R., 2,* 195.

26. Allen to McClellan, *O.R., 5,* 736–737.

27. Combined strengths of the Confederate Army of the Potomac and the Aquia District, *ibid.,* pp. 932–933. Johnston's figures (*Narrative,* pp. 80–81) check with *O.R., 5,* 1086.

28. McClellan's report, *ibid.,* pp. 6–8.

29. *Ibid., 122,* 611–612.

30. *N.Y. Tribune,* Nov. 2, 1861. On Oct. 19 McClellan (*op. cit.,* p. 170) wrote to his wife that Scott proposed to retire in favor of Halleck. A preference for Halleck would not have been inconsistent with letters that Scott had written to Cameron. On Aug. 12 he complained of McClellan's behavior, and on Oct. 4 a longer and more bitter letter gave details about McClellan's failure to make proper returns to army headquarters (*O.R., 15,* 5–6; *107,* 492–493). But Lincoln said in his message to Congress of Dec. 3 that Scott had repeatedly expressed himself in favor of McClellan as his successor (*ibid., 122,* 613).

31. Nicolay and Hay, *Lincoln,* III, 466, quoting an entry in Hay's diary.

32. McClellan, *Own Story,* p. 173. The letter has Scott leaving Washington on Nov. 3; but it may have been misdated, for a dispatch in the *N.Y. Tribune* implies he left on Nov. 2.

33. McClellan's order assuming command was No. 19 in Scott's series; that giving the change in General in Chief was War Department order No. 94. G.O. 98, Nov. 13, was the first order in the new style.

34. McClellan, *loc. cit.*

35. *N.Y. Tribune,* July 29, 1861.

36. Minutes of a council of war at Centerville between President Davis and Generals Johnston, Beauregard, and G. W. Smith (*O.R., 5,* 884–887).

37. "This is from an undoubted source—a secret agent of theirs," a Confederate agent in Washington wrote on Nov. 25 to Secretary of War Benjamin, in support of a tip; and on Nov. 30 an agent wrote: "I have every reason to believe, from all I can hear, that McClellan will certainly make a bolt at you next week. Watch him on every hand. Every device will be used to deceive you" (*ibid.,* pp. 978, 979).

38. *Harper's Weekly,* V, 674 (Oct. 26, 1861).

39. *N.Y. Tribune,* Sept. 26, Oct. 11, and Oct. 18, 1861.

40. *Ibid.,* Nov. 21, 1861; large picture in *Harper's Weekly,* V, 776–777 (Dec. 7, 1861).

41. *N.Y. Tribune,* Dec. 12, 1861.

42. *Ibid.,* Dec. 14, 1861; *Harper's Weekly,* V, 827 (Dec. 28, 1861).

43. *C.C.W.,* 1863, 2: 139.

44. Henderson, *Stonewall Jackson,* p. 438.

45. *O.R., 122,* 608–609.

46. A Washington dispatch of Dec. 26 to the *N.Y. Tribune* stated, "Doctors Leon and Marcy, brother of General Marcy, reached here today, having come on expressly from New York City to attend General McClellan and his Chief of Staff, who have been confined to their beds for several days."

47. Leech, *op. cit.,* p. 125.

48. Ballard (*Military Genius of Lincoln*, p. 110), quoting Ropes, remarks: "It was just the excellence of the army that made the President long for a man who would use it. When no plan for action could be found the President, sorely puzzled, had every reason to be despondent."

49. Swinton, *Army of the Potomac*, pp. 79–85. In the summer of 1864 Swinton submitted McDowell's manuscript to Lincoln, who stated that it was a true report of the war councils as he remembered them, but he believed he had not used the phrase "the Jacobinism of Congress" when speaking of the political situation.

50. *O.R.*, 5, 35–41. The Army of the Potomac is not mentioned in letters that McClellan quotes, and no indication is found as to when he gave up the Manassas plan. A remark of Swinton's (*op. cit.*, p. 69 n.) is pertinent: "Though General McClellan used to keep his own counsel, yet General McDowell tells me he was wont, in their rides over the country south of the Potomac, to point towards the flank of Manassas and say, 'We shall strike them there.'"

51. Leech, *op. cit.*, p. 135.

52. McClellan's report, *O.R.*, 5, 41–42.

53. Maurice, *Statesmen and Soldiers*, pp. 76, 77. Maurice later (Marshall, *Aide-de-Camp of Lee*, p. 23 n.) saw reason to doubt the full justice of his own criticisms of some of Lincoln's war orders.

54. Martin Sommers, "Why Russia Got the Drop on Us," *Saturday Evening Post*, Feb. 8, 1947; Sherwood, *Roosevelt and Hopkins*, chaps. xxiii, xxv, p. 615.

55. Ropes, "The Peninsular Campaign, General McClellan's Plans," *Mil. Hist. Soc. Mass.*, I, 77.

56. Maurice, *Statesmen and Soldiers*, chap. iv, "Abraham Lincoln and Grant." His chapter on Lincoln and McClellan further refutes the extravagant assertion of Ropes.

57. Fuller, *Decisive Battles*, pp. 184, 223.

58. McClellan's report, *O.R.*, 5, 42–45.

59. *Harper's Weekly* on Nov. 2, 1861, suggested editorially, "If General McClellan be the far-sighted general people believe him to be, he was prepared for what has happened, and is provided with a remedy."

60. *O.R.*, 5, 633–634.

61. Hebert, *Fighting Joe Hooker*, chap. iv, "In Lower Maryland"; *O.R.*, 5, 407–411. Of McClellan's refusal to endorse Hooker's plan, Hebert (*op. cit.*, p. 58) wrote in 1944: "From what we are learning today of the difficulties of forcing a beachhead and the exhaustive preparation for such a maneuver, it was probably all to the good for Hooker's subsequent career that his commander 'cooled off' his suggestion." But Col. Graham's landing and extensive inland movement entirely unopposed was more significant and relevant to Hooker's proposal than any landing operation in World War II. Graham made careful preparations; those of Hooker would have had to be more extensive, but suited to the defenses to be encountered, not to the highly organized beaches in Europe and the Pacific in 1942–1945.

62. Hebert, *op. cit.*, p. 60.

63. *Harper's Weekly*, V, 675 (Oct. 26, 1861).

64. Michie, *General McClellan*, p. 246. American military literature contains

few books that rank with this work. As a young engineer officer in the Civil War, Michie was very successful and drew commendation from Ulysses Grant. He became one of West Point's best known teachers and scholars, and his name also lives on in a stadium erected to an athletic son killed at San Juan Hill. McClellan's warmest friends agreed that Michie was impartial, judicial, and fair; but, in spite of mild language, he left little to McClellan as a field commander and spoke candidly of McClellan's strange mental constitution and emotional nature.

65. Blackford, *War Years with Stuart*, p. 71.

66. Henderson, *op. cit.*, p. 176. On the preceding page Henderson stated, "From the day McClellan took command the Army of the Potomac had done practically nothing." Eckenrode and Conrad (*McClellan*, p. 36) state, however, "The eminent G. F. R. Henderson fully approves McClellan's inaction at this time."

67. Leech, *op. cit.*, p. 120

68. Myers, *op. cit.*, p. 265, quotes Thomas G. Frothingham, in "The Peninsular Campaign of 1862," *Proc. Mass. Hist. Soc.*, LVII, 82–122 (Nov. 1923), as excusing McClellan's delay, and describes him as "an especially able and deep student" of the early part of the Civil War. But Frothingham makes only a superficial comparison of the military and troop-training problem of 1861 with that of World War I. His contention that "delay and preparation" were of "immense value for the North" ignores completely the great danger of foreign recognition of the Confederacy, which increased with every month that the Federal government failed to deal effective blows against the rebelling states; and it ignores also the dire situation in the Confederacy. Jefferson Davis (*Rise and Fall*, I, 476–477) wrote: "The winter of 1862 was the period when our ordnance deficiencies were most keenly felt. Powder was called for on every hand; and the equipments most needed were those we were least able to supply. . . . After the fall of 1862, when the powdermills at Augusta had got into full operation, there was no further inability to meet all requisitions for ammunition."

Maurice (*Statesmen and Soldiers*, p. 73) touches on the question, but does not mention the great difference between the Civil War and World War I in the types of training needed. He does point to the fact that the Germans put four new army corps into action within three months after the beginning of the war, and calls it a "remarkable feat of organization."

69. Douglas, *I Rode with Stonewall*, p. 113.

70. Leech, *op. cit.*, p. 128.

NOTES TO CHAPTER VI

1. Welles, *Diary*, I, 60–67.
2. *O.R.*, 5, 51.
3. Leech, *Reveille in Washington*, p. 133.
4. *N.Y. Tribune*, Mar. 13, 1862.

5. Blackford, *War Years with Stuart*, pp. 59–60. He put responsibility upon Johnston for drawing supplies from Richmond instead of locally; but Johnston (*Narrative*, pp. 98–99) stated he had protested vigorously against the practice.

6. *N.Y. Tribune*, Mar. 13 and 14, 1862.

7. *O.R.*, 5, 52.

8. *Ibid.*, pp. 896–897, 934, 941–942, 948–949. Secretary Benjamin indirectly revealed Johnston's strength on Oct. 13 (pp. 896–897) but refrained "as a matter of prudence" (p. 892) from mentioning the figure in a letter to Johnston on Oct. 7.

9. *Ibid.*, p. 1086.

10. Nicolay and Hay, *Lincoln*, V, 174.

11. Johnston, *op. cit.*, pp. 96–97.

12. Freeman, *Lee's Lieutenants*, I, 133.

13. Nicolay and Hay, *op. cit.*, p. 173; *O.R.*, 5, 51.

14. Macartney, *Little Mac*, p. 83.

15. President's War Order, No. 3, Mar. 8, 1862, in McClellan's report, *O.R.*, 5, 50.

16. *Ibid.*, pp. 55–56.

17. *Ibid.*, p. 753.

18. McClellan, *Own Story*, pp. 227–228.

19. Michie, *General McClellan*, p. 465.

20. Ballard, *Military Genius of Lincoln*, p. 105.

21. Macartney (*op. cit.*, p. 143) states that under such circumstances the greatest genius in the world could hardly have succeeded. Both Grant and Lee had to reinstate themselves after suffering popular disfavor, and McClellan, while General in Chief, telegraphed Halleck about putting Grant in arrest for fancied neglect of duty. Myers (*General McClellan*, p. 301) states that McClellan should have resigned when he found the administration was not giving him "unquestioned support." No general should expect *unquestioned* support until he has given some evidence that he can carry out plans as well as make them. Maurice (*Statesmen and Soldiers*, pp. 113–114) approves of the way Lincoln demanded of the well tested Grant an explanation when he thought Grant had made a mistake.

22. Ballard, *op. cit.*, p. 73.

23. *O.R.*, 5, 54.

24. *Ibid.*, 14, 15.

25. *Ibid.*, 5, 59–61.

26. *Ibid.*, 14, 57, 61–62. In a paper, "General McClellan's Plans for the Campaign of 1862, and the Alleged Interference of the Government with Them," *Mil. Hist. Soc. Mass.*, I, 86, it is stated: "Your committee regard it, then, as established beyond question that Gen. McClellan did not propose to comply with the requirements of the President; and they cannot regard the detention of Gen. McDowell's corps at Washington as an interference with the plans which Gen. McClellan had been authorized by the President to carry out." The paper made a careful study of all the pertinent orders and instructions—for which Ropes, the chairman, was well fitted by his legal training.

27. Ballard, *op. cit.*, p. 75.

28. Maurice, ed., *An Aide-de-Camp of Lee*, p. 19.

29. Henderson, *Stonewall Jackson*, p. 177.

30. Ballard, *op. cit.*, p. 111; Michie, *op. cit.*, p. 466. Michie asserts that the question whether McDowell's corps would have been of value to McClellan is fruitless, "because, under the circumstances of the time, it was not possible for the Administration to ignore the absolute danger in which Washington would have been placed had not McDowell been retained as a covering force."

31. *O.R., 14,* 14, 18, 25, 27–28, 38–39, 65.

32. *Ibid.,* p. 39. Wool informed McClellan, "The object of my orders were greater dispatch and to keep the men out of the hospital." Myers (*op. cit.,* p. 271) takes a different viewpoint about the command arrangements from that set forth here. Although as a rule the ranking commander has full authority over all troops and installations in a region where he is operating, there are important exceptions. The situation at Fort Monroe was, in fact, one of the puzzling ones in military operations. That Lincoln foresaw the difficulties was revealed by his efforts to anticipate them.

33. *O.R., 14,* 66, 68. The second dispatch ends, "I have moved up troops to protect McClellan's left flank. All goes on very smoothly. I do not believe the Army of the Potomac will find many troops to contend with."

34. *Ibid.,* p. 76.

35. *Ibid.,* p. 67.

36. Michie, *op. cit.,* p. 241.

37. *O.R., 14,* 71.

38. Michie, *op. cit.,* p. 239.

39. McClellan to Thomas, *O.R., 14,* 74.

40. *Ibid.*

41. John C. Palfrey, "The Siege of Yorktown," *Mil. Hist. Soc. Mass.,* I, 144, makes a long and careful examination of the charge that the Navy did not give as much assistance in the reduction of Yorktown as it might have done and finds it groundless. Michie also examines the question.

42. *O.R., 14,* 436, 437. Originally Magruder had 11,500 men; by Apr. 11 he had received 20,000 reenforcements, but detachments left only 23,000 for his long line, with no general reserve.

43. McClellan's report, *ibid., 12,* 14.

44. *Ibid., 14,* 74, 76–77.

45. *O.R., 12,* 14; *14,* 87–88, 72, 76.

46. McClellan's report, *ibid., 12,* 15. The total strength of the Army of the Potomac on Mar. 20 was 240,234, the figure including the commands of Dix (Baltimore), Banks (Shenandoah Valley), and Wadsworth (Washington) (*ibid.,* pp. 14, 26).

47. Ballard, *op. cit.,* p. 112.

48. *O.R., 14,* 455–456.

49. *Ibid.,* pp. 126, 130.

50. *Ibid.,* pp. 73, 78–79.

51. *Ibid.,* pp. 102, 103.

52. Barnard, *Peninsular Campaign*, p. 74.

53. *O.R., 14,* 134. McClellan's promptness was relative. For some comments, see Michie, *op. cit.,* pp. 256–258.

54. *O.R., 14,* 143.

55. *Ibid.,* pp. 148–149.

56. *Ibid.,* p. 143.

57. Michie, *op. cit.,* pp. 277, 281; Webb, *The Peninsula,* p. 87.

58. McClellan's report, *O.R., 12,* 28.

59. *Ibid., 14,* 176.

60. *Ibid., 12,* 30.

61. *Ibid.,* pp. 28–29.

62. *Ibid.,* p. 30.

63. *Ibid.*

64. *Ibid., 14,* 190.

65. McDowell to Stanton, May 25, *ibid., 18,* 233.

66. Ballard, *op. cit.,* p. 113.

67. On May 31 Kenly wrote a full and apparently reliable report of Jackson's attack, which he stated struck him between 1:00 and 2:00 P.M. (*O.R., 15,* 555–558).

68. *Ibid., 18,* 219.

69. *Ibid., 15,* 626.

70. *Ibid., 18,* 219.

71. Hendrick, *Lincoln's War Cabinet,* p. 292.

72. *O.R., 18,* 220–221, 226.

73. Frémont's career in 1861 in Missouri will be discussed in a later volume. In early May of 1862 he was advancing on Staunton while Banks descended the Shenandoah Valley. Frémont's leading troops under Brigadier General R. H. Milroy were defeated by Jackson on May 8 at McDowell, Virginia (25 miles northwest of Staunton). Frémont then moved to Franklin.

74. *O.R., 14,* 189–190.

75. *Ibid., 18,* 228–230.

76. *Ibid., 12,* 31–32.

77. Bill states specifically that McClellan had received orders to assault the Richmond defenses at once or return to Washington, with the implication that the date in question was the last of June; and he uses the phrase "Washington meddling" in the distorted way described (*Beleaguered City,* pp. 133, 128).

78. *O.R., 12,* 32.

79. *Ibid., 18,* 232.

80. *Ibid.,* p. 234.

81. *Ibid., 15,* 344.

82. *Ibid., 12,* 32.

83. Freeman, *Lee's Lieutenants,* I, 382.

84. *O.R., 18,* 247.

85. *Ibid., 12,* 33.

86. *Ibid., 14,* 189–190.

87. Michie, *op. cit.,* p. 247.

88. Francis W. Palfrey, *Antietam and Fredericksburg,* p. 134.

89. "The period which elapsed between the fall of Yorktown and the begin-

ning of the seven days' battles," *Papers, Mil. Hist. Soc. Mass.*, 1895 ed., I, 173. Palfrey continued, "The weather was fine from the 24th to the afternoon of the 30th, except that there was rain on the night of the 26th."

Eckenrode and Conrad (*McClellan*, p. 72) state that if McDowell's force had been added to McClellan the latter "would have been three times as strong as the Confederates and would have, in all probability, taken Richmond, ending the war." Actual strengths must be ignored. Controlled by exaggerated enemy reports and habitual fears, McClellan would surely have acted as he did.

90. *O.R., 14*, 530–531.

91. Freeman, *op. cit.*, pp. 220–221.

92. *Ibid.*, p. 223.

93. Michie, *op. cit.*, p. 302.

94. *Ibid.*, p. 312.

95. *Ibid.*, p. 313. Palfrey (*Papers, Mil. Hist. Soc. Mass.*, 1895 ed., I, 199), who was present in Sedgwick's division that crossed a shaky bridge to reenforce the troops on the south of the river, did not mention McClellan's illness, but said: "I am clear that he ought to have come upon the ground, and fought his own battle. He did not do this." McClellan's illness was certainly not serious.

96. *O.R., 12*, 130–131.

97. No casualties were reported for either the Fifth or Sixth Corps (*ibid.*, p. 762). The losses in the Fourth Corps slightly exceeded the combined losses in the Second and Third, which were essentially equal.

NOTES TO CHAPTER VII

1. *O.R., 15*, 643.

2. *Ibid.*, pp. 11–12.

3. *Ibid.*, p. 644.

4. *Ibid.*, pp. 643, 644.

5. *Ibid.*, p. 645. In a dispatch Stanton received at 2:30 P.M., May 24, Frémont had explained how very low his rations were; he had just secured beef, the only food he then had, and he wanted the authority to purchase 400 horses, which was given to him in Lincoln's order to move to Harrisonburg (*ibid.*, pp. 643–644).

6. *Ibid.*, Atlas, II, Plate LXXXV-1.

7. *Ibid., 15*, 646–647.

8. *Ibid., 18*, 627.

9. *Ibid., 15*, 647.

10. *Ibid.*, pp. 647–648.

11. Shields to McDowell, May 30, *ibid.*, p. 682.

12. Jackson's report, *ibid.*, p. 707.

13. Shields to McDowell, *loc. cit.*; McDowell to Stanton, May 31, *ibid., 18*, 299.

14. Harman to Jackson, *ibid., 15*, 721–722.

15. *O.R., 18*, 293–294.

16. Henderson, *Stonewall Jackson,* pp. 251–252.

17. *O.R., 15,* 707.

18. *Ibid., 18,* 279. For Shields's excellent reply, see *ibid.,* pp. 280–282. He told McDowell to inform Washington that he would be in Washington the next night, and asked, "General, have you any particular suggestions as to the course to pursue?" In reply McDowell said, "You will go forward with your whole division; none left behind for guards. Ord's division shall be on your heels if I can get them there."

19. *Ibid.,* p. 298.

20. Freeman, *Lee's Lieutenants,* I, p. 415.

21. *O.R., 15,* 649.

22. *Ibid.*

23. On May 26 Lincoln addressed a communication to Congress about a resolution censuring former Secretary of War Cameron. He stated that in the matter which had been referred to, he and all members of the cabinet were equally responsible (*ibid., 123,* 73–75).

24. *Ibid., 15,* 649–650.

25. McDowell to Stanton, quoting Shields, *ibid., 18,* 298.

26. *Ibid.,* p. 302.

27. In the long paper which McDowell presented to the Court of Inquiry appointed at his request to examine charges made against him later in the summer, he gave an account of all his operations beginning Apr. 1. Though he was trying to put his own record in as good a light as possible he did not even intimate that Shields should have marched on Strasburg on May 31 (*ibid., 15,* 283). The paper was written in Feb., 1863, and Shields was soon out of the army, having resigned because of the Senate's failure to confirm Lincoln's recommendation of his promotion. Actually Shields did not have his division well concentrated until the morning of June 1, having thrown part of it northward on a reconnaissance while other parts held roads to the south (Shields to Schriver, *ibid., 18,* 315). McDowell evidently approved of his action.

28. *O.R.,* Atlas, I, Plate XXVII–1, indicates it as a "common road" as distinguished from a "turnpike" or "stage road." Writing from Rectortown Shields spoke of "the Strasburg turnpike road" and "the Front Royal road" (*O.R., 18,* 280–281). His meaning is not clear.

29. Henderson states that the bridges had been destroyed (*op. cit.,* p. 270). Actually the railroad bridge was standing, as will be noted presently. A large-scale map of the Strasburg area in 1864 shows no road bridge at that time (*O.R.,* Atlas, I, Plate LXXXII–9).

30. Henderson, *op. cit.,* pp. 268, 267, where it is asserted that Shields "had done nothing more than push a brigade towards Winchester, and place strong pickets on every road by which the enemy might approach." The inference is unmistakable.

31. *Ibid.,* pp. 270, 269, 267, 288.

32. McDowell's statement to Court of Inquiry, *O.R., 15,* 283.

33. *Ibid.,* p. 677.

34. *Ibid., 18,* 314, two messages.

35. Shields to Schriver, 11:00 P.M., May 31, *ibid., 15,* 682–683. Freeman (*op.*

cit., p. 419) interpreted the action as occurring halfway between Front Royal and Strasburg; reference should be to *O.R.*, XII, pt. 3, p. 314. Shields's state- ment that the enemy was "pursued back in the direction of Winchester" indi- cates that the engagement was north of Front Royal.

36. On May 31 Banks had some troops in Martinsburg (*ibid.*, pp. 535–536).
37. *Ibid.*, *18*, 315.
38. *Ibid.*, *15*, 650.
39. Henderson, *op. cit.*, pp. 268, 265.
40. *O.R.*, *15*, 650–651.
41. Henderson, *op. cit.*, p. 270.
42. *O.R.*, *15*, 651.
43. *Ibid.*
44. Frémont's report, *ibid.*, p. 16.
45. *Ibid.*, pp. 540, 541. Freeman states (*op. cit.*, p. 407), "Not until June 9 were any of Banks's infantry re-equipped and ready for active operations." The claim is not supported by the reference given and is contradicted by several dispatches of Banks. On June 2 he wired Stanton that he had not lost over 1,000 small arms; the same day he stated that his advance was at Winchester, and that he had several regiments at Martinsburg; the next day he stated that Crawford's brigade of 3,000 men was expected in Winchester on the 4th (*O.R.*, *15*, 538, 539).
46. *Ibid.*, p. 653.
47. Carroll's report, *ibid.*, pp. 698–700.
48. Allan, *Valley Campaign*, p. 187; Freeman, *op. cit.*, pp. 439–440.
49. Carroll's report, *loc. cit.*
50. *O.R.*, *15*, 19.
51. *Ibid.*, p. 25.
52. Shields's report, *ibid.*, p. 685.
53. *Ibid.*, pp. 711–716.
54. Freeman, *op. cit.*, p. 461.
55. Frémont's report, *O.R.*, *15*, 21–22.
56. *D.A.B.* states that Shields was courteous in manner, graceful and humor- ous in debate, but that his temper was sharp, while he was arrogantly inde- pendent and was something of a demogogue.
57. Shields to Schriver, in Schriver to McDowell, *O.R.*, *18*, 367–368. On Oct. 3, 1862, McDowell wrote to the adjutant general of the Army, "Both the condition of General Shields' division and that of the roads and rivers, as represented by him, indicated anything [else] than the success he anticipated" (*ibid.*, *15*, 689).
58. *Ibid.*, *15*, 685, 688.
59. *Ibid.*, p. 23. Frémont said that his pontoon bridge was in use at Mount Jackson, but that plans were under way to build a bridge from local materials.
60. *Ibid.*, p. 655.
61. *Ibid.*, p. 24.
62. *Ibid.*, *18*, 367–368. In forwarding Shields's long dispatch Schriver told McDowell he did not think any of the corps could take the field in less than a fortnight, except King's division.

63. *Ibid., 15,* 683–684.

64. McDowell to Schriver, June 8, *ibid., 18,* 363, 364. McDowell said that Shields had forgotten his "instructions not to move his force so that the several parts should not always be in supporting distance of each other." At 9:30 A.M. Schriver passed the criticism on in about as plain language as a lieutenant colonel could use to a general with a dueling record.

65. Shields to Schriver, *ibid., 15,* 683–684; also report, *ibid.,* p. 686.

66. Herndon, *Life of Lincoln,* pp. 183–205.

67. *O.R., 15,* 689.

68. *Ibid., 18,* 414.

69. Hendrick, *Lincoln's War Cabinet,* p. 247.

70. *O.R., 18,* 420.

71. Freeman, *op. cit.,* p. 410 n.

72. Hudson, *Journalism in the U.S.,* p. 337. There were some papers that appeared only on Sunday, and a very few dailies issued Sunday editions. The war itself stimulated Sunday papers, but when the *N.Y. Tribune* brought one out, the remonstrance was so great that it was given up.

73. *N.Y. Tribune,* May 26 and 27, 1862. Stanton had telegraphed Banks (*O.R., 15,* 529): "Your telegram this morning received. We rejoice greatly at your safety. Do you need ammunition to enable you to dispute the enemy's crossing of the river, or anything else?"

74. Henderson, *op. cit.,* p. 263.

75. *O.R., 123,* 69–70, 72, 85, 86.

76. *Ibid.,* pp. 98–101.

77. Henderson, *op. cit.,* p. 263. He grossly exaggerates when he states that the governors of the thirteen states called on their militia to march to Washington. Actually some of the governors reported they had no militia available, and none of them said anything about *marching.*

78. *O.R., 123,* 101, 108, 109; Henderson, *loc. cit.*

79. Freeman, *op. cit.,* p. 409. Referring to Stanton's call for troops, he writes, "President Lincoln was relieved in spirit immediately." Without good authority this must be regarded as imaginative—like Henderson's statement about troops marching to Washington. Lincoln could call for troops whenever he wished; he did not have to wait for action by Stanton.

80. *O.R., 18,* 275–276, 279.

81. *Ibid., 15,* 573. Capt. James W. Abert was a regular officer of the topographical engineers, so that his estimate should have been accurate.

82. Casualty report, *ibid.,* p. 690.

83. James F. Huntington, "Winchester to Port Republic," *Mil. Hist. Soc. Mass.,* I, 336 (1895). This paper by the commander of a participating battery is an excellent illustration of both the value and the inadequacies of personal accounts. Huntington is in general very critical of Shields but does not question the orders he had received when he entered Front Royal. Of Carroll's failure to burn the bridge at Port Republic, he writes: "It was afterwards much debated whether General Carroll's orders were to burn, or hold, the bridge at Port Republic. So accurate a writer as the Comte de Paris asserts the latter. I know, for I have seen them, that Carroll's instructions contained no reference

to the bridge one way or the other. What he should have done about it, of his own volition is another matter" (p. 328). Naturally Shields said nothing in his orders about a bridge which he believed already destroyed. But he afterward criticized Carroll strongly for not burning it, writing to Schriver on June 12, "He held it for three-quarters of an hour and wanted the good sense to burn it" (*O.R., 15,* 683–684).

84. Shields to Schriver, *O.R., 15,* 684–685.

85. *Ibid., 18,* 368.

86. *Ibid.,* pp. 267, 279.

87. J. E. Edmonds, "The First Battle of the Marne," *Encyc. Brit.,* 14th ed., XIV, 931.

88. McDowell to Schriver, *O.R., 18,* 363; Schriver to Shields, *ibid., 15,* 690.

89. *Ibid., 18,* 364.

90. R. L. Dabney, *Jackson,* p. 429.

91. Freeman, *op. cit.,* p. 410.

92. *O.R., 15,* 685.

NOTES TO CHAPTER VIII

1. McClellan to Stanton, *O.R., 14,* 217.

2. *Harper's Weekly,* VI, 258 (Apr. 26, 1862), which, though it had generally supported McClellan, stated significantly: "McClellan has not yet commanded in a great battle as Grant, Buell, Lyon, Siegel, Curtis, and McDowell have, therefore his generalship in the field upon a large scale is to be tested. . . . Should he capture Richmond, every cloud of uncertainty rolls away from his name."

3. *O.R., 12,* 46.

4. *Ibid., 14,* 216, 217.

5. *Ibid.,* p. 219.

6. *Ibid., 12,* 46.

7. Eckenrode and Conrad (*McClellan,* p. 73) say: "While Lincoln sincerely desired McClellan's success and wished to aid him, Stanton hoped to be able to get rid of him before a decisive battle was fought. Stanton also desired success, but under a new commander." Nothing is given to support the strong contention about Stanton, and the statement as a whole is not in agreement with McClellan's assertion (*Own Story,* p. 242) that "the administration, and especially the Secretary of War," were inimical to him and did not desire his success. That charge included Lincoln, and it is not apparent how Eckenrode and Conrad clear him and leave Stanton guilty.

8. *O.R., 14,* 207, 138. On May 4 Stanton wired Wool, "The President desires to know whether your force is in condition for a sudden movement, if one should be ordered, under your command. Please have it in readiness." Wool's reply of the next day is as characteristic: "My infantry are ready to march at any moment, with provisions, ammunition, etc. I have one field battery ready for the field. If I had horses, I could fit out three fine batteries." He had given wagons to McClellan, and the deficiency might, he said, delay him "a day or two."

9. *Ibid., 12,* 634–635.

10. Myers handles the question carelessly, to say the least, in *McClellan,* pp. 284–285. He asserts that McClellan lost Blenker's division on Mar. 31, Wool's force on Apr. 3, and McDowell's corps in the course of the campaign. The first statement is accurate, the others are deceptive. Wool's force was not even on McClellan's return for Mar. 31. McDowell was lost at the start of the campaign, but most of his troops were returned during the course of operations. Barnard's statement that McClellan had expressed the wish to be rid of Blenker's division is discussed later.

11. *O.R., 14,* 239. The strength present and absent on Mar. 31 was 214,983 (*ibid.,* p. 53). Deduct 32,625 for Banks, 22,410 at Washington, and 1,459 at Alexandria; there is left 158,489, which checks closely with the figure for Apr. 1. Thus the latter figure includes Banks and McDowell.

12. The combined strength of Franklin's division, Fort Monroe command, and McCall's division was 32,360 present (*ibid.,* p. 239). In addition, the engineer brigade of McDowell's corps should be included. Taking its strength as 1,800, it is seen that there were sent to McClellan by way of restitution or replacement at least 34,000 men plus the seven regiments mentioned by Stanton (*ibid.,* p. 219), which gives a total certainly of 40,000 men. McDowell's strength present on Mar. 31 was 35,943 (*ibid.,* p. 53). Blenker's strength present should have been between 8,000 and 9,000 on the basis of 27,907 for Sumner's corps of three divisions. Consequently the number of men "present" who were withheld must have been a little under 45,000. On June 9 Dix reported to Stanton that after sending nine regiments forward to McClellan he had about 9,500 men left (*ibid.,* p. 219). This would indicate a possible greater contingent from Fort Monroe than was contained in the 32,360 figure above.

13. Marshall, *Aide-de-Camp of Lee,* p. 80 n.

14. *O.R., 14,* 201, 208–209.

15. *Ibid.,* p. 240.

16. McClellan to Stanton, *ibid.,* pp. 241, 253.

17. Eckenrode and Conrad, *op. cit.,* pp. 74–75. Bill states that by 1864 the population had increased three and a half times (*Beleaguered City,* p. 191).

18. Eisenschiml, *Why Was Lincoln Murdered?* p. 334.

19. *O.R., 5,* 51–52.

20. Some of his dispatches that give an exaggerated figure are included in the memoirs, so that McClellan suggests a great strength for Lee, without actually asserting it.

21. *O.R., 14,* 235–236.

22. *Ibid.,* pp. 225, 232–233. This does not look like the meddling of which Bill and others speak.

23. *Ibid.,* pp. 240–242.

24. *Ibid., 12,* 49.

25. *Ibid.*

26. Freeman, *Lee's Lieutenants,* I, 497.

27. *O.R., 14,* 232–234.

28. *Mil. Hist. Soc. Mass.,* I, 208–209.

29. *O.R., 14,* 589–590.

30. *Ibid.,* pp. 251–252.

31. *Ibid., 12,* 51.

32. *Ibid., 14,* 259.

33. *Ibid.,* p. 254.

34. *Ibid.,* pp. 257, 252–253.

35. *Ibid.,* p. 260.

36. *Ibid.*

37. *Ibid.,* pp. 264–265.

38. Freeman, *Lee,* II, 157.

39. *O.R., 13,* 662.

40. Marshall's papers (*op. cit.,* pp. 90–91), edited by Maurice, discuss the risk to which Lee's operation exposed Richmond. The claim that Lee could re-cross and attack McClellan in rear if the latter attacked Richmond is invalid, for the lower bridges were out. In a footnote Maurice quotes Lee's answer to Davis, "I will be on McClellan's tail," as the reply that Lee gave the Confederate President when the latter raised the question as to the safety of the city if Lee concentrated heavily against McClellan's right. There is no doubt that Lee was much disturbed on the night of June 26, for he sent repeated instructions to Magruder to hold his position at the point of the bayonet if necessary, and he was uneasy on June 28 also, according to Magruder's report. In his own report, Lee stated, "The bridges over the Chickahominy in rear of the enemy were destroyed, and their reconstruction impracticable in the presence of his whole army and powerful batteries" (*O.R., 13,* 494). The sentence disposes of the contention that Lee would have been on McClellan's tail if the latter had struck at Richmond.

41. *O.R., 14,* 265, 266.

42. *Ibid., 13,* 430.

43. *Ibid., 14,* 267, 268–269. Earlier in the day (1:20 P.M.) McClellan had informed Goldsborough that he was ordering supplies sent up the James and asked protection for them (*ibid.,* p. 267).

44. *Ibid., 12,* 61.

45. Bates, *Lincoln in the Telegraph Office,* pp. 109–112.

46. A return for June 20 gave the present-for-duty strength of the Army of the Potomac as 115,102 (total present, 127,327); present and absent, 156,838. Deducting the 9,277 present for duty at Fort Monroe from 115,102, leaves 105,825 men present for duty in front of Richmond.

Freeman (*Lee II,* 116–117) observes that there are no Confederate returns for June 20–25 and gives the estimates of four writers, which range from 80,762 to 86,500 as Lee's strength. He accepts 85,500 effectives as of June 26 and breaks the figure down into ten components, chiefly divisional. On the other hand, Myers accepts without any analysis the strange figures of Col. Livermore (*Numbers and Losses,* p. 86) for "effectives engaged": 91,169, Union; 95,481, Confederate.

For the Confederates Livermore worked back from a strength return for July 20 by adding the losses in the battles of June 25 to July 1, but without making allowance for the fact that during the period July 2–20 (a very active period of strengthening and refitting on the part of Lee), newly conscripted men were added, and many men returned, including sick and wounded.

47. Michie, *General McClellan*, p. 347.

48. McClellan's justification of his retreat in his memoirs (pp. 422–423) is weak. He completely ignores the possibility of seizing a position in front of Richmond and holding it. After raising the question of why he did not march on Richmond in view of the fact that most of the enemy was on the left bank of the Chickahominy, he wants one to believe that, because that did not seem advisable, he had to retreat.

Various Southern writers have defended McClellan. Thus Allan (*Valley Campaign*, p. 150), quoting from McClellan's report, argues that McClellan had to keep part of his force north of the Chickahominy because McDowell was ultimately expected; and he asserts that this contributed to McClellan's defeat. This ignores the fact that Lee had to divide his army in order to attack McClellan, and had the bulk of it on the wrong side of the river after Porter had retired.

49. *O.R., 14*, 250–251, 141.

50. For Pope's mission, see *ibid., 18*, 435.

51. Eckenrode and Conrad, *op. cit.*, p. 100. These authors make extraordinary claims for McClellan. The assertion that he "was in a class by himself" in logistics may have been true, but in another sense than was intended. Most commanders would have had a road reconnaissance made.

52. Freeman, *op. cit.*, pp. 243, 236.

53. *O.R.*, Atlas, I, Plate XIX-1.

54. *O.R., 12*, 64.

55. *O.R.*, Atlas, II, Plate XCII, Map 1, Section 1. The road from Long Bridge south past Samaria Church is well shown in McClellan's map, but the connecting road from White Oak Swamp is not shown, although the beginning of it is suggested. The roads are also shown on a less detailed Confederate map made in 1862 and 1863, bearing Lee's signature under date of Apr. 3, 1863 (*ibid.*, I, Plate XX-1).

56. Report of chief quartermaster, Brig. Gen. Stewart Van Vliet, *O.R., 12*, 159.

57. *Ibid.*, p. 158. Van Vliet's figures for forage indicated something like 28,000 animals. Even without taking careful account of cavalry and artillery horses it looks as if his figures for wagons may be high. Eckenrode and Conrad (*op. cit.*, p. 100) speak of 5,000 wagons and ambulances but cite no authority.

58. *O.R., 14*, 326–327.

59. *Ibid., 12*, 64.

60. Ingalls to Meigs, *ibid., 14*, 326–327.

61. Keyes's report, *ibid., 13*, 193.

62. Barnard's report, *ibid., 12*, 118–119.

63. Alexander's report, *ibid.*, p. 140.

64. When he wrote his report McClellan saw the difficulty he was in over roads. He stated with reference to June 30, "The engineer officer whom I had sent forward on the 28th to reconnoitre the roads had neither returned, nor sent me any reports or guides" (*ibid.*, p. 64). He was evidently referring to Alex-

ander and the two engineer officers that accompanied him, but they had *not* been given the mission of looking for roads to the James in addition to the Quaker Road. Alexander wrote his report on July 12, 1862; McClellan wrote his in Aug., 1863. In the intervening year McClellan naturally had forgotten details; but even if his statement had been true it would not have extricated him from his difficulty. What kind of staff officers did he have, and why had he not sent out others on June 29? As a matter of fact, Alexander had reported by noon on that day. McClellan also asserted that Keyes and Porter had not made reports about the roads they had used. Why should they? Corps commanders are busy men and should not have to do the work of the army commander. If McClellan expected his corps commanders to find their roads to the James and *report* on the routes, he should have so directed.

65. Keyes's report, *ibid., 13,* 193.

66. Porter's report, *ibid.,* p. 228.

67. McClellan stated definitely that the battle of Frayser's Farm was fought in order to protect his trains: "It was therefore necessary to post the troops in advance of this road [Quaker Road], as well as our limited knowledge of the ground permitted, so as to cover the movement of the trains in the rear" (*ibid., 12,* 64).

68. *Ibid., 13,* 431.

69. Franklin, "Rear-Guard Fighting During the Change of Base," *B. and L.,* II, 381.

70. Heintzelman remonstrated when informed of Franklin's proposed retirement, for his rear would then be threatened by Jackson, who could easily cross White Oak Swamp. Both Heintzelman and Sumner were expecting orders from McClellan, but took counsel together and withdrew.

71. *O.R., 13,* 493. At first Lee could not tell whether McClellan was retreating to the James or intended to cross the Chickahominy by lower bridges and go toward Fort Monroe. He stated that in the latter case he wanted to have the bulk of his army on the left of the Chickahominy, and so did not have Longstreet and A. P. Hill cross until he was assured that McClellan was not moving down the peninsula. If Longstreet and Hill had crossed on the 28th and it had been found later that McClellan was headed for Fort Monroe, their troops could have been a pursuing force, while Jackson, still north of the river, would have had a flanking column. This would have reversed the roles the forces had in the pursuit of McClellan to the James.

Lee sent Ewell to guard Bottom's bridge on the Williamsburg road and had cavalry watch the lower bridges. If he had had the bridges promptly destroyed, McClellan would have been much delayed in any move down the peninsula and could have been attacked at great disadvantage. Below the three bridges that were being watched the Chickahominy rapidly becomes a wide and difficult stream. Lee would have been playing reasonably safe with odds in his favor if he had sent Longstreet and Hill across the river on the afternoon of the 28th.

72. Freeman, *op. cit.,* pp. 163–165; Henderson, *Stonewall Jackson,* pp. 375–383. For an able discussion not in agreement with Henderson, see the letter from Wade Hampton in Marshall, *op. cit.,* pp. 109–112.

73. Frothingham, "The Peninsular Campaign of 1862," *Proc. Mass. Hist.*

Soc., LVII. Myers calls this one of the ablest analyses of the Seven Days' Battles ever written, in spite of the fact that Frothingham makes no reference to the Official Records. An example of Frothingham's distortions is furnished by the statement (p. 110), completely disproved by McClellan's own report, "McClellan had the country on the proposed line of march surveyed, and maps made, which were very necessary in such a country where maps were unknown."

74. Livermore, *Numbers and Losses,* p. 86; Freeman, *op. cit.,* p. 230.

75. Lee stated (*O.R., 13,* 494): "At Savage Station were found about 2,500 men in hospital and a large amount of property. Stores of much value had been destroyed, including the necessary medical supplies for the sick and wounded." Freeman (*op. cit.,* p. 264) says, "Lee had felt that McClellan had been brutal in destroying the medicine needed for the sick and wounded left behind at Savage Station."

76. *O.R., 14,* 272.

77. Surgeon Charles S. Tripler left with the senior surgeon who remained with the sick and wounded a letter addressed to "The Commanding General Confederate Forces or Commanding Officer." It closed, "A large amount of clothing, bedding, medical stores, etc., have been left both at Savage Station and at Dr. Trent's house" (*ibid., 12,* 191). The division of the supplies into two parts indicated a special effort to prevent destruction; and, whatever may have happened to those at the station, it seems unlikely that the part at Dr. Trent's house was not found. Tripler's letter should have been the basis of an accurate report to Lee.

78. *Ibid., 14,* 280.

NOTES TO CHAPTER IX

1. *O.R., 14,* 270.
2. *Ibid.*
3. *Ibid.,* pp. 270, 271.
4. *Ibid., 123,* 179–180.
5. *Ibid., 14,* 277
6. *Ibid., 123,* 181–182.
7. *Ibid.,* pp. 186–188.
8. McClellan to the Governor of New York, July 15, 1862, to the Governor of New Jersey, Aug. 1, *ibid., 14,* 323, 347. See Upton, *Military Policy,* p. 437, for both figures and discussion.
9. Upton, *op. cit.,* pp. 440–443.
10. *O.R., 123,* 185.
11. On July 14 a War Department order sought to remove some of the evils resulting from furloughs to sick and wounded men (*ibid.,* pp. 221–222). On July 31 an order annulled as of Aug. 11 all leaves and furloughs except those granted by the War Department. Every regiment was required to be mustered on Aug. 18, and lists of absentees were to be sent in. U.S. marshals, mayors, chiefs of police, postmasters, and justices of the peace were named "as special provost-marshals to arrest any officer or private soldier fit for duty who may be

found absent from his command without just cause and convey him to the nearest military post or depot" (*ibid.*, pp. 286–287).

Upton's *Military Policy*, in the chapter "Influence of the States in Depleting Our Armies," points to certain special evils, including state hospitals. It is doubtful whether a person with Upton's ardent disposition could analyze any complex question accurately and fairly.

12. *O.R., 12*, 185.

13. *Ibid.*, pp. 188–195.

14. Lincoln and Stanton to Seward, *ibid., 14,* 274–275. Fulton intimated very successful operations by the Federals to the *N.Y. Tribune;* but at 11:00 P.M. June 29 he informed it in a dispatch published the next day that the Secretary of War would release nothing.

15. *O.R., 14,* 274–275.

16. *N.Y. Tribune*, July 2.

17. *O.R., 14,* 277.

18. *N.Y. Tribune.*

19. *Ibid.*, July 7.

20. *Harper's Weekly,* VI, 450, 451 (July 19, 1862), article "McClellan" and editorial "Who Did It?" That the stopping of recruiting reflected popular feeling was shown in the editorial by the statement: "It must never be forgotten that we are learning to make war by experience. When it is the universal conviction that half a million volunteers are enough, a call for a million, upon the plea that the more the men the surer the result, would fall heavily upon the public ear." Recruiting was stopped before the Confederate conscription act was passed. It would seem that there must have been knowledge in the North that such an act was contemplated, though neither its passage nor its nature could have been predicted.

21. Quoted in *N.Y. Tribune*, July 9.

22. *Ibid.*, July 21. Livermore, *Numbers and Losses,* p. 46, gives "No. on Confederate Returns" as 401,392 on Mar. 3, 1862, and 463,891 on Jan. 1, 1863.

23. Blackford, *War Years with Stuart,* pp. 76–77.

24. *O.R., 14,* 279.

25. Halleck to Stanton, Stanton to Seward, *ibid.*, pp. 285, 276–277.

26. *Ibid.*, pp. 281, 286, 291–292, 294, 298–299, 301–303.

27. McClellan's report, *ibid., 12,* 73–74; Leech, *Reveille in Washington,* p. 176. McClellan made the direful prediction, "A declaration of radical views, especially upon slavery, will rapidly disintegrate our present armies."

28. *General McClellan,* p. 371.

29. On June 20 McClellan asked Lincoln's permission to lay before him his views on military affairs throughout the country, and asked for the numbers and disposition of troops not under his command. Lincoln replied the next day that he would be glad to have the general's ideas if it did not divert too much of his time and attention from the army under his immediate command, but security reasons made it inadvisable to telegraph information: "I would be glad to talk with you, but you cannot leave your camp and I cannot well leave here" (*O.R., 12,* 48). Perhaps it was failure to get the desired military data that led McClellan to take up politics as his "extracurricular activity."

30. *Ibid., 14,* 316. The letter was sent by a "confidential officer."

31. *Ibid.,* pp. 314–315.

32. Leech, *op. cit.,* p. 179.

33. *O.R., 14,* 295–297.

34. *Ibid.,* pp. 306, 299.

35. Lee's report, *ibid., 13,* 497; Freeman, *Lee,* II, 256.

36. *O.R., 18,* 473–474.

37. *Ibid., 16,* 50. A strong order on pillaging was issued on Aug. 14, and on Aug. 16 Ruggles directed Sigel to arrest the provost-marshal of Steinwehr's division on account of plundering and pillage (*ibid., 18,* 573, 577). The letter directed: "Parties caught plundering the country will be treated as common robbers and shot upon the spot, whenever and wherever found by the patrols from any army corps or any detachment sent out for that purpose. Commanders will be held responsible that they exercise proper restraint upon their men."

38. *N.Y. Tribune,* Aug. 1, 1862.

39. *O.R., 16,* 51, 52.

40. *N.Y. Tribune,* July 22.

41. *O.R., 18,* 500–501.

42. Halleck to McClellan, Aug. 7, *ibid., 14,* 359–360. This was an interesting official letter in reply to a personal letter.

43. The author recalls an extreme order on the subject of fraternization that was issued to some units in the Army of Occupation after World War I, which was recalled a few hours after issue, but which would probably have been quite generally ignored.

44. Lincoln wrote to Halleck, July 14 (*ibid.,* p. 321): "I am very anxious—almost impatient—to have you here. . . . When can you reach here?"

45. *Ibid.,* pp. 337–338.

46. The number given in the strength return as on special duty, sick, and in arrest was 17,828. In his report to Stanton, Halleck conveyed McClellan's opinion that the enemy's force "was not less than 200,000," and added that most of McClellan's officers concurred. Such an estimate should refer to July 26, after it was known that Jackson and Ewell had left (McClellan to Stanton, Pope to McClellan, July 20, *ibid.,* pp. 328, 329). On July 19 McClellan had informed Pope: "The enemy not within 10 miles of me in large force. Has fallen back to vicinity of Richmond and Petersburg. I cannot tell whether he has any designs on you or not."
   On June 26 Pinkerton presented McClellan a report stating, "The summary of general estimates of the rebel army shows their forces to be at this time over 180,000 men," and on Aug. 14 he presented another report stating, "The summary of general estimates shows 200,000 men to have composed the rebel army of Richmond about the time of the Seven-days' Battle" (*ibid., 12,* 269, 270). To the later report was appended a list of various estimates of enemy strength. They went as high as 260,000, so that McClellan had support for almost any opinion he wished to advance. Included was the statement, "Beauregard's forces are believed to be mostly in Richmond."

47. At the trial a few months later of Gen. Porter, Burnside testified (*ibid.,*

17, 1005): "Two-thirds of the officers of the Army of the Potomac with whom I met on the James River were favorable to the withdrawal of the army, and three-fourths of the general officers with whom I met and talked were favorable to the withdrawal; and an informal council of war, where I was myself present, decided that it ought to be done, a majority of the general officers in the council being in favor of the withdrawal. I came down on a steamer from Harrison's Landing, and of all the officers I met there was not one single one who did not urge upon and argue with me the necessity of withdrawing the Army of the Potomac from the James River."

48. Keyes to Meigs, *ibid.*, 14, 331–333. The letter contains some strong statements: "I find that a majority of the generals are beginning to droop. . . . I will say that to pen up more than 100,000 men and animals in a space so small that you can find no point of that space which is one mile distant from its outside boundary on the James River in the months of July, August, and September is to secure disease, weakness, and nostalgia as a certain crop." Although he wrote chiefly of existing conditions and future actions, Keyes said, "This army has lost golden opportunities." He added that if he could see Meigs he would explain how they had been lost. A postscript by Keyes states that he held the letter two days for further reflection. An indorsement of July 28 by Meigs referred the letter to Halleck.

49. Medical Director Letterman to Surgeon General Hammond, July 29, *ibid.*, p. 341. McClellan wrote to Lincoln on July 15 that the number of officers and men present sick was 16,619.

50. Lincoln wrote July 13 of being told that more than 160,000 men had gone to the army on the Peninsula (*ibid.*, p. 319). After making various deductions he had 45,000 men "still alive and not with it"; and he asked, "How can they be got to you, and how can they be prevented from getting away in such numbers in the future?" In his reply of July 15 (*ibid.*, pp. 321–322) McClellan admitted that many well men got away with the sick and wounded after the battles of Williamsburg and Fair Oaks. He stated: 'I can now control people getting away better. . . . Leakages by desertion occur in every army . . . but I do not at all however anticipate anything like a recurrence of what has taken place." The Confederate army also suffered badly from "absenteeism," but it was much easier for Lee's men to get away than for McClellan's on the Peninsula.

51. *Ibid.*, pp. 340–341. The President, in his letter of July 13 to McClellan, suggested that half or two-thirds of the men absent were fit for duty, and said, "If I am right, and you had these men with you, you could go into Richmond in the next three days." This statement may have been extravagant; but it shows that Lincoln did not believe that Lee had anything remotely resembling 200,000 men.

52. Something like 400 ships were required to supply McClellan's army, and doubling the number would have probably presented a very difficult problem. To withdraw the army rapidly, Meigs called in approximately 200 more vessels for temporary duty (Meigs to Tompkins, and Meigs to McClellan, *ibid.*, pp. 371–372). Even before the withdrawal had been decided upon, McClellan's insistent demand for more ferryboats was causing trouble (McClellan to Halleck—two dispatches—Meigs to Halleck, Meigs to McClellan, *ibid.*, pp. 351, 353–354).

53. Aston, *Marshal Foch*, title page.

54. Henderson, *Stonewall Jackson*, p. 172.

55. *Ibid.*, p. 432.

56. Meigs to Belger, *O.R.*, *14*, 341; Halleck to McClellan, *ibid.*, *12*, 76–77.

57. *Ibid.*, *18*, 524.

58. *Ibid.*, *12*, 80–81.

59. *Ibid.*, pp. 81–82.

60. *Ibid.*, pp. 82–84. Freeman (*Lee*, II, 276 n.) speaks of Halleck as prevailing upon Lincoln and Stanton to order the abandonment of the Peninsula Campaign.

61. *O.R.*, *14*, 359–360.

62. McClellan's report, *ibid.*, *12*, 80–90; especially dispatch of Aug. 19. The thing that would go furthest to clear McClellan of the charges of unnecessary delay would be Ingalls's letter of Aug. 15 to Meigs (*ibid.*, *14*, 377), stating: "We have embarked troops from this point to the full extent of our ability. Colonel Falls and others will tell you so. . . . Up to this moment the thing could not have been done faster."

63. Halleck's first instructions to McClellan about getting rid of sick and wounded clearly indicated that it was desired to have McClellan prepared for any move whatever that might be ordered (*ibid.*, *12*, 76–77). McClellan began to argue that he could not tell which of his sick, etc., to get rid of until he knew what move was expected of him. On Aug. 3 he stated: "As I am not in any way informed of the intentions of the Government with regard to this army, I am unable to judge what proportion of the sick should leave here, and must ask for specific orders" (*ibid.*, p. 80). This was just quibbling, for McClellan knew that the removal of his army was being considered. Although his attitude may not actually have been responsible for any delay, it is not strange that it aroused Halleck's suspicions.

Gen. Sumner's dispatch of Aug. 5 to Gen. John Cochrane in Washington expressed the conviction that "if we had a re-enforcement of 20,000 men we could walk straight into Richmond," and requested, "Do represent this in the right quarter" (*ibid.*, *14*, 356). McClellan may not have seen the irregular dispatch, but it bore the approval of his chief of staff. On Aug. 12 McClellan discussed an operation against Richmond in a message to Halleck (*ibid.*, pp. 372–373).

64. *Ibid.*, *12*, 86.

65. Frémont to Stanton, *ibid.*, *18*, 437–438.

66. *Ibid.*, p. 444. Sigel in a long letter to Pope's chief of staff on July 5 described the confusion resulting in large part from the fact that Frémont had taken many papers and documents with him (*ibid.*, p. 455).

67. Barnard, *Peninsular Campaign*, p. 20.

68. See *O.R.*, *18*, 439, for inspection report.

69. *Ibid.*, p. 523.

70. Piatt to Pope and Pope to Piatt, *ibid.*, pp. 475, 483, 485.

71. *Ibid.*, *14*, 325–326.

72. *Ibid.*, pp. 327–329.

73. *Ibid.*, *18*, 487.

74. *Ibid.*, pp. 487–488.

75. Bayard to Schriver, *ibid.*, p. 488.
76. Banks to McDowell, *ibid.*, p. 492. A longer dispatch was sent to Pope.
77. Banks to McDowell, *ibid.*, p. 494.
78. *Ibid.*, pp. 489–490.
79. *Ibid.*, *14*, 328.
80. *Ibid.*, *18*, 490–491. Banks reported that the orders to Hatch had been forwarded (*ibid.*, p. 492).
81. McDowell to Ruggles, *ibid.*, p. 496. There had been a delay of four days in the original plan for Hatch's move as communicated to McClellan on the 17th.
82. *Ibid.*, p. 514.
83. Henderson, *op. cit.*, p. 401.
84. Freeman (*Lee*, II, 264) says that Lee had contempt as well as personal dislike for Pope.
85. Strother, "Personal Recollections of the War," *Harper's Monthly*, XXXV, 278 (Aug. 1867). This article is drawn upon without explicit reference in all cases. Strother spent July, 1862, in Washington, interviewing refugees, compiling information about roads, streams, etc.
86. Freeman, *Lee's Lieutenants*, II, 6.
87. *O.R.*, *18*, 535, 527. Lee stated that the reenforcements he was sending "will exceed 18,000 men" (*ibid.*, p. 918).
88. *Ibid.*, pp. 535–536.
89. Crawford to General, Bayard to Schriver, *ibid.*, pp. 541, 544–545.
90. Strother, *op. cit.*, p. 283. The information came from one of the refugees Strother had interviewed in Washington. He passed the report on to Pope and recorded in his diary, "The estimate of Jackson's force he said accorded with his own opinions." Bayard also reported that he had learned from a Negro that Ewell had crossed the Rapidan (*O.R.*, *18*, 550).
91. Barstow to Duffie and Allen, Barstow to Bayard, *ibid.*, p. 549. Only one battery is referred to; Strother is authority for two batteries. It is to be recalled that Bayard was in McDowell's corps, not Banks's.
92. *Ibid.*, pp. 547–548.
93. Pope to King, *ibid.*, pp. 548 ff. For expeditions conducted from Fredericksburg, notably one by the Sixth Wisconsin with some cavalry and two guns, see reports by King, Gibbon, and Cutler, *ibid.*, *16*, 121–125.
94. Strother, *loc. cit.*
95. Bayard to Schriver, *O.R.*, *16*, 130.
96. Douglas, *I Rode with Stonewall*, p. 50.
97. Ballard, *op. cit.*, p. 89.
98. *C.C.W.*, 1865, 4:54, under heading "Miscellaneous." For a slightly different version of the order furnished by the officer who took it down, see Ropes, *The Army Under Pope*, p. 20.
99. Freeman, *Lee*, II, 264; Lee to Randolph, *O.R.*, *13*, 936.
100. Pope to Halleck, Aug. 13, 1862, *ibid.*, *16*, 133–135. He said Banks "was directed not to advance beyond [Crawford's position], and if attacked by the enemy to defend his position and send back timely notice." Pope did not accuse Banks of not following instructions, saying merely, "General Banks advanced

to the attack." He also said, "I cannot speak too highly of the intrepidity and coolness of General Banks himself during the whole of the engagement."

After Banks had given the Committee on the Conduct of the War the order he asserted had been written down at Col. Marshall's dictation, Pope wrote very critically of him to the chairman of the committee (*C.C.W.*, 1865, 4:47–49). But the order he said Banks claimed to have received differed significantly from the one Banks actually gave the committee. Pope also furnished (*ibid.*, p. 54) a letter of Dec. 26, 1864, in which Col. Marshall gave the order according to his recollection: Banks was not to attack unless it became evident that the enemy would attack him; then, "in order to hold the advantage of being the attacking party," he was to attack with his "skirmishers thrown well to the front." Jackson's aggressiveness makes this look like an order to attack.

101. The brief description of the battle is based largely on the reports of Generals Williams, Augur, Crawford, and Gordon (*ibid., 16*), for the Federal operations. For accounts from the Confederate standpoint, see Henderson, *op. cit.*, chap. xv, and Freeman, *Lee's Lieutenants*, Vol. II, chap. ii.

102. Ruggles to Sigel, *O.R., 18, 547*–548.

103. Strother, *op. cit.*, pp. 284–287; Milroy's report, *O.R., 16*, 142.

104. Spencer to Pope or Banks, *O.R., 18, 559*.

105. Schriver to King, *ibid.*, p. 558.

106. *Ibid.*, pp. 556, 558, 561, 564.

107. *N.Y. Tribune*, Aug. 11 and 12, 1862.

108. *O.R., 16*, 133, 135.

109. Freeman (*Lee*, II, 261) states that Lee ordered Jackson and Ewell to proceed by *rail* to Louisa, but gives no authority. Douglas (*op. cit.*, p. 120) says, "The General went on in advance and we were soon far ahead of troops and wagon trains on the road to Ashland." This sounds much like a road march, as do other incidents related. Freeman (*Lee's Lieutenants*, II, 7–10) describes the trial of Garnett for retreating with the Stonewall Brigade at Kernstown.

110. *O.R., 18, 918*–919; Freeman, *Lee's Lieutenants*, II, 12–15.

111. Strother (*op. cit.*, p. 295) wrote: "When Jackson, ascertaining himself confronted by our concentrated forces, went tumbling back across the Rapidan under cover of night, abandoning many wounded and stragglers by the way, and barely saving his baggage, calling for reinforcements, and thanking the Lord for the victory in the same breath, we are at a loss to imagine the grounds for his pious gratitude."

Henderson (*op. cit.*, pp. 415–416) concedes that the Federals had covered themselves with glory, but nevertheless endorses the claim that Cedar Mountain was one of the most brilliant Southern achievements of the war, basing the view largely on the fact that Jackson remained in possession of the field. This simple criterion had been rejected by Jackson after the battle of Kernstown.

112. Freeman, *Lee's Lieutenants*, II, 23. By this time the Confederates had plenty of wagons—many of which had been bought by Meigs. For Lee to Jackson, protesting excessive transportation, see *O.R., 18*, 923.

113. Freeman, *op. cit.*, pp. 13–14.

114. Bayard to McDowell, Porter to Halleck, *O.R., 18*, 562, 579; Freeman, *op. cit.*, chap. ii.

115. Douglas, *op. cit.*, p. 128; *O. R., 18*, 923–924.

NOTES TO CHAPTER X

1. *O.R., 18,* 560.

2. At 8:00 P.M., July 20, Halleck informed McClellan that Pope reported that he had learned from deserters that the enemy had only a small force in Richmond, and concluded, "I suggest he be pressed in that direction, so as to ascertain the facts in the case." Hooker, with his division and Pleasonton's cavalry, was directed to seize Malvern Hill on the night of Aug. 2; but the operation failed because of incompetent guides. A second attempt on the night of the 4th was successful (*ibid., 12,* 76, 77–78). The *N.Y. Tribune* of Aug. 9 contained a report of the abortive attempt from a correspondent who wrote on the 7th, "I do not think it in violation of parole to state, at this late date, that the movement upon Malvern was to have been made two days earlier."

3. On Aug. 7 at 9:00 A.M., Lee wrote to Jackson from near New Market, four miles from Malvern Hill on a direct road to Richmond: "I am here in consequence of the reported advance of McClellan's army. I have no idea that he will advance on Richmond now, but it may be premonitory to get a new position, reconnoiter, etc." (*O.R., 18,* 925).

4. *Ibid.,* pp. 561, 564.

5. *Ibid.,* p. 565.

6. Burnside to Halleck, *ibid.,* p. 566. In order to detain Union troops at Fredericksburg, the enemy made some demonstrations against it. In fact, Burnside closed his dispatch, "The enemy drove in our pickets a few moments since, but I do not believe they are in force in front of us."

7. Pope to Halleck, Aug. 6 and 11, Halleck to Pope, Aug. 12, *ibid.,* pp. 540–541, 561, 565.

Pope had first suggested a march by Cox, which certainly would have been hazardous. On Aug. 9 Cox called attention to the difficulty and danger. The distance was 220 miles and he stated: "The country for the first hundred miles is desperately rough. I know nothing of the rest." He suggested falling back to the Ohio and making a river and rail trip. On Aug. 11 Pope ordered Cox to keep 5,000 of his men in West Virginia, sending the rest forward as he had suggested. On Aug. 20 Cox telegraphed Meigs that he would be at Parkersburg on the evening of the 20th, "with 5,000 infantry, two batteries of six guns each, 300 cavalry, and the camp equipage and regimental trains complete, going to join General Pope" (*ibid.,* pp. 555, 560–561, 570, 577).

8. *Ibid.,* pp. 568–569; Ingalls to Sawtelle, *ibid., 12,* 86–87.

9. McClellan's report, *ibid.,* pp. 88–89, 90. A dispatch from Dix to Halleck at 4:00 P.M., Aug. 16, stated, "General Porter crossed the Chickahominy yesterday with his *corps d'armée* and is at Williamsburg" (*ibid., 18,* 579).

10. *Ibid., 12,* 88.

11. Porter to McClellan and to Halleck, *ibid., 18,* 579.

12. Henderson, *Stonewall Jackson,* pp. 423–427. Freeman's statement (*Lee,* II, 280), "Pope's ignorance of Lee's movements had caused him incautiously to present his adversary as fair an opportunity as ever a soldier was offered," hardly puts the situation accurately or fairly.

13. *O.R., 18,* 575–576, 588, 589; Meigs to Halleck, pp. 596–597. On the morning of the 17th Pope telegraphed: "Reports from various sources represent large force to be moving from Richmond to join Jackson. I think it very likely to be true. . . . Our position is strong, and it will be very difficult to drive us from it." Freeman's implication is that Pope's position was weak.

14. *Ibid.,* pp. 565, 569.

15. *Ibid.,* p. 590.

16. *Ibid., 14,* 378.

17. Ropes (*Army Under Pope,* p. 12) commented that McClellan's Peninsula Campaign "had been characterized by an assumption on his part that he was entitled to deal on an equal footing with the Government as a sort of contracting party."

18. *O.R., 18,* 590.

19. McClellan to Heintzelman, to Porter and Heintzelman, and to Burnside, *ibid.,* pp. 599, 606, 605.

20. Pope's report, *ibid., 16,* 22. Freeman identifies the regiment (*Lee's Lieutenants,* II, 60 n.).

21. Stuart's report, *O.R., 16,* 726; Freeman, *op. cit.,* chap. iii.

22. Pope's report, *O.R., 16,* 29. Pope referred to "an autograph letter of General Robert E. Lee to General Stuart, dated Gordonsville, August 13, which made manifest to me the position and force of the enemy and their determination to overwhelm the army under my command before it could be re-enforced by any portion of the Army of the Potomac." In a dispatch to Halleck of Aug. 22 Pope referred to the letter, again giving its date as Aug. 13 (*ibid.,* pp. 58–59). The date is manifestly incorrect because Lee was not at Gordonsville on Aug. 13. Freeman suggests Aug. 16 as the correct date (*Lee,* II, 287 n.).

23. Freeman, *Lee's Lieutenants,* II, 62.

24. *O.R., 18,* 590–591. Halleck stated that although he was trying to get troops to Pope as rapidly as possible, he might not be able to sustain him beyond the Rappahannock if he were attacked by too large a force.

25. Freeman, *Lee,* II, 287. For discussion of Lee's delay in concentration see *ibid.,* 284, 286, and *Lee's Lieutenants,* II, 61.

26. Henderson, *op. cit.,* p. 425, laid the entire delay on Fitz Lee and the capture of Major Fitzhugh. He evidently did not study Pope's dispatches or his withdrawal order, and may have relied too much on adverse criticisms in Gordon's *The Army of Virginia* (this work is discussed in Appendix VIII).

27. Freeman, *Lee,* II, 288.

28. The use of three columns recalls an amusing incident related by Strother, "Personal Recollections of the War," *Harper's Monthly,* XXXV, 279 (Aug., 1867). When Pope took the field his staff secured for their headquarters a cook who professed previous service with Longstreet, and who constantly advised, "Advance in three columns."

29. *O.R., 18,* 598.

30. Strother, *op. cit.,* p. 704 (Nov., 1867).

31. *O.R., 18,* 594, 595.

32. Pope to Halleck, *ibid., 16,* 56–57, and *18,* 603.

33. *Ibid., 18,* 609.

34. Reno to Pope, *ibid.*, p. 610.

35. *Ibid.*, *16*, 58–59, 57.

36. *Ibid.*, *18*, 611, 612.

37. *Ibid.*, pp. 611–612.

38. Porter to McClellan, *ibid.*, pp. 616–617. In a telegram to Porter on the 22nd, McClellan stated, "I sent Harris with a large supply of ordnance last night" (*ibid.*, p. 628).

39. *Ibid.*, pp. 615–616, 606. To McClellan's injunction Porter replied, "I guess we shall have no trouble to hold out for five or six days" (*ibid*, *107*, 755). The supplementary volume of the *O.R.* just referred to contains numerous interesting dispatches relative to Pope's campaign.

40. Cox to Stanton and to Pope, *ibid.*, *18*, 619, 629.

41. On the 21st W. P. Smith of the B. & O. informed Assistant Secretary of War Watson that cars for 4,000 men and all the artillery horses had been at Parkersburg that morning. The next day he gave assurance that there would be ample cars for the remainder of the command when it arrived by boat. On the 24th J. W. Garrett, president of the railroad, wrote with some satisfaction to Watson about the movement (*ibid.*, pp. 618, 629, 634–635, 650–651).

42. Bayard reported that cavalry, infantry, artillery, and wagons had crossed at Waterloo; Burnside reported to Lincoln that a messenger just in from Reno stated the enemy was massing large bodies of troops at Kelly's Ford (*ibid.*, pp. 626, 620).

43. The change in destination of the different corps was an important matter, and the main facts are as follows. On Aug. 21, 3:45 P.M., Halleck told Burnside that Assistant Secretary Tucker thought Heintzelman should go to Alexandria on account of draft of vessels, and told him to use his judgment. At 4:00 P.M. Burnside stated he had given instructions to redirect Heintzelman. On Aug. 22 at 6:40 P.M. he suggested to Halleck that other corps should follow Heintzelman, and asked if he should use his judgment. On Aug. 23 Halleck informed Burnside that Franklin would go to Alexandria, and told McClellan that he was still undecided as to Sumner. Sumner left Fort Monroe at 5:00 A.M., Aug. 26, for Aquia Creek; was at Aquia the next morning; was sent to Alexandria after some disembarking may have been done (*ibid.*, pp. 614–615, 621, 633, 682, 701–702, 691–692). Keyes's corps was temporarily held at Fort Monroe.

44. Pope's report, *ibid.*, *16*, 58–59.

45. *Ibid.*, pp. 30–31, 59.

46. Earlier in the day Halleck suggested to Pope that he attack the enemy in flank if the latter moved in force on Warrenton, but he said nothing about Pope's recrossing the Rappahannock (*ibid.*, *18*, 622).

47. At 2:20 A.M., Aug. 23, Pope reported the raid to Halleck, saying that considerable damage had evidently been done; but later he reported the damage as trifling (*ibid.*, *16*, 60, and *18*, 630). The raiders attempted to burn a bridge but were prevented by Federal infantry as well as the rain (Blackford, *War Years with Stuart*, p. 106).

48. Freeman discusses the slowness in getting seized papers into Lee's possession (*Lee*, II, 297; *Lee's Lieutenants*, II, 71). It is doubtful that there was

anything of value in them. The Washington decision not to land troops at Aquia Creek after Porter's corps would have been important information for Lee, but it had been only partially made on the 22nd. Pope himself was very much in the dark as to when reenforcements would reach him.

49. *O.R., 16,* 61.

50. Ruggles to Reno, *ibid., 18,* 623—a dispatch sent on the evening of the 22nd for Reno to Rappahannock Station where an attack was expected.

51. For march order, see *ibid.,* pp. 631–632.

52. Pope said: "I march at once with my whole force on Sulphur Springs, Waterloo Bridge, and Warrenton, in the hope to destroy these forces before the river runs down. . . . The rain still continues, and I think we are good for thirty-six hours."

53. Halleck to Pope, Aug. 23, *ibid.,* p. 630. Halleck cautioned Pope not to expect Heintzelman too soon, and also stated that Cox had not arrived.

54. *Ibid., 16,* 31, 63.

55. For details of the Confederate operations, see Freeman, *Lee's Lieutenants,* II, pp. 73–78, and Early's report, *O.R., 16,* 703–708.

56. *Ibid., 18,* 641.

57. In a letter to Pope on July 21, Banks told of the report of a native of Connecticut that Richmond people did not believe Jackson was going to the Valley, but would threaten Washington from Gordonsville so as to force the withdrawal of McClellan (*ibid.,* p. 491).

58. Miles to Pope, 9:00 A.M., to Halleck, 3:00 P.M., *ibid.,* p. 652; Garrett to Watson, pp. 650–651.

59. *Ibid.,* pp. 640–641, 653. The wording of Halleck's message, "Ascertain, if possible, if the enemy is not moving into the Shenandoah," seemed to indicate that he thought the move somewhat likely.

60. Halleck to McClellan, C. L. Snyder (operator at Warrenton Junction) to Kearny, *ibid.,* pp. 646–647, 643. Snyder requested an orderly to find Pope, saying, "It is very important."

61. *Ibid.,* p. 642.

62. *Ibid., 16,* 65–66.

63. *Ibid., 23,* 344, 421.

64. On Aug. 27 Halleck stated that three-quarters of his time was taken up with raising new troops and with matters in the West; on Aug. 7 he wrote to McClellan that nearly all his time was occupied with new drafts and enlistments (*ibid., 18,* 69, and *14,* 359–360).

65. *Ibid., 18,* 605.

66. *Ibid.,* p. 618. After his subsequent assignment to Minneapolis, Pope wrote to Halleck on Sept. 30: "I need not remind you that when you arrived in Washington I earnestly urged you, as I had before urged the President, to allow me to return to the West. I told you, as I had already told him, that McClellan could not be depended on to co-operate with me, and that I was sure he would fail me." Halleck did not challenge the statement although he replied at length.

67. *Ibid.,* p. 600.

68. In connection with Stuart's October raid into Maryland (*ibid.,* 28, 29–30).

69. Aug. 22, 3:45 P.M., *ibid., 18,* 620.

70. *Ibid.*, p. 627.

71. *Ibid.*, pp. 621–622, 639.

72. *O.R.*, *17*, 1020. The words were in a question put by Porter to Assistant Secretary of War John Tucker, whom he called as a witness. In cross-examining Tucker, the court asked: "When the accused was making his efforts to leave the Peninsula, did he know that he was to be placed under the immediate command of General Pope?" Tucker replied: "I cannot answer that question; I do not know that he did." Porter's position would have been strengthened if the answer had been an unqualified yes. He had been emphasizing the haste he had shown in embarking, and after the court's question and Tucker's answer there was room to believe that he had hastened because he thought he would have an independent command until McClellan arrived.

73. *Ibid.*, *18*, 645–648, 651.

74. On Aug. 22 Halleck addressed an excellent order to Kearny or the officer commanding Heintzelman's corps, at Alexandria, which read: "As fast as the troops of your corps arrive they will be pushed forward by rail to the Rappahannock to re-enforce General Pope. Col. H. Haupt, superintendent of railroads, will supply transportation on your requisition. Not a moment should be lost, as Pope's army is already engaged." On the same day he informed McClellan that there had been skirmishing the day before, that Heintzelman had been ordered to Alexandria and would be sent by railroad to the Rappahannock as rapidly as possible, and he also outlined future plans. On the 23rd he sent a long dispatch to Pope, indicating that both Heintzelman's and Porter's corps were to be reenforcements for him (*ibid.*, pp. 625–627, 630).

75. *Ibid.*, pp. 602, 608.

76. Halleck wrote to McClellan Aug. 20: "You asked [for] a private telegraphic cipher. It could not be given, as all telegraphic messages were required to be shown to the President, and Secretary of War" (*ibid.*, *14*, 379–380).

77. *Ibid.*, *18*, 562.

78. *Ibid.*, pp. 614, 613. It is possible that the messages passed each other.

79. *Ibid.*, pp. 654–655.

80. *Ibid.*, pp. 654, 653.

81. Bayard to Schriver, Schriver to Reynolds, *ibid.*, pp. 656–657.

82. *Ibid.*, p. 653.

83. *Ibid.*, p. 657.

84. *Ibid.*, *18*, 653, and *16*, 67.

85. Haupt, *Reminiscences*, with the personal sketch by Frank A. Fowler *O.R.*, *18*, 598.

86. *Ibid.*, 603 and (some interesting observations by Meigs to Halleck Aug. 18), 596–597.

87. *Ibid.*, pp. 624–625, 605.

88. Several telegrams by Haupt, *ibid.*, pp. 634–638. Kearny's criticism of delay, pp. 632–633, did not take account of Stuart's raid.

89. Haupt to Watson, *ibid.*, pp. 636, 638; Haupt, *op. cit.*, pp. 80–84.

90. *O.R.*, *18*, 649–650 (telegrams of 2:00 and 11:10 P.M.), 662–663.

91. Sigel's report sought to explain and excuse his actions (*ibid.*, *16*, 263–264). McDowell in his report criticized Sigel's report, which had been made public (*ibid.*, pp. 333–334).

92. *Ibid.*, pp. 347–348.

93. *Ibid.*, p. 67.

94. *Ibid.*, *18*, 665.

95. Freeman, *Lee*, II, 308.

96. McDowell to Pope, Barstow to Buford, *O.R.*, *16*, 348–350, and *18*, 669.

97. Haupt to Devereux, *ibid.*, *18*, 663.

98. *Ibid.*, *16*, 67–68.

99. *Ibid.*, p. 69.

100. *Ibid.*, *18*, 672.

101. *Ibid.*, pp. 682–683, 666. Halleck's interesting dispatch contains much information. He assured Pope there was not the least dissatisfaction with his operations on the Rappahannock, and spoke of the great amount of telegraphing he had to do.

102. Lee to President Davis, Aug. 24, *ibid.*, p. 942.

103. *Ibid.*, pp. 675–676.

104. Eckman to McDowell, 8:20 P.M., *ibid.*, p. 668.

105. T. C. H. Smith (aide-de-camp to Pope) to Heintzelman, 8:20 P.M., *ibid.*, *16*, 70. The 72nd N.Y. Infantry was sent under Capt. H. J. Bliss. For report see *ibid.*, pp. 450–451. Bliss seemed dissatisfied with what was accomplished, but there certainly was little he could do.

106. Of Hooker's movement the next day, the 27th, Henderson writes: "Hooker had been instructed to ascertain the strength of the enemy at Manassas, for Pope was still under the impression that the attack on his rear was nothing more than a repetition of the raid on Catlett's Station" (*op. cit.*, p. 441). This error is even worse than his previously noted accusation that Pope was ignorant of the danger he was in when on the Rapidan.

107. *O.R.*, *16*, 70. The telegram at midnight stated: "I telegraphed you an hour or two ago what dispositions I had made, supposing the advance through Thoroughfare to be a column of not more than 10,000 or 15,000 men. If [Lee's] whole force, or the larger part of it, has gone, we must know it at once."

108. *Ibid.*, p. 351.

109. *Ibid.*, p. 49.

110. The supplies and equipment were not only for Pope, but for the anticipated campaign to be undertaken after McClellan had arrived.

111. Freeman, *Lee*, II, 293.

112. There has been dispute about incidents connected with the order for Jackson's famous march. Freeman's account in *Lee*, II, 300–301, differs from that in *Lee's Lieutenants*, II, 82–83. According to the first work Lee *sent* for Jackson, to give him the order for the march; in the second account "Lee rode over to Jeffersonton, found Jackson, and in a brief conversation presented him such an opportunity as never had come to him." See also Douglas, *I Rode with Stonewall*, pp. 132–133. Freeman apparently does not accept the whole of Douglas's detailed account of a conference between Lee, Jackson, Longstreet, and Stuart on the afternoon of Aug. 24 at Jackson's headquarters.

Jackson's march was certainly ordered on the afternoon of the 24th; but a long letter that Lee wrote that day to President Davis does not touch upon it, although there is a brief reference to a further advance by the army in connection with a discussion of supplies (*O.R.*, *18*, 942).

113. *Ibid.*, p. 679.

114. *Ibid.*, p. 680.

115. Hancock to Halleck, Haupt to Halleck, *ibid.*, pp. 694, 695, 680. The last was sent at 11:00 P.M., after Haupt's first but unsuccessful effort to find a general.

116. For Scammon's report and the reports of Taylor's regimental commanders, see *ibid., 16,* 405–406, 539–544.

117. *Ibid., 18,* 699.

118. Col. Samuel L. Buck, 2nd N.J. Volunteers, *ibid., 16,* 540–541. Col. Buck spoke of the "unfortunate manner in which the brigade was ordered into action." He also paid tribute to enemy courtesy as follows: "Assistant Surgeon Clark, while attending the wounded on the field was taken prisoner by the enemy, treated in the kindest manner, and released in a few hours without parole."

119. *Ibid., 18,* 696, 688–689; Haupt, *op. cit.,* pp. 103, 98–99. At 1:20 P.M. McClellan sent Halleck a message showing that he was in Haupt's office (*O.R., 18,* 689). This corroborates Haupt's narrative, which was written much later.

120. Haupt, *op. cit.,* p. 107.

121. *O.R., 18,* 689, 690.

122. Haupt, *op. cit.,* p. 104.

123. *O.R., 18,* 691. McClellan's reply was received at 5:00 P.M. (*ibid.,* p. 692).

124. *Ibid.,* pp. 693, 702–703. McClellan's postscript stated: "Take steps to cover the retreat of any of Pope's forces that may come in your direction." The message was sent at 2:30 P.M.

125. *Ibid.,* p. 819.

126. Haupt, *op. cit.,* pp. 104, 103; *O.R., 18,* 704.

127. Haupt, *op. cit.,* pp. 99, 109–110.

128. *O.R., 18,* 690.

129. Halleck to Meigs, Aug. 22, *ibid.,* p. 628.

130. Sawtelle to Williams, *ibid.,* p. 664. An excellent summary of the shipping situation at 8:30 P.M., Aug. 25.

131. Rucker to Holabird, Aug. 23, and to Ransom, Aug. 25, *ibid.,* pp. 639, 662. The later dispatch stated that the animals would be started the next day by the pike. What became of them is not clear; they did not reach Pope.

132. Rucker to Ferguson, Haupt to Rucker, *ibid.,* pp. 705, 704.

133. Stoddard to Rucker, *ibid.,* p. 720.

134. General Orders, No. 188, *ibid.,* p. 568.

135. Leech, *Reveille in Washington,* p. 186.

136. Brooks, *Washington in Lincoln's Time,* pp. 8–10. The statue was placed on top of the dome on Dec. 2, 1863, and a salute of 100 guns was given the flag hoisted on the pole above the statue.

NOTES TO CHAPTER XI

1. *O.R., 16,* 353.

2. *Ibid., 18,* 684.

3. *Ibid.*

4. *Ibid., 16,* 33. Pope stated that he thought Franklin was at Manassas on the afternoon of the 26th.

5. Pope wrote to Porter at 7:00 P.M., Aug. 26: "Franklin, I hope, with his corps, will by day after to-morrow night, occupy the point where the Manassas Gap Railroad intersects the turnpike from Warrenton to Washington City" (*ibid., 18,* 675). It is not possible to reconcile the statement in the report with that in the letter. But there had been so many changes in the matter of re-enforcements that Pope could not have known the exact status or position of troops reaching Alexandria. On Aug. 23, the day after the Catlett raid, some fear was expressed about a raid or an attack upon Manassas (Haupt to Halleck, *ibid.,* p. 637; Col. L. B. Pierce—commanding a regiment of cavalry at Manassas—to Sturgis, *ibid.,* p. 632). The dispatch from Halleck to Pope dated Aug. 22, *ibid.,* p. 627, should be dated Aug. 27, and is given again with that date on p. 685.

6. *Ibid., 16,* 70–71, 35.

7. *Ibid.,* pp. 34–35.

8. *Ibid., 18,* 688, 685, 702.

9. *Ibid., 16,* 35; Hebert, *Fighting Joe Hooker,* p. 122.

10. Henderson, *Stonewall Jackson,* p. 443.

11. *O.R., 16,* 35 and *18,* 699–700.

12. *Ibid., 17,* 703–704.

13. Strother, "Recollections of the War," *Harper's Magazine,* XXXV, 710–712 (Nov., 1867), gives a very interesting and probably accurate account of Aug. 27, beginning: "Fair and pleasant. Rose early, and got my coffee."

14. Pope's report, *O.R., 16,* 35–36, 71–72. A shorter and somewhat different version of the order to Kearny, in *ibid., 18,* 704, contains the sentence, "As you value success be off by the earliest blush of dawn," which was not in the order as given in Pope's report.

15. Strother, *loc. cit.*

16. Freeman, *Lee's Lieutenants,* II, 103–105. The hours at which different elements of Jackson's command left Manassas are not stated.

17. Douglas, *I Rode with Stonewall,* pp. 135–136, and Blackford, *War Years with Stuart,* pp. 109–115, contain accounts of Jackson's operations.

18. McDowell's report, *O.R., 16,* 335–336.

19. *Ibid.,* p. 236. McDowell stated that, knowing that Longstreet would be coming through the Gap, he sent Col. Wyndham's 1st N.J. Cavalry there at an early hour, and afterward more cavalry and Ricketts's division. He knew that the spirit of Pope's order was to crush Jackson before Longstreet arrived, but he felt that holding Longstreet back was essential. The report was dated Nov. 6, 1862, In Jan., 1863, the question was reopened in the investigation of McDowell's actions that was held at his request. At that time he implied that Sigel should have given some attention to Thoroughfare Gap; but his order of early morning Aug. 28 does not support the plea very well. At the hearing Pope testified that he had said nothing about the Gap and that he regretted McDowell's precautionary action, for he did not believe that Longstreet would get through the Gap that day; but he said clearly that it was within McDowell's

discretionary power, in the situation in which he was, to act as he did (*ibid.*, *15*, 206).

At 11:30 P.M., Aug. 27, before the receipt of Pope's order of 9:00 P.M., McDowell wrote to Sigel that "a large division of the enemy under Longstreet left Salem at 4 P.M. for the enemy's position in the direction of Manassas" and could be expected to come through Thoroughfare Gap (*ibid.*, p. 304), and directed Sigel to take position near Haymarket and Gainesville ready to hold this force back.

20. McDowell's report, *ibid.*, *16*, 335, and Freeman, *Lee*, II, 307. Freeman states that the incident slowed Lee's march; McDowell, that Buford "sent in word . . . that he had cut the enemy's column and forced Longstreet to deploy between Salem and White Plains."

21. *O.R.*, *16*, 73; also Special Orders, *ibid.*, p. 70, giving priorities.

22. Ruggles to Lieut. F. J. Shunk, chief of ordnance, and to Col. Clary, chief quartermaster, *ibid.*, pp. 72, 74.

23. *Ibid.*, p. 73.

24. *Ibid.*, pp. 74, 360–361. In his report, dated Jan. 27, 1863, Pope stated that he reached Manassas about noon and "less than an hour after Jackson in person had retired" (*O.R.*, *16*, 37). At the McDowell Court of Inquiry he testified that the larger part of Jackson's troops left Manassas between 3:00 A.M., and 9:00 or 10:00, and that Jackson, after visiting a hospital there, left with a small escort about 11:00 (*ibid.*, *15*, 203). This agrees quite well with Pope's dispatch to Halleck on the evening of the 28th, in which he said Jackson had evacuated Manassas three hours before any Federal troops arrived (*ibid.*, *18*, 721).

25. Blackford, *op. cit.*, p. 116.

26. Freeman, *Lee's Lieutenants*, II, 103–104.

27. Pope's report, *O.R.*, *16*, 36–37. The question is rendered difficult by doubt as to when various elements of Jackson's command left Manassas. Blackford unfortunately gives no information as to when Jackson withdrew or when he completed the occupation of the Sudley Springs position. Douglas (*op. cit.*, p. 136) is equally disappointing, saying merely, "On the morning of the 28th, Jackson put his command in position near Sudley's Church." In 1887 Mosby stated with great positiveness that Jackson left Manassas before daylight, except for a cavalry rear guard (*B. and L.*, II, 528). For some interesting testimony, with a map, concerning the movements of McDowell and Sigel on Aug. 28, which was put into the McDowell Inquiry Record, see *O.R.*, *15*, 257–260.

28. Henderson, *op. cit.*, p. 451.

29. *O.R.*, *18*, 720–722. Other dispatches, written just before, were headed "Near Bull Run" (*ibid.*, *16*, 75). Strother (*op. cit.*, p. 713) stated definitely that Pope's headquarters that night were on the Centerville-Warrenton turnpike, from which the Groveton action was observed at a distance of three or four miles.

30. *O.R.*, *18*, 713.

31. *Ibid.*, p. 714 and elsewhere.

32. *Ibid.*, pp. 705, 706.

33. *Ibid.,* pp. 707, 708.

34. *Ibid., 16,* 406.

35. *Ibid., 18,* 710.

36. *Ibid., 14,* 367.

37. *Ibid., 18,* 706.

38. *Ibid., 14,* 342.

39. McClellan to Halleck, Aug. 4, and to Stanton, *ibid., 12,* 81, and *14,* 264.

40. *Ibid., 18,* 629.

41. *Ibid.,* pp. 706, 710. For Halleck's long answer of the 29th to Stanton, see pp. 729–741.

42. Pope's report, *ibid., 16,* 37–40, 74–76; McDowell's report, *ibid.,* pp. 357–359, and his testimony in the Porter courtmartial, *ibid., 17,* 902–911; Sigel's report, *ibid.,* pp. 265–267; Heintzelman's report, *ibid.,* pp. 412–413, are in general the sources for the battle of the 29th.

43. Freeman, *Lee,* II, 314–316.

44. *O.R., 16,* 76.

45. *Ibid., 18,* 730. The editors of the *O.R.* supplied the day.

46. Pope's statement at the Porter trial about Longstreet's expected arrival did not agree with his joint order to McDowell and Porter. At the trial (*ibid., 17,* 851) he said that he had "expected the movement of Longstreet certainly during the afternoon of the 29th. General Buford, with his cavalry, was in that direction, and I knew that he was watching for the movement, and expected him to report as soon as he could ascertain anything about it. At 4½ o'clock I had not received any report from him. He was at that time under the command of General McDowell." Pope did not state that he received a message from Buford at any time.

47. Strother, *op. cit.,* p. 715. Speaking of what was taken as a cloud of dust, Strother said, "I was afterwards informed it was an artillery duel between the cavalry forces of Stuart and Buford."

48. Freeman, *Lee,* II, 323.

49. *Ibid.,* p. 326.

50. Douglas, *op. cit.,* pp. 137–138.

51. *O.R., 16,* 416, 419.

52. *Ibid.,* p. 18.

53. *Ibid., 17,* 875–883.

54. Captain Pope stated at the trial: "In a conversation which I had with General Porter, after his reading the order, he explained to me on the map where the enemy had come down in force to attack him, and had established a battery" (*ibid.,* p. 876). Porter did not question the statement. One battery would not have indicated a very strong force.

55. *Ibid., 18,* 735.

56. *Ibid., 16,* 465.

57. *Ibid., 17,* 998–1001.

58. *Ibid., 18,* 733. Burnside forwarded the letter to Halleck by telegraph at 5:15 P.M.

59. Halleck to McClellan, *ibid.,* pp. 722–723.

60. *Ibid.,* p. 722. A difficult problem is presented by Halleck's message to

McClellan (given on p. 722 with the date Aug. 29, and in McClellan's report, *ibid.*, *12*, 97, with the date Aug. 28). The reference to the arrival of Sumner's corps indicates that the date was the 28th, but the reference to Porter's letter shows it must have been the 29th! Whatever the date may have been, Sumner camped on the 28th on the road to Centerville. That McClellan expected orders for him to proceed to Manassas is shown in the next note.

61. Sumner's testimony, *C.C.W.* (1863, 2; 366–367); Marcy to Sumner, Aug. 29, 2:00 P.M., *O.R.*, *18*, 727. This is a very important dispatch and says: "it was supposed when you were ordered last night to hold your command ready to move this morning that you would be required to march to Manassas. The general commanding directs me to say that he wishes you to continue to hold your command in readiness to march, as he is expecting orders every moment from Washington, and he expects that you will move up the river to occupy position on this side of the river." The word "required" is significant, and McClellan's wish to have Sumner detained seems evident.

62. Halleck to McClellan, 3:00 P.M., *ibid.*, p. 722.

63. At 5:25 P.M. McClellan wired Halleck that he had started Sumner to Arlington and the Chain Bridge but indicated that he could be stopped (*ibid.*, p. 723). Sumner stated he moved to the aqueduct bridge at night. For a favorable report about Pope's situation, see Franklin's dispatch to McClellan, in McClellan to Halleck, *O.R.*, *18*, 723–724.

64. *Ibid.*, *12*, 98. McClellan's dispatch began: "The last news I received from the direction of Manassas was from stragglers to the effect that the enemy were evacuating Centreville and retiring toward Thoroughfare Gap. This is by no means reliable." His caution at accepting good news from Pope contrasted with his readiness to accept bad. The Confederates had indeed given up the temporary hold they had of Centerville on the 28th.

In a dispatch that did not show the hour, McClellan's chief of staff informed Haupt that Pope was at Centerville and that supplies could go through without meeting much, if any, opposition. The reply was sent at 3:40 P.M. (Haupt, *op. cit.*, p. 114).

65. The dispatch to the President was sent fifteen minutes before Halleck had sent his dispatch to McClellan, telling him to dispose of troops as he saw fit.

66. *O.R.*, *12*, 98.

67. *Ibid.*, *18*, 723. For all the delays in Franklin's movement, see Halleck to Stanton, *ibid.*, pp. 939–941.

NOTES TO CHAPTER XII

1. *O.R.*, *18*, 741. Franklin's dispatch is given *ibid.*, *16*, 17.

2. *Ibid.*, *16*, 40–41.

3. *Ibid.*, pp. 19, 42. Pope wrote to Halleck, "The whole of the heavy reenforcements which attacked us on Saturday, passed down the road from Gainesville during the whole afternoon and night of Friday." His report stated that, "during the whole night of the 29th and the morning of the 30th, the

advance of the main army under Lee was arriving on the field to re-enforce Jackson," and that reenforcing troops continued to arrive during the afternoon of the 30th. Pope's final report was colored by testimony at Porter's trial, and cannot be accepted as conclusive evidence as to what he thought on Aug. 30.

4. *Ibid., 18,* 766.

5. Strother, "Personal Recollections of the War," *Harper's Monthly,* XXXV, 717 (Nov., 1867).

6. *O.R., 18,* 744, 754, 747, 742.

7. McDowell's report, *ibid., 16,* 340.

8. *Ibid.,* pp. 361, 340.

9. The best accounts seem to be Sykes's and Warren's reports, *O.R., 16,* 481–484, 502–504.

10. Freeman, *Lee,* II, 332. It is possible that teams were hitched, or even that guns were limbered.

11. According to Strother (*op. cit.,* p. 710) it was the first time Pope had shown any excitement during the campaign.

12. *O.R., 16,* 343, 78.

13. Strother, *op. cit.,* pp. 720–721.

14. *O.R., 16,* 344, 270, 483.

15. *Ibid.,* pp. 78–79.

16. Freeman, *op. cit.,* p. 337.

17. Franklin to Halleck, *O.R., 16,* 536, reporting much confusion and many stragglers.

18. *C.C.W.,* 1863, 2:367.

19. *O.R., 18,* 749.

20. *Ibid., 16,* 80.

21. *Ibid.,* pp. 78, 324–325 (itinerary of Banks's corps).

22. Banks to Halleck, Ferguson to Rucker, *ibid., 18,* 743, 768. The multiplicity of weapons that had to be provided for is shown by an ammunition requisition (pp. 767–768).

23. *Ibid., 16,* 79.

24. *Ibid.,* p. 81.

25. *Ibid., 12,* 101–102.

26. Halleck to McClellan, *ibid.,* p. 102.

27. *Ibid., 18,* 771–772, 774.

28. *Ibid., 23,* 464, 335.

29. *Ibid., 18,* 773.

30. *Ibid., 12,* 102–103.

31. *Ibid., 18,* 773, 774. In an effort to make the command situation clear, a War Department order had been issued on Aug. 30 (*ibid., 12,* 103).

32. *Ibid., 12,* 103.

33. *Ibid., 12,* 103–104, and *18,* 786.

34. *Ibid., 16,* 82.

35. *Ibid., 18,* 768–769. The date Aug. 30 is certainly incorrect. Porter spoke of a dispatch by Pope, which is dated Aug. 31, 10:45 A.M. (*ibid., 17,* 80), as written "to-day." Other statements in Porter's letter show it was written on the 31st.

36. For the original, see McClellan Papers, Library of Congress, LXXV, 15328-15329. It bears the hour 9 P.M., which is not on the version in the *Official Records*. Nor did the editors of the latter indicate that they had added the signature of the writer, although they had supplied the name of the addressee. The letter as printed differs only in minor ways from the original. A search of the War Records in the National Archives has failed to reveal the copy of the letter that was used for the *Official Records*. The letter does not appear in McClellan's *Own Story*. The issue of *O.R.*, Serial 18, which contains it, commenced on Aug. 20, 1885 (*ibid.*, *130*, p. iv); McClellan died suddenly on Oct. 29 of that year, leaving his completed work.

37. Strother, *op. cit.*, p. 714.

38. *O.R.*, *18*, 706-707.

39. Pope to Halleck, Oct. 20, 1863, *ibid.*, p. 821. The word "intercepted" would seem to rule out reference to Porter's letters to Burnside, even if Pope knew about them.

40. Jones to Bragg, Sept. 2, *O.R.*, *28*, 589. Gen. Sam. Jones at Chattanooga forwarded a dispatch he had received from Adj. Gen. Cooper, dated Sept. 2, copying Lee's undated message, which may have been sent as late as Sept. 1. To Lee's telegram Cooper had added, "General Lee is pursuing the enemy."

41. *Ibid.*, *16*, 81, 82.

42. *Ibid.*, *17*, 841. Smith's testimony was of a positive nature, and began with an account of an interview he had had with Porter on the afternoon of the 28th over ammunition that had been sent to Porter's corps. After giving a statement he had made and Porter's reply Smith told the court: "I do not know as it is evidence to give the spirit in which this was said—the way it impressed me. Those remarks were made in a sneering manner, and appeared to me to express a great indifference. . . . This conversation, from General Porter's manner and look, made a strong impression on my mind. I left him, as I have said, after an interview of about ten minutes, and rode on, arriving at our headquarters on Bull Run just as we entered them and pitched our tents for the night. After my tent was pitched, and I had had something to eat, I went over to General Pope, and reported to him briefly what I had done in regard to the ammunition. I then said to him, 'General, I saw General Porter on my way here.' Said he, 'Well, sir.' I said, 'General, he will fail you.' 'Fail me,' said he, 'what do you mean? What did he say?' Said I, 'It is not so much what he said, though he said enough; he is going to fail you.' These expressions I repeat. I think I remember them with exactness, for I was excited at the time from the impression that had been made upon me. Said General Pope, 'How can he fail me? He will fight where I put him; he will fight where I put him;' or, 'He must fight where I put him; he must fight where I put him'—one of these expressions. This General Pope said with a great deal of feeling, and impetuously and perhaps overbearingly, and in an excited manner. I replied in the same way, saying that I was so certain that Fitz John Porter was a traitor, that I would shoot him that night, so far as any crime before God was concerned, if the law would allow me to do it. I speak of this to show the conviction that I received from General Porter's manner and expressions in that interview. I have only to add that my prepossessions of him were favorable, as

it was at headquarters, up to that time. I never had entertained any impression against him until that conversation. I knew nothing with regard to his orders to move up to Kettle Run, and I knew nothing of any failure on his part to comply with any orders" (*ibid.*, p. 889).

43. At 8:50 P.M., Aug. 29, Pope sent a very peremptory order for Porter to report to the field of battle (*O.R., 16,* 18).

44. Pope stated, "The attack of Porter was neither vigorous nor persistent" (*ibid.*, p. 42). It is difficult to tell how much weight can be given the assertion, as representing what Pope thought at the time of the battle. But see *supra*, p. 351, for remark about Porter's casualties.

Apropos of Lee's intention to attack about 1:00 P.M., Strother wrote (*op. cit.*, p. 727), as if quoting Lee's chief engineer: "He was anticipated by Porter's attack, which, being but feebly urged, soon failed, and afforded the golden opportunity for the grand counter-attack." It is to be noted that what Strother recorded in 1867 about the arrival of Lee with Longstreet's command and the Confederate dispositions on Aug. 30, as communicated to him by Lee's staff officer, was very accurate.

45. Col. Speed Butler, aide to Pope, made a report of remarks that Griffin made, reflecting both upon Pope and upon other superior officers (*O.R., 16,* 18).

46. *Ibid.*, pp. 82–83.

47. *Ibid.*, p. 367.

48. Sumner's testimony before *C.C.W.* (1863, 2:367).

49. *O.R., 18,* 796–797. McClellan's report, written a year later, cannot be accepted on his interview with Halleck without some question. He stated: "During this interview I suggested to the General in Chief the necessity of his going in person or sending one of his personal staff to the army under General Pope, for the purpose of ascertaining the exact condition of affairs. He sent Col. Kelton, his assistant adjutant-general" (*O.R., 12,* 104). A quite different aspect is given the matter when it is recalled that Pope urged Halleck to come out and see the heavy straggling in McClellan's troops. Halleck replied, "It is impossible for me to leave Washington."

50. *Ibid., 16,* 415.

51. *Ibid., 18,* 797.

52. *Ibid., 16,* 86–87.

53. Haupt, *op. cit.*, pp. 116–117.

54. Dennett, *Lincoln and the Civil War*, pp. 44–46.

55. Nicolay and Hay, *Lincoln*, I, xii.

56. Burnside also forwarded to McClellan a dispatch of Porter's written at 2:00 P.M., Aug. 28, which began, "All that talk of bagging Jackson, etc. was bosh" (*O.R., 18,* 732–733).

57. In a letter to Halleck from St. Paul, Oct. 20, Pope wrote: "Did not both you and the President know before the battles at Manassas, from Porter's intercepted dispatches, that he was likely to do precisely what he did? The President himself told me so" (*ibid.*, p. 821). While there is uncertainty about "intercepted dispatches," there is none about those that came from Burnside.

58. McClellan's report, *ibid., 12,* 104.

59. The strength return for Aug. 10 gave 12,710 "present" in Morell's and

Sykes's divisions (*ibid.*, *14*, 367). Warren's report gave the strength of the Fifth N.Y. as 490 when the action began (*ibid.*, *16*, 502).

60. Special Orders, No. 218 (Headquarters of the Army), *ibid.*, *18*, 807.

61. *Ibid.*, pp. 802, 801.

62. McClellan, *Own Story*, pp. 532–533, 535 (quoted with comment by Nicolay and Hay, *op. cit.*, VI, 26–28).

63. *Ibid.*, p. 537.

64. *O.R.*, *16*, 344.

65. *Ibid.*, *18*, 808.

66. General Orders, No. 16, Aug. 15, *ibid.*, p. 574. This modified an order of Aug. 6, which had prescribed that 100 rounds be habitually carried, and had stated that captains who were negligent would be arrested and reported to the War Department for dismissal (*ibid.*, *16*, 52–53). The change showed that Pope could correct mistakes, though he should have known that 100 rounds were too many for soldiers to carry habitually.

67. *Ibid.*, *18*, 808.

68. *Ibid.*, pp. 808–809.

69. *Ibid.*, *28*, 169. The order bears an indorsement saying it had been delivered to Halleck at 10:00 P.M. It is signed by Stanton, but Nicolay and Hay (*op. cit.*, p. 28) state the original was written in Lincoln's own hand.

70. *O.R.*, *18*, 810.

71. *Ibid.*, p. 811.

72. *Ibid.*, p. 813.

73. *Op. cit.*, p. 567. The losses in the Army of the Potomac were not particularly heavy—4,728 out of a total of 14,462 killed, wounded, and missing (*O.R.*, *16*, 263).

NOTES TO CHAPTER XIII

1. Dennett, *Lincoln and the Civil War*, p. 47.

2. McClellan wrote (*Own Story*, p. 242): "Add to this consideration that I had now only too good reason to feel assured that the administration and especially the Secretary of War, were inimical to me and did not desire my success."

3. Fuller, *Generalship of U. S. Grant*, p. 1.

4. *Ibid.*, p. 2.

5. About the uncertainty of the morning of Aug. 30, Strother wrote in his "Personal Recollections," "for some time after the General walked to and fro, smoking and anxiously engaged in solving the difficult problem involved in the contradictory evidence he was continually receiving" (*Harper's Monthly*, XXXV, 718, Nov., 1867).

6. *O.R.*, *14*, 63.

7. *Ibid.*, *18*, 812–813.

8. The *N.Y. Tribune* of Sept. 2 contained a dispatch from its correspondent at Centerville, 5:00 A.M., Aug. 31, stating: "I do not think there was a brigade

that could not, as it came from the field, show its distinct regiments, or rather a nucleus of each regiment to whose standard ere it had marched a mile its scattered men gathered." The dispatch was copied in *Harper's Weekly*, VI, 599 (Sept. 20, 1862). That there were many stragglers was admitted.

9. Myers so describes it in *General McClellan*, p. 311. Henderson summarizes Pope quite unfavorably in *Stonewall Jackson*, pp. 482–483. On the other hand, Ropes calls Pope "a vigorous, active, resolute man," and concludes his *Army Under Pope* (p. 171), "When he met his antagonists he fought them with a courage and persistency which extorted their admiration." For a discussion of Gordon's adverse volume—from which Henderson probably drew—see Appendix VIII.

10. Pope to Halleck, *O.R., 18*, 822.

11. *Ibid.*, p. 818.

12. Michie, *General McClellan*, pp. 393–394. Michie gives an excellent discussion of the problem that faced the President and the cabinet.

13. Stanton to the Rev. Heman Dyer, *O.R., 28*, 725–728 (also see Flower, *Stanton*, pp. 157–161, and Gorham, *Stanton*, I, 428–432). Of the President's War Order No. 1 Stanton wrote: "It is not necessary, or perhaps proper, to state all the causes that led to that order, but it is enough to know that the Government was on the verge of bankruptcy, and, at the rate of expenditure, the armies must move or the Government perish. . . . Many, very many, earnest conversations I had held with General McClellan, to impress him with the absolute necessity of active operations, or that the Government would fail because of foreign intervention and enormous debt."

On Charles Marshall's expression of the confidence in the South that foreign recognition would come by Feb., 1862, Gen. Maurice comments, "This is the best explanation of which I know of Lincoln's action in issuing, on January 27, 1862, his much criticized War Order No. 1" (*An Aide-de-Camp of Lee*, p. 23).

14. *O.R., 18*, 739–741.

15. *Ibid.*, pp. 812–813.

16. Palfrey, *Antietam and Fredericksburg*, p. 17.

17. Strother, *op. cit., Harper's Monthly*, XXXVI, 290 (Feb., 1868).

18. Dennett, *op. cit.*, p. 49. Hay recorded Sept. 5 that Lincoln had said to him: "The other day I went down to Alexandria and found General McClellan's army landing. I considered our armies united virtually and thought them invincible. I went home and the first news I received was that each had been attacked and each in effect beaten. It never had occurred to me that any jealousy could prevent these generals from acting for their common fame and the welfare of the country." As a description of the battle, the President's statement was rather inaccurate.

19. Michie, *op. cit.*, p. 395.

20. Dennett, *op. cit.*, p. 47.

21. Margaret Leech states in *Reveille in Washington* (p. 197) that McClellan performed something like a miracle. Blackford's *War Years with Stuart* (p. 139) makes exaggerated statements about Second Bull Run, so far as the Federal actions were concerned.

22. The record of the Court of Inquiry is in *O.R.*, *15*, 36–332. On the charge of drunkenness, the court stated (p. 331): "The court denounces the charge of drunkenness against General McDowell as ridiculous. The fact is that there is no man in the land more free than he from all taint of such vice. Among temperate men he is proved by the testimony to belong to the most temperate and even abstemious."

23. Special Orders No. 3, Sept. 6, *ibid.*, *28*, 197–198.

24. *Ibid.*, *27*, 144–145. Freeman's statements in *Lee* and *Lee's Lieutenants* do not agree with that of General Lee or with each other. In *Lee*, II, 354, he writes, "On September 5–6, the head of the columns prepared to cross the river," but in *Lee's Lieutenants*, II, 153, he writes of "the passage of the Potomac on September 4–7." Lee's word "between" has been replaced by "on.

25. *O.R.*, *28*, 198.

26. *Ibid.*, pp. 199, 200.

27. *Ibid.*, p. 201.

28. In *N.Y. Tribune*, Sept. 9.

29. Dated Sept. 15 in *Harper's Weekly*, VI, 610 (Sept. 27, 1862).

30. *O.R.*, *28*, 210, 211.

31. *Ibid.*, p. 212.

32. *Ibid.*, p. 211.

33. *N.Y. Tribune*, Sept. 8, 1862.

34. Editorial in *Harper's Weekly*, VI, 594 (Sept. 20, 1862).

35. *O.R.*, *28*, 214–215, 218–219, 222–223.

36. *Ibid.*, p. 270.

37. *Ibid.*, p. 266, 269.

38. *Ibid.*, p. 268.

39. *N.Y. Tribune*, Sept. 12 and 13.

40. *O.R.*, *28*, 254.

41. *Ibid.*, p. 266.

42. *Ibid.*, pp. 254–255.

43. *Ibid.*, p. 272.

44. *Ibid.*, pp. 225, 226–227.

45. Ruggles to Sigel, Aug. 16, about marauding parties from Steinwehr's command, *ibid.*, *18*, 577. The order is on p. 573.

46. Soldiers can be legally punished only according to the Articles of War, and there is no justification for such an order as Pope's. But it could have been carried out by any officer or soldier who caught a man in the act of plundering, with nothing said about it. On the other hand, there was no chance whatever that a court-martial would order a man shot for marauding. Article of War 87 stated that the death penalty could not be inflicted for offenses where it was not explicitly mentioned; and it was not mentioned in Article 54, under which a marauder could have been punished. It was absurd to think that the necessary two-thirds of any court would vote for a sentence which they knew was illegal.

47. Strother gave a good description (*op. cit.*, p. 275). Press correspondents also reported at length.

48. *O.R.*, *28*, 601–602; also Freeman, *Lee*, II, 356–357. Freeman states,

"The address doubtless was written by Col. Charles Marshall, a Marylander."

49. Freeman, *Lee's Lieutenants*, II, 154, 155; *Lee*, II, 340.

50. Silas Cosgrove, "The Finding of Lee's Lost Order," *B. and L.*, II, 603, puts the finding of the order close to noon.

51. *O.R., 28*, 281.

52. *Ibid., 18*, 800, 802. White's evacuation of Winchester was investigated at the direction of the Secretary of War by a military commission, whose proceedings are given in *O.R., 16*, 766–805. The commission found that he had acted with capability and courage, and that there was no ground for censure. His report to Halleck on the evacuation, dated Sept. 6, is given ahead of the proceedings.

53. *Ibid., 28*, 181, 198, 199.

54. *Ibid., 27*, 43, 44. McClellan's report dates the dispatch Sept. 19. A note states the copy in the War Department is dated the 11th.

55. Lee's report (*ibid.*, pp. 144–153) and Freeman's *Lee*, II, chap. xxv, contain discussions of his purposes in invading Maryland and in moving to Hagerstown.

56. Freeman's *Lee*, II, 359, gives 53,000 as the force which Lee took into Maryland. Palfrey (*op. cit.*, p. 7) puts the number "present for duty" as between 40,000 and 50,000.

57. Freeman, *Lee's Lieutenants*, II, 145, 149, and chap. viii.

58. *O.R., 28*, 603–604, gives the original order in its entirety. The lost copy did not have the first two paragraphs, which had nothing to do with the march; it is given in McClellan's report, *ibid., 27*, 42–43.

59. Freeman, *op. cit.*, pp. 147–148.

60. Lee's army was not divided into corps, though he was handling it as two corps, with Longstreet and Jackson commanding temporary divisional groups. After he had joined the army, D. H. Hill had been under Jackson. Copies of Special Order No. 191 evidently went to all divisional commanders, but nothing was said about their *distribution*. Not being sure that D. H. Hill had a copy of the order which would cause him to march with Longstreet, Jackson made a copy with his own hand and sent it to Hill, who thus received two copies. The lost copy was the one he had received direct from army headquarters, and would probably have been protected more carefully if a second had not come. The incident shows the importance of having all orders show their distribution. According to Freeman (*op. cit.*, p. 161), Jackson made the extra copy as the best way of showing Hill that he was cognizant of his transfer to Longstreet's command. A one-sentence note would have done that. Hill afterward sought to maintain that the only copy of the order he had received was the one from Jackson, which he later was able to produce (*ibid.*, pp. 715 and 161 n.).

61. For many years it was stated that Lee had been informed that McClellan had come by a copy of his order, but Freeman in *Lee*, II, 369 n., rejected the story as not having proper support. The rejection caused convincing evidence to be put in his hands, and in his second account of the Maryland campaign he accepted the story and gave the evidence in full (*Lee's Lieutenants*, II, 173, 201, 715–723).

62. *O.R., 28,* 211.

63. Ballard, *op. cit.,* p. 125.

64. *O.R., 27,* 45–46.

65. Palfrey, *op. cit.,* pp. 20, 29–30. He stated there was no means of fixing the time when McClellan received the lost order, except that it was before 6:20 P.M. Although McClellan's report did not include his noon dispatch to Lincoln, it was in *C.C.W.,* 1863, 2: 485. Cosgrove's article," The Finding of Lee's Lost Order," had not yet appeared.

66. *Ibid., 28,* 281–282.

67. Freeman, *op. cit.,* pp. 718 (memorandum of a conversation with Gen. Lee by E. C. Gordon), 162.

68. Palfrey, *op. cit.,* pp. 44 n., 47 n.

69. Strother, *op. cit.,* pp. 276–277.

70. McClellan, *Own Story,* p. 572. Except for the omission of a comma the sentence repeated a statement McClellan had made in his report, *O.R., 27,* 42.

71. McClellan's report, *ibid.,* p. 45, does not give the time more definitely than "morning."

72. Statement of the courier, Capt. Charles H. Russell, before the commission examining into the surrender of Harpers Ferry, *ibid.,* pp. 720–721, 723.

73. *Ibid.,* pp. 723, 726, 45.

74. *Ibid.,* p. 45. Strother (*loc. cit.*) wrote of trying to find a citizen of Frederick who would take a message to Miles "for pay or patriotism." Although he was unsuccessful, the chief of the secret service had found a messenger; but he wrote nothing of three.

75. *O.R., 27,* 374–376.

76. Michie, *op. cit.,* p. 497.

77. For an account of the defense, see Freeman, "The Test of Lafayette McLaws," *Lee's Lieutenants,* II, chap. xi.

78. *Ibid.,* p. 192.

79. Reports of Gen. Cox and Col. Scammon, *O.R., 27,* 459, 461.

80. A total of 32 as against 26 in the 17th Michigan, which had more wounded (*ibid.,* pp. 186–187).

81. For an account of the defense, see Freeman, "Harvey Hill's Battle," *op. cit.,* chap. x.

82. Myers, *General McClellan,* p. 290; Michie, *op. cit.,* p. 409; Strother, *op. cit.,* p. 279.

83. *Op. cit.,* p. 39.

84. *O.R., 28,* 294–295.

85. McClellan, *Own Story,* p. 583.

86. *O.R., 27,* 53.